SIGN, STORAGE, TRANSMISSION
A series edited by Jonathan Sterne and Lisa Gitelman

ISE

DUKE UNIVERSITY PRESS   DURHAM AND LONDON   2013

JAPANOISE

MUSIC AT THE EDGE OF CIRCULATION | David Novak

© 2013 Duke University Press
All rights reserved
Printed in the United States of
America on acid-free paper ∞
Designed by Amy Ruth Buchanan
Typeset in Quadraat by Tseng
Information Systems, Inc.
Library of Congress Cataloging-
in-Publication Data appear on the
last printed page of this book.

Frontispiece: Hanatarashi
performance at Toritsu Kasei
Super Loft, August 4, 1985.
Photo by Satoh Gin.

Supplemental media examples and
further information are available at
www.japanoise.com.

This work is licensed under the Creative
Commons Attribution-NonCommercial-
NoDerivs 3.0 Unported License. To view
a copy of this license, visit http://creative
commons.org/licenses/by-nc-nd/3.0/ or
send a letter to Creative Commons, 444
Castro Street, Suite 900, Mountain View,
California, 94041, USA. "Noncommercial"
as defined in this license specifically ex-
cludes any sale of this work or any
portion thereof for money, even if the sale
does not result in a profit by the seller
or if the sale is by a 501(c)(3) nonprofit
or NGO.

CONTENTS

Acknowledgments | vii

Introduction | 1

1   Scenes of Liveness and Deadness | 28
2   Sonic Maps of the Japanese Underground | 64
3   Listening to Noise in Kansai | 92
4   Genre Noise | 117
5   Feedback, Subjectivity, and Performance | 139
6   Japanoise and Technoculture | 169
7   The Future of Cassette Culture | 198

Epilogue: A Strange History | 227

Notes | 235   References | 259   Index | 279

ACKNOWLEDGMENTS

This book would not exist without the participation and encouragement of many talkers, listeners, thinkers, players, organizers, collaborators, and friends. I am deeply indebted to Fujiwara Hide, Kelly Churko, Filth the Sleep, Higashiseto Satoru, Tabata Mitsuru, Gomi Kohei, Haco, Ishii Akemi, and Aoki "Pinky" Satoru for opening their homes, stores, practice spaces, and home recording studios to me, and especially to Hiroshige Jojo, Mikawa Toshiji, Ôtomo Yoshihide, and Akita Masami for sharing their perspectives and their writings on the worlds of Noise they created. I could not have asked for a better cohort of interlocutors in Osaka and Kyoto, and I thank Ishibashi Shôjirô, Matt Kaufman, Onishi Aya, Yamazaki Maso, David Hopkins, Go Shoei, Yamamoto Seiichi, Jeff Bell, Christopher Stephens, Mitch Kinney, Nishikawa Bunshô, Môri Katsura, and Toyonaga Akira for leading me further underground in Kansai. It was a privilege to have worked alongside the staff of Bridge and the Festival Beyond Innocence, especially Uchihashi Kazuhisa. My time in Japan was also invaluably enriched by talking and performing—and talking about performing—with Kato Hideki, Nakajima Akifumi (Aube), Unami Taku, Ito Atsuhiro, Akiyama Tetsuzi, Nakamura Toshimaru, Uemura Masahiro, Kudo Tori, the late Iwasaki Shohei, and the late Tano Koji.

For the North American portions of my research, credit goes to Art Pratten, the late Hugh McIntyre, and all of the members of the Nihilist Spasm Band and the staff of the No Music Festival, Ron Lessard, Jessica Rylan, Clay Lacefield, Kyle Lapidus, Mark Weitz, Sam McKinlay, Carlos Giffoni, and everyone at No Fun Fest; Chris Goudreau, Chris Cooper, Seth Misterka, and Dan Greenwood, who brought me deeper into Noise on the East Coast; and on the West Coast, Daniel Menche, Greg Saunier, Matsuzaki Satomi, Mason Jones, and Seymour Glass.

My advisor Aaron Fox was an unflagging source of intellectual inspiration and support in my doctoral work at Columbia University; Steven Feld, Ana María Ochoa, Marilyn Ivy, and John Pemberton were also profoundly involved throughout. I cannot credit them enough for their insights, and I am deeply indebted for their attention and confidence. Thanks also to Chris Washburne, Ellen Gray, George Lewis, Brad Garton, and the Center for Ethnomusicology. This project germinated at Wesleyan University, where I am grateful to Mark Slobin, Sumarsam, Alvin Lucier, and Anthony Braxton for their generosity. Other mentors have given valuable encouragement, including Tim Taylor, Louise Meintjes, Jonathan Sterne, Anne Allison, Ian Condry, Bonnie Wade, Sherry Ortner, Mike Molasky, David Samuels, Tom Porcello, Jairo Moreno, Martin Stokes, John Szwed, and Alan Cummings. My exceptional graduate cohort provided forthright critique through many years of friendship. Amanda Weidman, Amanda Minks, Joshua Pilzer, Brian Karl, and Matt Sakakeeny were particularly unfailing in their willingness to engage with my writing, and I'm thankful for countless conversations with Farzaneh Hemmasi, Maria Sonevytsky, Lorraine Plourde, Michael Fisch, Toby King, Jeff Snyder, Paul Hogan, Ryan Skinner, Niko Higgins, Morgan Luker, Ryan Dohoney, Melissa Gonzalez, Paul Yoon, Cynthia Wong, Tyler Bickford, Anna Stirr, and Lauren Ninoshvili.

I gratefully acknowledge the sources of funding and support that enabled me to research and write *Japanoise*. The Fulbright Foundation, the Social Science Research Council, and the Mellon Foundation sponsored my fieldwork in Japan and North America; writing was supported by the Society of Fellows in the Humanities at Columbia University, the Lane Cooper Foundation, the Warner Fund of Columbia University Seminars, and the Academic Senate of the University of California, Santa Barbara. Primary fieldwork in Japan was carried out under the auspices of JUSEC; thanks to my sponsors Yamada Yoichi and Hosokawa Shuhei, and to Kansai Geijutsu Daigaku for hosting my Fulbright research. Yamamoto Yuka, Nathaniel Smith, and Odai Kiyomitsu provided help with research and translations, and I also benefited from critical readings by Anne McKnight, Miura Hiroya, and Sakuramoto Yuzo.

This book has benefited from the input of audiences at many talks and presentations. I thank all of the participants and respondents at the 2009 Listening In, Feeding Back conference, and Eileen Gillooly, Jonah Cardillo, and my fellow fellows at the Heyman Center for the Humanities at Columbia University; the members of the AAA Music and Sound Interest Group; and audiences for workshops and talks at UC Berkeley, NYU, the University of Pittsburgh, Princeton University, the Art Institute of Chicago, the Hagley Museum and Library, the University of Rochester, UCLA, Brown University, the University of Oklahoma, Duke University, and the Radio Nacional de Colombia. At UCSB, further thanks go to faculty, graduate students, and staff in the Music Department, as well as the Center for the Interdisciplinary Study of Music, the Ethnography and Cultural Studies Research Focus Group, the Interdisciplinary Humanities Center, and my affiliated colleagues in East Asian Languages and Cultural Studies, Film and Media Studies, and Anthropology.

I feel extremely lucky to have received the careful attention of two anonymous reviewers at Duke University Press, both of whom provided extensive and extremely helpful guidance in the revision of this manuscript. From the first, Ken Wissoker has been a wonderfully enthusiastic and encouraging presence, and his guidance was always on target. Liz Smith, Jade Brooks, Laura Poole, and Amy Ruth Buchanan expertly shepherded the book through production. Thanks to series editors Jonathan Sterne and Lisa Gitelman (not least for giving me the chance to say that I am putting something out on SST). Duke also deserves recognition for their exceptional support of new forms of scholarly publishing, and for allowing this book to be published under a Creative Commons license that enables its open digital distribution. Thanks also to the photographers who contributed materials and permitted their work to be reprinted on these pages, to Derek Gottlieb for the index, and to *Popular Music* for portions of chapter 3 that were published there in an earlier form (in "2.5 x 6 Metres of Space: Japanese Music Coffeehouses and Experimental Practices of Listening," vol. 27, no. 1).

I've learned most everything from my family, friends, and fellow musicians. James Fei has been a constant source of information, goodwill, and sonic challenge for many years, especially in our live electronic duo Maestros, whose performance tour in Japan was a particularly bright spot of my fieldwork experience. Jeremy Novak provided an endless repository of new/rare/old/strange sounds and kept me playing as a member of the Live Dymaxion Interpretation Society. Toby King, Little Timmy Pearson, Brent Cramer, Josh Pilzer, and Danny Fisher endured many bar rooms and lugged much equipment with me in Habit Trail. Thanks to WKCR and Erin Chun for special broadcasts based on portions of my research, and to WFMU, WESU, and KCSB for hosting performances and interviews.

My sons Gus and Finn are the newest sources of noise in my life; they keep my blood flowing and my ears listening (and sometimes ringing). And my companion and friend Jen Gherardi helped me more than I can say.

INTRODUCTION

This place is a classic underground spot: falling apart at the seams, bohemian quirkiness of the fake wood walls reminiscent of a postwar Middle American home bar in the basement, fan spinning creakily above us, all sorts of random swaying things hanging from the ceiling. But it feels like something special is going on tonight as two musicians begin jamming their equipment together, hurriedly plugging distortion pedals into tape echoes into amps, shoving guitar cases and suitcases behind the bathroom door, as the room fills to overflowing. A fire hazard for sure. People standing all over, more in back by the bar than the twenty or so lucky enough to cram into mismatched chairs around a handful of tables in front of the stage. There're only fifty people here at most, but it feels full, packed to overflowing, and the energy is charged. A young woman asks one of the performers if she can take his picture—sure, of course—a recording of harsh ringing sounds, crashing metal (a bowed cymbal?) plays over their setup. Though the lights are still up and people continue to talk, one performer seems as if he is beginning to play, shaking his table to create static, triggering buttons on a homemade electronic instrument. Crackles of filtered electricity begin emerging from the PA speakers suspended above the stage, really just a carpeted area that might ordinarily fit a set of drums or a piano. Someone quietly hoots in preparation from the back—one of the performers nods—are they are ready? Is this still the CD? They stand and poke at their pedals; nothing happens. Is it broken? Is this on purpose? An intermittent crackle continues in the background, one performer replugs his pedal and makes some noises, testing, testing. The other continues adjusting a broken Korg "Stage Echo" tape delay and smacking a few more sounds out. He asks for more sound in the monitor, and turns, pushing a CB mic up against his amp to squeal some sharp feedback. In the brief moment of stillness before the blast of Noise begins, he finally turns to the audience, and stone-facedly announces "Konban wa": "Good evening." (We're about to start.)

|||||

Japanese Noise legends Hijokaidan are crammed into the tiny broadcast booth of CHRW, an independent radio station in London, Ontario. The group is in town for a rare overseas appearance at the 2003 No Music Festival, an annual event hosted by the long-running local troupe Nihilist Spasm Band (NSB), who have brought Hijokaidan over from Japan to play alongside a roster of important North American Noise acts in this small Canadian city. "I've been playing Hijokaidan all day," the DJ announces; "people are probably crashing their cars all over town!" Actually, it had been a fairly laid-back morning in London. After breakfast at NSB member Art Pratten's house, everyone posed for photos in the backyard with his pet snake, and then piled into different cars to drive through the snowy streets to the anonymous university building that housed the CHRW studios. Inside the studio, the host begins his interview with a typical opening gambit, inquiring about the origins of the band. It's a reasonable place to start, since most listeners of this quite experimental station probably don't know much about the twenty-year history of Hijokaidan; even the otherwise well-informed host repeatedly mispronounces the band's name. But Mikawa Toshiji, serving as the group's informal spokesperson because his English is best, claims that he can't remember exactly when they met. A long time ago, anyway. Instead, he speaks of his own discovery of free improvisation, punk rock, and German "krautrock" records, discussing his favorite groups and pointing out that a common interest in these recordings is what brought the members of Hijokaidan together. The host turns the conversation back to Japanese experimental groups like Kosugi Takehisa's important group Taj Mahal Travellers and saxophonist Abe Kaoru. Weren't these influences for Hijokaidan? Wasn't there an important local music scene? But Mikawa says that they weren't listening to those Japanese groups. "Maybe years later, after we started, then we heard about them." The host asks several further questions intended to elicit some kind of historical narrative about the group's development in Osaka, the invention of the Noise genre in Japan, and their connections to a local Japanese Noise scene. Mikawa talks about one of Osaka's baseball teams. A half hour soon passes, and the host's well-intentioned attempt to introduce these legends of Japanese Noise to the radio audience is almost over. "Well," he announces into the mic as he cues up a track, "if you want to know about Hijokaidan, you'd better come down to the Forest City Gallery tonight and check 'em out for yourself." Then he leans over to press play and slides the fader up on a wall of Noise.

|||||

"Now that it's everywhere, how do you decide whether a piece of noise-rock is good or bad?" This was the question posed by "Aestheticizing Noise," a panel at the 2005 CMJ Music Marathon in New York City, a independent music industry conference where critics, label owners, and promoters gathered to discuss the future of Noise. For the panelists, most of whom had been involved with promoting concerts and circulating recordings for many years, the growing recognition of Noise was both exciting and confounding. The genre, everyone agreed, was becoming increasingly popular, although no one seemed to know exactly what to call it—"noise-rock," "noise music," or just plain "Noise"—or could predict if the buzz might lead to anything more than chatter. Detroit's Wolf Eyes were now on the cover of international music magazines; New York's No Fun Fest was gathering unprecedented crowds. For some, the rapid pace of its current circulation meant that Noise's day had finally come as a new form of extreme music. For others, its exposure practically guaranteed that it was all over. People weren't going to get it, and Noise would no longer exist in a way that really mattered. Whatever was happening now wasn't real Noise.

|||||

A sheet of paper flutters against the door of a dive bar on a deserted downtown street in a mid-sized Northeastern city. The 8.5 × 11 flyer, crudely designed with hand-drawn black-and-white text, announces a live Noise show featuring two performers from the area, as well as a Japanese artist on a brief tour of the United States. Inside the bar, two distinctly separated groups of people are clustered in the small space. On one side, a motley group of college-age stragglers are scattered around the room, some standing directly in front of the PA, others leaning against the walls. On the other side, some regulars are huddled together wondering what's going on, trying to get as far away from the amplifiers as possible, and obviously ruing the invasion of their local watering hole by these ear-blasting misfits. The Japanese performer is climbing up a pillar in the center of the room, directly above a tableful of random electronic gear that has filled the room with screeching feedback for the last fifteen minutes. He leaps from the pillar onto the table, falling backward as his equipment scatters across the room, and slowly stands up as the Noise fans applaud and roar their approval. In the sudden silence, someone sitting in the back of the bar shifts his weight on his stool, swiveling over and cupping his hand against his mouth to shout: "We don't understand what the hell you're doing!" One of the local performers looks up from another small table, where his gear is already half-plugged together in preparation for the next set, shoots a grin at the Japanese performer, and yells back: "It's Noise—you're not supposed to!"

|||||

I've got my headphones on, listening to "Electric Peekaboo" from the 1993 Merzbow record *Brain Ticket Death*, trying to make sense of the sounds I hear. The track begins with a one-second blast of sound, which shifts sharply downward in pitch before abruptly cutting out, as if taking a breath before releasing the long, harsh, continuous scream of Noise that follows. Sounds are split between the left and right speakers, creating two separate but interrelated layers of texture; other sounds are quickly panned between the two speakers to create a sense of movement in the flat landscape of the stereo field. Filters sweep across the distorted sound field, rippling through a stream of harsh frequencies. Beneath these timbral changes, there is another loop of sound, which repeats a two-second fragment of muted static. The distorted feedback begins to break up as some amplifier in the chain reaches the limit of its capacity. A microphonic feedback is introduced in the background, and the sound begins to short out as a thin hissing sound momentarily fills both channels. A new loop lurches into both channels at once, emitting a spitting chatter for two seconds and then submerging into a low hum. A vocal sound, like a moan, appears underneath the layers of feedback; it is unclear to me whether this is actually the sound of a human voice or some resonance created in the feedback process, or by a filter, or another pedal. Suddenly the Noise just ends, leaving me suspended in the buzzing stillness. A final burst blasts through the system, as if I've been unplugged from myself. But none of this really describes it at all: the overwhelming feeling of it, the shocking effect of the transitions between sounds, the shiver that runs up your spine when the Noise cuts out. It's been three minutes, forty seconds—or a decade of listening, depending on how you look at it—and I am still struggling to hear what is going on.

FROM MUSIC TO NOISE

Over the last two decades of the twentieth century, Noise became a musical discourse of sounds, recordings, performances, social ideologies, and intercultural affinities. It connected a spatially and culturally diverse network of musicians and was embodied through the affective experiences of listeners. It was exchanged as an object of transnational musical circulation that touched down in particular places and eventually came to be imagined as a global music scene. Noise, too, is connected to many contemporary histories of aesthetic form and ideology, especially in new electronic, experimental, and underground styles of music. In short, Noise has become a kind of music, but one that remains distinctly and compellingly different in its circulation as "Noise," "Noise Music," and "Japanoise." In this book I tell the story of Noise as a circulation of popular music. This Noise I write with a capital N to identify the specific sounds, places, times, and people that I have tuned into in my ethnographic work, all of which taught me to recognize its cultural presence.

I write this particular story of Noise out of my encounters with practitioners and listeners in extended fieldwork in Japan and North America from 1998 to 2008.[1] In Osaka, Kyoto, and Tokyo, I conducted interviews with musicians, listeners, and club and label owners; observed and participated in performances; and talked about recordings in the places where they are produced, sold, and heard. I also learned through fieldwork (and several preceding years of informal contact) in experimental scenes in New York City, San Francisco, Providence, and London, Ontario, that connected with North American musicians and listeners.[2] The description of Noise in this book, then, is neither a general term of discourse nor an abstraction of critical theory. It is directly informed by my experiences in these times and places, in encounters with people and close observations of musical production and reception in practice. All of this brings me to relate how Noise has taken shape as a cultural force on the ground, even through the displacements of transnational circulation that often make it hard to identify. Over the years, I heard many different accounts of its creative purpose and historical origins, recorded disputes about its cultural and musical status, and listened to its changing sounds as it moved on the margins of many different styles. I learned about techniques of Noise performance, production, and distribution, about aesthetics of listening and ways of describing sound. Noise was more than a theoretical catchall for any musical or cultural idea that exceeded the boundaries of representation. It had become a world in itself.

Although my perspective was rooted in these particular moments, events, and dialogues, I also recognized that it would be impossible to compress my view of Noise into an ethnographic depiction of a contained musical community, whether local or transnational. Despite the fact that people described it as a mode of pure sonic experience, I found no way to isolate Noise to a singular musical form—a "Noise-in-itself" that might be hermeneutically unpacked as a consistent stylistic project. Its aesthetic history was continually submerged in layered cycles of mediation, always reemerging changed, somewhere else. Listeners and musicians created different biographical, historical, and aesthetic narratives. Some stories connected a certain group of actors, though not always in the same place and time, and others were isolated in their own individual versions of Noise. A coherent picture of Noise sometimes appeared when these particular views lined up with one another; they inevitably glided apart soon after these rare moments of convergence. My project, then, was to describe this feedback and attempt to follow its subjects through all of their movements and changes. Noise, I discovered, can only exist in circulation. Noise displaces the home ground of ethnographic research as much as it challenges the representations of musical history. It does not settle in a distinct place or group of people, and its fragmented mediation makes

6 | Introduction

it difficult to depict its ethnographic terrain, even as global or multisited. Practitioners change their names and sounds often, and local audiences rarely coalesce into consistently recognizable scenes, even in a single city. Noise is bound to other histories of style that draw its sounds, if only temporarily, into their sphere of influence. Beyond Noise's consistent loudness, it is just as challenging to describe the sonic features of Noise as a musical form. It is often unrelentingly harsh, but also ambient and dynamic; it can be improvised and freely played or deliberately prepared, edited, and through-composed; it can include recognizable elements of other musical practices and use existing instruments, or be entirely non-referential in the invention of original live electronic sounds. Wordless Noise has no original linguistic center, and even its names—the English loanword Noizu in Japan and Japanoise in North America—conspire to attribute its source somewhere else.

I entered this loop by attempting to follow the flow of Noise between North America and Japan. But the circulatory centers of Noise shifted many times from the late 1980s through the turn of the millennium. In these rapid fluctuations—from place to place, impulse to impulse, person to person, moment to moment—Noise became a wave. Its movements resonated with the overlapping hopes, demands, and desires of friends and strangers scattered across the world, even as their exchanges amplified the cultural distortions, breakdowns, and delays that I describe in these pages. Taking a definitive authorial position within this circuitry is impossible. So, to begin, I turn back to an earlier point on my spiraling path into the feedback of Noise.

A PLACE I CALLED "JAPAN"

I first traveled to Japan in 1989, having dropped out of college to teach English, study Japanese and koto performance, and find the culture that I had only just begun to encounter in my texts on Japanese history, literature, and religion. The best way to really find out about these things, I thought, was to live in Japan and discover them for myself. I moved to the former medieval capital of Kyoto, a bustling mid-size city known as much for its modern arts and contemporary intellectual culture as its cultural and religious history. I found a tiny apartment, and began to search for informal English teaching work and to explore this new place, armed only with the Japanese language I had crammed in a summer intensive

Introduction | 7

course at UC Berkeley. Kyoto was and is a spectacular city full of historical landmarks and markers of traditional Japanese society. But it was also a bewildering mix of cultural materials that I already knew from home. Many of the things that immediately captured my attention were already familiar, if somehow transformed in "the Japanese version." Many highly particular local practices were deeply embedded in the surround of transnational capitalism (i.e., the recent custom of eating at Kentucky Fried Chicken on Christmas Day). Common sources of media, especially music and television, seemed to create a similitude between my own experience and the cultural frames of modern Japan. Some points of coincidence even triggered deeply held memories, though I hadn't known that my existing knowledge of media would be intrinsic to my daily life in Japan.

For example, I quickly rediscovered the *Star Blazers* animated TV show, with which I had been obsessed as a child in late 1970s Buffalo. I had watched these cartoons after school on our black-and-white TV in full ignorance of their Japanese origin. But in Kyoto, the familiar characters and images appeared everywhere in new detail, and I felt a strange rush of unwarranted nostalgia for this native production.[3] In Japan, *Star Blazers* was *Uchû Senkan Yamato* (*Space Battleship Yamato*). It had been one of the first full-fledged smash hits of Japanese anime, beginning as a TV series in 1974, years before I began watching in grade school. In the anime-obsessed corners of Akihabara in Tokyo or Den-Den Town in Osaka, or pasted into the corners of flyers for punk rock shows, a bewildering proliferation of images from *Uchû Senkan Yamato* appeared: acetate stills, comics and retrospective books, models and representations of the series' characters (whom I knew under their Americanized names of Derek Wildstar, Mark Venture, Dr. Sane, General Krypt, and so forth). I had come to Kyoto to learn about local culture, but most of my social connections began through some kind of mutual—or perhaps merely overlapping—knowledge based in transnational channels of popular media. From the shared-but-different childhood memories of *Uchû Senkan Yamato* / *Star Blazers*, my acquaintances might move to a discussion of computer software, to debates about favorite Beatles songs, to obscure independent films, books, and recordings. Even language was a mix of familiar and new; with some friends I spoke in Japanese, whereas others preferred to speak in English. Perhaps these mediated contexts were natural points of contact for cosmopolitan intercultural communication. After all, we were, I thought, part of a global network that sought out naturalized connections in popular media and technology. But perhaps equally naturally, our shared experiential ground did not always line up.

Despite familiar things in my Japanese surroundings—ideas and images, social and technological frameworks, and even my own language—there were also many things that remained out of my field of perception. Unknown things filtered back in, forcing me to reconsider how I sorted out those aspects of culture that I acknowledged as Japanese. Certainly, I recognized the fascinating difference of Japan, embedded in Kyoto's history and traditional aesthetics. But I began to focus on other, noisier, aspects of cultural representation that had escaped my recognition. In my own fandom of *Star Blazers*, I hadn't known the show as Japanese, although its starcraft kept the imperial name *Yamato*. The futuristic narrative of *Uchû Senkan Yamato* transformed the famous World War II warship, excavated from the ocean floor, into a star cruiser that traveled the galaxy to save Earth from imminent self-destruction. *Yamato* had been the lead ship of the Imperial Navy, sunk in a suicide mission off the coast of Okinawa in the closing months of the war. This complex reference to wartime Japan had remained submerged in its new sites of reception, even as the battleship was dredged up, resurrected, and made into a science fiction epic for a new international audience.

As the mediated galaxies of "Japanimation" expanded further in the 1990s, new narratives of contemporary Japanese culture slowly came to the surface. Media studies scholar Iwabuchi Kôichi describes the 1990s as a shift from the cultural "odorlessness" that marked the early entry of Japanese media and consumer technologies into global circulation (Iwabuchi 2002, 2004). Japanese hardware had revolutionized the world market for electronic commodities in the 1970s and 1980s, including sound technologies like transistor radios, FM synthesizers, and the Sony Walkman, all of which carried little scent of Japan into their transnational markets. The cultural software of Japanese animation, comics, video games, and other audiovisual materials in the 1990s, on the other hand, began to bear more than a whiff of Japaneseness to faraway places.

What was specifically Japanese about these products, and what it meant for them to be recognized as distinctively cultural, remained unclear. But as "Cool Japan" penetrated the global market, attributions of cultural origin were fed back into a whole range of Japanese popular media—even, as I show here, into a seemingly cultureless Noise. Like anime, which is embedded in a history of foreign film technologies but has come to repre-

Introduction | 9

sent a distinctive local style, Noise's Japaneseness is the outcome of a specific transnational mediation with the United States that shaped Japan's "long postwar" (Gluck 1993; Harootunian 2000). Japanese anime became "Japanimation," Japanese pop became "J-pop," and Japanese underground music began to be circulated overseas as "Japanoise."

This cultural feedback was a long time coming. In the 1980s, Japan was both the apex and the enigma of global modernity, especially among North Americans transfixed by the contrast between the nation's emerging economic power and its idiosyncratic local practices. Japan was a fascinating and threatening landscape of extremes that juxtaposed traditional culture against ruthless technological efficiency. Symbols of Japanese difference abounded, from group calisthenics in auto plants to futuristic relationships with personalized robots, as well as more absurd and unsettling contexts of fetishistic cuteness and violence, reduced cartoonishly to the consumer excesses of mechanized toilets and the public perversions of sexually explicit comic books. Japan was reported as a retrograde society steeped in state corruption and corporate control of individual subjectivity, twisted by its own national repression of wartime violence into a rationalized nightmare of technocapitalism. It was the site of an idealized foreign tradition, but also a bizarre world of arbitrary postmodern hybridity. Japan became the "mirror of modernity," whose avant-garde refractions of the West filtered out through the incommensurable prism of the "Japanese version" (Vlastos 1998). Like so many others, I glimpsed this fantastic imaginary Japan through the images, objects, and sounds that spun out of its seemingly untraceable media mix. But it was not until I came back to the United States that I discovered Japanoise.

BIG IN AMERICA

The genre of Japanoise emerged around 1990, as transnational systems of media distribution were undergoing significant change and expansion. On my return from Japan that year, I was surprised to discover that a musical aspect of "Cool Japan" had begun to be invoked in the United States by the names "Noise," "Noise Music," "Japanese Noise," and eventually "Japanoise." Japanese music had finally become a force in North American media, and Noise was rapidly becoming known as its central genre. Still, I had never heard of Noise or any of these seemingly new groups, although most were located in Kansai, and even in Kyoto, where I had been living for a year. What was happening here? There were certainly other Japanese productions that might have been more likely to cross over to foreign audiences. In fact, most popular music in Japan already sounded very much like Western pop music. Many rock and pop artists used English phrases in their songs, while some others (e.g., Matsuda Seiko) recorded albums entirely in English, with North American producers and guest stars, in a deliberate attempt to court an overseas audience. But Noise, which finally broke through where so many attempts had failed, trickled in through underground channels far from the mainstream of corporate J-pop that dominated the mass media. Japanese underground music had begun to enter into North American reception several years earlier, with a steady flow of experimental cassettes building up throughout the 1980s. The expansion of transnational media distribution in the early 1990s became a confluence for a stream of Japanese independent recordings. By the turn of the millennium, Japanoise had come to define a new transnational music culture.

Japanoise surfaced in North America from within a larger framework of reception that included not just Noise but "noisy" Japanese music. A host of recordings by strange Japanese groups had begun to filter into independent distribution: Boredoms, Haino Keiji, Melt Banana, Omoide Hatoba, Ruins, Ghost, Grind Orchestra, Acid Mothers Temple, Ground Zero, Space Streakings, Zeni Geva, and others. Many recordings picked up by North American fans in the 1990s were by punk, hard rock, and hardcore groups from the Kansai region, especially Osaka. Osaka's citizens have historically been recognized within Japan for their outspoken aggressiveness, direct local language, hedonistic enjoyment of leisure, and outrageous sense of humor. Given this outgoing expressive character, it was not surprising that extreme, intensely performative musical styles were associated with the city. Osaka encouraged edgier, more experimental attitudes, as well as amateur performance spaces and recording projects. But the region was also a logical site for transnational connections to the Japanese underground because it was isolated from the centralized national media in Tokyo. Although domestic distribution remained difficult for Kansai artists into the 1990s, overseas networks of independent music had begun to mediate the development of a local underground scene in Osaka.

Shonen Knife was one of the first groups to fire the imagination of North American listeners. The Osaka band featured three Japanese women — reportedly "office ladies" who seemed as remote from any punk rock scene as possible—singing songs about public baths, Barbie dolls, bison, chocolate bars, and goblins called *kappa*, using the three-chord stripped-down punk form of the Ramones. In North American reception, Shonen Knife seemed to be the perfect musical example of modern Japan's paradoxical mediascape; something about them was wonderfully off. While the trio approximated familiar styles, their songs were quirky, amateurish, and somehow fundamentally "alternative" to the more familiar original. The group simultaneously reinforced and confused Western stereotypes, both of Japanese women and of one-way models of intercultural imitation, with their absurdist-but-genuine version of outsider punk rock. Shonen Knife's first official U.S. release was the reissue of their LPs *Shonen Knife* and *Pretty Little Baka Guy / Live in Japan* on U.S.-based Gasatanka/Rockville Records in 1990.[4] But this snapshot of the "new" Japanese underground had already been released twice, first in Osaka on Zero Records in 1983 and then again as an informally copied and circulated cassette tape on the tiny U.S. indie label K Records in 1986. This was newness amplified by a time lag, a musical difference ordered within the cultural imaginaries of global media. The sounds of the Japanese underground were familiar, but excitingly mysterious. They were recognizable, but somehow unfixed and somewhat unintelligible. They were ready to turn into Noise.

By the early 1990s, recordings by Hijokaidan, Incapacitants, C.C.C.C., Solmania, Masonna, Monde Bruits, Astro, Aube, Government Alpha, Pain Jerk, K.K. Null, K2, MSBR, Geriogerigegege, Violent Onsen Geisha, and Merzbow had swept into North American reception. College radio stations and independent record stores circulated releases from Osaka's Alchemy, Public Bath, Japan Overseas, and New York's Shimmy Disc and Tzadik labels. Underground fanzines like San Francisco–based Mason Jones's *Ongaku Otaku* informed fans of the archetypal examples of Noise and helped them assemble a rudimentary map of its generic boundaries in Japan. North American tours, especially by Merzbow and Masonna in the mid-1990s, allowed select fans to experience Japanese Noise live and relate legendary stories for those who missed the chance. It was increasingly possible to talk about a "Japanese Noise scene," and maybe even see some of its representatives in live performance. By the time I really began to tune into what was going on, the layers of feedback from North American reception—in which almost any Japanese underground music had come to be described as Noise—had already shifted the ground for Japanese musicians.

"Noise Music" was already widely in use as a general term of difference in North American underground music. But new confusions between the overlapping terms of "Noise," "Noise Music," and "noisy music" became crucial for bringing Japanese media into North American reception. In the 1980s, "Noise Music" described a broad range of "noisy" artists that could also be described as "experimental," "industrial," "hard-core," "postpunk," or "no wave" (e.g., the NYC-based bands Sonic Youth, Suicide, Glenn Branca).[5] "Noise Music" was a loose, metageneric term for all of these diverse underground sounds that were too noisy to be absorbed into a commercial mainstream or recognized as a distinct musical movement. Noise was everything on the margins of musical genres: recordings with no consumer market, sounds that could never be confused with any kind of normal music. But with the sudden appearance of Japanese Noise, much of what had previously been called Noise became "noisy music," to be distinguished from a purer form of Noise, which was represented by new sounds from Japan. Japanese recordings were increasingly differentiated from local "Noise Music" by the phrase "Japanese Noise Music," and finally the neologism "Japanoise." In the alternative media networks of the 1990s, Noise was now something that came from Japan. The invention of the term *Japanoise* further supported the North American belief that the distant Japanese Noise scene was bigger, more popular, and more definitive of the genre.

Many Japanese artists argued that their music was not, in fact, Noise and began to distinguish their projects from other Japanese work that could more properly be described as Noise.[6] Osaka's Boredoms, for example, became one of the most widely known examples of Japanese Noise in North American reception, although the group has argued vehemently against being considered a Noise band. Still, those hearing their first U.S. release, *Soul Discharge* (issued in 1990 by Shimmy Disc) could be forgiven for thinking that "Noise" was a pretty good description. The recording was a Dadaist cut-up of pop music styles, performed at top speed with an absurdly aggressive, over-the-top energy. Lead singer Eye Yamatsuka (now Yamataka) babbled nonsensical sometimes-Japanese sometimes-English vocals over warped guitar, bass, electronics, and two drum sets in a montage of hard-core and *musique concrète*. The cover depicted a ragtag band of both women and men dressed in scuba gear, draped with junk electronics, long hair and shaved heads, toy sunglasses, and multicolored fluorescent clothing. Boredoms' absurdist play with their musical influences and even their names—Eye, Yama-Motor, Yoshimi P-we, God Mama, and so on—reiterated their unknowability.

Boredoms began touring the United States, playing tiny clubs for in-the-know aficionados of experimental rock. Eye connected to New York's experimental music scene through the downtown composer John Zorn, first in Zorn's group Naked City and later in the duo project *Nani Nani*.[7] The band collaborated with underground legends Sonic Youth and opened for Nirvana at the height of their major-label exposure. In 1994, Boredoms played the hugely influential Lollapalooza tour, bringing their intense, cacophonous stage act to crowds of young concertgoers across the United States at the apex of alternative music. The group was signed to Reprise, a division of Warner Bros., for the U.S. release of *Pop Tatari* in 1993, and their older Japanese releases were reissued overseas. Over the next decade, Boredoms left their major label distribution in the United States, changed their name to Vooredoms, then back to Boredoms, then to Boadrum, and splintered into several side projects with an ever-more confusing discography.[8]

Boredoms is certainly a very noisy band, and many members of the group had strong social and creative links with local developments of Noise in Japan. Before forming Boredoms, Eye had been part of the influential Noise duo Hanatarashi, whose performances in 1980s Kansai have become legendary.[9] Although individual members had strong connections to Noise projects, they did not consider Boredoms as Noise. Eye began to inform North American audiences of the differences, insisting that Boredoms was not Noise, just "noisy." In explaining the distinction, he occasionally mentioned groups like Merzbow and Hijokaidan, which, he explained, could accurately be described as Noise. Of course, Eye had no intention of explaining Noise. But the term spun out of his surrealistic deflections of inquiries about Boredoms' relationship to Japanese culture, to other forms of music, and to contemporary subcultures in the United States. His vague references demanded further knowledge of the elusive category, and listeners began to seek out the real Japanese Noise.

NOISE IS DEAD. LONG LIVE NOISE

The North American reception of the 1990s opened a brief window for Japanese musicians and listeners to imagine a new Japanese underground back home. Local Japanese receptions of overseas success are often characterized by the phenomenon of *gyaku-yunyū*, or "reverse importation," through which Japanese artists become validated at home after gaining status on a foreign stage.[10] International success sparked a brief surge of interest in the local Kansai Noise scene, even to the extent of briefly putting Noise artists on national television in the mid-1990s. For a hyperindividualist, largely amateur, and secretive group of performers, the sudden demand for exposure was potentially devastating. Japanoise connected Japanese artists to an audience they would never have reached without the intervention of North American reception. But they had to position their Noise within explicit claims of cultural authorship. As overseas feedback looped back to Japan, local musicians and listeners again shaped their cultural boundaries around a foreign Noise.

When I returned to Japan in 1998 to begin my ethnographic research, I was surprised to hear that Noise was already dead or had never existed in the first place. Many prominent performers, along with fans, record store and club owners, writers, and other participants, told me that there was no use attempting to search for it, explain it, or even bothering to describe it. They continued to produce and release recordings and put on regular performances for a core audience of long-term listeners. But they claimed that the idea of Noise was a misunderstanding generated by confused fans who had taken things too seriously. Still, over the course of that initial research trip in Osaka, I attended electrifying Noise concerts; had long conversations about the history of the Kansai Noise scene in the 1980s; met first-, second-, and third-generation performers; and flipped through the bins marked "Noise" at local record shops, where owners wrote lists of important recordings and groups and customers joined in with their own advice. I strained to make sense of a chorus that seemed to speak with two voices: one shouting, "Noise is dead," the other whispering, "Long live Noise."

Any story of Noise must account for the transnational circuitry of its subjects, and also acknowledge their dogged pursuit of antisocial, antihistorical, antimusical obscurity. This multisited struggle against cultural identification makes Noise extremely difficult to place. Despite a concentration of exceptional performers, Noise is by no means exclusive to Japan. Noise is practiced in pockets of the United States, Canada, Europe, Australia, and Latin America; in recent years, there have been Noise festivals in China, Taiwan, and South Korea. Some link the historical development of Noise to earlier British industrial music (Whitehouse, Throbbing Gristle, SPK), American experimental rock (Velvet Underground, NYC "downtown," Los Angeles Free Music Society, "No Wave"), and free jazz

(Albert Ayler, the late John Coltrane, and several 1970s improvisational collectives), as well as European postwar electronic synthesizer composition and tape music, contemporary projects of sound art and experimental music.[11] Performers have often described Noise as a global form that transcended specific cultural influences, spinning out of a primordial human creativity. But for two decades, Japan was where Noise stuck—not because Noise was invented there, but because it was driven home in transnational circulations that continually projected its emergence back onto Japan. Although there are many other contexts, I focus on North American receptions, largely in the United States but also in Canada. These are not places where the products of Japanese Noise artists were merely "received." Japanoise, I argue, could only have been produced through this mediated feedback between Japan and North America.

For the relatively scattered and isolated population of North American listeners and musicians, imagining the Japanese underground was deeply significant. The idea was ripe with potential for experimentation and international camaraderie, as well as the challenges and surprises of cultural difference. Meanwhile, a lack of local recognition had driven Japanese recording artists to bypass regional distribution in search of a transnational audience. Listening from afar, North Americans imagined the Japanese Noise scene as a cohesive, politically transgressive, and locally resistant community—in other words, a version of their own ideal musical world in an unknown cultural space. But its Japanese subjects lived in different cities, often did not know of each other's work, and were more oriented toward overseas reception than the constructions of a local cultural identity.

Japanoise represented a global music scene forged in circulation. Its fragmented publics were connected through miscommunications, distortions, and established channels of intercultural "untranslation."[12] Eventually, the "grass is greener" projections of North American and Japanese participants did cultivate a long-term exchange, as each side imagined—wishfully, and often wrongly—that the other had a larger, more engaged, and somehow more real Noise scene. Even as Noise loosened the links between musical sources and local cultural origins, it began to represent an original project of global culture in itself. But its feedback also questioned if there could be such a thing as culture at the roots of circulation after all.

FEEDBACK: CIRCULATION AT THE EDGE OF MUSIC

Circulation lies at the theoretical center of this book. Even as I describe Noise through its circulation, I want to challenge the comparative models of exchange that represent circulation as something that takes place between cultures. I privilege the concept of feedback to emphasize that circulation itself *constitutes* culture. Feedback is a critique of cultural globalization, a process of social interpretation, a practice of musical performance and listening, and a condition of subjectivity. By focusing on the transnational context of popular music, and the specific case of Noise, I show how technological mediation transformed the global scale of cultural exchange, even as it undermined its historical continuity. Ethnographies of media affirm that culture travels and also demonstrate how people experience its movements, and how different interpretations feed back to creative sources.[13] But describing circulation does not mean merely showing how cultural forms enter into production in one place and emerge changed in reception somewhere else. Output is always connected back to input in transformative cycles of feedback. Seeing the cultural power of media *in circulation* means recognizing the mediation of culture *by* circulation. Feedback, in turn, shows how circulation always provokes something else.

Circulation typically describes the distribution of material goods and currency, but its models of economic production and exchange are embedded in a discursive framework that extends to the dissemination of social knowledge, news, ideas, and other productions of cultural content. Increasingly, *circulation* is used to characterize intercultural relationships, paths of migration, aesthetic and expressive forms, and ideologies and imaginaries of cultural globalization. Global "flows" and "scapes" seem to correlate all of the multisited transactions of the contemporary world as interrelated networks of goods, people, and images across space and time (Appadurai 1996; Castells 1997). But circulation can sometimes appear as a transparent background for exchange, rather than a cultural production in itself. Against this, Benjamin Lee and Edward LiPuma have argued that circulation is not just the "movement of people, ideas and commodities from one culture to another." Instead, circulation represents "the performative constitution of collective agency," and a distinct "cultural process with its own forms of abstraction, evaluation, and constraints" (2002:192–93). Circulation is not just movement and exchange, but performance and process. Its forms do not simply progress from one place, person, or sociocul-

Introduction | 17

tural context to another. Circulation is a nexus of cultural production that defines the things, places, and practices within its loops.

If circulation is a culture-making process, what kinds of culture does it make, and what kinds of cultural subjects? What happens when circulations break down? Or, more accurately, what happens when they break down, start up, and break down again in an irregular off-kilter trajectory? What happens to things that are not swept into the paths of intercultural dialogue, to the incremental differences that disappear or hide away? Is everyone always already "in sync" with circulation, simply by being within reach of its ever-expanding grasp? Circulation can easily be compressed into a totalizing entity of global culture. But the feedback I describe in *Japanoise* shows that its circuits can never be fully contained in networks of collective agency or communication. Instead, Noise performs circulation as an experimental force, which is compelled to go out of control.

The cultural movements of circulation reproduce historical relationships of power and trace out the institutional routes of center–periphery formations. Circulation also generates powerful forces of newness and difference that change these structures, and sometimes fundamentally shift their meanings (Urban 2001). Global networks can seem to extend space and place "beyond culture," to reshape conceptions of self and other, home and travel, contact and adaptation, continuity and change (Gupta and Ferguson 1997). In this, circulation depicts the cultural politics of globalization as an ever-adapting framework of interactive relationships. But the subjects of circulation are not so easily discovered. They are always moving somewhere else, changing situations and being changed by them. Sometimes they reappear where they were before, and sometimes they are diffused into unstable patterns that spread out into a field of differences. Although most circulations cannot accurately be described as purely local or national, few are truly global. They aren't always communicational and can be difficult to characterize in terms of interaction, dialogue, expression, or agency.

Circulation is full of "missed encounters, clashes, misfires, and confusions" in what Anna Tsing calls the "friction" of global interconnection (Tsing 2005). These circuits are hard to trace because they do not move smoothly or include everything they might seem to. They don't complete their revolutions; they break down or spiral off into the distance. Some cycles cannot endure the erosion of repetitions; others were never linked in in the first place. It is crucial to recognize that these irregular exchanges go on even as they fail and their objects are transformed or destroyed. People discover other meanings in culture as it unravels, disconnects, and folds in on itself.

Feedback is circulation at the edge. An edge is a special kind of being-in-place; it marks the transition between something and nothing. Edges are limits, and also shape-defining margins. To be at the edge, as Edward Casey puts it, is to exist in the "in" of the "in-between," in the instant between one time and another (Casey 2008).[14] An edge cuts and changes whatever it encounters. It is where movement must stop or turn in a different direction; it is where people plummet into the abyss, or learn to fly. Things end, and begin, at this place—but nothing stays at the edge forever. Edges mark the boundaries of empty space, but they also represent the transformational places where new possibilities open up again.

The edges of feedback are temporal as well as spatial. In any given circuit of exchange, "to reintroduce uncertainty is to reintroduce time; with its rhythm, its orientation and its irreversibility" (Bourdieu 1980:99). A time lag can radically change the meaning of circulation: it can turn music into Noise and back again. Michael Warner describes how the "punctuality" of circulation orients publics toward their own mediation. Newspapers, for example, are printed, reviewed, and cited at a given frequency; this repetition brings individual readers into a specific relationship of reception. Each particular media cycle creates its own self-reflexive social knowledge, turning a history of "exchanges into a scene with its own expectations" (Warner 2002:66). Postmodern media theory has focused on the global simultaneities created by the ever-increasing speed of circulation (e.g., Harvey 1990; Jameson 2001 [1991]; Lyotard 1984; Soja 1989). But temporalities of exchange depend as much on slowdown, interruption, and mutual exclusion. New media pile up to the point of overload, collecting in bottlenecks that strain the capacity of public distribution. Local infrastructures radically distort transmissions by adding more and more noise to the signal (Larkin 2008). Feedback, then, does not reduce to dialogue between cultures. It shows that circulation defers and distorts communication, even as it enables new possibilities for connection.

Noise spins out of its productive miscommunications. The historical concept of communication included a range of meanings, only a few of which related to interaction between discrete subjects. As John Durham Peters has pointed out, communication could include indeterminate acts of reception (e.g., partaking in Holy Communion, which made the recipient part of a religious body without any personal expression); it could involve the transfer of a sourceless energy or the unconscious appropriation of an idea for another use. In the twentieth century, broadcast and recording media recast communication as a dialogic world system that could connect different cultural voices through an ever-improving technological network.[15] But the copresence of global connection also involves miscommunication, confrontation, and mutual breakdown. The mistake of communication theory, Peters argues, is "to think that communications will solve the problems of communication, that better wiring will eliminate the ghosts" (Peters 1999:9). In fact, the wired world generates more spectral voices than ever, and more Noise.

MUSIC AS MEDIA

One aim of this study is to complicate historical narratives of popular music through the repetitions, delays, and distortions of technological mediation. I show how the jagged distribution of Noise set the stage for new waves of musical creativity, as its recordings were discovered and rediscovered by scattered listeners around the world. Noise's perennial newness is generated by its irregularity in the time frames of popular media. It is out of sync with the speedy schedules of corporate industry, and also with local scenes of independent music and histories of avant-garde aesthetics. The newness of any musical genre is determined by the time it takes to become familiar, as it "breaks" in different sites of reception. Music is produced and distributed; it is heard and then named, identified, and placed in comparative relationships with other styles. The clock starts again as a new style is slowly broken into the world. It becomes known as it is distributed, historicized, diversified, and then, perhaps, lost, buried, and recollected in nostalgia.

But as media circulation opens access to an increasing catalog of global forms, its time lags and delays continue to amplify the effects of cultural difference. Distance and isolation are exploited to create separate markets within the misalignments of transnational distribution. When an American musician or band is described as "big in Japan," this means that their music has run its course everywhere else. It is surprisingly popular in this unlikely place only through some sort of unnatural accident or coincidence, which seems to spring from the gaps between its original culture and its foreign reception. But global popular culture is not staged on a unidirectional timeline, like a telephone game in which a message radiates outward, slowly losing its original authority and meaning in its expansion to distant, separate contexts, from which it never returns. It is constantly remediated through the transformations of feedback. As time lags and inequalities become part of circulation, they break new ground for musical creativity and generate new forms that are folded back into the loop.[16]

Mass-mediated genres of popular music are increasingly recognized as productions of cultural difference, as well as hegemonic objects of transnational capitalism. Social critics have long feared that the spread of technological media would eliminate global diversity. For ethnomusicologists, the rapid postwar expansion of recorded and broadcast music threatened a "cultural greyout" of the world's musical resources (Lomax 1968). As media influenced the content of local knowledge and traditional instruments were replaced with electronics, separate music cultures might even cease to exist, as distinct expressive forms are consolidated into a homogenous global mass. In fact, the opposite has occurred: cultural difference has fed back into musical circulation with a vengeance. Popular music remediates local identity, sometimes as a fusion of transnational musical aesthetics adopted by ethnic and subcultural groups, and other times as an unfused essentialism of cultural nationalism.[17] Regional pop stars symbolize new political movements; "world music" channels the transcultural creativities of urban cosmopolitanism; and hybrid pop genres are heard as sonic hallmarks of mimetic influence and intertextuality.[18] Recorded music has become integral to contemporary senses of place and identity. Recordings inspire local revivals and provide material for emerging archives of cultural memory even as their sonic contents are remixed into new forms and alternative interpretations of history. In this feedback, it is difficult to describe any popular music as distinctly local, original, or independent. Local musical cultures have not disappeared. But they are constantly reproduced and remediated in dialogue with other new projects of listening, performance, emplacement, and selfhood.

To illustrate how musical cultures are formed in circulation, I describe a diverse range of listening practices that brought Noise to the ears of a transnational audience. These creative receptions are not necessarily exclusive to Noise or to its audiences in the United States and Japan. As recordings became ubiquitous to musical knowledge in the twentieth century, listening was transformed on a global scale. The "audile techniques" of recorded sound—the technological isolation of listeners, the construction of private acoustic space, the introduction of historical forms into mass culture, and the complex relationships of sonic "fidelity" between copies and original sources—were particularly crucial in forming the aural subjectivities of "alternative modernities" (Gaonkar 2001; Sterne 2003). Charles Hirschkind, for example, has described how cassette-recorded sermons in contemporary Egypt constructed a political public sphere of "ethical listening," and Amanda Weidman discusses the impact of phonographic listening on transmission and performance practices in South Indian Karnatic music (Hirschkind 2006; Weidman 2006). Recordings generated new discourses of collection and connoisseurship, as well as diverse contexts of mediated performance (e.g., remixing and reperforming recorded music in dub, hip-hop, karaoke, mashups, and so on).[19]

Narratives of global media often focus on the displacement of circulating forms from their original sites of creative production. But audiences bring music back to place through their own sonic explorations. Noise fans create maps of recordings—guides to record stores, lists of essential tracks and albums, indexes, charts of performance sites, and collections of sounds—that chart the underground networks connecting Tokyo to New York to Osaka and point to distant horizons of creativity. Recordings become points of access to a hidden world of sound that echoes beneath the surface of everyday life and moves scattered listeners to imagine the space of a global music scene. Through their geography of consumption, they transform the creative landscape of Noise: fans become musicians, receptions become productions, and techniques of listening turn into frameworks of performance.

In *Japanoise*, I trace the feedback between recorded media and performance in contemporary musical experience. Sensibilities of recorded sound are an especially crucial common ground for audiences separated by geographic, linguistic, economic, and cultural divides. To close the distances of global circulation, listeners and performers alike become deeply invested in the personal embodiment of sound. Absorbed in sound, they bring recordings into their senses, and then feed their experiences back into public discourse as a mediated form of musical knowledge. Live performances of Noise create an intensely powerful sonic atmosphere that inhabits public space with a private emotional sensibility. The sheer loudness of Noise can produce sensations of interiority, and live shows are valued for this immersive experience, especially in the tiny "livehouses" of urban

Japan, where audiences are suffused in an intense environment of overwhelming volume. But Noise's "liveness" emulates the sonic production of recordings, which create an equally powerful aesthetic of "deadness" in individual experiences of sound. Listeners identify the special qualities of Noise through its embodied sensations (e.g., "harsh"), which are incorporated into special techniques of production and mastering that can make Noise recordings sound loud at any volume.

Another goal of this book is to examine the role of technology in the formation of cultural subjects. Here, feedback stages the technocultural subjectivity of Noise, which takes shape in its sonic practices of creative destruction. In Noise, disparate things get plugged together. Outputs go back into inputs, effects are looped together, and circuits are turned in on themselves. Sounds are transformed, saturated with distortion, and overloaded to the point that any original source becomes unrecognizable. Controls no longer do what they are supposed to; each discrete function is tied to the next in a fluctuating, interrelated mass of connections. Sound seems to generate itself. In the next moment, the circuit is overturned, the gear is wrecked, and the network is destroyed.

Feedback generates a powerful ambivalence around the terms of musical authorship.[20] Individual practitioners began making Noise in isolated experiments with consumer electronics, which eventually overlapped in performance systems based in "circuit-bending," overload, and distortion. In the process, they bent the linear narratives of musical history into an unpredictable, self-reinforcing network. But if performers celebrate the inventive possibilities of technological participation, they also debate its violent effects on individual sensibilities. Their electronic feedback embodies a human–machine relationship that is uncertain, excessive, and out of control. Noisicians forced their listeners to witness the technological overload of individual consciousness in consumer societies. The millennial narratives of Japanoise extended the aesthetic modernisms of futurism and surrealism to the symbolic power of 1980s industrial music and postapocalyptic anime. This technocultural critique fused Noise to Japanese culture through a global imaginary in which postwar Japan has become iconic of the destructive impact of modern technologies. In this process, Japanoise was linked into Japanese cultural politics through geopolitical histories that are anything but random.

THE JAPAN OF JAPANOISE

Japan has been particularly important for enculturating the sourceless feedback of Noise, particularly in overseas reception as Japanoise. But how is Japanoise Japanese? Throughout this book, I contextualize Noise in Japan, usually among particular individuals and communities in Osaka, Tokyo, and Kyoto from the mid-1980s to the mid-2000s. I conducted the bulk of my fieldwork with Japanese musicians, fans, producers, and other social agents, and I observed particular local networks and documented particular practices of performance, recording, and listening in Japanese sites. My narratives of Noise generally document its creative developments in Japanese contexts and its subsequent receptions in North American ones. Because of this ethnographic focus, it might be possible for readers to think that I am arguing that Noise is, in fact, a Japanese genre with a discrete local origin. Foreign reception may have merely distorted its true native voice, which remains buried beneath the static. Or, given its place in a history of intercultural mistranslation, Japanoise might be a pure invention of Western Orientalism: even the name recalls the appropriation of Japanese traditional culture in the "japanoiserie" of turn-of-the-century French aesthetics. But I am not arguing that Japanoise is a singular local entity or that it was generated only by foreign misappropriation. Its cultural character reflects an intricate historical relationship with the United States, through which Japan has been constructed as an antisubject of Western modernity.

Japan's modernization is deeply linked to the military and political interventions of the United States, but its popular cultural forms are often represented as if they had been spontaneously generated in situ. As Iida Yumiko has stressed, the particularizing realm of the aesthetic has been central to Japanese national identity. Japan's modern status was mediated through Western appreciation of its art and culture, so that "Japan" "became an aesthetic construct of the modern universal world" (Iida 2001:14). Narratives of postmodern Japan as an aesthetic surface provoked the search for its deep structures of cultural origin, even in its most derivative commercial forms. Even Japan's most blatant borrowings and imitations of Western culture could be perceived as reflective of a unique native subjectivity.[21] Japanimation, J-pop, and other forms of J-culture have helped American audiences reimagine Japan within a global technological commons that connects modern publics even through their differences. But even as Japanese products are spread across the world in music, cinema, food, games, and technologies, Japan has not reappeared. What emerges instead is Japanoise.

Encounters between the United States and Japan have historically been unequal, but unequal in particularly repetitive, cyclical ways. Japanese cultural productions constantly affirmed the constitutive influence of the West while insisting on an autonomous unique status. The particular asymmetries of Japan's "off-center" perspective became embedded in its modern intellectual and literary development (Miyoshi 1991). Consumption of American goods was politically institutionalized in postwar Japan, promoting a fantasy of "bilateral" relations within the hegemonic power of the United States (Yoshimi 2003). As a result, the Japanese public is deeply familiar with American-made popular culture, but even as Japan's powerful media industries find a growing market in Asia, crossovers to the United States have been rare. Japanoise seemed to reverse this lopsided movement, even if its flow from Japan to the United States was irregular, enigmatic, and untranslated. My extension of Japan studies into a context of transnational reception, then, is also a step toward globalizing American studies through the circuits of Japanese media.[22] In both contexts, distinct projects of cultural and subcultural identity emerged from shared but separate loops of consumption.

Scholars of popular music show that Japanese productions of jazz, rock, hip-hop, hardcore punk, and reggae have generated transcultural critiques of race and ethnicity, cultural authenticity, consumerism, and national politics (Atkins 2001; Bourdaghs 2012; Condry 2006; Hosokawa 1994; Matsue 2008; Sterling 2010; Stevens 2007). Japanese forms valorized American constructions of postmodernism, minimalism, and techno-futurism. Contemporary Japanese art was strongly influenced by overseas selection of its most exceptional avant-garde forms—the fashion of Miyake Issei, the striking and bizarre performances of Butoh and the Gutai group, and the "superflat" art of Murakami Takashi—even as its reception often covered over historical relationships of influence and political interconnection (Kondo 1997; Looser 2006; Marotti 2013; Murakami 2000).[23] America's "Japan Panic" of the 1980s inspired deeply productive fantasies about dystopian futures in cyberpunk novels and films, which influenced productions of Japanese manga and anime (Brown 2010; Morley and Robins 1995; Napier 2000; Tatsumi 2006). "Millennial monsters" such as Pokémon and toys like the Tamagotchi reflected the absorption of Japanese cultural forms into "enchanted commodities" of flexible capitalism, which triggered a wave of participatory identification among postindustrial youth in the United States (Allison 2006).

In tracing these bidirectional movements of "Japan," I do not claim that Japanese culture does not exist or that all local differences have been completely saturated in Noise. But Japanoise must be glimpsed through these reflective relationships, which project its global adaptations against its radical cultural incommensurability. Japanese modernity is haunted by narratives of disruption and displacement, which produce infinite speculations about what is or is not still present of its culture. "Discourses of the vanishing," as Marilyn Ivy puts it, raise endless questions about whether an autonomous Japanese culture can still exist, or ever existed in the first place. The newness and constant emergence of modern Japan are the flip side of this anxious inquiry, as the inexplicability of Japanoise creates "a crucial nexus of unease about culture itself and its transmission and stability" (Ivy 1995:9).

FEEDING BACK INTO ETHNOGRAPHY

Ethnographic writing, too, can be as much a force of ambiguity as of explanation. The displacements of feedback are essential to how I write about Noise, even though they contribute to an unsettling mode of ethnography. I will not touch down in particular sites for long. I do not break down its forms into separate Japanese and American components or distinguish its publics through frameworks of class, race, and gender. I have not attempted to give complete accounts of the historical relationships between groups or to synchronize Noise as a timeline of events within the boundaries of a local music scene. Even as specific individuals become recurrent presences that loop through the text, I do not recount their biographies or profile their stylistic contributions within a larger repertoire of Noise. Although I describe Noise on the level of sound through its intricate performance and recording practices, this book does not explain the irreducible sonic particularities of "the Noise itself." In taking this dislocated position, I am complicit with Noise's unstable circuitry of cultural representation.[24] My story of Noise is fragmented and partial; it is marked as much by what it occludes as by what it reveals. It is a strange moment to author a monograph about a hidden form of popular culture, as even its deepest underground flows appear to be laid bare in an age of open access, crowd-sourced information, and participatory media. After decades in which Noise was a powerful mystery, its forms are now widely available; it is easy to search for its sounds and find some version of its history. The continuous transformation of Noise has made an ethnographic approach essential in my account of its movements, as it surfaced and submerged back into circulation over two decades.

Japanoise describes the productivity of an experimental culture whose scattered subjects privilege distortion and disintegration over authentic sources of expression. To take Noise seriously in its creativity—rather than compressing its diverse forms into a theoretical abstraction—means paying attention to how people create it, listen to it, and experience it in their lives, without freezing its dynamic movement in place. I enter into Noise through performance, recording, and listening; through talking to people about their goals and personal sensibilities, and then discovering the ways their experiences have and have not lined up with others; by tacking back and forth between different places and returning over years to recognize how things have changed. I often zoom out to look at these points of contact from a distance. This is not to authorize a global perspective on Noise as a whole, or to provide a long view of its historical development, or to inscribe its generic boundaries. Instead, I spiral into the particular sounds, sensations, and things of Noise and spin back to its scenic networks and stories. If not ethnography "on the ground," then, this is ethnography "in the circuit," following Noise through the overlapping, repetitive channels of its social and sonic feedback.

It may seem strange that I have chosen this marginal experimental form as a frame for the broadest scales of cultural globalization. But Noise shows that many central ideas about global culture are formed on the fringes. My intention is not to give Noise authority through its mystical position of obscurity. On the contrary, I argue that Noise, despite its marginality, lies at the heart of global media circulation. We have begun to listen to Noise. What we hear is not just a short-circuited interruption of local cultural meaning or an echoing stream of random postmodern static stripped of its communicative possibilities. Noise is a feedback loop of deep and multilayered significance, which brings the sounds of a distorted world back into earshot.

CHAPTER 1

SCENES OF LIVENESS AND DEADNESS

There are about forty-five people in here, bathing in the blast of Noise right now: a group of older fans, some college kids already holding CDs they've purchased from the merchandise table, a handful of foreigners (mostly Canadian and American), and a lot of familiar faces among the regulars, local performers, and store and label owners here for the show. These all-Noise concerts usually happen about once a month in Tokyo, in different venues. The livehouse, 20,000V, is set up like any small hole-in-the-wall rock club, a poorly maintained, boxy room in the basement—actually, two floors down in the subbasement—of an anonymous building on the main shopping street in Koenji. It's about a hundred square feet, and there are huge black wooden speaker enclosures chained to the ceiling on either side of the stage; flyers on the walls for both current and past hardcore, scum, punk, and Noise shows; a tiny bar in the back by the toilets selling cups of beer; and a little table near the door where recordings by the evening's performers are sold.

I stand about halfway toward the front of the room, slightly to the side of the stage, in line with one of the huge towers of speakers. MSBR is on stage now, and he is very interesting to watch. His body movements are much more conservative than those of the energetic eighteen-year-old Long Islander Viodre, whose thrashing set preceded MSBR, but his hands are always moving: constantly adjusting pots and faders, starting and stopping sounds, changing them, pushing against pedals, and switching them off and on with the base of his hand. In comparison with tonight's other performers, MSBR's Noise is more multilayered and rhythmic, and he is almost completely still as he sits in the center of an earsplitting whirlwind of sound. He cuts in and out of an analog delay, shuttling through a spacey blur as he shifts out of one timbre and into another, never letting any texture linger for more than five or ten seconds. Everyone is rapt, falling into the steady flow of sound. No one talks; no one *could* talk if they wanted to. . . . Besides, it costs ¥4,000 (about US$50) to get in, so you can't afford not to get it—you just listen.

Indeed, everything about this audience shows that they already know what they are doing here, as they stand scattered about the floor of the club, now watching the next band, Nord, blasting through the speakers, two huge thickets of incense burning on stage as blue light illuminates the performers from behind. The low-end vibrations are inside my chest, forcing my lungs to compress as I exhale slightly, involuntarily, along with the blasts of sound. Nord is so *heavy*, pounding deep drum sounds, droning moans with electric clatter over it all, and as the atmosphere intensifies, growing louder, the lights begin to come up—white, glaring spots in my eyes as their set crashes to an end.

Finally, the famous harsh Noise duo Incapacitants takes the stage. It's so loud I can't breathe—they vibrate the air inside my mouth, in the back of my windpipe, as the volume grows and grows. I fear for my eardrums despite the wadded-up balls of wet toilet paper I stuffed in my ears as the set began, and I retreat a few meters to the back of the tiny room where it's slightly—barely—quieter. Two or three others have done the same, but most press closer to the center as Mikawa and Kosakai crash their sounds against us. One Noise musician I recognize is right up in front, directly in front of a speaker, bouncing his head and shoulders back and forth, and occasionally thrusting his arms out in front of his body toward the musicians, vibrating tautly in place.

Mikawa is crushing a contact mic under a bent square of steel, tilting it back and forth to shift the oscillating loops of feedback emerging from his system. Kosakai shakes the mic in his hand in front of his Marshall amp, his entire body rattling and jerking as if he is holding onto part of some powerful being that is trying to escape his grip, as a quaking stream of high-pitched noise spins out of the speakers. Mikawa leans over in front of a smaller Roland amp, each of their heads down on either side of the stage, faces to their tables now, leaning on them, shaking them—or are they being shaken? Kosakai crashes to the floor in a jumble of electronic parts as his table collapses—the lights come up harsh and bright, shining right at us. Suddenly the sound is cut, the lights switch off a second later, and we are left in a strange void of darkness and silence, soon broken by sporadic applause and shouts of approval, as the performers shut off their amps and abruptly stumble off stage, exhausted, tripping over the morass of wires on the floor.

|||||

Noise is about liveness and deadness, both in performance and in the technologically mediated sound of recordings. Live Noise performances can produce extraordinarily powerful embodiments of sound that help audiences imagine a community of Noise listeners, both locally and as a global "scene." How can we understand these experiences of sound as part of Noise's circulatory context? Listeners most often encounter Noise through individual experiences with recordings, and even the liveness of Noise concerts is geared toward isolated receptions of sound. The feedback loop between liveness and deadness, then, is about the co-constitutive relationship between performance and media in the lives of listeners. But this loop runs parallel to another kind of feedback—between making sound and feeling its effects. Liveness is about the connections between performance and embodiment, which transform passing moments into repeatable encounters of listening. Deadness, in turn, helps remote listeners recognize their affective experiences with recordings as a new aesthetics of sound and listening in the reception of Noise.

In this chapter, I illustrate Noise's liveness and deadness in several different contexts of experience. I describe liveness in the places of Noise performance, in the embodied practices of Japanese Noisicians—particularly the legendary Incapacitants—and in the affective experiences of individual listeners. Liveness is further embedded in Noise through the production and circulation of media. Noise recordings were foundational in the growth of performance networks, especially in North America. Noise is embedded in techniques of production that aestheticize its overwhelming sound into recorded qualities of loudness and harshness. Finally—although, of course, there is no end to this loop—the sonic values of deadness in Japanese "harsh" Noise recordings become a poetic resource for listeners, who reanimate the scene of live Noise performance. The density of the experiential relationship between recordings and live performance in Noise follows from the displacement of musical communities and scenes in circulation. Where is the real place of Noise? What do the sensations of liveness and deadness mean to different Noisicians and listeners? What kinds of emotions are produced in the sensational liveness of Noise? How are recordings woven into translocal receptions, especially for those far from any accessible live scene? How does recorded media help listeners connect their isolated listening to social performance?

Ethnographers often privilege live performance in narratives of musical culture. For many researchers, live music is where authentic musical experiences happen, and performances represent sites of dialogue and interactivity that stand in stark contrast to the displacements of recorded media. Thomas Turino attributes an especially heightened musical sociality to "participatory performances," especially flexible, improvised gatherings (jam sessions, sing-alongs, etc.) where the collective "doing" of music is stressed over the "end product that results from the activity" (Turino 2008:28). Live music evokes an immediate—and apparently unmediated—experience that is musically authentic, culturally distinct, and sometimes politically resistant. Amateur performance is the foundational source of continuous, collective sociomusical knowledge, and its transmissions may contain the remnants of a traditional oral "music culture." Recordings, on the other hand, rationalize music beyond the productive space of social relations into separate forms of "studio art" that are passively consumed.

The experiential binaries of this scenario do not offer much to redeem the participatory experience of mediated listening or justify the centrality of recordings in everyday musical life. Musical circulation becomes a mediated *kulturkreis*: live performance stands at the bull's-eye of creative production, but its social force is gradually diffused through waves of technological mediation. At best, recordings become disembodied placeholders for authentic culture. At worst, they are a virtual dead end that dislocates people from the living realities of music. Certainly, the physically and temporally immediate context of performance gives live music a deep social presence and a sense of "here and now" in face-to-face interaction. But social experiences of live music can be profoundly individuated and often depend on embodied knowledge acquired through personal experiences with recordings. Just as performance is not always productive of social copresence, "dead" recordings do not necessarily separate listening communities into atomized consumers.

Recordings and performances constantly overlap in perceptual space but spin out into different contexts. In his influential book *Liveness: Performance in a Mediatized Society* (1999), Philip Auslander showed that contemporary live performance depends on the integration of technological media to create its cultural presence. Meanwhile, liveness is inscribed in studio production techniques that sonically represent the copresent space of musical communities in recordings (Meintjes 2003; Porcello 2005). Media, then, are not just the remote end product reflecting the original context of musical production. Recordings make sense of music for listeners, and constitute different socialities of performance and musical community. And just as online virtual worlds do not need to correlate to offline contexts to become real places, recordings do not have to connect "back" to performance practices to actualize musical experiences (Boellstorff 2008).

It is important to recognize that liveness is not a natural by-product of live performance. Liveness is not simply the transcendent feeling of "being there" at an exceptional concert among an appreciative audience. It is an affective relationship between embodied experiences of the "real" world and individual "virtual" encounters with technological media. As Jane Feuer (1983) argues in her work on live television, liveness cultivates a feeling of immediacy and interaction with televisual events. Liveness helps viewers actualize the extreme fragmentation of space inherent in broadcasting and allows them to share the experience of a media event even as it happens somewhere else. In this, liveness is both a technique of media production and a social habitus that naturalizes technological mediation through embodied practices of reception (Couldry 2004).

In bringing these relationships of musical place, performance, and media to the surface, the subjects of Noise put a great deal of stress on "the scene." The context of the local music scene has been central to historical imaginaries of independent music and exerts a powerful hold on its publics (Bennett and Peterson 2004; Kruse 1993). For scattered listeners who do not share face-to-face interactions, the idea of the scene can evoke a "diasporic," even "tribal" network of participants, which can bring musical sociality into a globally mediated context. The notion of the scene was especially useful in complicating earlier notions of musical subcultures that imagined alternative social identities through art, fashion, and language (Hebdige 1979). Will Straw (1991) used the term to describe the social construction of local communities in decentralizing practices of circulation. In his useful formulation, a scene is not a physical site or network but a fluid and flexible mode of performance that helps listeners navigate the industrial contexts of music production. Yet music scenes sometimes boil down the essence of a local community to a singular authentic site, where unmediated social relations are musically enacted. This is not to deny the symbolic power of the scene. The very idea is deeply motivating for fans who imagine, listen for, seek out, read about, talk about, and poetically conjure an original space of liveness, which appears to somehow transcend its own mediated networks.

But in Noise, deadness makes the scene live. Its listeners perform musical worlds through recordings: they repeat their sonic experiences, or put them on pause; they turn sociality up or down, or shut it off; they trigger individual memories and imagine impossible continuities between disparate places and times. But they also bring a sonic imaginary into cultural circulations, which extends beyond their own private audition. They conjure places across the globe, possibilities buried in the past, and feelings beyond social representation. Listeners slowly connect their own private sensory knowledge to the broader discourses of Noise, and more—they feel these sounds and emplace them in their own lives in ways that create new worlds of experience. And, as I will show, they can use these experiences of recordings to enliven the place of performance, by feeding their isolated listening into the scene.

FEELING THE SPACE OF THE LIVEHOUSE

In Japan, a small music club is called a "livehouse" (*raibuhausu*), a Japanese neologism that describes a site in which *raibu* ("live," meaning live musical performances) take place. In many ways, livehouses set the tone of music scenes in Japanese cities. The spatial fit between a livehouse and an audience is very important to the affect of liveness, because the feel of any performance is affected by the size of the venue. Noise is almost always performed in a relatively small livehouse, and occasionally (but rarely) in outdoor concerts or multipurpose art spaces. Because organizers take a personal risk in paying the venue for tickets in advance, attendance is important and carefully managed.[1] In several years of fieldwork, I rarely saw a local Noise "live" sell out, but neither were the tiny places much less than full: with occasional exceptions, Japanese Noise audiences vary from around twenty to fifty attendees. Most livehouses of this size are not dedicated to a single kind of music but accommodate many different fringe music audiences. As a result, Japanese livehouses become "big tents" for a diverse range of overlapping underground scenes.

The energetic, "packed" feeling of public space in Japanese cities creates a famously dense, focused ambience, and this affect follows through to the feel of its performance sites. In his study of Japanese hip-hop, Ian Condry describes the deeply social context of the *genba*, the "actual place" of live music where cultural production is "made real" in affective experience (Condry 2006). This sense of place is crucial for creating local social identifications for global genres like hip-hop, which are often constructed through recordings produced elsewhere. The focused attention of listening in an enclosed space helps construct the boundaries of a local audience as well as a separation from the general public. In Japanese cities, small livehouses sometimes occupy basements or higher floors of office buildings with little overflow into the outside world, rather than in street-level zones set aside for entertainment. The "actual place" of local performance is clearly delineated from ordinary life: you are either in or out.

Foreign performers are often impressed (and sometimes confused) by the close attention Japanese audiences give to performers. Many have commented on the intensity of livehouse spaces, despite the fact that audiences were not necessarily any larger than at home. One Chicago-based musician who frequently performs in Japanese venues described this atmosphere in terms of the density of feeling in the small rooms: "In a way, playing in Japan feels pretty good as a musician, because the place is always packed—there might only be fifteen people, but it's packed—and you sort of feel like, 'Wow, there's a scene happening here!' I mean, it's not much when you look at how many people live in Tokyo, or when you go to see a basic rock show in a bigger livehouse. But there is a feeling of some sort of connection with a scene, even though it's small . . . because everyone is stuffed into the same place, whether it's a big place or a small place, people are always stuffed in." In a Japanese livehouse, even a small audience can occupy the space in a way that feels crowded, creating the feel of the scene, just as the crowd creates the feel of the city. The liveness of these moments promises the continuity of sociality beyond the walls of the livehouse, feeding back into the everyday lives of the listeners. Liveness is created simply by being in these special spaces, where people return over and over again to embody the scene. Livehouses conjure and narrate musical worlds through this experience of repetition, which depends on the longevity of local performance spaces.

Local clubs are crucial in many histories of popular music, and are sometimes viewed as the actual source of new musical styles.[2] Although there have been few clubs dedicated exclusively to Noise, there are some especially significant spots. For example, since the late 1980s, the livehouse Bears has been an important site for Noise, hard-core, experimental music, and extreme rock and has almost singlehandedly enabled the survival of underground music in Osaka.[3] The tiny club, located in the back streets of the Namba district, is owned and managed by Boredoms guitarist Yamamoto Seiichi, who tirelessly accommodates an endless series of extreme performances, from teenage newcomers to the classic "old school" Noise of its annual Noise May Day. Other clubs in Osaka, many of them larger and better equipped, have come and gone over the years. In the meantime, Bears has slowly become famous as a center for Japan's experimental rock, punk, and Noise. "Even if the building got burnt down," says Yamamoto, "we would continue it in a shack" (Yamamoto 1998). Bears' reputation was crucial for spreading the word about Osaka's Noise boom in the 1990s, through musicians' stories about the club and compilation recordings (such as the Japan Overseas CD *Bears Are Not Real*).

But livehouses do not often generate this distinctive sociality by being distinctive in themselves. The music scene that travels best is produced in anonymous spaces, where liveness can be reassembled and remembered in many different environments. Many livehouses deliberately cultivate a neutral, temporary state of occupancy. Unadorned black-painted rooms situate the audience between two blocks of speakers; the PA reamplifies the onstage equipment in a sonic field that emulates a gigantic home stereo system. In Japan, when people temporarily invest their energy in a particular spot, that place is described as a *tamariba*: a "haunt" or "hangout" that is both a space of gathering and a transitional cultural formation, like a temporary social club. A tamariba creates a point of occupancy between place and event and between public and private sociality. This is the liminal liveness of a waiting room, the feeling of standing in the crowd at a food stall or newspaper stand, or a gathering of acquaintances on a street corner.

The sensibility of liveness can be developed only through the repetitions of personal experience. Liveness helps audiences "realize" an undistinguished performance space as a chosen site of heightened activity. When people assemble in livehouses, they briefly inhabit what Hakim Bey calls a "Temporary Autonomous Zone," which "liberates an area (of land, of time, of imagination) and then dissolves itself to re-form elsewhere" (Bey 1991:100). Liveness is the affective context of these momentary "uprisings" that violate historical social narratives with unique moments of experience: although they cannot happen every day, over time they "give shape and meaning to the entirety of a life." These repetitive but special encounters with music become a kind of circulatory placemaking. Liveness leads people from the heightened musical space of the livehouse to isolated moments of quotidian listening and back again.

PERFORMING LIVENESS: "YOU WON'T BE ABLE TO TELL WHAT'S WHAT"

Performers become immersed in Noise through an emotional sensibility that connects their individual performances to overwhelming experiences of sound. In thinking about the virtuosity of live Noise performance, I unwillingly drag one particular memory to the surface: the moment I attempted to scream together with the Hijokaidan vocalist Hiroshige Junko in an open session at the No Music Festival in London, Ontario. Someone had suggested that we improvise briefly as a pair; Junko agreed, but I had forgotten my instruments and gear. I foolishly decided that I would just grab a microphone, seized with the idea that it would be great just to scream along with the famous Noise screamer. But I was struck dumb a few milliseconds later, when Junko opened her mouth and emitted an amazingly earsplitting sound. Instantly overcome, I tried my best to make some kind of noise: after all, I thought, how hard can it be to just scream? But I could hardly hear myself at all. My weak, undifferentiated sounds underscored the intensity of her volume; the pure harshness of her timbral focus; the mix of constancy and deliberation with the shocking sense of being overwhelmed and out of control. In other words, I was experiencing the deep affective consciousness of Noise's liveness, so apparent in Junko's incredible scream. Her screaming, I knew in a sudden flash—and then with a wave of nausea and humiliation, as I became conscious that we had just begun our "collaboration"—wasn't just screaming, and Noise wasn't just "making noise."

Noise performance is a spectacular mode of liveness, which seems especially extreme when contrasted with the disciplined listening of experimental music performance. Noise performance is musical experimentation writ large: the biggest, loudest, and most intense invocation of sonic immediacy imaginable. Despite the scene-like sociality of its performance contexts, Noise's liveness is embedded in distinctly individual—even if diffused and refracted—sensibilities of sound. Listeners stress the subjective embodiment of Noise's overwhelming volume. Its extreme loudness has become definitive of its special live performance (although similar aesthetic fields, as I discuss later, are common to popular music, especially heavy metal and hardcore punk music). The sensation of volume produced in Noise performances overwhelms listeners and performers alike. Although they encounter this overwhelming volume together, the separation of their emotional responses plays down the collective space of experience, instead focusing attention on internal confrontations with the sound of Noise.

The ability to produce overwhelming volume is perhaps the most obvious difference between Japanese and North American performance contexts. In North America, most Noise performances take place in nonprofessional venues, with hastily assembled and underpowered equipment. In some places, the demand to confront audiences with volume can lead to literal confrontations over the production of sound. I have attended performances that were shut down by club staff and repeatedly heard both musicians and audience members complain that the sound system was not loud enough for Noise. Sometimes performers deliberately test their equipment at a quieter volume during their soundcheck to turn up to fully distorted levels in performance. Arguments over the appropriate volume level can even lead to physical confrontations with concert staff: one performer, frustrated with the club's unwillingness to turn up the PA, simply walked over to the sound engineer and pushed him over, saying, "This is how we need to sound." In contrast, Japanese shows are conducted in livehouses where the staff is expected to create the best possible sound environment. Even the smallest clubs in Japan are equipped with absurdly powerful equipment and trained live sound engineers. This allows concerts to take place at crushing volumes, which bolsters the international reputation of Japanese Noise performance as the purest and most powerful context of Noise.

Japanese Noise is strongly identified with extreme live performance,

Scenes of Liveness and Deadness | 37

and groups like Incapacitants have become symbolic agents of Noise's liveness in transnational circulation. Despite the fact that many overseas listeners have never attended a Noise show in Japan, Japanese and foreigners alike regularly describe Japanese Noise as the furthest threshold of its performance style. Japanese Noisicians are particularly famous for the intensity of their live acts. It is not uncommon for sets to end with a performer collapsing on the floor, smashing a piece of equipment, or pushing over a tableful of electronics. Not all performers have such demonstrative stage acts. Many performances are conducted from a seated position, with the performer hardly moving at all beyond what is necessary—reaching out an arm to turn a knob in a minute gesture, or moving a contact microphone slowly across the surface of another object. But Japanese Noise established its reputation through its most radically physical performers, particularly Incapacitants, whose ultradynamic shows have become legendary. For most Japanese artists, overseas tours are rare, and Incapacitants have only played a handful of shows outside of Japan. But although most North American fans may never attend a show by these artists, knowledge about their performance is widespread. Stories of over-the-top shows help distant listeners connect recordings to the liveness of the *real* scene—which, for most fans, whether in Japan or North America, is always elsewhere.

Incapacitants generate an intense emotional energy (figures 1.1–1.3). Mikawa Toshiji and Kosakai Fumio react expressively to every sound, convulsing with frantic gestures as if possessed by their own Noise. Mikawa compares the group's live shows to sporting events like professional wrestling, whose performers stage a conflict that produces the feeling of violence without actually engaging in any kind of truly violent confrontation. He says that about twenty minutes into the shows—which is usually near the end of many Noise performances—he is overtaken by a rush of adrenaline akin to a runner's high. Although he says that his movement does not directly affect his sound, Mikawa claims that the sound is *felt* differently when he moves: "I move a lot, don't I? But it has nothing to do with the sound. Probably I would be able to produce the same sound without moving. But it would be *different*—probably to the audience, it would be *totally* different" (Mikawa 1999:25). Mikawa's performance is enfolded into his own experience of listening. Witnessing his movements, too, changes the experience of the sound. His Noise does not actually change through his gestures, but it is felt differently. Mikawa vibrates with the brute force of his own sensory overload, enacting the responses of a body out of control.

His performance is immediate, visceral, and outwardly directed, but self-consciously reactive at the same time.

In their live performances, Incapacitants embody the private sense of being overwhelmed by sound. They show the effect of Noise on their own senses, even at the very moment of its creation. This liveness short-circuits the distance between the listener and the sound, folding them back together in its affective feedback loop. Noise emerges simultaneously "out there" and "in here," inside your body. The audience member does not simply hear this sound in space but *reacts* to its sensations within a private sensory world. Noise's liveness is a circuit of energy that is purely internal and admits no outside space; in this, it is less like listening to music and more like the sensation of an electric shock. Liveness becomes an involuntary encounter with the *feeling* of Noise within one's body. Incapacitants transform these profoundly individuated sensations of personal overload into an observable performance.

Mikawa's physical reactions mirror the involuntary response of the listener, and the changes in his gestures follow an inexorable buildup in the power of the sound. Mikawa and Kosakai progressively increase their movement over the course of the performance, slowly expanding the intensity until their bodies appear out of control. Mikawa may begin trembling, stabbing pedals with sharp, violent gestures, while Kosakai starts to shake violently and begins doubling over, his body wracked with spasms, shouting into a mic that emits screeching feedback. As the Noise builds, Mikawa grips the flimsy table holding his gear and begins to shake it—or rather, the table begins to shake when his shaking body takes hold and tries to steady itself—and the pedals begin to bounce up and down and crash into one another. Finally, he pushes down on the table, and the folding legs first buckle and then slide underneath, and the table collapses. Mikawa is on top of his gear, amazingly still connected as he sprawls across his electronics, his body undulating in spasms as his hands continue to strike at pedals, now on his knees holding one up in his shaking hands, turning the knobs until the sound is at a peak, wide-open distortion at full volume. He ends the performance abruptly, perhaps by cutting off the power on his amplifier or by disconnecting a cord in his setup by collapsing across the pedals on the floor.

Incapacitants feed their internal physical reaction to sound back into the soundmaking process. Their liveness becomes an involuntary encounter with the private feeling of Noise: it is separately felt but experi-

1.1. Incapacitants. Photo by Jon Spencer.

enced by all within range, whether performers or listeners. Incapacitants perform a mode of sensory feedback that Maurice Merleau-Ponty called the "double sensations" of the body, which "catches itself from the outside engaged in a cognitive process; it tries to touch itself while being touched, and initiates a kind of reflection" through which people recognize their bodies in the process of embodiment (Merleau-Ponty 1962:93). They embody the overwhelming effects of their own sound and bring their physical responses into the loop of soundmaking. Mikawa and Kosakai become immersed in this disorienting environment and are inevitably overcome by Noise. In an ideal performance, says Mikawa, "you will reach boiling point, and then when you build up sounds, you won't be able to tell what's what" (Mikawa 1999:25).[4]

Incapacitants' extreme performances stand in stark contrast to their personal ordinariness (figure 1.4). Many Noise fans, even those who have never seen the group, have heard that Mikawa works a bureaucratic job in a major Japanese bank. His offstage life, they say, is exceedingly mundane. He dresses as a typical *sarariiman* (corporate worker, "salary man"); he commutes to work from a suburban home; he coaches his children's soccer

1.2. Mikawa. Photo by Jon Spencer.

1.3. Kosakai. Photo by James Hadfield.

1.4. Incapacitants before their first appearance in New York City, May 2007. Photo by Natasha Li Pickowicz.

league. Kosakai, who works in a government office, is equally approachable and friendly off stage, despite his possessed demeanor while performing. This knowledge about Incapacitants' workaday existence has become legendary among Noise fans. The quotidian life of a Japanese banker becomes a blank slate of social normalcy, against which the power of Noise is revealed through its transformative effects on the humble bodies of ordinary people.

The ordinariness of Incapacitants confirms that anybody—any body, no matter how unlikely—can be swept up into the power of Noise. There is something classically comical about the physicality of the duo, with tiny Mikawa spasming and collapsing on one side of the stage, flanked by the comparatively huge Kosakai flinging his arms into the air like a giant, shaking a fed-back, wailing telephone pickup, his broad stomach shaking and vibrating. These physical disparities, and the open secret of their ordinariness outside of this underground world, simply reinforce the overwhelming power of Noise's liveness. By showing their two vastly different and separate bodies producing and simultaneously being overtaken by sound, Incapacitants confirm the bodily disorientation of listeners. Even those who generate this sound in live performance are folded into a liveness that exceeds ordinary life.

GETTING INTO IT: VOLUME, POWER, AND EMOTION IN NOISE

The sensations of Noise's liveness are amplified by the individual embodiments of its performers. But off stage, listeners, too, stress individual conditions for feeling the sound. At a Hijokaidan concert at Kyoto's Taku Taku, I witnessed a man suddenly begin to thrash around in the back of the room about twenty minutes into the performance, eventually crashing to the ground. Unsure if he was in the throes of an epileptic fit, I looked over to see local Noise performer Hayashi Naoto sitting on top of the man, holding him down so that he would not continue to strike out, apparently involuntarily, into the crowded space around him. After the performance, I learned that this man often came to Kansai Noise shows and was an old acquaintance of Hayashi and others. Hayashi brushed off the abnormality of his reaction, saying simply, "He got into it." "Getting into" the liveness of performance, of course, is a marked ritual of musical sociality. Just as the search for obscure recordings distinguishes a specialized listener, the choice to "get into" Noise performance highlights an individually embodied knowledge. Noise etches hard lines between those who inhabit its unapproachable space of sound; between those who feel it—even if that feeling is involuntary—and those who do not. In some ways, the sense of participating in a powerful musical experience is made "live" as much by those who choose *not* to "get into it," but to "get out of it."

Noise performance breaks down the public scene of live music audiences into their subjective encounters with extremely high volume. The only choices are to stay to feel it or to leave. At the beginning of many Noise performances, the audience splits in two: in an instant, some press closer to the stage and the speakers, and others retreat to the back of the room. Listeners must decide, almost immediately, whether they can tolerate the overwhelming volume. Those who remain must find a way to appreciate this sound—to construct some valuable framework of personal experience through it—or they are forced from its presence. Unlike the nuanced contours of a good live sound mix, which brings a crowd together in a shared public atmosphere, Noise concerts flatten the space with overwhelming loudness. Extreme volume divides the common social environment of music into individual private thresholds of sensation. A really

1.5. Masonna at Festival Beyond Innocence, Osaka, 2012. Photo by Kumazawa Telle.

good Noise show confuses you, separates you from your acquired knowledge, and makes you wonder what's going on. It is easy to know that a Noise performance will be loud, but successful Noise performances still feel shockingly and unexpectedly so.

In 1994, I went to see Osaka Noise artist Masonna (figure 1.5) perform in a small underground club in San Francisco. Like many North American independent music fans, I was familiar with noisy bands such as Boredoms, Melt Banana, and Ruins, whose records I had listened to for years, had already seen perform live on North American tours, and like many others, believed were exemplars of Japanoise. I was expecting an over-the-top, virtuosic display of fast, loud, code-switching rock deconstruction, so I was surprised to find the stage practically empty, with no instruments anywhere to be seen. After a few minutes, the background music on the PA cut off, and a tall, thin man, with long hair and huge sunglasses practically obscuring his entire face, walked on stage, carrying a microphone on a stand. He immediately pulled the mic and stand apart and whirled the stand around in one hand, grabbing the mic in the other, then smashed the stand down to jettison his body into the air; landing on the stage on his knees, he began to shout. I had seen such onstage theatrics before, of course. But the Noise that emerged was unlike any voice I had ever heard, any sound I had ever heard. I wasn't sure I liked it, but then I never thought about liking it or not. I was witnessing it, feeling its intensity, receiving it, dealing with it. Sudden, crushing blasts of pure distortion whirled into my ears, and the Noise was just happening, sweeping into my mind.

Masonna transformed his voice into Noise, feeding the microphone back through a process of extreme distortion. His shouts became clipped bursts of overloaded sound, doubled and extended by a delay that displaced the sounds into stuttered blasts of static. These vocal sounds fused into a rattling background of harsh metallic fuzz, which was created by frantically shaking a highly amplified box filled with coins. I could not parse this sound into its constituent parts, as either the result of electronic processing, amplification, or "natural" voice—his voice was distortion, and distortion was his voice—and then it suddenly stopped, and a strange decompression and blankness seemed to rush into the room. Masonna dropped the mic and walked off stage as quickly as he had entered, and I slowly recovered myself. The entire performance had lasted only four minutes, but I felt as if I had taken a long journey, fallen asleep, or passed out, and was just coming to my senses.

Even in the crush of the crowd, this kind of loudness foregrounds individual experiences of Noise. Masonna's performance forces listeners to check themselves, to feel the limits of their physical reaction: "How long can I take this? Am I enjoying this feeling? Is this what I am supposed to feel?" I was driven within myself, paying close attention to my sensations to understand what I was experiencing. "What does this person *feel* that he needs to make this kind of Noise?" asked one friend after witnessing a Masonna performance for the first time. But questions of artistic intention quickly feed into other, more personal questions: "What do I feel, and why am I here to listen?" Years later, Yamazaki told me that he believed Noise is "a natural feeling for humans," and that any listener could understand it immediately on hearing it. But, he stressed, the feeling of Noise does not move "from inside to outside"; it is not a form of musical self-expression that communicates the inner feelings of a musician to an appreciative lis-

Scenes of Liveness and Deadness | 45

tener. In Masonna performances, Yamazaki said, "I create the tension by myself. The audience just submits to it."

ON THE SENSATIONS OF NOISE

Standing in the ringing, strangely empty aftermath of a show in the backstreets of Osaka, a friend told me something of how the loudness of Noise worked. We had seen many Noise performances together, but this was one of only a handful of times that he had voluntarily addressed his experience. At the beginning of a good Noise show, he said, the volume "just sucks all the air out of the room," leaving the listener suspended in sound: "You can feel your whole body react [he snapped his body back as if suddenly startled] when they start—the sound fills your mind completely and you can't think. At first you're just shrinking back, until you overcome that and let it go, and then you're in it and you're just being blown away." Noise's affective power requires this visceral embodiment of its extreme volume. When the sound begins, your body starts, instantly short-circuiting the public space of sound into internal response.

Theodore Gracyk, in his work on the sonic paradigms of rock music, describes the "noise" of loud music as a tool for overcoming the entrainment of distanced listening: "When not functioning as mere background, loud music can break us out of our sense of detached observation and replace it with a sense of immersion . . . where traditional aesthetic theories have often offered an ideal of disinterested contemplation or 'psychical distance,' the presence of noise can overcome the respectful, reverential aspects of distancing" (Gracyk 1996:106). The effects of extreme volume also have physiological effects on the way sound is heard. Very loud sounds are perceived as closer and clearer because they are compressed in the auditory canal under higher levels of acoustic pressure. This distance-erasing intensity of loudness is highly valued among fans of heavy metal, hardcore, and punk performance styles that exploit the effects of volume to create a powerful "in-your-face" sound (see Berger 1999; Kahn-Harris 2007; Shank 1994; Walser 1993). The association of loud sound with affective power occurs in other genres of "extreme" music in Japan as well, as Jennifer Matsue notes in her study of hardcore punk in Tokyo, where performances were described positively as *pawaa ga ippai* (full of power) (Matsue 2009:127). The liveness of loud music sometimes creates coherent subject positions within otherwise fragmented and decentralized musical subcultures. In the words of one fan remembering the 1980s punk scene in Austin, Texas, the sensation in the crowd "felt like we were going towards this one big happy tormented family" (Shank 1994:131).

In Noise, volume flattens out the scene to foreground the idiosyncrasies of individual sensation. Noise fans and performers sometimes describe their experiences at live performances as a state of hypnosis, dreaming sleep, or trance. This immersion in volume is not a moment of social collectivity but a personal encounter with the overwhelming presence of sound. The stress on sensory immediacy does not mean there is no social "there" there. Listeners obviously make great efforts to discover the subterranean sound of Noise, and their ongoing attendance at Noise shows marks them as part of a distinct local core of fans. But most Noise listeners describe performances through their individual reactions to sound, rather than the actions of performers or general audience responses. They describe the performance with abstract superlatives that relate the force and magnitude of its effects on their own bodies. Shows are sometimes described as "brutal" and "painful." Noise performers sometimes choose names for live projects and recordings that characterize these qualities of endurance as the involuntary suffering of pain, illness, and violence (e.g., Sickness, Pain Jerk). These are private feelings that cannot be described by ordinary terms of musical enjoyment and taste. Instead, Noise's liveness becomes a totally individuated experience of sound that cannot be translated to others. Its modes of listening detach from normative social contexts of musical appreciation.

The terms that describe Noise, both in Japanese and English, tune into the negative beauty of sublime experiences with sound.[5] They often connote excess and overflow of the senses, especially in words that refer to volume, such as *dekai* (enormous), *ookii* (big or loud), or *tsuyoi* (powerful). For example, another common word, *sugoi*, means "too much," and is akin to the word *awesome* in English. *Sugoi* can simply translate to "great" or "incredible," and in general speech is often used to modify other terms (e.g., *sugoku ookii*: "great sound/incredibly loud"). But its use among Noise listeners refers directly to the affective force of a sound and to the listener's overwhelmed response. As a sound that is "too much," the awe-inspiring, overflowing aesthetic of Noise stresses the individual encounter that cannot be recuperated back into social life.

At first blast, the overwhelming volume of Noise seems like a throwback to musical romanticism. The performance of Noise returns listeners to the epiphanies of the self that are compromised by technological mediation, stressing all of the heightened moments of emotion that bring them back to the uniquely irreducible context of live musical experience. But the transcendent individual experience of Noise's liveness is conditioned by the deadness of recordings. Through techniques of sound production and mastering, Noise recordings emphasize qualities of loudness, harshness, and presence that confront the senses at any volume. How can a recording communicate these involuntary sensations of volume, since it can be turned up, turned down, and even shut off at any point? What happens to the overwhelming embodiment of Noise when it is put under the control of the listener?

Next, I turn to the way Noise producers "master" the aesthetics of recorded Noise and describe how listeners learn to talk about deadness through the reception of recordings. First I want to show that liveness, too, is a technical quality of recorded sound. Liveness is always produced in relation to deadness; a "live" sound is a sound that is "not dead." Without further intervention into the listener's experience, most modern recordings would not sound live. Instead, their liveness is the outcome of a process of technological mediation by which recordings are made "not dead."

RECORDING LIVENESS

"Live"-sounding studio recordings often evoke an original site of musical performance. But liveness is more than a technological effect; these are sounds that create a mediated "sense of place."[6] Often, recorded liveness is created through reverberation, a kind of "soundprint" of physical space that can help listeners perceive a recording as live. Sometimes reverberations represent the resonance of a particular sounding space: a live-sounding room is one in which the reflective characteristics are audibly imprinted on the sounds recorded in that place (think, for example, of the squeak of basketball sneakers on a gymnasium floor). "Reverb" effects do not always derive from a particular acoustic environment. Electronic effects of echo and reverb evoke another kind of reproducible liveness, which is also heard by listeners as a particular aural context.[7] Studio recordings must reconstruct the space of liveness as a technical field of sound quality. Skillful producers are capable of generating particular qualities of reverberant liveness that listeners recognize in the spatial feel of a recording (Doyle 2005; Zak 2001). For example, the liveness of drum sounds recorded by noted engineer Steve Albini has led generations of bands from around the world to travel to Chicago to record in his studio. But the sound of Albini's liveness extends far beyond this particular space. Distant bands can reference this history of musical creativity by working elsewhere to reproduce the reverberant qualities of the iconic "Albini sound."

The musical place of liveness is deeply challenged by tensions around the authenticity of recorded media. Liveness helps listeners reimagine a public space of musical performance threatened by the context of technological reproduction. But this mediated liveness can obscure the particularities—of the lives, places, and cultural contexts—that recordings represent. Louise Meintjes's ethnography of South African recording studies, for example, describes the liveness of electronic reverb as part of a technologically mediated "sound of Africa" (Meintjes 2003). The interactions of Zulu musicians and outside engineers combine to create an illusion of live performance that develops sonic tropes of authenticity to represent local culture. This "African" liveness conjures for listeners a natural "space of contact with the performer" in a mediated circulation where nothing so transparent could possibly exist (Meintjes 2003:127).

Deadness, on the other hand, places the listener back into the displaced context of private audition. Instead of conflating sound with social space, deadness feeds the listener's attention back into the iconoclastic details of mechanical reproduction. The difference between "live" collectivity and "dead" immediacy, then, is not merely the difference between two distinct sound aesthetics, one connected to studio recordings and the other to performance. Deadness is a direct embodiment of technological reproduction in individual experiences of music.[8]

The rise of deadness traces back to early developments of communication technologies. The telephone initiated a demand for the reduction of noise to increase the intelligibility of sonic details, which was quickly extended to the "high-fidelity" sounds of music in broadcast and recorded media. As reverberant liveness faded as an aesthetic ideal, collective sites for listening began to appropriate the "dead" contexts of technological mediation. In the concert hall, deadness re-created the private experience of the bourgeois listener. The effect of this individuation is well illustrated in the transformation of public concert hall architectural design from the turn of the century until the early 1930s (Thompson 2002), which increasingly conformed to the model of an isolated listener. Reverberation in concert halls was reduced to an optimal level through innovative acoustic design and the increased use of sound absorption materials.

Managing these relationships of liveness and deadness became equally crucial in the craft of mixing in modern recording. Most multitrack studio environments are "dead," and the sounds recorded within must be "enlivened" in postproduction. Because each track is recorded separately, the mixing environment does not emulate the holism of collective space but creates a balance between live and dead sounds. A well-mixed record recreates the representational effects of live performance in a tightly controlled mix environment that isolates each sound and degrades the reverberant qualities of liveness by giving equal stress to the directness and clarity of individual sounds (Porcello 1998). But a truly dead-sounding recording bypasses the imprint of social space altogether in favor of direct connection to sound.

Noise recordings, almost without exception, are extremely dead. Even when they are recorded from a live performance, it is uncommon for Noise recordings to impart any sense of place that could represent the listener's or musician's position within a room. They are meant to sound as if the Noise was already inside your head—as close and "in your face" as possible. Deadness points attention to the environment of reproduction rather than to the original place of creation. Many Noise recordings are made by plugging the output of the electronics system directly into a recorder, without the resonance of room ambience or any other sonic attributes of the performance site. This method (sometimes called "direct injection") bypasses the space of mixing to connect the recording media directly with the sound source. Noise recordings do not omit social space to more clearly control the production of separate musical signals; rather, they cultivate a holistic sound field of deadness, through which listeners become immersed in their internalized receptions of Noise.

In the remainder of this chapter, I describe how deadness is incorporated into Noise recordings, and how its sonic aesthetics have influenced the formation of a transnational audience. In the process of "mastering" Noise recordings, we see how the dense qualities of its liveness—its thresholds of disorientation, overwhelming volume, and internalization of sonic experience—are mediated by its aesthetics of recorded deadness. These techniques of sound production influence Noise listeners, who have developed ethnopoetic terms for deadness to describe the "harsh, "extreme," and "ambient" qualities of Noise. By learning to recognize and evaluate their responses to these recordings, listeners create a form of knowledge production in their reception, which eventually feeds back into the affective context of live performance.

AS LOUD AS POSSIBLE: MASTERING NOISE'S DEADNESS

In the heat of a Tokyo summer in June 2007, I crowd into Gomi Kohei's tiny apartment along with Mikawa and Kelly Churko, a Canadian Noise artist and sound engineer who has been living in Tokyo since 1997. We are listening to the premasters for an upcoming split release by Incapacitants and Gomi's project Pain Jerk, culled from live recordings of their performances at the 2007 No Fun Fest, a major annual Noise festival in New York City. Churko's laptop screen is broken, and we've had to plug the computer into Gomi's old Sony TV, which is so blurry that the titles of the file folders are barely readable. Somehow the process seems appropriate to Noise, to use such a low-tech system for such a highly technical process. Every now and then, Churko asks Gomi and Mikawa what they think about the frequencies represented in the stereo master:

> "Can you bring it more up front [*dekai*] . . . ?"
> "More high end [*takai*]? More bass [*teion*]?"
> "Hm. Yeah—just turn them all up."
> "Like—*puuuwaaaan* [an onomatopoetic term connoting power and impact, something like "pow"]."
> "As *harsh* as possible, right?"
> "Right."

The original live recording was made on a faulty digital audio tape (DAT) taken directly from the soundboard, and there's a lot of crackling digital distortion. On any other recording—that is, any recording of music—this amount of distortion would render the tape unusable. But as Churko works, the recording is distorted again and again until the original distortion is overloaded into a crushing curtain of up-front treble-y harshness. The sonic fault of the live recording becomes another noise buried within the Noise. Although this additional layer of distortion was not intentionally created, this random artifact of the live recording was nonetheless fed into the chain of electronic transformations that represented the space of its liveness: the buzz of ungrounded current flowing, the sizzle and fuzz of amp distortion, the sudden impulse of a distorted shout, all of it absorbed into the compressed, flattened deadness of Noise.

A few weeks later, Churko showed me several techniques for mastering Noise, as he worked on another recording, this one by the Kansai Noisician Guilty Connector. He expanded the effects of the existing distortion on the final mixdown by "EQ-ing" sounds to make the treble frequencies more apparent and by using compression to further flatten the dynamic range.

> Churko: It's totally maxed out. . . . . you can't even see the wave [in the stereo waveform used in Churko's mastering program] because it's all maxed out all the time. For [Guilty Connector], he wants it to be harsh, and that's his only priority in the sound. . . . Just make it brutal and harsh and loud and that's it.
>
> DN: But it's already really harsh and loud; how do you make it harsher?
>
> Churko: Just by adding EQ [equalization]. It's like on your own stereo: [If] you don't like the sound, you change the EQ and suddenly it sounds better. You turn up the treble, you can make the sounds more pure and piercing. You're not *actually* making it louder; you're making it *seem* louder. You can turn the stereo down, but it will still sound loud.

Mastering is the last stage of recorded sound production, in which the final version of a recording is altered for the particular media format on which it will be released. For most music recordings, mastering a recording consists of maximizing its volume through compression, as well as affecting the balance of the existing frequencies with equalization. In many ways, mastering a recording is an inscription of creative individual listening, as a professional listener "prints" their subjective interpretation onto the recording to create the final musical result. In keeping with the aesthetics of live Noise, mastering takes the effect of this subjective listening to an extreme, so that mastering can radically alter the sound of the original recording. Although mastering typically makes all recordings louder, Noise mastering maximizes loudness to the point of overload, introducing new layers of distortion and high-frequency harmonic presence.

Mastering Noise, Churko says, is like experiencing the performance again in slow motion and then isolating and amplifying the moments of its deadness. Churko begins by distorting the entire final mix, turning up the volume to its maximum level, so that the sound "clips," flattening the

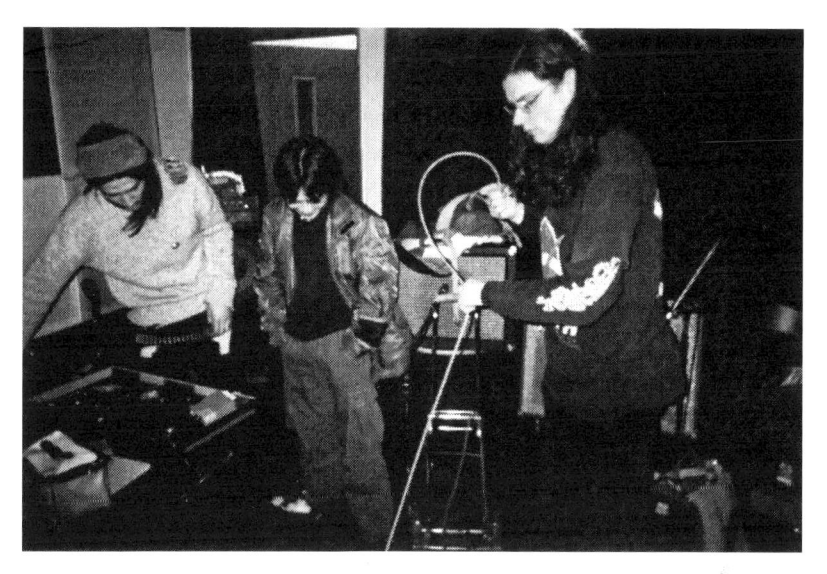

1.6. Kelly Churko (right) setting up equipment, with Filth the Sleep (Guilty Connector, left) and Yoshida Yasutoshi (Government Alpha, center). Photo by the author.

soundwave against the ceiling of the amplification device. The clipping of the amplifier compresses the sound by lowering the peak levels to round off the dynamic curves; all sounds, quiet or loud, then emerge at the loudest possible volume. He then begins to EQ the recording, pushing the stereo mix through filters to make it seem even louder and flatter. Mastering the deadness of Noise is not a process that emphasizes or balances certain sounds in relation to others. The objective is full frequency overload: to bring everything up at once, to make the entire sound feel as close to the listener as possible.

Noise recordings feel closer because they exaggerate high frequencies to emphasize what engineers describe as "presence." Presence increases the perceivable effect of volume without increasing the decibel level and makes the music feel closer—more "present." In sound engineering, *presence* usually refers to a timbral contour that creates an effect of immediacy by boosting the upper midrange frequencies (especially around the area of one kilohertz, known as the "critical band" of frequency perception).[9] As Jeremy Wallach describes it, presence is a marker of "electrosonic excess" that orients listeners toward the materiality of sound and makes them conscious of its effects on their senses (Wallach 2003). Presence makes listeners aware that they are listening to a recording and reorients their perception toward its particular sonic qualities, especially sensations of loudness. Studies of equal loudness contours (also known as Fletcher-Munson curves) have shown that raising the volume of a sound significantly changes the range of sensitivity of the human ear. A louder sound is heard as "flatter" across the frequency spectrum and will be perceived as closer, fuller, deeper, and "brighter" (more high frequencies).[10] Because "present"-sounding recordings are equalized to mimic these changes in perception of loudness, they can seem louder than they really are, even at low volumes. Exaggerating this psychoacoustic effect can reduce the perception of distance between the sound and the listener, which makes Noise recordings feel more "immediate."

Churko's story of his own first experience with a Noise recording—Merzbow's harsh Noise classic *Venereology* (1994)—highlights the shocking effects of Noise's sonic presence:

> I was astonished, because at first it was just this noise, this texture, and I thought, "Well, when's the band going to break in?" You know, I thought it was an intro, and pretty soon there's going to be a riff or something. But it ended up that thirty minutes later, nothing had changed; well, a lot of things had changed, but overall, it hadn't changed at all. I was making this curry and I started to get this headache, and then it started to feel like my teeth were being wired shut, and then it felt like I was getting stabbed in the back—and I thought, "Oh, this is pretty cool!"

Churko's inclusion of a seemingly unimportant detail—that he was cooking for himself while listening—illustrates the transcendent feeling of overwhelming immediacy for which Noise's deadness is valued. He initially treated the CD as a musical supplement to his everyday activities and attempted to listen while simultaneously taking care of his evening chores. But the sound interrupted and overcame his senses, cutting him off from his ordinary life and from the possibility of distracted listening. Churko recalls the surprise of his initial perception of Noise ("thirty minutes later, nothing had changed") and then immediately qualifies this with the knowledge developed through a decade of listening and performance ("Well, actually, a lot of things had changed").

Venereology was one of the first Noise recordings to appear in the North American retail market. Although the CD contained almost no supplementary information, the deadness of its sound began to teach first-time listeners how to appreciate Noise. It was released in 1994 by the tiny independent label Relapse, just at the moment that U.S. independent labels began to find distribution in national retail outlets. Relapse's description of *Venereology* as "extreme" reflects the emergence of Japanese Noise into a U.S.-based independent circulation in the 1990s. "Extreme" quickly became a term closely associated with Noise, and one Australian label named itself Extreme Recordings.[11] One North American Noise fan told me that he bought *Venereology* because "it had a sticker on it that said 'This is the most extreme CD you will ever hear'": "What shocked me was that it was so loud. It was the loudest CD I had ever heard. It produced a sensation of total panic when you put it on. You immediately reach for the [volume] knob, and for a moment, there's just sheer panic . . . but then I would get hypnotized. I had it turned up pretty loud, but I really wasn't particularly focused on it. But it just invaded my senses anyway." Relapse's claim of *Venereology*'s extremeness was backed up by the mastering techniques used on the CD. With the cooperation of a technician at the pressing plant, the CD was mastered at the highest possible level. In fact, the sound levels were so high that the release was technically illegal, violating federal limitations on the dynamic level allowed on CDs (a fact that was widely reported by the label in advertising the recording). Although the volume of playback ultimately remains under the control of the listener, *Venereology* showed a new audience how Noise was supposed to feel.

Expanding on the idea of Noise as extreme music, Noise recordings often exploit frequency ranges that test the endurance of the listener. Even when played at a fraction of the decibel level at which it would be experienced in a livehouse, a good Noise recording feels overwhelmingly loud. For example, Guilty Connector filters the sounds of highly amplified metal plates to emphasize extremely high-frequency sine waves, which create a piercing, ringing sonic contour. He calls this method *shibaki*, from the Kansai-language slang term *shibaku*, which means to beat or strike (someone). In shibaki Noise, high-frequency clusters are swept across the treble range, shifting the contour of the sound, like waves of shimmering tone color in an ocean of distortion. Noisicians selectively develop terms such as shibaki to describe their personal techniques of sound production, and listeners eventually created their own ethnopoetics for the affective qualities of Noise recordings.

The most common descriptor for Noise is *harsh*. Because "harsh Noise" represents an extreme sonic experience, this quality has become the symbolic center of Noise's deadness, as well as a subgeneric term associated with Japanese Noise. Because they were first developed in North American reception, these terms are in English, but they have been widely adopted by Japanese listeners as well. Many active fans qualify their appreciation of Noise with this term, saying, "I really only go to pure harsh Noise shows," or they evaluate a recording positively by noting that its sound was "really harsh." Churko characterized "harsh" Noise as more common in Japan than in North America. Among three closely related examples—all on the Osaka-based Alchemy label—he described two as "harsh" and the third (albeit more ambivalently) as "ambient":

> Churko: [Harsh Noise] is like maximum Noise all the time. Harsh Noise is not dynamic. Incapacitants is harsh, Masonna's harsh; it's so loud, all the time. Especially in Japan, people know what's harsh, and that's what they're looking for most of the time.
>
> DN: *So what's not harsh Noise?*
>
> Churko: Like . . . Aube wouldn't be, because it changes; it's almost ambient noise. It's noisy at times, but then it climaxes and comes back down.

Although certain formal differences of style are noted (ambient Noise "climaxes and comes back down"), the ability to distinguish harshness is located in embodied personal knowledge ("people know what's harsh"), rather than in identifiable structures of sound.

Although these terms were created as references to recorded sound, they also can be used to identify live sound productions. The harsh Noise artist Masonna often shakes a metal can filled with coins, which is amplified enormously and put through a series of electronic effects. To this filtered noise, he adds the "peaky" sounds of heavily distorted and delayed shouting, giving a sharp dynamic contour that adds to the overall harshness of the Noise. The "ambient" sound of Aube, on the other hand, reflects a more gradual approach to timbral and dynamic change, developing a single sound field over a long period of time. His performances are far longer than Masonna's, often lasting thirty to forty-five minutes, building and then tapering off slowly ("it climaxes and then comes back down") rather than ending abruptly.[12]

Harsh, then, might seem to distinguish a set of formal traits that could help characterize Noise through its particular qualities of sound. But more than describing specific differences of sonic texture, listeners use these terms to relate the sensational effects of Noise. For example, Canadian Noise artist Sam McKinlay (a.k.a. The Rita) described "wall" Noise (sometimes represented by the acronym HNW, for "Harsh Noise Wall") to me to explain how different sound aesthetics could be perceived within the larger field of harsh Noise. McKinlay considers wall Noise as the purification of "classic" Japanese harsh Noise into a more refined "crunch," which crystallizes the tonal qualities of distortion in a slow-moving minimalistic texture. Crucially, McKinlay defines wall noise primarily through the sensory feedback it produces in the listener: a "euphoric state" of deadness that should "manipulate the listener into evaluating and finding value" in the different sounds of Noise within a Noise recording (McKinlay 2006). Wall Noise, then, is not merely a refinement of the harsh Noise sound; it describes a particular way of *feeling* sound through recordings.

This discourse of embodied listening eventually fed back to Noise's live performance. Ethnopoetic terms for deadness helped a North American listenership imagine their experiences as part of an international "Noise scene." One way that fans connected was through the identification of harsh Noise recordings, first in direct correspondence and in fanzines, and later in online forums like the well-known harshnoise.com discussion board, where categorizations of Noise sounds, legendary stories of Noise "stars," and lists of "best" and "harshest" Noise releases among listeners are posted. Long-term listeners can readily identify different styles of harsh Noise and can capably distinguish between the recorded sounds of individual performers. The ability to differentiate between harsh Noise textures — and even recognize that different aural valuations are possible — is a hard-earned skill requiring many hours of isolated listening. Nonlisteners, on the other hand, might hear these same sounds as an uninterpretable static (e.g., "the signal's gone dead"). This knowledge of recordings helped experienced listeners recognize that it was possible to appreciate and embody the sensations of Noise in a mediated form. But it also emphasized an emergent context of musical experience, in which individual responses to recordings create the interpretive conditions of liveness.

This special relationship between liveness and deadness is what gives Noise the heightened quality of "having an experience," to invoke John Dewey's use of this phrase. Dewey distinguishes "an experience" from the general stream of experiences in everyday life by its integral holism and self-sufficiency, which is "constituted by a single *quality* that pervades the entire experience" (Dewey 1980 [1934]:37). We recognize "an experience" as "the closure of a circuit of energy" between "doing something" and "undergoing something"; between knowledge of the self and interaction with the world. As a form of sonic experience, Noise's deadness is no more the product of recording technologies than its liveness is created solely by live performance. Both are part of the consummation of lived experience. In the feedback between recordings and live performance, musical sociality "can be crowded into a moment only in the sense that a climax of prior long enduring processes may arrive in an outstanding movement, which so sweeps everything else into it that all else is forgotten" (Dewey 1980 [1934]:56).

To close this chapter, I loop back to the scene of liveness to describe Incapacitants' first-ever performance in North America in 2007. Connecting the trajectories of liveness and deadness shows how Noise audiences have reanimated their individual encounters with recorded media as social performances of listening; deadness feeds back into liveness again. Within this feedback loop, the affective links between recordings and performance create the foundations of modern musical subjectivity.

FROM DEADNESS TO LIVENESS

The annual No Fun Fest, a four-day Noise concert festival organized by the New York–based Noisician Carlos Giffoni, became increasingly well attended over the years since its inception in 2003, hosting some of the largest audiences for Noise performances ever assembled. The 2007 Fest was an exception by any standards. Anticipation for a roster of international Noise performers, including five from Japan (Merzbow, Haino Keiji, Incapacitants, Yoshimi P-We, and Pain Jerk) as well as artists from Europe and around the United States, has filled the remote club in Red Hook, Brooklyn, to its 600-person capacity (and then some) with Noise fans, many of whom have traveled long distances to be here. The onstage performances take place upstairs, but the basement of the Hook is an equally active site. Small labels and record stores have lined the room with tables, and the tiny space is packed with fans poring over an enormous array of recordings for sale in every format, as well as obscure fanzines and a few homemade electronic devices. For the four days of the festival, the Hook becomes the center of an unprecedented scene. If one could encircle this cramped space, it would contain within its borders not only the largest archive of Noise media in the world but also a significant proportion of the North American Noise listenership.

Although Incapacitants' recordings had become legendary among North American fans over two decades, the group had never performed in the United States before this point. The pair had scheduled a show in New York City in fall 2001, but the concert was canceled at the last minute in the aftermath of the September 11 attacks on the World Trade Center. When the word got around that Incapacitants were booked for the 2007 No Fun Fest, Noise fans around the country were ecstatic, and the duo's appearance became the most talked about aspect of the upcoming concert. In fact, the festival was originally planned for March, but because Mikawa could not rearrange his work schedule at the bank, Giffoni rescheduled the whole event for May to accommodate Incapacitants. All of this added to the heightened sense of anticipation around the duo's spot on the Friday lineup, and tickets for that night were sold out weeks in advance.

On the evening of the performance, the crowd builds slowly throughout the evening, eventually filling the club beyond capacity. The excitement is palpable throughout the building, as fans press closer and closer to the stage. Incapacitants are the ninth and final band on the schedule, and by the time Mikawa and Kosakai step out onto the stage to begin setting up their gear at 1 AM, the audience is psyched up beyond belief. As the duo moves their small equipment tables out to the center of the stage and begins to plug their gear together (to the suspenseful background of Ifukube Akira's *Godzilla* soundtrack that some brilliant smartass is playing through the sound system), they shoot anxious glances out at the surging crowd. The audience is already applauding and shouting; they have begun to crush against the stage, pushing forward until they cannot move any farther. On stage, a ring of people, including most of the performers and anyone else with the nerve to jump up and squeeze onto the side of the stage, fills in every inch of the floor not occupied by Incapacitants and their gear. This is a rare moment, and everyone knows it; video cameras are everywhere. One man at the edge of the stage smashes a can into his forehead over and over, grimacing performatively as a thin stream of blood trickles down from his scalp. Another, spotting Gomi from Pain Jerk taking photographs of the crowd from behind the amps on stage, shouts "*Gomikawa Fumio!*" (the title of a 2002 collaborative recording that combined the names of Pain Jerk and Incapacitants members). Most of the people in the crowd stand their ground, waiting in silence, but there is an increasing wave of motion passing from the back of the room to the front, as more and more people try to push through to get closer to the stage. Some hug the edge of stage, with their heads directly in front of the PA, and others climb up to stand next to the speakers. I have found a place on the side of the stage to record video, from on top of one of the massive bass cabinets on the floor, and I have set up my tripod so I can pan back and forth between the stage and the audience (although this position will not last long).

The *Godzilla* soundtrack fades out as Incapacitants complete their setup and walk a few steps away from their tables, Kosakai reaching back to adjust one more knob. The crowd cheers and applauds. As Kosakai and Mikawa return to stand in front of their tables, lit by a plain spotlight, there is a pause of a few seconds. Someone in the crowd yells out the name of a 1993 Incapacitants album — "Quietus!" and another immediately responds with "CMPD!," in reference to the 1996 CD *New Movements in CMPD*; someone else calls out "D.D.D.D!," the title of a rare 1995 cassette-only release. A voice from the side — comically adding to the incongruity of shouting out Noise "song requests" — adds "George W. Bush!" and someone in the back immediately snaps back "Hitler!" Then Mikawa turns up the volume on his mixer; a crackling, static-y distortion spits out of the amps as he leans over to shout into a cheap plastic mic, and screeching feedback fills the room. The crowd lifts up a few inches, and immediately launches forward toward the stage as hands fly into the air, some clenched and shaking, others holding cell phones and cameras that unleash a flurry of flashes from all directions.

Kosakai is doubled over, rattling a mic in one hand as he twists a knob with the other; Mikawa smashes his elbow into a metal sheet on the edge of his table, then points a shaking finger at the audience, glaring directly ahead. Someone in the middle of the crowd throws themselves on top of the others, and the audience is so tightly packed together that they immediately fill the gap, pushing his convulsing body slowly toward the stage, where Chris Goudreau (a.k.a. Sickness) and a few other volunteers push him back until he is finally hauled back down into the crowd. There is nowhere for him to land; Incapacitants stand in a ten-foot circle, surrounded by fans on all sides. Behind them, someone pushes forward into the back of Kosakai's amp, briefly disconnecting the power as Giffoni and another Noisician on the side of the stage rush forward to plug it back in seconds later; more and more people push forward until the crowd is like a wave, spilling out onto the stage (figure 1.7).

1.7. Incapacitants and crowd at No Fun Fest, 2007. Photo by Michael Muniak.

Mikawa puts a contact mic into his mouth and begins to shout muffled unintelligible sounds, distorted beyond recognition. A roar comes from the crowd, and now the people in the front are unable to stand up; they are leaning forward, falling on top of one another, and some begin to jump up to crouch at the edge of the stage. By about fifteen minutes into the set, the crowd is piling up onto the stage, and Goudreau and a few other volunteer stagehands are literally holding them back from falling onto Incapacitants. I have abandoned my post on top of the bass cabinet and use the folded tripod to hold my camera up over the sea of heads as more fans push forward onto the stage. Mikawa stands still, vibrating, staring out at the crowd, pouring with sweat now as Kosakai raises both fists in the air, smashing two homemade electronic boxes together over his head. He inches forward on the stage, and the crowd reciprocates, bending forward and shaking like grass in a strong wind, reaching out and almost grabbing the squalling mics out of his hands. Mikawa throws his body in circles at the edge of his table, and Kosakai staggers forward to the edge of the crowd; he spins around to face the back of the stage, raising his arms in the air. He stands there, briefly, pushing back against the crowd—as if stand-

Scenes of Liveness and Deadness | 61

ing in their place for a moment—before throwing his body backward into the audience, whose roar drowns out the last few seconds of Noise before Mikawa snaps off his mixer and the show is over.

After many years of mediated listening, the North American Noise audience brought the distinction of their carefully crafted deadness back into the live scene. They were ready to experience the overwhelming sound of Incapacitants' impossibly harsh Noise and to perform their knowledge of its overwhelming sensations of deadness in the context of liveness. In many ways, the response of the crowd—surely one of the largest Noise audiences ever assembled—overwhelmed the performance on stage. At points, the sound of the crowd was even louder than the Noise from the PA, colliding with the energy of Incapacitants' liveness and throwing it back with even greater force. The organizer Carlos Giffoni pointed out the irony of this reversal: "It's funny, because they started in Japan as these extreme performers who were always confronting the audience, pushing forward with this intensity—but now it's like the audience becomes the extreme characters! They were playing and the crowd was almost falling on top of them!"

The intense liveness of this instantly legendary live performance was quickly fed back into Noise's mediated circulation, both in online networks and in the production and reception of recordings. On the morning following their performance, countless video clips and photographs of the show were posted on YouTube and Flickr, shot from many different perspectives within the crowd.[13] Even now, one could practically create a 3D reconstruction of the show from the enormous collective archive of video and still photography taken that night. Within a few days, the online discussion boards and other music blogs were full of reportage about the event, with most attendees confirming that the show was the "harshest ever." A few months later the Pain Jerk/Incapacitants split CD *Live at No Fun Fest 2007* (the mastering of which I described earlier) was released on Giffoni's No Fun Fest label. Pain Jerk's track was called "Hello America (excerpt)," and Incapacitants titled theirs "The Crowd Inched Closer & Closer."

This singular scene of Noise's liveness then spun back out again into ordinary life. I caught up with Incapacitants at their next performance in Tokyo, two weeks after the No Fun Fest, and asked Mikawa what he thought about the show. "Great, of course, the audience was great," he responded quickly, nodding his head. Then, after a brief pause, he added, "but the sound system was too weak." The crowd for this performance at

Showboat in Koenji (featuring Incapacitants headlining a bill with touring North Americans The Rita, Impregnable, Tralphaz, and Oscillating Innards) only numbered around twenty-five people. As I videotaped the performance from the back of the small livehouse, I was struck by the comparison with the overflowing audience at No Fun Fest. At Showboat, I could keep the tiny crowd entirely within the frame. The small in-group of international Noise performers and hard-core local fans were clustered between the speakers in front of Incapacitants, who vibrated and shook in the center of the tiny stage. But the audio on my recording came out completely distorted; the sound was just too much.

CHAPTER 2

SONIC MAPS OF THE JAPANESE UNDERGROUND

Go from wherever you started to JR Shinjuku Station. Get out of the train and find your way to the east exit. Go past the giant Studio Alta television towering over Yasukuni Street. Go past the Seibu station entrance and head under the tracks, beneath the train overpass. Directly across the street from you is Omoide Yokocho: "Memory Town," a grubby, jam-packed cluster of narrow alleys filled with tiny eating and drinking shacks, never rebuilt since the hard postwar recovery, when it became a center where Tokyoites gathered to drink and forget. Go past the high-rise hotel and pachinko parlor, kitty-corner to the multistory Sakura camera shop, across from the skyscraper district. Take a right at the next corner, and you will be standing in the echoing center of a miniature world of media—one of the densest concentrations of record shops anywhere.

But you would never know it from what's right in front of you: the same ramen noodle shops, *konbini* corner stores, pharmacies, and soft drink machines that you can find on any central street in urban Japan. More than a hundred record stores share this corner of Shinjuku, tucked away on the upper floors of office buildings, around corners, or up back staircases. Nishi-Shinjuku holds a consumer archive of popular music history engraved in vinyl, in niches occupied by expert collectors who take up shop in the back rooms of emptied-out office buildings. These scavengers crept in after previous inhabitants—accountants, small export businesses, and attorneys of the postwar economic miracle—had failed or moved a few blocks over or a few stations away.

Nishi-Shinjuku's stores are rotating archives of microgenres like French yeye, Brazilian tropicalia, bootlegs of German psych—and of course, Noise. Stores like Baby Pop, Beat Collector's, Jet Set, Warehouse, Hal's, Yellow Pop, Psych-up, and Los Apson are crammed into rooms that measure ten or fifteen jô (a unit of measure corresponding to the size of a tatami mat, about twelve by fifteen feet), with record bins lining the walls and a small desk or table. There the solitary owner sits, minding the room, filling the space with the definitive sounds of his taste, perhaps selling a few records a day to his small but dedicated clientele.[1] Small, handmade wooden signs, some with LP covers stapled to them, placed on the edge of the sidewalk along the main street in front of the building or alleyway each afternoon—at 1 PM, or 3 PM, or whenever the owner shows up—are the only indications of where to go and how to find your way. Unless, of course, you already know exactly where you are going.

My entry into Japan's musical underground fed back into my mediated music-cultural knowledge, recollected in the overwhelming stockpiles of these niche record stores in Tokyo, Kyoto, and Osaka. I began my research in Japan by contacting performers, in the expectation that these contacts would eventually lead me to other musicians and eventually to map connections between Japan and North America. Locating these communities of practitioners, I presumed, would help me narrate Noise through its personal networks of performance, friendship, and internecine rivalry. A close-up look at the local social scene might flesh out, or perhaps overturn, some of the nascent impressions I had developed from listening to recordings in the United States—which could only be inadequate representations of the real Japanese scene.

However, my interlocutors often did not direct me to other artists, or to prominent performance sites, jam sessions, gathering spots, or, indeed, to any obvious social marker of a locally emplaced music culture. Instead, I was directed to record shops as primary public sources for information or aesthetic commentary. Performers insisted that if I *really* wanted to understand the boundaries of their Noise, I should visit a particular record store to put their stuff in the right context. A store manager, they occasionally claimed, might be more likely to recall the details of their own musical past anyway: "[So-and-so at Record Store X] can tell you about that record, he put it out . . . I think they've still got a copy up there, I forget." Meetings regularly led off with a visit to an important record store, and often the scheduled interview never occurred, displaced instead by connections made over the bins in tiny record shops around town. Questions about the local origins or individual histories of Noise trickled into talk about foreign scenes and influential obscurities. "Here," a Noise artist might say, pushing a copy of a rare Texas psych LP into my hands, "you should really check this out first."

I soon realized that the endless references to influential recordings and their sites of distribution were not meant as a diversion from the real scene. Rather than being led away from the knowledge I sought, I was being oriented toward the edge of a media circulation that defined the local landscape of Noise, as individual paths of listening were woven into an underground "geography of consumption" (Jackson and Thrift 1995). Recordings created a circulatory imagination of Noise that helped outsiders work their way inside, by notating the flow of sounds, labels, covers, collections, narratives, and compilations. Collections of Noise recordings laid the groundwork for imagining this alternative musical landscape. Listeners map the uncharted territory of popular music onto the spaces of the global city, seeking the subterranean places where new sounds are made and new scenes found. But when they try to navigate the horizons of a distant underground, they find themselves already looped into the spirals of its transnational movement.

Ethnographies often open with maps. Maps focus the distant reader's attention on a special, specific place that becomes the ground of cultural exegesis. I began this chapter with a view from central Tokyo, a site that focuses global views of Japan as a hypermodern uber-cosmopolis of overflowing media consumption. But Noise cannot be localized, even within the boundaries of a megacity.[2] Its landscapes juxtapose different urban sites—Tokyo, Osaka, New York—into a transculturated montage of underground music. The underground is the ultimate "inside" space of musical sociality. It represents a zone of deep creativity that seems only to be known by insiders, who collectively inhabit this subterranean world. But the inside view of Noise is scaled to distant perspectives, in which "a view from above remains a view from elsewhere, a view which in making the city *other* must correspondingly employ metaphors of otherness" (Stewart

1993:79). Even when they attempt to reveal a particular landscape on the ground of localized experience, maps make sense of the world from afar.

A map also creates a desire for what it is not: a local, immediate experience of the world. Sonic maps of media circulation feed back into representations of particular sites, networks, and social groups; depictions of musical place feed back into travel and intercultural connections; and the transnational circulation of recordings feeds back into on-the-ground views of local Noise.

MAPS DRAW THE OUTSIDER

Every map charts a place from a particular point of view and orients the traveler toward his or her destination. Although mapmakers may attempt a neutral form of knowledge creation, cultural and human geographers argue that relations of power are embedded in all cartographic representations.[3] Within a map, "social structures are often disguised beneath an abstract, instrumental space" that "produces the 'order' of its features and the 'hierarchies of its practices'" (Harley 2002:281). The ordering force of cartography allows the mapmaker to appropriate knowledge of a local world by rescaling its boundaries. The "visual-spatial realm," as Henri Lefebvre notes, "has a vast reductive power at its practical disposal," as maps reduce historical specificity and sacrifice ambiguity to represent the "perception of an abstract subject" (Lefebvre 2001 [1974]:312). The proposed neutrality of a map does not merely structure the subject positions of its readers; it affects their orientation within a landscape of knowledge. Maps compile multiple "senses of place" to represent the world, compressing multidimensional resources of cultural perspective into a single plane of objective information (Feld and Basso 1996). A map not only provides information to explorers, it helps them organize the social knowledge they already possess.

People place themselves in a landscape by using social, linguistic, and aesthetic resources derived from lived experience. Keith Basso's work on place-names shows how collective knowledge can render regional landscapes in ways that are not easily read by outsiders (Basso 1992, 1996). Basso's Western Apache interlocutors "speak with names" to anchor the feelings and memories that define local places. Describing an event that occurred at a place called "whiteness spreads out descending to water" is authoritative because the naming achieves maximum communication with minimal materials. Storytellers rely on embodied knowledge of specific places, encouraging listeners to use the same resources to "travel in their minds." Western Apaches use these narratives of personal experience to navigate the boundaries of a specific cultural world. When these stories are recorded and circulated as representations of local culture, they become maps that identify resources for an outsider for whom this world is unknown and strange. As people begin to move back and forth between cultural perspectives, different views of landscape and discourse seem "close at hand and tangible in the extreme," yet "each in its own way appears remote and inaccessible, anonymous and indistinct" (Basso 1992:220). Maps gather these independent local resources—stories and counternarratives, timelines and family trees, catalogs and repertoires of memory—and use them to create an abstract space of objective knowledge uncoupled from the variations of lived experience.

Regardless of location, a map allows its readers to look at the world from a distance. As Pierre Bourdieu describes it, a map is "the analogy that occurs to an outsider who has to find his way around in a foreign landscape and who compensates for his lack of practical mastery, the prerogative of the native, by the use of a model of all possible routes" (Bourdieu 1977 [1972]:2). Maps do not represent the landscape as a continuum of affective social relationships. They prioritize the outsider's view, compiling local worlds to make them knowable from a distance. This might suggest that embodied knowledge of place is entirely unrelated to the representational work of cartography. But some contexts—think, for instance, of a ship's captain out at sea—are simply too large to be navigated without a map. These circulations require the global view of the stranger, whose position in a group, as Georg Simmel put it, "is determined by the fact that he has not belonged to it from the beginning, that he imports qualities into it, which do not and cannot stem from the group itself" (Simmel 1950 [1908]:402).

Global cities, particularly those of urban Japan, are often described as landscapes of cosmopolitan overflow that can neither be mastered nor fully understood as representations of local culture. Although these places have been mapped relentlessly, they are always drawn apart. The placelessness of Tokyo has become an especially iconic territory for the modern outsider "lost in translation."[4] Roland Barthes's famous and controversial *Empire of Signs* mapped the semiotics of Japanese culture from his alienated position within this foreign city. But this is a Tokyo refracted through the view of a stranger, a "system which I shall call: Japan" (Barthes 1982 [1970]:3).

For Barthes, who did not speak or read Japanese, "the largest city in the world is practically unclassified, the spaces which compose it in detail are unnamed" (Barthes 1982 [1970]:33). He begins by acknowledging the futility of detailing the social realities of Japan. However, he documents his attempt to travel through this unmarked territory as a productive experience in itself: "it suffices that there be a system, even if this system is apparently illogical, uselessly complicated, curiously disparate" (Barthes 1982 [1970]:33). *Empire of Signs* represents the perspective of the prototypical stranger finding his way in the familiar-but-alien streets of the Japanese city.[5] As Barthes wanders through Tokyo, weaving through incommensurable signs toward its empty cultural center, he discovers that "the content is irretrievably dismissed . . . there is nothing to *grasp*" (Barthes 1982 [1970]:109; emphasis in original). His embrace of confusion and distance is undoubtedly provocative and might be easily dismissed as irrelevant to local knowledge. But this free movement through unrecognized cultural space is exactly what a map is meant to enable. Unlike the accumulations and overflows of everyday life, a map renders the local scene by reducing the specific details that clutter an objective view (what Edward Tufte describes as "chartjunk"; Tufte 1983). As long as they understand the technical orientation of maps, strangers can move forward without becoming lost in a proliferation of details.

Reading maps is an everyday practice for cosmopolitan insiders, too, because maps have become part of the work of belonging to the endless cultural space of a global city. This effect is particularly apparent in Japanese cities, where the absence of street names posted on signs makes addresses of no practical use in finding a location. Osaka or Tokyo denizens, intimately familiar with their routes to work or favorite spots in the city, still require maps to locate a place they have never visited, even if these new places are within a hundred yards of their home, or the train station where they depart for work each day. The daily writing of maps reminds the inhabitants of the city that they are strangers, directing their attention to new formations in a world that changes around them from year to year. "Walking the streets of the city," says Jinnai Hidenobu, "one is treated to repeated changes in the cityscape . . . the unexpected is always waiting" (Jinnai 1995:5). Cosmopolitans juxtapose "home" and "travel" to construct this reflexive space of cultural intimacy discovered through the experience of strangeness.[6]

The underground is an especially productive and unsettling place to call home. "Home," as anthropologist Michael Jackson points out, is a "double-barreled" word. It "is always lived as a relationship, a tension" between "a part of the world a person calls 'self' and a part of the world he or she sees as 'other'" (Jackson 1995:122). Home "involves finding somewhere in one's own world from where one may put oneself in the place of another" (Jackson 1995:122). Mapping the circulation of underground music helps listeners imagine new trajectories toward frontiers of indescribable sound, toward a distant horizon that always lies ahead. But a listener can make sense of this subterranean landscape only after they have already, in some crucial way, entered its undocumented territory from the edge.

Knowing music is a way of mapping the world, too. But how does one enter into a world of Noise? Recordings simultaneously orient listeners toward a promised destination and sketch out its boundaries. They are both compass and map. Curators and collectors chart the local features of an emergent underground: its styles, histories, formal structures, social networks, and sonic boundaries. But why do the coordinates of this distant musical landscape—the "Japanese Noise scene"—come to matter so much to listeners who will never touch down on its home ground? When most scenes are predicated on bringing you "inside" the music, how has the map of the outsider become the constitutive perspective on Noise?

LANDSCAPES OF UNDERGROUND CITIES

> The city is built
> To music, therefore never built at all
> And therefore, built forever.
>
> —Alfred Lord Tennyson, "Gareth and Lynette"

How is a scene seen from outside? For distant explorers, the place-names of New York City's neighborhoods—the Lower East Side (abbreviated L.E.S., and pronounced *eru ii esu*), the South Bronx, Williamsburg—become fulcrums of desire that resonate with social imagination. As the map of New York City in *Afutaa Awaazu* (*After Hours*) magazine shows, the representation of a music scene correlates to specific itineraries of connection and discovery (figure 2.1). In this case, writers from the Tokyo-based magazine

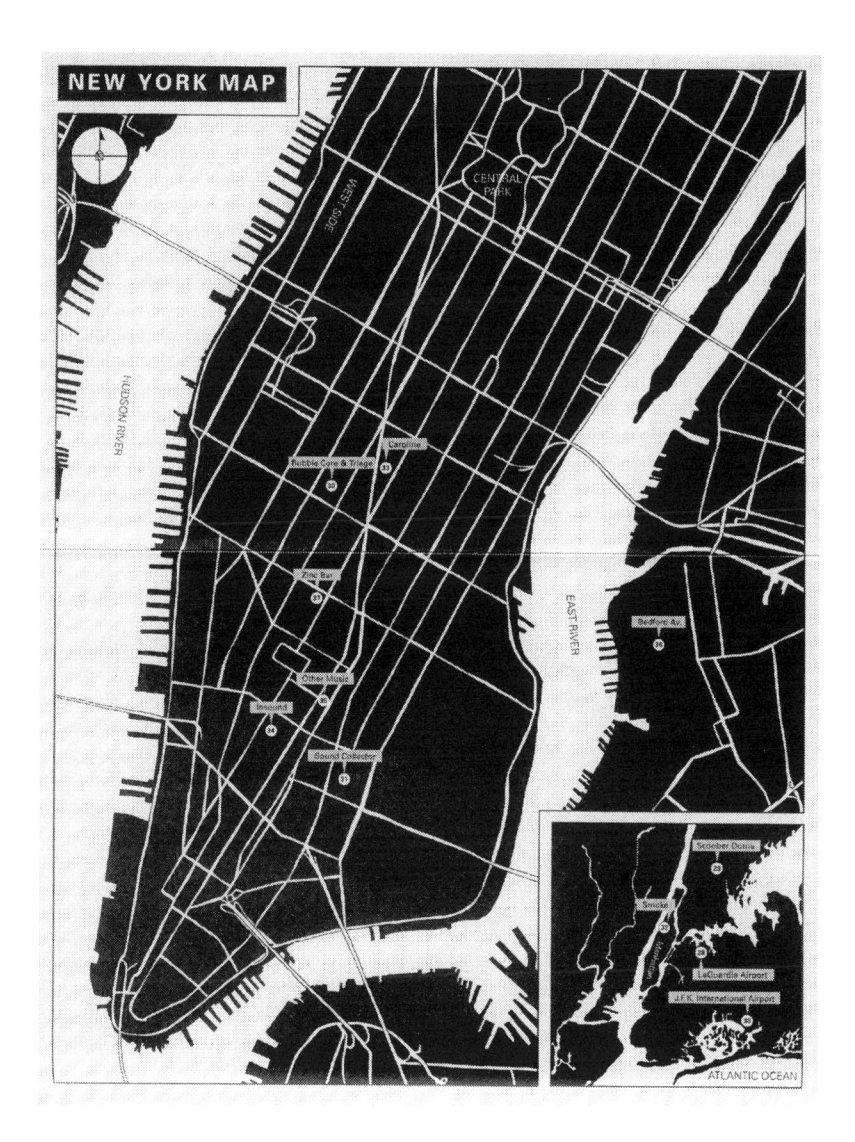

2.1. *Afutaa Awaazu*'s New York City. Courtesy of *After Hours* magazine.

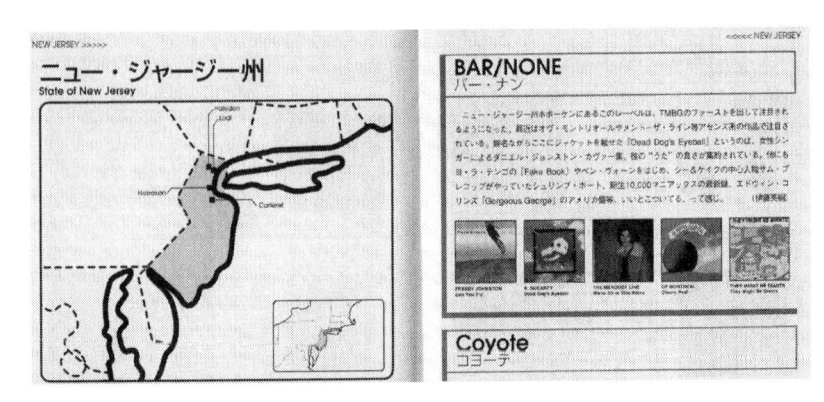

2.2. *Cookie Scene's U.S. Indii Poppu Mappu*, New Jersey.

visited New York, as well as Chicago and Paris, to connect with the local independent music scenes in each city. The resulting issue contained reports for Japanese fans on their experiences, with a set of photos published under the title "The Harvest of This Trip."

Ôsuki Takayuki's article "Shikago to Nyûyôku Shiin no Genjô" ("The Present Situation in the Chicago and New York Scenes") describes the project's goal as clarifying the operation of U.S. indie networks by interviewing everyone involved in creating the scene. The level of detail included not just musicians but label owners, distributors, store owners, and so on, supplemented by a compilation CD included with the magazine. Ôsuki and his comrades, by virtue of being Japanese explorers, describe themselves as alienated and distanced from their points of entry into the North American underground. But they are also already connected to these networks by their consumption of local recordings, and so can recognize the specifics of the indie musical landscape by mapping their existing knowledge against the terrain of new discoveries. In a section humorously titled "Are! Nande Konna Tokoro ni Iru no yo?" ("Huh?! Why the Hell Are We Here?"), Ôsuki describes the first day of exploration, when "three Japanese, unshowered, without having drunk any coffee or eaten any bread," arrived in New York; twenty minutes later, the trio were in an acquaintance's car on the way to a show (Ôsuki 2002:19). By immersing themselves in what they already knew to be the "local scene" through this access point, the writers followed a chain of pre-developed contacts to conduct interviews with members of the city's independent music scene. By the end of their visit, the cartographers' position moves rhetorically from stunned to embedded, and the group can return to Japan with the harvest of their "sentimental journey" to the American urban outposts of a global music scene.

For Japanese listeners in the 1990s, the world of the North American underground was traced out in the selections of independent record stores; with the reviews in local *minikomi* ("zines"); with distant addresses printed on the backs of imported releases that spoke of far-off local scenes. In the *U.S. Indii Poppu Mappu* (U.S. Indie Pop Map; figure 2.2) published in the fanzine *Cookie Scene* in 2000, indie labels were discussed state by state, with charts of each state's vital statistics and then discussions of its seminal labels, followed by short descriptions of selected releases from each label. For each state, the map provided a brief historical narrative of its definitive styles and bands and their contribution to the creation of the larger national independent musical underground. Each mapped place corresponded with a specific style, reasserting the locality of recorded production that is unraveled in decentralized circulation. But the desire for a consistent localization of musical style often led to conflations and inaccuracies. For example, Bar None is pinpointed in New Jersey, where the label is located, although most of its artists are spread across the country.

Depicting the local sources of underground music allowed Japanese fans to map their remote consumption of media back onto specific places of musical production (figure 2.3). In the *U.S. Indii Poppu Mappu*, New York is presented as the capital of the U.S. underground, with a definitive local style emerging from 1960s experimental pop group Velvet Underground, whose sound is echoed in later local groups Yo La Tengo and the Feelies, and in the production techniques of Shimmy Disc label owner Mark Kramer. The important 1978 "No Wave" compilation *No New York*, the downtown transformation of free improvisation at the Knitting Factory nightclub, and early 1980s hip-hop are all reiterated as styles that could only have emerged from this particular place. But the user of the *U.S. Indii Poppu Mappu* does not need to visit New York to navigate this scene. Rather, the reader explores the U.S. Indie Pop Map through the diverse range of musical products already available—and separately known—at home.

The desire to explore the world by consuming recordings feeds back to local productions of musical identity that map the sounds of a city's scene. During the 1990s, the music scenes of cities like Seattle, Minneapolis, and Austin were represented from multiple perspectives, from multinational music industries to alternative media productions to regional arts organizations.[7] In many ways, the U.S. indie scene was a piecemeal con-

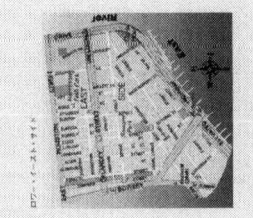

2.3. "Lower East Side" from *Avant Music Guide* (Sakuhinsha, 1999).

struction of scattered listeners, who contributed different views of local developments. Magazines like do-it-yourself (DIY) punk standard *Maximum Rock'n'Roll* often printed local "scene reports," written by insiders in each city's music community. The Louisville, Kentucky, scene report, for example, might include descriptions of concerts by visiting bands, new releases by local labels, openings and closings of record stores, and anecdotes about the town's well-known punk fans. By gathering several of these reports in each issue, *Maximum Rock'n'Roll* provided its readers with glimpses of scattered communities around the United States, compiling a national underground from various on-the-ground views. These fragmented perspectives carved out the routes of underground media networks, describing how local music is "released" into circulation, and how narratives of the music scene return home through distant consumers.

MAPPING THE JAPANESE RECORD STORE

When Noise recordings first began to be circulated in the 1980s, independent record stores were places where listeners took their first steps into the underground. Even at the end of the first decade of the 2000s, brick-and-mortar storefronts (albeit tiny and often transient in location) are crucial for cultivating knowledge about niche music scenes. This is especially true in Japan, where underground music scenes are almost always associated with at least one local record store dedicated to a hyperspecific audience. Japanese fans often use "map books" such as the annual *Rekōdo Mappu* (Record Map) to find stores that carry a specific type of music. In Japanese cities, such places rarely advertise in magazines or newspapers and may be identified only by an obscure name on an apartment building doorbell. Even for Japanese city dwellers, a particular store or club may be legendary but notoriously difficult to locate, seemingly lost in an out-of-the-way corner despite its location right in the center of the city.[8] Record maps help local listeners discover these stores by showing their positions in relation to the nearest train stations and providing a comprehensive list of the stores for any city in Japan. Next to the small map for each store, the book describes the typical genres and price ranges, and the total amount of LPs, CDs, and cassettes they carry (whether new or used) (figure 2.4).[9]

Another way to navigate the landscapes of recorded music is the *reiberu-bon*, or "label book," a type of music resource commonly used by Japanese music fans (figure 2.5). Label books compile lists of recordings on a specific label or group of labels and display photos of each release's cover along with very brief descriptions of its contents. Although these lists may be vital for describing the surface features of musical history, label books tell the reader little of creative narratives, local cultural contexts, or the aesthetics of sound. Hosokawa Shuhei and Matsuoka Hideaki point out that Japanese discographies emphasize photographs of the album covers and are less like archival documents than shopping lists, displaying rare collectible LPs as if they were immediately available for purchase. Lists guide the shopper, grading records to the specific knowledge of the consumer by indicating the appropriate "level" of the records and CDs, "whether 'beginner,' 'advanced listener,' or 'dedicated collector'" (Hosokawa and Matsuoka 2004:160). The progression toward completeness motivates many collectors, and mapping out the range of available recordings is often crucial for informing a listener's understanding of a particular music scene.[10]

For most North Americans, too, knowledge of the Japanese under-

2.4. *Rekôdo Mappu 2000*, entry for Modern Music in Shimokitazawa. Image courtesy of Gakuyo Shobo, Tokyo.

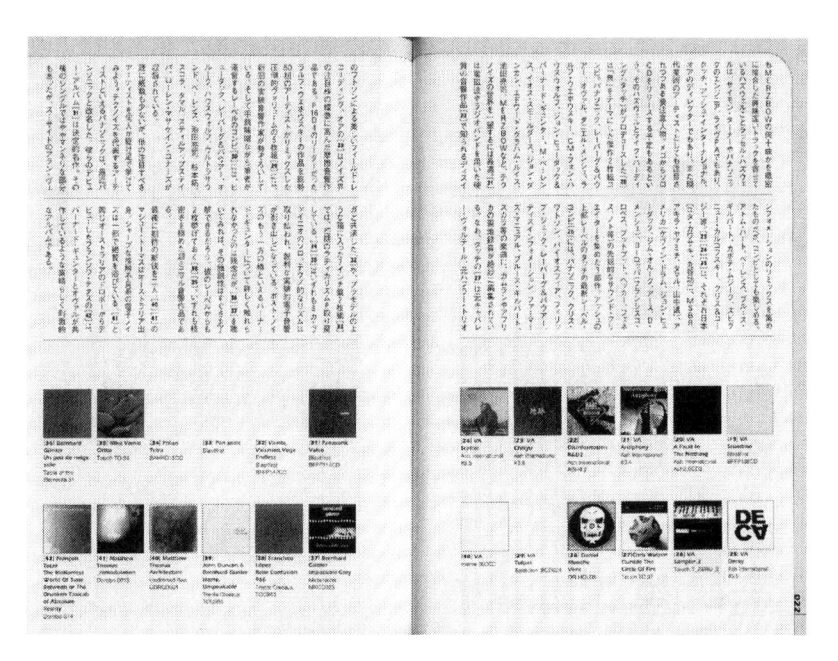

2.5. "Technoise" entry in *Avant Music Guide*.

ground would always only be partial, and this fueled the desire for "on-the-ground" reports. One issue of the fanzine *Ongaku Otaku* (Music Junkie) featured an article by Jimmy Dee with maps to legendary Tokyo record stores (figure 2.6). Dee discusses the primary genres featured in each store and sometimes provides a brief description of the interior or a photo of its doorway on the street. For example, he introduces Setagaya district's Modern Music as a "Tokyo landmark . . . small, packed to the ceiling with books, magazines, records, tapes, CDs, videotapes new and used," and notes that "they always have flyers on the wall for upcoming shows, etc." (Dee 2001:62). Even as he reveals the important locales for experimental music in Tokyo, Dee reencodes the mystery that leads fans to seek out these places for themselves. His introduction describes Japan's underground culture as "downright submarine"; a disorienting, intense, labyrinthine world where "casual involvement is difficult, if not impossible" (Dee 2001:62). Emphasizing the instability of Noise's musical territory, he warns that "places go in and out of business, move, change names, and so on, so please be prepared for surprises . . . opening hours, websites, even landmarks may differ from what you see below" (Dee 2001:62). He charts an underground landscape that promises privileged access to deep mean-

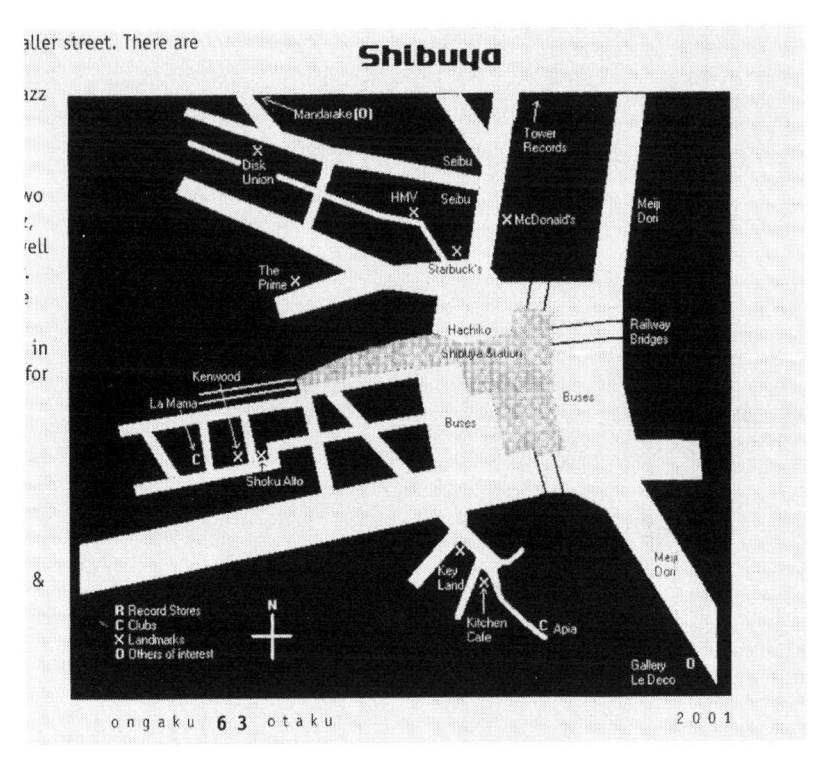

2.6. *Ongaku Otaku*'s map of Shibuya. Courtesy of Jimmy Dee.

ing while simultaneously upholding its wildness, transience, and unknowability. Finally, he warns that this map will inevitably erase itself, as a temporary document of a marginal popular culture.

There is a strange juxtaposition at the core of Dee's map of the Tokyo underground. Many of the sites identified as landmarks are global corporate chain stores, such as McDonald's, Starbucks, 7-Eleven, and so on, which are familiar to Japanese and American mapmakers alike. These underground record stores and clubs, which haunt the margins of commercial exchange even in the heart of Tokyo, offer the possibility of uncharted local ground beneath the "shared" corporate markers of globalization. To map the underground, then, is to reveal a hidden layer of experience beneath "ordinary" consumer space. Its obscure networks motivate the map reader to imagine — and then explore — the depths of a unique and separate place, even within an urban territory covered over by ubiquitous markers of transnational capitalism.

The underground would be no place without some portal of entry to its mysterious local secrets. The record store became a doorway to musical knowledge that could be unlocked through media consumption, but it was also a destination in itself. Both Japanese and North American fans regularly credited their discovery of Noise to particular record stores that helped them begin to map out their own pathways into the underground. Especially in the 1980s and early 1990s, independent store owners ordered records and cassettes directly from the labels in small batches, basically mirroring the practice of individual fans on the larger scale of commercial retail. As a result, store managers were free to make eclectic decisions in choosing their stock, and their personal selections could exert a great influence on local listeners.

Matsuzaki Satomi (Deerhoof) found her way into the San Francisco underground through a small Tokyo community of tape traders and specialized record stores:

> Someone gave me a tape of this music by a band called Caroliner [a.k.a. Caroliner Rainbow], which I later learned was part of a scene on the American West Coast. I got really interested in this, and started asking around, "What is this 'American West Coast' music?" and some friends showed me record stores like Paris Peking, Los Apson, smaller stores like that. Before that I used to go to Vinyl, and some other more general stores around there [JR Shinjuku Station]. But Los Apson had really good descriptions of the music that they'd write on a sticker and put on each record, and they could tell you all about the record.

The staff of these tiny niche market stores helped Matsuzaki find recordings that fueled her interest in California's experimental music scene. In 1989, she went to see Caroliner, a San Francisco–based band, perform on their now-legendary tour of Japan with Osaka's Boredoms.[11] She began to correspond with lead singer Grux, who sent her Noise cassettes from Bay Area groups. Grux invited Matsuzaki to come over to San Francisco for a visit, and she took him up on his offer in 1994. During her visit, she casually tried out for the local experimental rock band Deerhoof, although she had never played music before. The audition went well, and she joined the band as the singer and bassist.

By mapping the underground on their shelves, record stores offered a portal for encounters with a new world of sound. Japanese releases began to trickle into North America and Europe in the 1990s. In those pre-Internet days, the difficulty of finding information about foreign artists, coupled with the expense of purchasing imported recordings, made the global view of underground music very opaque. Mapping a distant scene required financial sacrifice in addition to the difficulty of actually finding releases in local stores. In a mid-1990s article, British music writer David Ilic rhetorically questioned his obsession with Rough Trade's Japanese import section: "The idea of handing over a 20 pound note for one CD and not getting any change used to be unthinkable. But for the last few years it has been my reality. Pursuing the Occidental's Orient via the Japanese import racks at Rough Trade's London shops . . . is a bank-breaking business; and unless you're familiar with *kanji*, Japan's complex form of script, you might not even be sure who or what is on some of the records you're buying. So why do it?" (Ilic 1994:37). Ilic's answer, of course, is that these sounds are just so good, and so different, that their discovery is worth the money and trouble. But the inverse was also true: the effort demanded by the search for obscure records—and the promise of participation in an underground network that spanned the globe—created a musical world worth searching for.

As I uncovered more of the connections between my North American and Japanese interlocutors, I found that many long-term relationships traced back to initial contacts developed through label owners, distributors, or record store managers. These curators of Noise circulation introduced fans with shared interests, became confidants and champions of musicians and new musical styles, issued recordings, and often promoted and sold tickets for shows in local livehouses.[12] Eventually, their relationships formed a rudimentary distribution network for independent music recordings. Curators made rare records available to distant outsiders and provided them with an overview of obscure musical worlds. Just as often, a single person could represent an entire local network, even from behind the scenes.

Higashiseto Satoru, for instance, manages the Namba branch of Osaka's Forever Records (figure 2.7), writes for local magazines, runs the small Hören record label, and has been a vital force in connecting North American and Kansai-based musicians. Higashiseto's influence as an arbiter for the Osaka Noise underground is well known, despite his humble occupation as a clerk at Forever Records for over twenty-five years. His curation of the local scene—as a ubiquitous presence at experimental concerts, a contact for foreign collectors, a champion of new recordings in the racks of his store, and a promoter and interpreter for international col-

2.7. Higashiseto Satoru at Forever Records in Namba. Photo by the author.

laborations—helped give countless overseas fans a view of the emerging Osaka Noise scene.

Throughout the 1980s and 1990s, Higashiseto advertised a list of rare records in several small internationally distributed experimental music fanzines, many of which focused on the exchange of cassettes, and developed correspondences with foreign musicians and fans who were seeking Japanese rarities and independent releases. On many occasions, when a well-known performer visited Osaka from North America, they would either already have developed a relationship with Higashiseto through the mail or have been referred to him by a friend.[13] Through the networks he mapped out in his dual role as a local promoter and an international record distributor, Higashiseto enabled many important connections that brought Osaka into the loops of transnational underground circulation in the late 1980s. In one instance, he helped then-unknown Boredoms secure a position as the opening band for New York experimental rock band Pussy Galore in their Osaka performance in 1987. A year later, fellow New Yorkers Sonic Youth also requested Boredoms for their opening act in Japan. These relationships boosted Boredoms' national exposure and eventually led to their North American tours with Sonic Youth, Nirvana, and other bands in the early 1990s.

The search for obscure records helped North American listeners orient themselves toward the oblique frontiers of a distant Japanese scene. Seymour Glass (a self-chosen pseudonym), publisher of the important Noise zine *Bananafish*, was introduced to Japanese Noise through regular phone conversations with Ron Lessard, owner of RRRecords, a small store with a mail-order catalog in Lowell, Massachusetts. As their relationship progressed, Glass would order a copy of a record on Lessard's recommendation, knowing that the releases he suggested would be new, strange, different, and rare. To illustrate this, he reenacted a typical phone conversation with Lessard: "I used to mail order cassettes from him in the mid-'80s, and I'd call him up and say, you know, 'Recommend something.' And he'd say: 'Well, I got this really weird band from Japan called Hanatarashi. But it's kind of expensive, you know, 18 bucks . . .' 'Is it good?' 'Yeah, yeah! It's REALLY weird. It's the most over-the-top shit I've ever heard.' 'Oh, yeah, better give me one of those.'" For his part, Thurston Moore of Sonic Youth describes how he gradually gained a sense of the Japanese Noise scene by seeking limited-edition Noise cassettes during tours in Japan. As labels began to issue more and more material, he soon found that the borders of his personal map of Noise were beyond containment:

> When Sonic Youth went to Japan I spent every free minute tracking down noise cassettes. The music began appearing on CD and I started gathering those as well. Enthusiasts in America, the U.K. and Europe began to release cassettes of Japanese noise: Boredoms, UFO Or Die, Masonna, Ruins, Bustmonsters, Omoide Hatoba, Zeni Geva, Volume Dealers, Incapacitants, Hanatarashi, Gerogerigegege, Violent Onsen Geisha, Hijokaidan, Aube, Pain Jerk, Merzbow, MSBR, Magical Power Mako, Fushitsusha, and many, many more. It all reached a peak in about 1992–93. Many of the same noise-artists continue to release brutal hyper-electronic noise cassettes and CDs. I want them to stop . . . Sometimes I think I'm going to have a nervous breakdown when I receive notice that Vanilla, G.R.O.S.S., Alchemy, P.S.F., Mom 'n Dad, Public Bath, Japan Overseas, Beast 666, Forced Exposure, Nux, Endorphine Factory, My Fiancee's Life Work, Coquette, etc, etc, etc have released a new Merzbow or Incapacitants cassette, CD, LP or 7. (Moore 1995:12–13)

This overflowing proliferation of limited-edition Noise recordings in the 1990s overwhelmed the outsiders who sought to catalog the emerging

NOISE MAY-DAY 2003
special limited edition CDR

your copy #

0 2 /50

Jojo Hiroshige with John Boyle and Aya

Masonna

Pain Jerk

Incapacitants

<collected rare & unreleased tracks>

2.8. *Noise May-Day 2003* limited-edition CD-R.

Japanese Noise scene. Its discovery also forged new loops of exchange between listeners. Noise CDs, records, and cassettes accrued value through their rarity, which encouraged rapid-fire trades and informal redistributions among fans, with many listeners auditioning and copying each copy of a recording. In Japan, Noise shows are sometimes promoted by producing a limited recording (perhaps as few as fifty copies), available at the venue on the night of the show only (figure 2.8). These often compile otherwise unavailable or unreleased tracks by the artists performing that evening and inevitably sell out in the first few moments after the door is opened.

In the 1997 Hijokaidan release *Noise from Trading Cards*, Alchemy Records owner Hiroshige Jojo ironically references the power of collectors to define the landscape of circulation. The album features a cover photo of Hiroshige in his card-trading shop surrounded by shelves of valuable baseball cards, sales of which generate the financial means to operate his unprofitable Noise label (figure 2.9). By revealing the interrelation between his two businesses, Hiroshige links the clientele for Noise recordings to a parallel universe of collection. He pulls back from the local view of musical creativity to reveal its roots in a broader world of fetishistic consumption.

2.9. *Noise from Trading Cards* (Alchemy Records, 1997).

WELCOME TO DREAMLAND

The search for hard-to-get recordings helped to place Japanese Noise at the furthest edge of underground music. An actual visit to Japan, of course, remained an extremely uncommon experience for the majority of overseas listeners. In this context, compilations became an essential way to map the Japanese Noise scene. A compilation is a set of tracks by different performers, often used to represent a particular stylistic history or aesthetic niche. Compilations encouraged distant listeners to imagine an unknown musical territory. They are maps within maps, which mediate the sonic landscape of Noise as a collective project of "various artists." Just as maps guide foreign travelers, compilations represent local musical knowledge for a public of outsiders. But compilations zoom in on the scene by reducing its specific features in favor of global legibility.

Noise compilations have been deeply influential among overseas fans, regardless — or perhaps as a result — of the fact that they often present distorted views of musical communities. Compilations of Japanese underground music are commonly presented as comprehensive samplers of a

2.10. *Japan Bashing*, vol. 1 (Public Bath, 1990). Design by Ohno Masahiko, permission of Public Bath Records.

regional scene, with titles such as *Tokyo Flashback, Land of the Rising Noise,* or *Extreme Music from Japan.*[14] But compilers may be motivated by any number of concerns in selecting a specific mix to represent a regional scene. Compilations might showcase a group of artists, encourage collaborations between different artists, or help promote a label, club, or magazine. Some were conceived as "best of" collections, mixing artists from different locales, generations, and levels of experience. Often these glimpses from above did not line up with local perspectives, and the scenes they mapped for others did not always exist as such.

For North American fans, one of the first compilations that put the Japanese underground on the map was *Japan Bashing*, vol. 1 (figure 2.10), a seven-inch EP issued in 1990 on the Osaka-based independent label Public Bath, run by American expatriate David Hopkins. The EP collected separate tracks from four different bands: Boredoms, UFO or Die, Hanatarashi, and Omoide Hatoba. Although all four bands are presented as discrete entities, each group was composed from the same small pool of musicians (Eye Yamatsuka, for example, was in Boredoms, UFO or Die, and Hanatarashi, and Yamamoto Seiichi was in Boredoms and Omoide Hatoba). But for those overseas fans without knowledge of its recursive social construction, *Japan Bashing* represented a cross section of Osaka's underground.

Public Bath quickly became crucial for North American listeners looking for a view into the Japanese scene. Hopkins had moved to Japan in the early 1980s and began distributing recordings of Osaka underground groups to U.S.-based independent distributors such as Revolver and Subterranean a few years later. His connections in Osaka are unquestionably deep, and his three-decade-long involvement earned him a rare expert knowledge of the Osaka underground. But Public Bath did more than merely represent the isolated features of an existing Japanese scene; it helped chart its landscape for North American listeners, and in doing so changed its terrain. In choosing artists for the subsequent editions of *Japan Bashing*, Hopkins decided not to advocate any particular style. "Because I was eclectic," he told me, "I knew everybody. Jojo [Hiroshige of Hijokaidan] and Eye [Yamatsuka of Boredoms] don't talk, but I'm friends with both of them, so I could put them both on my label." Hopkins's eclectic compilations slowly became a map that guided a new transnational consumption, which fed back into the formation of the Japanese scene.

Even if they did not represent a coherent local community, compilations became central to the transnational cartography of Japanese Noise. Mason Jones, the San Francisco–based compiler of the 1995 Relapse CD *The Japanese-American Noise Treaty* (figures 2.11 and 2.12), told me that even if a band didn't necessarily fit with others on the release, "I had to give preference to the bands that I was friends with. If I knew a Japanese artist well, it would have been unthinkable not to include them on the compilation." Although Jones organized his compilation in ways that reflected his awareness of Japanese social rules, he had already begun to remediate the local scene in a new transnational context. The only liner notes for *The Japanese-American Noise Treaty* consisted of the included artists' postal addresses. Many of the artists contacted one another for the first time after the recording was released, and listeners and other musicians from overseas wrote or sent recordings. As the list begat the network, the map became the territory.

Another early compilation of underground Japanese music that received international attention was titled *Welcome to Dreamland: Another Japan* (figure 2.13), released in 1985 on the Celluloid label. The record was compiled by guitarist Fred Frith, who met most of the included musicians during his

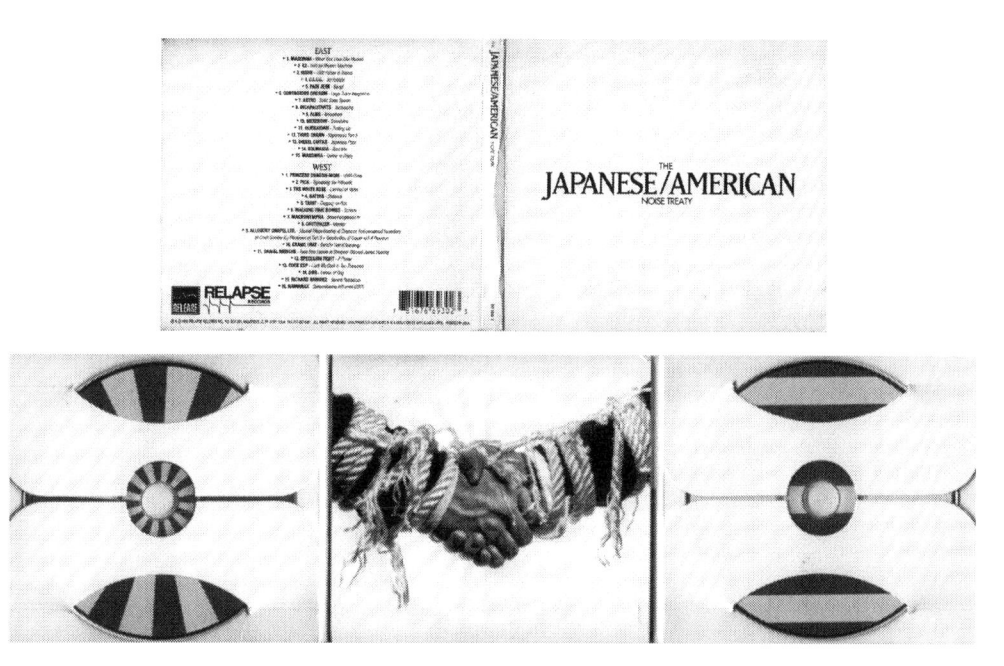

2.11 and 2.12. *The Japanese-American Noise Treaty* CD (Relapse, 1995).

highly influential tours of Japan in the early 1980s (documented in the 1980 film *Step across the Border*). After deciding on his favorites, Frith mixed the sessions himself at a Tokyo studio, gathering the groups to record original music and including many luminaries from both Tokyo and Kansai, as well as some lesser known musicians. Frith clearly anticipates misinterpretation of the record as a canonizing project. In his liner notes, he states that the compilation was not intended to "sample" the Japanese underground, or even to represent any particular group or style of music: "This is not a record company sampler and it doesn't represent a 'school' of music. It isn't an overview and it isn't complete. The musicians do different things at different times with different people. Most of them have day jobs. They certainly don't feel that they belong together. . . . Not much of it [this music] is heard outside of Japan. Some of it doesn't fit and won't go away" (Frith 1985). In attempting to head off possible misreadings, Frith argues that the scene does not exist. But no underground would be worth exploring if it did not somehow remain out of sight.

The first track on *Dreamland* adds another layer of obscurity. Listed as a collaboration between famous Tokyo experimentalist Haino Keiji and a group called Fake, the track was actually composed by Frith as a collage

2.13. *Welcome to Dreamland* LP (Celluloid, 1985).

made from leftover scraps of separate studio recordings, which included all of the different groups and individuals on the compilation. His remix superimposed these spatially and temporally distinct sound sources into a montage against which Haino then improvised an additional part. By design, then, this unsettled assemblage simply "doesn't fit"—within its own musical world as much as with anyone else's. Yet because of its uncategorizable nature, it "won't go away."

Even if it presented itself as a "fake" record of a local community, *Dreamland* encircled an imaginary version of the Japanese underground. Although Frith deliberately avoided any specific logic of organization, the selected tracks nonetheless traced out the contours of an emergent knowledge. Because *Dreamland* represents music "from Japan," the record provided an otherwise unattainable view of local creativity. As the liner notes assert, "not much of it is heard outside of Japan"—but, of course, whether these recordings were ever heard *inside* Japan is equally unclear. *Dreamland*, as one reviewer put it, is "an aural snapshot of a once-active underground ... it reeks of familiarity, but is simultaneously a whole other planet" (Stillman 2002:27). The outside listener visits this dreamland through the ears of an ambivalent guide, trusted all the more for his open-ended, arbitrary position on the sonic frontier.

THE CURSE OF DISCOVERY

In a 1994 essay, published in 2002 in the underground music magazine *G-Modern*, Mikawa Toshiji of Incapacitants criticized overseas compilations for creating and enforcing the categories of "Japanoise" and "Japanese Noise." Mikawa argued that "Japanese Noise" was presented to foreign audiences as a landscape of radical incommensurability, which forced Noisicians to define themselves against an Orientalist projection. His examples are the covers of *Extreme Music from Japan*, *Land of the Rising Noise*, and *Come Again II*, all of which feature explicit and sometimes violent sexual images. Charnel House's *Land of the Rising Noise* "depicts a photo of a doll, which looks coquettish but androgynous, dressed in a kimono, baring one shoulder and staring languidly at the lens" (Mikawa 2002 [1994]:43), whereas the British artist Trevor Brown's cover art for *Come Again II* shows a naked and beaten schoolgirl wrapped in bandages against a wall of blue tiles, a hypodermic needle in her arm and a tube draining blood from her nose.

Many of the Japanese performers on these compilations were frustrated and disturbed by the artwork chosen to represent the Japanese Noise scene. Shocking images of sexual bondage and physical violence were used on the covers of several early recordings by Japanese Noise artists in the 1980s—primarily Merzbow, most famously on his *Music for Bondage Performance* CD, which featured artsy black-and-white photographs of women bound in the Japanese rope-tying bondage technique called *kinbaku*.[15] Associations with deviant sex quickly became an important part of overseas knowledge about Japanese Noise, especially in the 1990s as *hentai* (strange/perverted) anime filtered into underground media circulations (e.g., the infamous *Urutsukidoji* film series depicting "tentacle sex"). Noise artists in North America began to use images inspired by Merzbow, often borrowing from Japanese pornography, and occasionally juxtaposing scenes of extreme sexuality against the backdrop of modern Japanese cities or other Japanese cultural symbols.

Japanoise became a mirror ball of distorted perspectives that could only refract the projections of an outsider back into their own view. "Looking at these covers," Mikawa argues, "it wouldn't be totally irrelevant to say that the bias that is preoccupying the producers is encapsulated in these images. That Noise should remind us of some sort of torture; and then, that being exposed to these sounds transforms torture into pleasure; and then, that idea is related to these images that evoke [torture] victims; then it goes without saying that—beyond the diversity of the works included— the images add a framework to these compilations, which takes power over the minds of their buyers" (Mikawa 2002 [1994]:43). Mikawa goes on to point out that this distorted reception of Noise was mapped onto to its creative sources, as Japanese artists were forced to define themselves in relation to a "Japanese Noise" scene, then changed their work to avoid being categorized under these terms. He describes this feedback as a "curse" (noroi) buried in the cartography of "Japanese Noise," which derives from the "original sin" of depicting its landscape in the first place: "Regardless of whether one accepts these visual choices or is disgusted by them, the use of these images has affected the minds of the individual artists on these albums, who could not play a part in the decision to use them. . . . So now, what has been represented as 'Japanese Noise'—at first by exaggerations based on the lack of sufficient information in the early period, then labeled with attributes that summarized the group from the distant perspective of overseas reception, and then represented by the glut of information in later periods—is forced to define itself" (Mikawa 2002 [1994]:43).

"But if this categorization is indeed a curse cast upon 'Japanese Noise,'" Mikawa concludes, "it is possible to re-transform it to shed labels once given . . . to continue going out of control, to an extreme, at an incredible acceleration is actually a redemptive impulse that 'Japanese Noise' is saddled with, even when one is not conscious of it." The distorted images of Japanese Noise are woven into its intercultural feedback, and traced over and over again to form new paths: "Misunderstandings spread like a wave. . . . The latent anomaly expands as it is continuously exposed to an uneven mixture of the brilliant and mediocre, endlessly increasing and decreasing like a spiral" (Mikawa 2002 [1994]:43).

The map feeds back into itself; it changes the territory. Deeper exploration, of course, creates a need for more detailed maps. Maps emplace our dreams of other musical cultures, even as they loop back to fill them in with our own expectations and desires for revelation. Recordings lead explorers underground to the obscure edges of cultural production, toward the limits of the known world. The frontier of Noise endlessly advances into uncharted territory.

At the vanishing point of the local music scene, the mystery of a global underground is projected onto another place beyond the horizon. In this mediated landscape, "there is always some unknown against which a more familiar reality can be mapped, to which appeal can be made for some new kind of authenticity" (King 1996:136). Eventually the traveler reaches the edge: a no-man's-land of newness and difference, whose borders are isomorphic with its own undiscoverable forms. Beyond here, there be Noise.

CHAPTER 3

LISTENING TO NOISE IN KANSAI

It was late, and we were wandering up a side alley away from the light and clamor of the main market road that leads away from the station. I was woozy after several drinks of strong Okinawan liquor that Tabata Mitsuru and I had been drinking at an *uchiage*, a collective gathering of musicians after a performance. "I'm going to miss the last train," I complained, as we headed farther into the darkness, away from the rumble of the trains. "Don't worry about it," mumbled Tabata, pointing to a tall hedge that ran along the wall of a nearby house, "I've slept back there a couple times when I missed the train . . . besides, we're almost there, and we can hang out and listen all night. Unless it's closed . . ." We stopped before the door of what looked like an abandoned storefront, its large window completely pasted over with record album jackets, their images so faded that only blurs of blue ink remained. Some peeled off the wall in shreds, like remnants of old posters from some long-past political campaign. The door, too, shed bits of old magazine pages as we swung it open to step inside. As my eyes adjusted to the darkness, I could see that the interior walls and ceiling were the same, covered with faded images and torn posters behind shelves cluttered with junk and bottles of Jinro *shôchû*, a Korean rice whiskey, marked with the names of the regulars by whom they were claimed. A shadowy figure stood behind the counter—really just a barrier formed by the piles of seven-inch records he was playing—as he bent down to replace the needle on the turntable. The dark, distorted "psych" rock music of 1970s *angura* (underground) Japan blasted out into the room and filled it for the next five hours as we waited for the night to pass. Two tables were occupied, and the third was stacked to the ceiling with records, but a couple of stools jammed into the counter were free. Tabata shouted my name to the master, his name to me, pointed to one of the stools, grinned, and nodded his acceptance of the unspoken offer of drinks. We sat and were absorbed in the music.

Listening to recordings is the crucible of modern musical creativity, and its practice is filled with as much interpretable meaning as the sonic objects themselves. This is as true in Japan as anywhere; but in Japan, there are music *kissa*. Throughout the twentieth century, music cafés, or *kissaten*—which, in their modern form, are something like the place I visited with Tabata—have been special places where urban Japanese come to develop musical knowledge. The subterranean environment of these hidden spots for listening to new forms of music, especially the famous postwar *jazu* (jazz) kissa, helped Japanese learn how to be modern through the rapid importation of foreign media and technology. Jazu-kissa, as popular music scholars have described, were strongly focused on stylistic canonization, which produced a formalized mode of hyperattentive listening (Atkins 2001; Derschmidt 1998; Hosokawa 2007). Experimental or "free" spaces for listening, in contrast, reorganized local media consumption to create new forms.

This chapter describes the emergence of Noise as a postwar history of Japanese media reception. I compare the distinctive modes of listening in postwar jazu-kissa with those of a "free space" called Drugstore, which was central to Noise's development in Kyoto in the 1980s. The two contexts of listening are in many ways quite different. The jazu-kissa became a powerful space of nostalgic canonization and specialized knowledge of foreign media; in Drugstore, reception turned into performance and the local production of original Noise. Japanese popular music is often read through the hegemonic impact of Western media that produces an endless chain of copycats and subjugated fans of imported musical forms. But here I show how localized listening can produce new creative performances and sites of intercultural participation. The remediations of Noise did not remain isolated in local reception but created a new sound from foreign musical materials. Listeners created unique performances and eventually put their own Noise into circulation.

Drugstore's clientele included many of the early Japanese Noise practitioners, whose reception of underground music planted the seeds of Noise in Kansai. From within their collections of strange, "wrong," and impossible-to-classify recordings, they imagined a category called Noise and began to produce it for themselves. Drugstore listeners coalesced into performing groups, as well as the label Alchemy Records, which represented the Osaka Noise scene in the 1990s. In what follows, I detail these early days of Noise to show how Osaka became a center of Noise's cultural production through transnational circulation, despite its marginality within Japan. In Japan, Osaka has always been out of the mainstream, but in the 1990s it became the emblematic city of the Japanese underground for a worldwide audience. Alchemy and other local labels forged a distribution network that bypassed Japan to circulate Kansai Noise overseas, where North American listeners renamed it "Japanoise."

Listening is essential to the complicated construction of musical knowledge in contemporary Japan. On one hand, hyperattention to foreign recordings articulates the cultural marginality of Japanese participation in transnational media. On the other hand, listening could also divert the imbalanced flow of imported music into a new form of Noise. I focus on the invention and performance of Noise in Kyoto and Osaka in the 1980s, but I do not claim that Noise is the product of this singular place and time. On the contrary, the story of Drugstore shows us that Noise's creative origins cannot be excavated from "behind the music," where the true story of a local scene waits to be finally revealed. Its experimental modes of listening constantly turn musical history back on itself, transforming distant sounds into new forms of Noise.

INSIDE THE JAZU-KISSA

Jazu-kissa is generally rendered in English as "jazz coffeehouse" or "jazz café," but this translation is not quite right. They are not much like European cafés; they are more insular underground establishments that exist on the border of public and private space. They serve more whiskey than coffee, and the self-selected customers—circles of friends, really—come to consume music recordings as much as beverages. Jazu-kissa are first and foremost places to listen. Although the tiny spaces occasionally feature live musical performances and are open to anyone, they often feel like a private living room or even a secret society. Like other tiny *nomiya* (drinking spots) sequestered in the back streets of urban Japan, they can be difficult to find. This is especially true of jazu-kissa, which exhibit a subterranean ambience that marks these places as special listening sites for a specific subculture of music fans. Even the earliest music listening cafés in urban Japan were associated with radical social changes of modernity and were symbolic of public discourses about foreign culture.

Though cafés have been popular in Japan since the Meiji Restoration, *ongaku* (music) kissaten (later colloquially shortened to kissa) originated in the 1920s with *meikyoku* kissaten, within which customers listened to Western classical music accompanied by female hostesses (Takahashi 1994). Miriam Silverberg describes the growing public presence of the Japanese café waitress as a symbol of the nation's emerging relationship with Western models of modern metropolitan life.[1] This shift was musically marked with the introduction of American jazz, which became the default music for the niche of music kissaten I describe here. By the mid-1930s there were forty thousand cafés throughout the nation, packed with crowds of sophisticated youth whose new social ideals were exemplified by the controversial jazz age social figures of the *moga* (modern girl) and *mobo* (modern boy) (Silverberg 1993:125). As such, kissaten have long been sites for Japanese cosmopolitans to experience the nation's emergent modernity. Jazu-kissa took this reception a step further, to introduce new listening practices that linked the unfamiliarity of foreign culture to the integration of sound reproduction technologies into everyday musical knowledge. Ongoing connections between Western music and social reform culminated in the postwar association of jazz with an emergent Japanese democracy, which became a powerful undercurrent in the flood of foreign media and technology flowing into postwar Japanese cities with the U.S. occupation forces (Atkins 2001).

The music played in jazu-kissa became increasingly specialized in the subterranean environments of the postwar intelligentsia.[2] Although they shared with earlier music cafés a refined, salon-like atmosphere of intellectual connoisseurship, jazu-kissa soon became the centers of a growing countercultural imaginary, incubating in the cloistered, slightly hedonistic insularity of these dimly lit, contemplative spaces of listening. In the 1960s, the jazu-kissa became a symbolic meeting ground for student radicals, much like Greenwich Village folkhouses where progressive politics and music tastes were interwoven. Jazu-kissa became centers of alternative media distribution, hosting film screenings, lectures, and meetings. On rare occasions, they transformed themselves into performance venues for live music, sometimes ranging beyond jazz to rock and blues. Although a few jazu-kissa provided space for local performers, the majority focused exclusively on playing records, and by the mid-1970s this range had narrowed to a very specific set of imported jazz recordings.

Today, the handful of remaining jazu-kissa in Japanese cities seem nostalgically unchanged from these formative postwar decades. The music is bebop and later "out" jazz, the atmosphere is darkly poetic, and the format is still vinyl LP (almost exclusively imported releases by artists like Charlie Parker, Thelonious Monk, Dave Brubeck, and also the "free jazz" of John Coltrane and Albert Ayler). A substantial surcharge on drinks ensures that the few seats in the tiny establishments are not occupied casually, but are for serious listening only. Silence is often mandatory, as listeners sit in rapt appreciation over their blend coffees and whiskeys; a new sound heard on each visit, a new piece of the giant puzzle of style. Jazu-kissa like Tokyo's Shiramuren, a tiny shop crammed above a storefront in a rundown back alley in Shinjuku, still hold "concerts" each Sunday afternoon as listeners fill the seven stools along the bar, silently sipping whiskey as free jazz blasts from enormous monitor speakers a few feet above their heads.[3] Such events epitomize the special kind of virtuosic listening that emerged alongside the industrial distribution of imported recordings in postwar Japan, aspects of which were later appropriated and altered in the experimental genre-breaking practices of Noise.

For Ôtomo Yoshihide, now an influential experimental guitarist and turntablist, the local jazu-kissa was at first an "ideal place to hang out and kill time while cutting class" in his hometown of Fukushima (Ôtomo 1995:4). It had been opened by a young Tokyoite, who moved north after burning out on the political and social quagmires of the city's countercultural scene in the late 1960s. Meeting with this exile from the capital's bohemian underground and listening to records together daily "opened a window into the cultural scene of Tokyo," where Ôtomo has spent his adult life (Ôtomo 1995:4). His description of a typical 1970s jazu-kissa is particularly evocative of its cramped, media-filled environment: "2.5 by 6 meters of space. That and a pair of huge JBL or Altec speakers, a couple hundred jazz records and a bar counter were all that was necessary to open your basic jazu-kissa.... Avant-garde jazz, manga [comic books], music and culture magazines, notebooks filled with the opinions of young leftists, concerts every one or two months, and 8 millimeter film shows" (Ôtomo 1995:4). The combination of carefully managed tastes and strictly maintained rules for listening made some jazu-kissa resemble counterculture *juku* (cram schools) for underground music, where social interaction was forbidden as records were played at incredible volumes. It was standard practice to play through an entire side of an LP at a time, so the course of an evening's listening progressed in twenty-minute "lessons," one following another, which introduced neophytes to narratives of style within the genre and sharpened the knowledge of experienced clients.

During the 1950s and early '60s, foreign jazz records were not widely available in Japan outside of U.S. Army bases, and the typical way to acquire them was to import directly via international post, which was prohibitively expensive for individual fans.[4] Listening collectively at a jazu-kissa was the only affordable way to become a knowledgeable fan of the latest music. Competition in seeking out new and different records became a matter of survival for the jazu-kissa in Japanese cities, because whichever one acquired the first copies of a recent release would draw the cutting-edge audience who needed to hear the newest sounds as soon as possible. Acquiring a functional knowledge of the jazz genre meant constantly keeping abreast of new releases, which could be a formidable task when important recordings were released on small and independent labels. Jazu-kissa owners began to search out private sources for supply, and some began to write to dealers in the United States, arranging for new releases to be shipped directly via airmail. Such arrangements helped build translocal U.S.–Japan chains of mail order and collection, developing early independent distribution routes and interpersonal relationships based on international exchange of recordings.

Listening attentively to recordings in jazu-kissa represented the best means for aspiring Japanese musicians to connect to the outer world of American jazz. Musicians would go to hear new and rare records, and sometimes they attempted to transcribe the solos as they listened for hours on end. The mandatory cup of coffee (or glass of whiskey), however, could be extremely expensive, so listeners would stay for as long as possible, making the most out of their opportunity to audition a rare LP, which might well be their only chance to do so. The atmosphere of some popular jazu-kissa could resemble a performerless concert hall, and in

3.1. Display of LP covers in *jazu-kissa*. Photo by the author.

the most hard-core jazu-kissa, listening in complete silence was standard practice. The careful, serious listenership of the jazu-kissa created a model for tightly focused, attentive Japanese audiences. But in the relatively small world of jazz fans in postwar Japan, the cultivation of live music performance, whether by local or foreign performers, did not follow directly from the appreciation of recordings. Rather, they curated a mediated knowledge of jazz by listening deeply into an exclusive repertoire of recordings that managed the music's local meanings and values.

A single jazu-kissa could exert a great amount of influence over the reception of a particular recording, and the opinion of its "master" (*masutā*) might make or break the local reputation of a foreign artist. The master usually owns and manages the kissa, and is often the only employee, serving drinks, small snacks, and most important, controlling the selection of music and talking with the clientele. Jazu-kissa masters are widely regarded as the pinnacle of expertise in the styles of music featured in their establishments, and they are often called on by critics and reviewers to corroborate data. The authoritative character of the master is somewhat analogous to the position held by a teacher in Japanese society, and the behavior of the clientele is like that of students, who develop loyal and exclusive relationships with a single jazu-kissa and its master.[5] The kind of silent, attentive listening practiced in the most conservative jazu-kissa carries the aura of an orally transmitted music lesson, in which a student learns a repertoire by hearing the teacher play and discuss each piece in hierarchical order.[6] Jazu-kissa, then, were less often places to socialize than places to be "socialized, evangelized, and indoctrinated into the mental discipline of jazz appreciation, and to a deeper understanding of the music's message and spirit" (Atkins 2001:4).

The social space of the jazu-kissa was also undoubtedly one of male privilege and prestige, which concentrates expertise in the figure of the master: as the gendered term implies, masters are almost always male.[7] Gender divisions are common to consumer identifications with sound reproduction technology in Japan, and the discipline of listening takes place within a masculine social hierarchy.[8] The master's evaluations of specific recordings and opinions of a particular stylistic era or group of artists are widely reproduced among his clientele. The master is considered to be in total command of his record collection; requests are rarely made, except by extremely long-term customers. His carefully presented taste and knowledge place him in a fetishized, practically magical relationship with his records. The elevated aura of the master is well captured by Bill Minor's remembrance of Hashimoto Tsuneo of Nagoya kissa Jazz Aster, "standing directly in front of a rack of LPs encased in transparent plastic covers, the room's light—reflected on them—producing the effect of some sort of flickering, glistening halo surrounding his head" (Minor 2004:239). The underground authority of the jazu-kissa, then, is coded in this special mastery of a foreign musical genre through a unique local interpretation. The terrain of jazz is presented here as an "out" music that also reproduces very "inside" hierarchies of social control.

The master is also a host, and the art of creatively producing and shifting the mood with records is considered a consummate skill. Fukushima Tetsuo, owner of the famous Shibuya jazu-kissa Mary Jane, on learning that I had been a student of the composer Anthony Braxton, played Braxton records all night, dramatically and proudly relating the story of how he had put the famous saxophonist at ease during his stay in Japan in the early 1970s:

Braxton came in. I knew immediately who he was, of course. He sat down and I got him a drink—I was playing some Sonny Rollins. . . . I could tell he was uncomfortable with it, I could feel the tension from him—the music was inappropriate [*chigau*, lit. "It was wrong"]. I ran behind the bar, crouched down by the record shelves, searching—no, not that one—what could it be? And then—hm, I wonder . . . I found it. Lennie Tristano. As the Rollins side ended, I brought it up slowly—this was it. His face changed; there was a relaxed feeling. Later, when he left, he told me he hadn't been comfortable in Japan until he came to this place.

Several aspects of Fukushima's story inform us of the cultural links between emotional sensitivity and critical knowledge in the space of the music kissa. That he "immediately knew" Braxton is presented as important, if natural; but the real demonstration of the master's mastery is represented by his ability to channel the correct music for his guest. Even without direct communication, Fukushima's sensitivity, coupled with his skillful application of specific knowledge, allowed him to select a recording that provided his sensitive customer a contemplative listening space that was transcendent of both cultural boundaries and rival musicians.

This special space for listening could also be overwhelming: "the darkness, the tremendous volume of the music, the motionlessly listening guest, and the frequently strict and authoritarian master . . . all added to the impression that one entered a very special, almost religious room, a completely different world" (Derschmidt 1998:308). In a book of reminiscences of 1960s Tokyo jazu-kissa, Ôshima Yu describes entering a kissa in Kichijôji, a neighborhood in West Tokyo that remains a center for underground music: "I was seventeen, and I was shocked by the volume of the music. The huge speakers trembled, and even the chair I sat on trembled under the force of the sound waves. . . . I saw a bearded guy listening with closed eyes, and some other men quietly reading their books. To me, that dark and smoky room seemed rather unhealthy" (Adoribu-hen 1989).[9] The darkness of the space, the unhealthy obsession with music, the overwhelming volume, the intellectual detachment contrasted with the total enclosure of the space of audition, where one "listened with closed eyes," trembling with intensity and power—all of these emphasize the shock of the music's newness and stress a complete absorption in disciplined listening that remains highly valued among Japanese underground music fans.[10]

The social mediation of Japanese listening resonated with an aura of discovery and surprise. But this crafted sensibility helped Japanese listeners reposition their place on the margins of modern music. A sense of extraordinary intensity was lovingly created in the 1960s kissa of underground urban Japan, dark corners that provide a space of total and overwhelming difference from the everyday world. The promise of an alternate musical experience within the flow of media—in which transcendent, isolated audition could connect almost telepathically to a global audience of deep listeners—became crucial for Japanese experimentalists oriented toward a transnational circulation.

How was this controlled, genre-focused listening remediated into an antigeneric Noise in Kansai's "free" spaces for listening in the 1980s? While jazu-kissa listeners tuned into the signal of a distant original jazz, experimental music listeners in Kyoto's Drugstore began to perform their own Noise. Before I return to this story, I briefly outline the historical influence of recordings on the conditions for musical reception in modern Japan. Recordings encouraged new modes of social performance and created new experiences of listening for an emerging mass culture in Japan. Because the technological centers of musical production were located overseas, recordings emplaced local knowledge in the context of transnational circulation. The original was always somewhere else and had to be brought into range.

THE PLACE OF RECORDED MUSIC IN MODERN JAPAN

The emphasis on recordings was not merely something that happened to Japan, something that made listening "modern" by virtue of technological reproduction. Rather, mediated listening itself was a crucial ground for the staging of Japanese cosmopolitanism. Japanese listeners were encouraged to substitute recordings for live music, and many important critics argued early on for the superiority of records as an alternative to musical performance. Despite their countercultural aura, jazu-kissa were engines of this postwar turn that privileged imported cultural materials.[11] In the context of foreign media, local music was separated from the broader norms of consumption. Attending a live performance was marked as a specialized and constrained musical experience, which stood in contrast to the seemingly universal musical standards of recorded media.[12] Privileged attention to recordings was in evidence among early modern Japanese publics from the turn of the century and grew exponentially in the era between the wars. The gramophone made its first inroads with the establishment of the Victor Talking Machine Company in Yokohama in 1927, and expanded into a growing consumer market in the 1930s.[13] For the emerging bourgeois consumer, the broader exposure to music recordings occurred at the same moment that Japan began to learn foreign popular music styles in earnest. Modern musical subjectivity meant developing new techniques for listening to foreign media.[14]

Early Japanese debates about recorded music show that the hegemony of Western musical styles had already established a distanced context of listening that could only be solved through increased attention to imported media. Hosokawa Shuhei and Matsuoka Hideaki, for example, historicize the problem of local musical authenticity by contrasting two between-the-wars-era music critics. Whereas Otaguro Motoo disdained the experience of listening to classical music recordings as superficial and "canned," Nomura Araebisu suggested that noisy and distracting concert settings compromised the genuine listening experience, stating that a purer appreciation of "sound itself" was afforded by gramophone recordings. The argument for the superiority of technologically mediated listening was reinforced by Japan's distance from Western centers of musical knowledge and creativity. Like other Japanese classical music fans in 1931, Nomura wondered whether "it was really better to listen to a live performance of a mediocre Japanese violinist or a superb recording of a virtuoso like Fritz Kreisler" (Hosokawa and Matsuoka 2004:154). Deep listening to an authentic imported recording helped Japanese audiences jump the gap between distant contexts of production and local sites of audition.

Japan emerged from World War II through hegemonic models of political and economic reform that increased public media consumption on a rapid scale. Japanese citizens were urged to embrace new communication technologies, especially radio and television, as part of the nation's geopolitical realignment with the United States (Nakayama, Boulton, and Pecht 1999; Partner 1999).[15] By the 1960s, Japan occupied a central space in the manufacture of media technologies such as transistor radios and tape recorders. But locally created music—whether in traditional genres or in the emergent realm of popular culture—was heavily undercirculated in comparison with imported music. Through their contingent participation in the advance of an uneven geopolitical sphere, postwar Japanese were massively overdeveloped as musical consumers. Whether the genre was jazz, pop, or classical music, Japan was a nation that listened to new sounds from outside.

How did Noise spin out of this localized attention to foreign recordings? In the second half of this chapter, I describe the transformation of jazu-kissa listening practices in the small Kyoto free space Drugstore, which contributed to the initial naming of Noise and its early development as an original performance style. The idea of Noise encouraged Kansai performers to produce their own recordings, which fed back into transnational circulation as an emergent Japanese genre. Through its identification with localized productions in Osaka and Kyoto, Noise is often seen as an invention, sui generis, of Japanese authors. But in fact, the emergence of Noise performance was part of a remediation of foreign recordings. In this tiny space for listening, a nascent group of Noise practitioners gathered to listen to a mix of marginal, almost unclassifiable recordings drawn from Western experimental, free, and "progressive" psychedelic rock. By recontextualizing these recordings as the inspiration for a new genre of Noise, the clientele of Drugstore began to feed their own listening back into transnational circulation.

MAKING NOISE IN DRUGSTORE

In Japan's major cities during the 1970s, music kissaten developed for a diverse variety of popular genres, especially rock and experimental music. Influenced by the growing angura (underground) theater groups and university cooperatives that flourished in Japanese urban bohemian life, informal and often short-lived "free" kissa sprang up spontaneously alongside alternative performance and art spaces. Like their counterparts in Europe and North America, the emphasis in the Japanese angura scenes was on action, self-definition, free expression, and personal independence.[16] In the late 1960s and early 1970s, jazu-kissa housed a stream of radical student organizations, avant-garde performances, film screenings, and theater groups. Many significant moments in the history of underground music in Japan occurred in jazu-kissa, as artists like Takayanagi Masayuki and Abe Kaoru began to take improvisation into uncharted territory. As the activist counterculture became more diffuse in the 1970s, jazu-kissa began to represent an increasingly nostalgic mode of reception and slowly disengaged from local activity in favor of remote fandom. By the 1980s, many jazu-kissa had become musical "museums," locked in memorialized grooves of collection and recollection.[17] As jazu-kissa gradually grew more codified within this historically oriented listening, experimental "free" (*furii*) kissa stressing creative participation fostered the growth of local performance networks.[18]

Free spaces for listening diverged significantly from the social standards of the jazu-kissa, and their clientele might not describe these places as kissa at all, or only with tongue firmly in cheek. Most were more like art spaces, squats, or social collectives than coffeehouses or bars. They were short-lived, antiauthoritarian, and loosely organized, with little of the strict regulation of the jazu-kissa. These spaces expanded the role of listening to new purposes and incorporated broader ranges of new musics. Free rock, progressive rock, and heavy music kissaten popped up around Kyoto and Osaka, such as *Niko-niko-tei* (Smile Shop), *Jam House*, and *Chigai-hōken* (Extraterritoriality). In these looser forms of kissa (where talking was encouraged), bands were formed, concerts were planned, and impromptu performances were enacted. Women exerted a much greater presence, and the role of the master was diffused as management duties were spread among a volunteer staff.

Throughout my fieldwork, Kansai musicians regularly referred back to one tiny yet influential Kyoto "free space" called Drugstore (figure 3.2), where many current performers met for the first time.[19] Despite the fact that Drugstore only existed for a few years, operated on an almost random schedule, and had a maximum capacity of fewer than twenty people, it maintains a mythical status for Kansai's Noise practitioners. A tiny room with no heat in winter and few amenities, the space was located at the western corner of the city in Nishijin, an old kimono-manufacturing district where rent was cheap. Almost all of the musicians who later came to define the Kansai Noise scene—and eventually represented its sounds internationally—met frequently at Drugstore to share their rare LPs, experiment with electronic sound and film equipment, and discuss music. The usual genre of choice was experimental *purogure* (progressive) rock, largely electronic and ambient groups from Germany and Britain (such as Guru Guru, Neu, Kraftwerk, and Tangerine Dream). However, Drugstore's selection was eclectic and was not limited to purogure, but included any *henna* (strange) recording available, including hard rock, electronic music, and free improvisation from Europe. The strangeness of experimental music kissa did not end with the selection of strange music, but surfaced in new techniques for listening in which recordings were looped, played

3.2. Doorway to Drugstore, 1976. Photo by Hiroshige Jojo.

at different speeds, and sometimes mixed together in a sonic collage. At Drugstore, one didn't listen to "experimental music" per se; rather, one listened experimentally.

Drugstore was established in 1976 as a *kanpa* (short for *kanpaniya*; "campaign") shop, maintained by donations from customer-members that did not require an ordinary business license. The workers were all volunteers, many of whom were students at nearby universities such as Doshisha and Kyoto University. Mikawa Toshiji first encountered Drugstore after being directed there by record store clerks while searching for a rare German rock album (UFO by Guru Guru). "I heard there was a 'store' where you could actually listen to such rare albums," Mikawa remembered, but on finally arriving he was shocked at its extraordinary weirdness: "As you opened the unwelcoming door, the inside space was divided vertically, like a bunk bed, and the ceilings of both spaces were too low to even stand up straight. The space was covered with purple shag carpet . . . it was a profoundly mysterious space. It was there that I was able to hear UFO for the first time; kids today cannot understand how impressed I was then . . . I encountered so many people in there who, to some degree, determined my future life" (Mikawa 1994).

Over time, the special atmosphere at Drugstore led the clientele to form a tight-knit social circle that produced a number of performance groups. Most were short-lived, but others formed the basis of a long-term music community and eventually fostered the transnational circulation of Noise recordings. Hiroshige Yoshiyuki (a.k.a. Jojo), a founding member of Hijokaidan (Emergency Stairway), started the influential Noise label Alchemy Records through friendships he made at Drugstore: "They played all kinds of stuff—progressive rock, experimental music, free jazz—but really loud. You could project films, or bring in your own records to play for your friends. I met all of the members of my first band Daigoretsu [Fifth Column], Mikawa [Toshiji], Nakajima [Akifumi], Ishibashi [Shôjirô] . . . and that's where I met Hide and we formed Ultra Bidé." Fujiwara "Bidé" Hide, leader of the influential early Noise band Ultra Bidé, first found Drugstore while he was still in high school, slowly discovering experimental rock through imported records. Fujiwara's hunt for records led him throughout the city of Kyoto and eventually to Drugstore:

> There was really only one small import record store. Jeugia, in Fujî-Daimaru department store at the corner of Shijô and Teramachi—I bought a lot of German rock, Velvet Underground, Captain Beefheart. It was pretty easy to get those records, but then I started getting into music that was harder to find, and there was no information, no fanzines back then. I'd read the liner notes; Pink Floyd had a gig with Soft Machine. "Hm. Who's Soft Machine?" Then go look for that record. When I found Drugstore, they had all the records like that—and it was all college students and older people, and some "cool" guys . . . I was like, "wow!" I was totally into it. That turned me into a real maniac [maniakku].[20]

Fujiwara was Drugstore's youngest and most outgoing customer, and he enthusiastically threw himself into the space as a second home, trading records with fellow customers and making connections throughout the city.

Ishibashi Shôjirô (currently one of Kansai's main independent music promoters and owner of experimental label F.M.N. Sound Factory) was an occasional staff member when Fujiwara suggested that Drugstore should host a live music performance mixed in with the usual listening sessions: "One day Bidé said, 'let's do a live here!' so we set it up for him. But I think only about twelve people could fit inside once the group was set up, so it was really just us [the staff and musicians]. We would have solo saxophone stuff, free jazz, or electronic stuff—we couldn't do a band really, with drums or anything like that. Most of the time the customers didn't really care about what we were doing or anything. You know, no one would come just to hear us. We would just do sessions whenever we felt like it."

Ishibashi told of an evening when the group based an experimental performance around a *nabe* meal, a hotpot dish in Japanese home cooking that evokes an intimate space of collective sociality. A nabe is cooked bit by bit by diners who gather around the boiling pot in a circle, slowly adding seafood, *mochi* (rice cakes), vegetables, and noodles and removing each piece when cooked. In this case, electronic music gear was attached to the hotpot, triggered by the actions of the diners as they ate to create a *denshi nabe* (electric, or in this sense, electronic, hotpot): "One night we came in and wired up our nabe pot to some synthesizers, so when you touched anything in the pot, it would set off sounds. Like, contact mics were put inside, just at the edge of feedback, so when you touched the food inside the pot—*Whaaaaaaaa!* There were all these sounds going off all the time from the synthesizers as people added things to the nabe. Actually, thinking back on it now, it was pretty dangerous! That was our version of *sokkyô ongaku* [improvised music]." Eventually, these haphazard experiments crystallized in a more deliberate public performance of feedback. But in the initial stages, performance was loosely blended with listening, with sessions circling around a small group of the most interested customers that cultivated their creative sociality in spontaneous events like the denshi nabe.

Ishibashi, Fujiwara, and Hiroshige, along with Mikawa Toshiji, Takayama Kenichi, Nakamura Junko (who later married Hiroshige), Zushi Naoki, Hayashi Naoto, and others in the core of Drugstore patrons, began forming ensembles to perform in other spaces in Kyoto and Osaka, often bringing experimental actors and *butoh* dancers they had met in the space on stage as well. The group maintained Drugstore's amateurish, improvisational spirit in their performances, appearing without fixed instrumentation or compositions—sometimes without even practicing in advance—and employing a changing cast of performers, most of whom had never played an instrument before. Hiroshige Jojo described an early gathering called Daigoretsu (Fifth Column), a predecessor to his famed Noise band Hijokaidan, as a "secret team" that did not perform publicly but assembled together ("like ninjas") to create something—anything, something different every time—then disperse. "Daigoretsu wasn't a *group*, really; more of a space, or something. Hm, was it a group after all? We had ten or twelve members, and we played almost every day, but with no organization—just 'Hi. Let's play something.' It was pure improvisation, but not just music. Any kind of action was okay. We would just play percussion, or make noise, or read poetry, or make a magazine—it was a very strange group. We had no live performances. It was just for us, just 'at home.' It was like a strange mythical team." In addition to private experimental gatherings like Daigoretsu, the Drugstore clan began also to experiment with renaming the sounds they appreciated as Noise. Eventually, Hiroshige remembered, he learned to narrow the products of his improvisational actions down to Noise as well: "I decided to play Noise, like we played in Daigoretsu sometimes—but *all* the time."

Although the name *Noise* eventually came to refer to their own sounds, the term was first developed in listening sessions at Drugstore. Before becoming a description for a specific genre, "Noise" was a general assignation for any off-the-map sounds; weird records, so extreme-sounding that they escaped generic categories of music. According to Ishibashi, the term was introduced by Hijokaidan member Mikawa Toshiji, who always referred to his favorite strange records as "Noise," regardless of their original generic context: "It was Mikawa, really, who started using the term Noise to talk about all the henna records he was bringing into Drugstore. Whatever he liked, Whitehouse, Stockhausen, Nihilist Spasm Band; all of that was 'Noise.' So then Hijokaidan started and of course they were 'Noise,' too. So actually, they were influenced by some other noisy stuff, but Noise as a category was started by Hijokaidan, and then they started Alchemy [Hiroshige's label]."

As both a catchall designation for difficult, hard-to-get recordings and a specific reference to the group's creative output, the idea of Noise gathered uncategorizable sounds and located them in the ears of a single group of listeners. Drugstore's listening gathered recordings from the margins of multiple musical genres—which had been named and organized somewhere else—and junked the previous categories to rename these sounds as Noise. Before the group had ever made Noise in performance, the sound of Noise had been remediated through their listening.

Drugstore's experimental listening stood as a deliberate rejection of the jazu-kissa's connoisseurship of historical expertise and repertoires of genre. Ishibashi insisted that in spite of its importance, Drugstore "was just a space . . . not like a jazu-kissa with a special history of the music, and sort of, how it was built bit by bit, and how it eventually became something. It [the music at Drugstore] didn't *become* anything, it just stayed *strange*." To "stay strange" required diverging from the genre-oriented, archival listening of the jazu-kissa, and also demanded the constant creation of new relationships between sounds. The Drugstore group began to add their own local Noise to the experimental blends of their record collections. Members brought in cassettes from isolated experimentalists from around Kansai, adding these tapes of underground Osaka and Kyoto artists to the mix. Drugstore began to attract occasional visitors from the influential Tokyo listening space Minor and other free spaces around Japan, and listeners started to branch out to program local performance events.[21]

One of the regular customers at Drugstore was the leader of the student *zenkyôtô* (all-campus joint struggle committee) at nearby Doshisha University.[22] Through this connection to the student government, Fujiwara began to book shows at Doshisha and then at venues throughout Kansai, including Eggplant in Osaka and Taku Taku and Jittoku in Kyoto (both of which occupied abandoned sake breweries). Several shows took place in the legendary Seibu Kôdô, a large hall on the western grounds of Kyoto University that had been taken over during the student power movement of 1968. Seibu Kôdô had remained vaguely autonomous from the university since the protests and remained open to the public. By the mid-1970s, it was an important space for experimental theater, lectures on radical politics, and occasional performances by Kyoto's early experimental rock bands, especially politically minded rock groups such as Datetenryu, Zunô Keisatsu, and the controversial Hadaka no Rallizes.[23] By booking the emerging Noise bands into these venues with underground legends of free music like Haino Keiji, Fujiwara began to link the listeners at Drugstore into an existing local performance scene.[24]

In 1980, Drugstore's circle of experimentalists released their first recordings, documented on the compilation LP *Dokkiri Rekôdo* (Shocking Record), collectively released by the musicians themselves. The record featured an early version of Fujiwara's Ultra Bidé, along with postpunk groups Henshin Kirin, Aunt Sally (featuring lead singer Phew), and Inu (featuring Machida Machizô, a.k.a. Machida Kô).[25] Hayashi Naoto, another Drug-

Listening to Noise in Kansai | 109

store listener, started Unbalance Records during the same year to release the sonically extreme Kansai compilation *Shûmatsu Shorijô* (Sewage Treatment Plant), as well as the first Hijokaidan LP. Because there was no other possibility of distribution, Hayashi and Hiroshige delivered the records and homemade cassettes to small independent record stores in Osaka and Tokyo by hand. They soon found this method too difficult, and the music was judged too harsh and extreme for most stores. But the label lasted long enough to hold an all-Kansai performance event called Unbalance Day at Loft in Shinjuku in 1981. Hijokaidan member Mikawa describes the Tokyo audience's reaction as "extreme culture shock": "[They] laughed with blank amazement at the sheer Kansai-ness of Hijokaidan . . . at the same time they were unable to look away, transfixed as though by some terrifying sight" (Mikawa 1992).

Hijokaidan added new elements of extreme performance to go along with their extreme sounds (figure 3.3). Members threw raw fish guts and garbage at the audience, destroyed equipment, and urinated and vomited on stage.[26] Drawing from the loose collective at Drugstore, Hijokaidan was composed of a large and flexible group of members, some making sounds, others doing actions. Their performances quickly became legendary, but the group was soon banned from most local performance spaces. Some within the group wanted to stay focused on the sound anyway. "As all kinds

3.3. Hijokaidan, circa 1979. Photo by Jibiki Yûichi.

of noxious pandemonium unfolded right in front of my eyes," Mikawa remembered later, "it was often very difficult to concentrate on creating my sounds . . . inside I began to long to focus on creating pure Noise."[27] In the face of this block on performances, Hijokaidan turned to recordings, which narrowed the group down to the more sonically oriented members. Over the next few months, they amassed a large collection of homemade recordings. The problem then became how to get them out.

FROM OSAKA ALCHEMY TO JAPAN OVERSEAS

With the help of Hayashi, Hiroshige started a new label, Alchemy Records, which eventually bypassed Tokyo to bring Noise to an international audience. Since the label's founding in 1983, Alchemy's success led overseas audiences to focus on the Kansai region, particularly Osaka, as the center of the Japanese Noise scene. But within Japan, Hiroshige explains, being located in Osaka was an enormous barrier to national distribution: "I started Alchemy because I just kept seeing Noise artists quit because they couldn't get a record released. Kansai is strange, because almost all the media is in Tokyo, and Osaka is just not considered a place for culture. In Kansai, we can do new things, really good things, but it's just impossible to become a success." Historically, Osaka has been known as a mercantile city, with a salt-of-the-earth population known for hard work and thrift, an explosive sense of humor, a rough local dialect, and excessive eating and drinking. These regional characteristics of spontaneity and directness may have attracted North American listeners, who responded to the forthright Osaka style. Although Osaka is famous for its special cultural attributes, the Kansai region is politically and economically marginalized within Japan. Kansai's popular music has been especially underrepresented. A few local independent labels had existed in the area during the early 1970s, including URC (Underground Records Club) started by Hayakawa Yoshio, the guitarist for the famed psychedelic band Jacks. But URC folded in the mid-1970s, and by the 1980s there were no local options for independent music production. Since the music industry was located in Tokyo, the only way to release Kansai acts was to start a new label that remediated local Noise for a transnational audience.

In 1983, after a brief stint in Tokyo running an unsuccessful video distribution company, Hiroshige decided that he had developed enough connections to start an independent music label in Kansai. Despite his connections with well-known Tokyo underground groups like the Stalin, Alchemy had little representation in Tokyo record stores. Hiroshige decided that even if Noise was ignored within Japan, it could find its way to a global listenership. "I decided to release all of the strange music from Kansai, and distribute it everywhere. I was into the idea of alchemy [renkinjutsu]: that you could make money from junk.[28] Our sound is junk, but we can record it, release CDs, and make money. That's alchemy . . . something that's not even art, something with no message. That's also alchemy . . . the feeling we get from our junk." To begin this transformation, Hiroshige had to reach beyond Tokyo, beyond Japan, to plug into a transnational network of listeners. Over the course of the next decade, Alchemy's distribution to underground audiences in North America looped back into Japanese reception to create an Osaka "Noise boom" in the 1990s.

Because the cost of foreign distribution was extremely high, the North American circulation of Alchemy Records was necessarily limited to small numbers. U.S. distributors sold imported CDs for up to $20 to retail stores, who marked the releases up to around $25. A record by Hijokaidan might sell for the same price in both Japanese and North American stores, but the North American copy would not produce any profit for Alchemy. In the late 1980s and early 1990s, longtime employee Ônishi Aya told me, Alchemy was forced to limit its overseas distribution, creating an imbalanced market for Japanese Noise: "We sell CDs for ¥2,800 here [in Japan], but we have to sell it for $14 in America. That's still considered too expensive, but we had to do it that way if we wanted to introduce the music to other countries, even though we didn't make any money from it . . . we could never even do a run of 1,000 copies straight away, just press them a little at a time; maybe after a while, we might reach 1,000 and stop." Alchemy provided free CDs to college radio stations and reviewers on request and managed to arrange some limited distribution to underground record stores in North America. By the mid-1990s, the North American audience had grown to the extent that Hiroshige could no longer manage the demand through mail-order correspondence. Alchemy and other small Kansai-based labels found it almost impossible to collect revenues from U.S.-based independent distributors, and they began to look for another way to distribute their releases in North America.

In 1994, Go Shoei began to consolidate the output of Kansai independent experimental labels in a small local distribution company called Japan Overseas, which distributed Alchemy's releases to North American stores in a quarterly catalog. At first, Go simply listed local recordings released by various local underground labels, emulating record dealers who circulated lists of "wanted" or "offered" rare records for sale. As interest grew, she began adding short, descriptive blurbs for each release, and soon overseas fans and record collectors began to write to request noncatalog items. The catalog quickly became the "Japan contact" for U.S. fans seeking obscure, undistributed Japanese releases. Japan Overseas also gave coherence to the North American view of the Osaka underground, since Go carried at least one record by each of the important local Kansai bands. Even though Japan Overseas was primarily a middleman for local Japanese labels, the catalog consolidated the category of "Japanoise" for North American reception. Go decided to simply make Japan Overseas into a label of her own, working directly with local groups and paying for the pressing herself. She arranged for her releases to be pressed at record and CD plants in the United States, which allowed her to sell Japan Overseas releases in North America for the same prices as domestic releases. Because Go priced her releases competitively, she was able to arrange for retail distribution in the United States with Forced Exposure, Revolver, Caroline, and other distributors.

Recordings by performers like Masonna, Solmania, and Monde Bruits began to appear on the shelves of North American independent record stores in the mid-1990s. For a growing group of Noise-focused listeners, every new release from Japan Overseas was another piece of the Japanoise puzzle. These recordings reverberated in the imaginations of American listeners as the "Osaka Noise scene," just as the sounds of bebop had represented America for Japanese listeners in the postwar jazu-kissa. An English-language zine called *Exile Osaka*, written by Brooklyn expat Matt Kaufman, reported on the Kansai scene for North Americans. But *Exile Osaka* was widely read in Japan as well, and Kaufman eventually became an important local authority on Kansai Noise. Back in Japan, record stores began to carry more underground and local independent music, and niche stores in Osaka like Forever Records, Maru ka Batsu, Time Bomb, and King Kong featured sections on Kansai Noise. The "Kansai Chaos Guide" *G-Scope* captured the local scene with a monthly performance calendar, descriptions of new recordings, and details of Kansai bands' overseas tours. Local livehouses like Fandango, Sun Hall, and Club Water began to fill up with enthusiastic young audiences for Noise shows.

A handful of Drugstore-like places for listening popped up as well. In 1995, an all-Noise "bar" opened on the third floor of an office building in

3.4. Yamazaki "Maso" Takushi (Masonna) in Alchemy Music Store, Shinsaibashi, Osaka. Photo by the author.

south Osaka. Bar Noise fit around ten customers at a time in a small room that blasted Noise recordings over the stereo (and even served a "Noise cocktail" that, according to critic Higashiseto Satoru, "tasted so bad that you could never finish it"). The ersatz "Noise kissa" hosted only a few performances during the year of its existence, but Bar Noise became legendary through Japan Overseas' issue of a compilation CD called *Bar Noise Full Volume Live Vol. 1*. At the end of the 1990s, Alchemy Records opened a retail outlet dedicated to selling Noise and experimental music in Shinsaibashi, managed by Yamazaki "Maso" Takushi (a.k.a. Masonna; figure 3.4). Customers lingered over the racks in the tiny shop, listening as Yamazaki mixed new Alchemy releases with rare records of Japanese psych or new recordings from Noise artists around the world.

LISTENING IN

I have foregrounded the story of Drugstore to stress the creative work of listening in creating new forms of music, and the role of recorded circulations in reframing musical knowledge. The practices of reception initiated by the jazu-kissa spread out into new social interpretations, which ranged from conservative sound-preserving institutions to genre-destabilizing experimental performances. While both jazu- and free kissa emphasized the interpretive power of listening, each produced different relationships to musical history. Jazu-kissa did not begin as socially conservative institutions. Eventually, desire for the pure original signal of jazz tuned out the possibility of local productivity, in favor of a historical canon whose boundaries lay somewhere else. Drugstore, on the other hand, reframed the stakes—and the possibilities—of listening by gathering Noise from the fringes of foreign media. But because it is constituted in circulation, the history of Noise can always be turned back on itself in new contexts of interpretation.

Hiroshige does not insist that Drugstore and Alchemy represent the only sources of Noise or that Noise is strictly a product of Japanese authorship. However, he points out an important divergence between Japanese and North American discoveries of Noise. Because they encountered Japanese records already named as Noise, he argues, North Americans simply reinforced this received category through their listening: "[At Drugstore], our experience was totally different. We heard a lot of different kinds of music, we learned a lot from records, and we didn't know about something called 'Noise.' But after the 1980s, they [Americans] knew about 'Noise' from us. We didn't know about Noise music, so we made the first Noise music. If you know that there is such a thing as 'Noise' when you're making it, well—that's different, isn't it?"[29] Hiroshige's bold claim that all Americans heard about Noise from Alchemy Records is unquestionably hyperbolic. But he points to something basic about the spirit of listening that continues to drive Noise beyond its own categorization. It is the desire to push experimentations with sound and performance beyond the canonization of musical genre, which remediates recorded music away from fixed histories and into the creative reinventions of feedback.

Like history itself, the interpretive practice of listening is always balanced on a tipping point. On one side of the edge, musical identities disappear altogether in endless revisions and appropriations; on the other, they are sealed in the conservative nostalgia of canon formation. Although Drugstore may have served as the crucible for one important group's experimentations, its story should not be taken as the definitive origin myth of Noise. When Drugstore closed in the early 1980s, it had only been open a few years, operating with a loose schedule and a varied clientele. The tiny spot was only one among many places where the idea of Noise was dreamed up and put into circulation. But a powerful sound bubbled out of this local circle of listeners, gathered around the nabe pot in an unheated room in winter. Only after this alchemical transformation—which turned recordings into performances, and then back into more recordings—could they bring their own Noise into the world.

> What else is this collection but a disorder to which habit has accommodated itself to such an extent that it can appear as order?
>
> —Walter Benjamin, "Unpacking My Library"

CHAPTER 4

GENRE NOISE

IS NOISE A MUSICAL GENRE?

Let's start this loop again. When I began my initial fieldwork in Japan in 1998, I expected to fill in the blank space in my mind that opened up whenever I imagined the category of Noise. Because I kept encountering recordings that were called "Noise," "Noise Music," or "Japanoise," I thought that I might begin by narrowing in on its specific musical features, historical developments, and stylistic traits. Noise was named as a genre, so it must be categorizable through some common musical characteristics. But the sounds and performances that fell under the umbrella of Noise were too inconsistent to be characterized with quick-and-dirty summaries of sound aesthetics, audiences, or regional histories. Even in flipping through the fixed categories of record store bins, I found myself in even mushier territory. If there was a section that contained Noise, it held other items named differently, bumping up against "experimental music" and also "free rock," "glitch," "out," "junk," and many other names I hadn't counted on. The genre name seemed like an afterthought, a glorified "Misc" bin in which to throw the detritus that did not fit anywhere else. But then, without some recognizable difference from other forms, how could Noise become known as a musical genre of its own? In the context of these overflowing categorizations of music, why name something Noise?

I first attempted to discover the boundaries of Noise on my preliminary fieldwork trip to Osaka in 1998. "You can't take it seriously," said Noise artist Yamazaki Maso (a.k.a. Masonna): "Noise isn't a kind of music. Masonna is just me doing my thing. I don't even listen to other stuff called Noise." "Most Noise artists think of their work as rock music, as a kind of extreme rock music," said Higashiseto Satoru, Kansai record store worker and long-term promoter of local experimental music. Across town, Hiroshige Jojo, Noise legend and owner of Alchemy Records, told me "Noise is just Noise. It has nothing to do with any other music." Still others set it all aside as *chigatta ongaku*: "weird," "strange," or more literally, "wrong" music. "I'm not interested in calling it 'Noise,'" said Noise fan Ishii Akemi, shouting over the PA in the Osaka livehouse Bears. "For me, this is just a sound that I like, because I'm always looking for things that are strange and different, and this stuff makes me feel like that." Some went further, saying Noise was not worth studying because it wasn't really music and would not hold up to any real attempt to understand it as such. "It's just a name." For many musicians (and these were often the most dedicated long-term participants), Noise did not even merit a name. "It's not serious," they told me, adding, "I just play for myself," and then "it doesn't matter."

Still, in both North America and Japan, the name keeps coming back. Musicians and listeners refer uncritically to Noise, Noise Music, and Japanoise as terms of musical genre. Others continue to insist that Noise is not music at all. Most practitioners argue that Noise does not possess any defining characteristics beyond its incommensurability with any existing form of music. These claims of total opposition, of course, are familiar from modernist avant-garde projects of antiart, which attempted, often vainly, to keep emergent forms of expression from being subsumed into the dialectics of historical categories (Bürger 1984; Huyssen 1986; Krauss 1986; Poggioli 1968). But despite Noise's antigeneric position, its immersion in popular music has been fundamental to its creative identity. Noise became a genre through its antagonistic feedback with Music, which split its generic difference into two interrelated loops. The first loop inscribed Noise in total separation from Music and all of its distinctive categories. In the second, Noise was integrated into circulation in the form of recordings and eventually distinguished as a musical genre of its own. Though I describe Noise's generic forms through this circulatory discourse, I do not mean to suggest that Noise's differences are *only* discursive. I have already argued that Noise is broadly recognized for its distinctive, if diverse, inventions of sound, performance, and modes of listening. But in the context of its recorded circulation, Noise's interventions into genre ideology also provoked a "language about music" that produced "interpretive, theoretical, and evaluative discourses surrounding musical experience" (Feld and Fox 1994:32).

In this chapter, I discuss two distinct archetypes of Noise—the Canadian group Nihilist Spasm Band and the Tokyo-based Merzbow—to illustrate how its generic history emerged in the transnational reception of recordings. Both examples are claimed as the original creators of Noise by different audiences and at different points in circulation. The Nihilist Spasm Band began performing in the 1960s as a local project of artists and self-identified "nonmusicians" in London, Ontario. It was not until the 1990s that Japanese audiences reissued the group's almost-forgotten recordings—which had barely been distributed in the first place—and designated the Canadians as "godfathers of Noise." Akita Masami, on the other hand, arose as the idol of Japanese Noise for North American audiences through his hyperproductive release of recordings as Merzbow throughout the 1980 and 1990s. By scattering his work across a global field of independent labels, Akita slowly became the central reference of the Noise genre, and to date he represents its biggest (and perhaps only) international star. Transnational receptions of Merzbow as "Japanoise" allowed his work to appear both as a new Japanese genre and as a cultureless form of antimusic.

Before I turn to these legendary characters, I want to show how a network of performers and listeners laid the groundwork for Noise's emergence as a genre, even as they aimed to avoid its categorization. Noise is always emergent and endlessly new, too new even to define. It is distinguished by its incommensurability with all standards of musical beauty. This antigeneric position may appear to be a simplistic *refusnik* version of aesthetic radicalism—just a vain attempt to make the grand concept of Music obsolete with the blunt, brute force of Noise. But even as an antigenre, ideas about Noise generated new experiences of musical sound, definitions of musicianship and musical practice, and performances of musical culture. Noise became a nexus of romantic aesthetics that reinstated the potential of Music to become an unknowable, mysterious, indescribable world of pure sonic experience. Noise made Music new, over and over again, by reiterating its potential to escape meaningful classification.

Famously, Mikhail Bakhtin showed how genre discourse is essential to the dialogic production of cultural meaning. Emerging categories are developed, explained, and compared with others in an endless cycle, in which "a new genre heightens the consciousness of old genres . . . to better perceive their possibilities and their boundaries" (Bakhtin 1986:229). To give Noise the power of its total difference, it had to remain meaningless and separate from all other musical genres, even from "independent music." Yet by being recorded and circulated, Noise was fed into the discourse of musical genre and eventually became recognized as a meaningful form of music in itself.

NOISE IS MUSIC, NOISE IS NOISE

The genre ideology of Noise was formed in the feedback between two apparently irreconcilable positions: "Noise is Music" and "Noise is Noise." Shimomoto Taku, a Kyoto musician who began making Noise in 2001, told me that Noise could not exist in the same space as Music. In the presence of Music, the pure element of Noise would be destroyed: "It's either pure Noise, or it's Music. Mixing Noise with Music, or using Music in Noise, makes the whole thing Music; and then it's all Music, not Music with Noise. It's a thing with its own existence—otherwise it becomes an 'effect' [*efekuto*, as in "sound effect" or electronic musical device], like playing a wah-wah pedal in the middle of a song." Shimomoto insists that Noise must maintain purity in its difference from Music. Any mixing whatsoever will render Noise as a musical effect that would corrupt the possibility of its own independent meaning. This demand for purification sometimes produced deep interpersonal conflicts, as Noise's antigeneric status enabled practitioners to make claims of total independence from musical history, and from each other.

In 1996, the cofounders of the Northhampton, Massachusetts, cassette label Soundprobe split over a debate about the boundary between Noise and Music. As I have described, Noise is often made with electronic systems of feedback and other special techniques associated with experimental or independent music. Many practitioners argue hotly against Noise's integration into these other categories. "At the time," cofounder Seth Misterka told me, "I was kind of confused about what 'Noise' was. At first, I thought of it as very energetic electronic music. . . . I was pretty much defining it by what my friends were doing." This led to a confrontation with his labelmates over a flyer for an upcoming show and eventually to Misterka's departure from Soundprobe: "I had printed some concert programs that said 'Support Independent Music.' . . . [Cofounders Dan Greenwood and John Brown] were really mad about it. . . . They hated everything except Noise. And the concert was more about what I was doing musically, and most of the groups were playing instruments. . . . I thought of Noise as a branch of experimental music, but they thought of Noise as Noise." Greenwood and Brown, on the other hand, invoked the category of Noise to prevent their unique creative work from being integrated into Music. More often, practitioners dismissed talk about musical names and described all genres as meaningless.

Genres can only exist in relation to one another: they take on their meanings through social interpretation. But the discourse of genre is not made of ideological binaries, in which "Noise" and "Music" would simply be pragmatic, conventional ways to separate fundamentally different types of sound and performance. Charles Briggs and Richard Bauman have argued that generic intertextuality is a form of creative agency, in which specific interpretations are performed within a fluid web of social references, identifications, and historical contexts (Bauman and Briggs 1999, 2003; Briggs and Bauman 1992). Genre changes the logic of association between the narrative elements, sensations, and settings of music, even as the mass-mediated distribution of recordings extends sound beyond local contexts of performance. The "texts" of Noise—its recordings, sounds, histories, experiences, cultural placements, and archetypal figures—become interrelated through its genre discourse. Practitioners constantly shift the terms of their relationships with other musical forms and also contest Noise's own separations from Music.

For example, I attended a 1996 performance in Portland, Oregon, by the local performer Daniel Menche, who scraped metal objects and bricks across a contact microphone, which was processed with feedback and heavy amplification. I could have identified the performance as Noise because of its extreme sonic material and lack of instruments. Most things described as Noise do not conform to normative structures of musical sound, such as consistent pitch and rhythm, patterns of melody, recognizable words, use of recognized musical instruments, and so forth. But even before I attended the concert and heard these sounds, I had already come to associate Menche's work as Noise through generic frameworks that arose in circulation. His recordings were grouped with Noise releases in catalogs, included on Noise compilations, described as Noise in magazines and in retail stores, and so on. Menche, however, was ambivalent about identifying his work as Noise. He viewed the anti-Music debate as yet another counterproductive attempt at categorization:

> Once you say it's Noise—that opens up, like, a huge monstrous gray area—like, well, what the hell is anyone talking about? And . . . it . . . yeah, I can see how some people can call it Noise . . . but I don't take any pride whatsoever in any type of labeling, whether Noise or Music. And if anything, I'd say, "Well, fine, I'm a musician, that's what I do." You know, you get right down to it—fine, so be it, you know? Some people take so much pride in it, like "Oh, I'm Noise, I do Noise, I do anti-Music." Great, fantastic, lovely—I don't care.

Menche's distaste for musical names is not unique to Noise. Most musicians are well aware that their agency is at stake when their output is named under the terms of genre. To be hailed as Noise is to be recognized as a form, however different, of Music. "The music that is labeled," Ingrid Monson argues in her study of improvisational music, "is somehow the one that carries less prestige, the one that is considered less universal" (Monson 1997:101). Genre discourse shows how musical identifications are constructed through a conflicted process of interpellation, which calls subjects into being through a normative social order that is impossible to refuse (Althusser 1971; Butler 1997). Alternative discourses, like those that resist the constraints of Music with Noise, are eventually recognized as generic productions in themselves. Through this recognition, Noise is constituted as a term of musical circulation and its practitioners are incorporated into the regulatory coherence of Music.

Musical genres become what they are in technological as well as social mediations. Seymour Glass, publisher for experimental music fanzine *Bananafish*, argued that Noise immediately takes on the shape of Music in the moment it is circulated as a recording. "You're still pressing multiple copies of it on a format that traditionally carries music. It's LPs and CDs. And those things usually carry music, and we file them with our other musical objects, we read about them in our musical magazines, we hear them on our musical radio stations, so it's actually more like music than anything else. You can listen to it more than once. So saying 'it's not Music, it's Noise' is sort of like saying [in a bored tone] 'is it jazz rock, or is it prog rock, or is it fusion?'" In other words, Noise can never escape musical classification by remaining separate from Music. It can only retain its difference by becoming equivalent to Music through the technological format of recordings. Recordings allow listeners to act as if Noise were a kind of Music, while simultaneously knowing that it is not.

Listeners were brought into the networks of modern communication by learning to distinguish noise from signal. Friedrich Kittler has claimed that the categorization of noise was essential to the "discourse networks" of mechanical reproduction. Recordings allowed musical time to be preserved and repeated, and opened the human sensorium to previously inaccessible worlds of music. They also produced and captured layers of noise, which demanded that listeners reframe their perception of sound in the context of technological mediation. Before music could be accepted in its mediated form, "noise itself had to become an object of scientific research," which brought music into discourse as "a privileged category of noises" (Kittler 1999 [1986]:25). But music's coming-into-being as a physical commodity also meant that noise also took on a new material form, as an accidental production of meaningless sound that could be distinguished against intentional forms. Once noise was set outside of the semantic content of communication, its character began to be defined in affective and aesthetic terms. The scientific analysis of noise at the end of the nineteenth century set the stage for later discourses of Noise as a distinct musical genre.

In the field of musical acoustics, noise's difference was measured by its physical and physiological characteristics. Hermann Helmholtz famously characterized noise as a "rapid alternation of different kinds of sensations of sound" (1954 [1877]:7). Unlike musical tones, noise frequencies do not repeat the same vibratory pattern over and over. They are inconsistent, unpredictable, and difficult to measure and represent accurately. Helmholtz defined these complex signals as "nonperiodic" waveforms, exemplified by the sounds of splashing water, and the whistling of wind.[1] Nonperiodic waveforms are not necessarily unmusical—most percussion sounds, for example, are nonperiodic. In fact, noise sounds are an intrinsic element in musical signals, such as the scrape of a bow on a violin string or the puff of air that precedes a flute tone.[2] Some kind of noise, then, is present in most musical sounds, but noise sounds are not heard as musical unless they are incorporated into musical structures.

Helmholtz, then, showed that noise could be technically separated from the intentional character of musical sound. Although noise was objectively identifiable as a separate category of sound, it was difficult to develop further systems of analysis. Beyond being nonperiodic, the distinct acoustic characteristics of noise are hard to define, even as physical waveforms. As Torbin Sangild notes, noise is "impure and irregular, neither tones nor rhythm—roaring, pealing, blurry sounds with a lot of simultaneous frequencies" (Sangild 2002:4). This inconsistent wall of sound is sometimes described by the abstraction of white noise, an ideal sonic entity that contains all audible frequencies at equal levels at once. But the category of noise did not develop into a discourse of sound through the abstractions of scientific measurement. Listeners could only recognize noise through its interference with music and communication. As Douglas Kahn succinctly puts it, noise became "that constant grating sound generated by the movement between the abstract and the empirical" (Kahn 1999:25).

Even if noise sounds could be absolutely distinguished from musical sounds through their physical characteristics, "noise" was not heard as such until it became an essential aspect of technologically mediated sound. As musical messages began to issue from horns and speakers, listening meant separating meaningful signal from the overlay of noise. Noise was interference that should be minimized as much as possible, both by technological improvements and by active listening that tuned out the existence of noise. The audile techniques of modern listening were not just about identifying the authentic musical content of recordings, but "about enacting, solidifying, and erasing the relations of sound reproduction" in social life (Sterne 2003:274). To listen to musical content through technological noise was to limit one's sonic perception—to create knowledge within an interpretable range of possible meanings. As listeners parsed musical messages from recordings, the defining framework of mediation disappeared into the background.

Throughout this process, the category of noise moved from a natural order of noise sounds to an unclassifiable static. Isolating the meaningless layers of noise meant tuning into a world of music that could be discovered, named, and understood even in its mechanical reproduction. As noise gave music a new meaning, recorded music made noise meaningless.

It could become meaningful itself only if it took on the material form of music. Noise had to be recorded—and then named as a genre of recorded music—to return to musical discourse.

FROM *NO RECORD* TO "GODFATHERS OF NOISE"

How did the circulation of Noise recordings—even as its listeners insisted on its lack of connection to other forms of music—generate a new context of musical genre? For decades, Noise recordings were distributed with very few clues as to their historical origin, often in limited editions by labels that folded after a handful of releases. A Noise recording might disappear practically moments after its emergence, and then surface again years later, far from its original source, renamed and radically recontextualized by a new audience. The far-flung reception of Noise recordings in transnational circulation eventually demanded a history for the genre.

One possible version was discovered in the "foundational" recordings of the Nihilist Spasm Band (NSB), whose members have since become internationally known as the "godfathers of Noise." For years after its formation in the 1960s, the Nihilist Spasm Band was a world unto itself, which might never have been connected to the global imaginary of Noise. They made recordings casually, as random messages in a bottle, sent out into an unknown reception. Decades later, the Nihilists came to define Noise's generic development for a Japanese audience in ways that redefined their past and redirected their future. The group initially developed their Noise in a marginalized context of local performance, which they imagined as wholly separate from any larger musical scene. Through the redistribution of their recordings in the 1990s, they were retroactively named as the progenitors of the now-transnational Noise genre.

The group began performing in 1965 in London, Ontario, as the "official band" (and most of the members) of the absurdist Nihilist Party of Canada (figure 4.1). The party formed itself in all-night "hang-out" sessions in the downtown art studio of member Greg Curnoe, talking and playing records at full blast.[3] The Nihilists began performing when volunteers from the crowd were asked to provide a soundtrack for a film called *No Movie*; they began by banging bottles together and playing kazoos. "Then," member Art Pratten told me, "we started building instruments, and the number of people who wanted to continue with this diminished to about eight. And they just didn't know when to stop, you know?" Over the next twenty-five

4.1. Nihilist Spasm Band in Greg Curnoe's studio, London, Ontario, 1966. From left: Bill Exley, John Boyle, Greg Curnoe, Murray Favro, Hugh McIntyre. Left foreground: Art Pratten. Photo by Don Vincent, courtesy of Bernice Vincent.

years, the group performed every Monday night, confounding audiences even as they became a beloved local institution. Throughout, the band's creative focus was almost entirely dedicated to the building of new instruments and their weekly "bar band" performances for friends. The Nihilists did not consider themselves musicians; they "made noise" purely for their own amusement as they went about raising families and working their jobs.[4]

The Nihilists did release a handful of recordings. The first—predictably titled *No Record*—was issued in an edition of one thousand copies on the small independent label Allied Records in 1968. "Bringing out a record, we thought, was sort of what bands do, so we should do one, too," said Pratten, "but we pretty much gave them all out and forgot about it right away." They were indifferent, he claims, to the fate of their recordings. Instead, they emphasized their amateurish isolation and avoided, as their jacket notes put it, "any knowledge of music they might have outside of the band." The group's second recording, *Vol. 2*, came out ten years later, and again the Nihilists remained ambivalent about where the copies ended up. Instead, they focused on their local performances, playing for friends and their own amusement and declining to tour. Aside from their Monday night slot—first in the bar of the York Hotel in downtown London and later in the Forest City Gallery—the Nihilist Spasm Band's main venue was their annual No Picnic for friends and relatives.

At some point in the late 1980s, friends began to mention that the group's records were now being called "Noise." The few available copies of *No Record* were being sold as a Noise rarity in record shops and were occasionally being reviewed and described as a document of early Noise in fanzines. The group was amused by the reappearance of their old recording as a historical hallmark of the new genre. They accepted their affiliation with Noise precisely because the name seemed perfectly meaningless, a nondescriptive label of their indescribable difference. Pratten described Noise as merely the latest in a long series of abstract neologisms: "We never called ourselves anything. We kept getting told that we were—oh, what was it—we were things like 'something rock' for a while, then we were 'proto-punk' and for a while we were some sort of 'radical jazz.' Then when 'Noise' came along, we said 'whew, that's a good *name!*' And 'Noise' is a category we've got no problem with. We've never said we were *in* it—but we're happy to be whatever anyone says we are. 'Noise' is fine." For Pratten and the rest of the Nihilists, the name "Noise" simply removed their sounds from consideration as an offshoot (if an especially "radical," "hybrid," or just "bad" version) of any other musical genre by creating an impossible category of music. "We never thought of being part of a movement," Pratten told me, "that's something other people do for you . . . I feel no impulse to defend it as music." Entering into transnational media circulation in the 1990s brought the group's recordings into a new context of reception, first in Japan and then back in North America.

In the early 1990s, members of the NSB were contacted by Hiroshige Jojo, leader of Kansai Noise group Hijokaidan and owner of the foundational Noise label Alchemy Records, which released several new albums by the group throughout the decade. Hiroshige had been a fan of the mysterious group since the late 1970s, but it wasn't until 1991—when Alchemy was beginning to develop ties with North American distributors—that he decided to contact the band to ask if they would contribute a track for an international Noise compilation. Ironically, the group's stalwart localism helped facilitate this international exchange, because they still received

4.2. Nihilist Spasm Band as "godfathers of Noise" on Japanese television in 1996. Courtesy of Zev Asher.

mail at the same address printed on their 1968 LP. As Hugh McIntyre told me, the letter from Hiroshige was the first time NSB learned that their records had traveled beyond their small circle: "Sometime around 1990, I got a letter from Japan. And it was from Jojo, saying that he loved the Spasm band, and he was familiar with our stuff, and he wanted a track to contribute to a compilation, which he called, I think, *World Music* [Alchemy Records ARCD-042, 1992]. They got the address from our '70s album, and we had had the same addresses the whole time . . . we all had a good laugh that somebody in Japan knows us! We had no idea who else was on the label, what kind of music, whatever. [Hiroshige] said he'd pay for everything; we'd still never met each other." In 1993, Alchemy released the group's first CD recording, titled *What About Me?* The recording hurled the Nihilist Spasm Band into Japanese distribution, where they were rediscovered as the progenitors of Noise.[5]

In 1996, the Nihilists toured Japan, where they performed alongside several Noise artists also on the Alchemy label; the tour was presented as a rare opportunity to hear the historical roots of Noise. They appeared on national television (figure 4.2), were interviewed by local underground magazines, and, in their Osaka performance, were preceded by a Nihilist

Spasm Band tribute band called Spasmom. But the Nihilists quickly discovered that the Noise of the Alchemy groups didn't exactly line up with their own Noise. McIntyre reported that although the band was thrilled to connect with Japanese artists, they were ambivalent about the generic associations: "It's very different from what we do. A lot of them would claim to be inspired by us, but it wouldn't sound like us. It was just the *idea* of making Noise [that connected us], not anything more." The NSB had accepted the term *Noise* as part of their insistence on the naïveté that separated their performances from Music. They argued their difference from other Noise bands in the same terms. While most Japanese Noise is often performed with electronics and is quite "serious," the NSB described their performance as "a parody of a real band": they had a vocalist, who at least spoke, if not sang, and their invented instruments were based on horns, strings, and drums. Rather than presenting Noise as a separate, pure form of sonic expression, the Nihilists used their collective musical "ineptitude and disorganization to confront cultural expression in all of its forms." As John Boyle explained, "it was never intended to *sound like anything*—we just played like that to avoid being drowned out by the others."

Soon after their return from Japan, the Nihilists made a belated entrance into the North American Noise scene. They went on their first U.S. tour (timed to coincide with some members' retirement from work at age sixty-five), playing Chicago, Buffalo, Rochester, Cleveland, and New York City. Back in London, the group's annual No Picnic evolved into the No Music Festival, which has since hosted an international roster of performers, including Wolf Eyes, Thurston Moore, and Knurl, as well as Japanese artists Hijokaidan, Incapacitants, and Aube. The Nihilists became the subjects of a 2000 documentary film (*What About Me?*; dir. Zev Asher), and the band has released eight more recordings since their 1996 Japanese tour (including two on Alchemy: *Live in Japan* and *Every Monday Night*) as well as additional reissues of their older work. A few years after the tour, Aya Ônishi, former drummer of Sekiri and employee of Alchemy Records, joined the band in London as a "permanent visiting member."

JAPAN AS A GENRE

It is no coincidence that Japan played such an important role in defining the generic form of recorded Noise. Japanese popular culture has been integrated into transnational media circulation for over a century, but its musical genres continue to be distinguished from those of the West. In Japan, contemporary popular musics are typically named with English loanwords transliterated in *katakana*, the script for foreign words (e.g., *rokku, jazu*).[6] Even the most general words for music are doubled with additional Western terms, so that both *ongaku* and *myûjikku* can be used to refer to music in its broadest sense (Johnson 1999). This juxtaposition results from the failure of the modern ontological separation of Japanese culture into native and foreign categories. In the case of Japanese music, two culturally separated metagenres—*hôgaku* and *yôgaku*—are used to categorize all musical forms as either Japanese or Western traditions. But as its modern cultural production was integrated into a circulation that presumed the universality of Western forms, Japan itself became a site of generic difference.

In popular music, "Japanese" genres assume some form of cultural separation from global centers of production. Even in Japan, local forms of popular music are specifically identified as Japanese, even in forms like J-pop that are clearly derivative of a transnational mediasphere.[7] Despite its obvious mimetic relationship with Western pop music, J-pop is considered Japanese because (as one friend put it when trying to explain J-pop's qualities) it is "just for us." There are many other examples of localizing genre names in global popular music (e.g., Rock en Español, Indipop, and so forth). On one hand, these genre names describe some kind of equivalence between regional and global media. On the other, they exceptionalize local productions and separate them from universal categories of popular music. The J of J-pop, then, is not meant to denote any essential Japanese sound but instead relates the localized scale of production and its cultural separation from global norms of popular music.[8] Conversely, the adoption of the English-language word *Noise*, transliterated as *Noizu*, allowed Japanese performers to stress the universality of their work. There is a constellation of specific Japanese terms for noise, noise sounds, or noisy situations—*sô-on, zatsuon, nigiyaka, urusai*, and others—that could have been used instead of *Noizu*. But a Japanese name would have implied a Japanese context of production, whereas the English loanword kept the genre in a broadly conceived circulation.[9]

Even the broadest of genre categories can be reinterpreted differently for local receptions. In the 1980s and '90s, the phrase "independent music" developed in North American circulations, first to distinguish the do-it-yourself productions of small-scale labels and then to name the new stylistic movement of "indie rock" (Azerrad 2001). "Indie" music's conflation of structural and aesthetic independence depends on a monolithic discourse of "mainstream" popular music, which is invoked to "provide a 'center' for other, 'alternative' or 'marginal' genres" (Brackett 2003:241). Japanese reception added an additional level of meaning to "independent music" that furthered its generic marginality. In Japan, independent records from North America and Europe are most often sold in smaller stores that deal exclusively with imports. Due to the protectionist licensing of the Japanese music industry, independent records were usually not included in the registered licensing packages of multinational media distribution networks (e.g., JASRAC, the Japanese Society for the Rights of Authors, Composers, and Publishers).[10] As a result, the same small urban record stores that carried exclusively imported foreign records were also the primary retail outlets for Japanese independent labels not affiliated with industrial channels. As "independent music," a local recording would be shelved next to imported Western pop music, putting Japanese indies into the context of a global scene.[11]

In some cases, it is the unfocused anonymity of a new musical genre that creates its appeal. Ben Chasny (6 Organs of Admittance) describes the mix of mystery and challenge he felt when seeing the label "acid folk" on a box of records in a photo of a famous underground record shop (Modern Music in Tokyo, which also houses the experimental label PSF):

> Through the Forced Exposure catalog, I found out that [the label] PSF had these compilations called Tokyo Flashback. And on the third one, there's a picture of the guy sitting in what I guessed were the PSF offices [actually the Modern Music storefront], and there's records stacked to the ceiling, a total mess, with this box in the front that's labeled "acid folk." I remember thinking, I don't know what's in that box, and I don't exactly know what it would sound like, but whatever it is, it's probably really great. I want to make music that you could put in that box. So I just made what I was looking for. (Chasny 2005:14)

Different receptions create different emplacements of genre. In the United States, a record by British group Test Dept. or the American group Three Day Stubble might be named "experimental" or "industrial," or just lumped into the "miscellaneous" bin. Among Japanese listeners, these recordings were grouped with others as a new genre labeled "Junk." Like Noise, "Junk" reorganized a diverse set of translocal materials for a new consumption. "Junk" might include "lo-fi" rock recordings from the

United States, German industrial records, or a Tokyoite's homemade electronic music, all of which could be re-placed as a new genre in Japanese import/indie record stores. Unlike "Noise," the genre name "Junk" never circulated outside of Japan. Most alternative genre names are transient and remain marginal, as local counterfactuals to histories produced elsewhere. But in some cases—like Japanoise—new genre names are taken up in a global context of circulation.

THE MOST EXTREME MUSIC IN THE WORLD

At the same time that Japanese audiences discovered the historical record of Noise in the Nihilist Spasm Band, North Americans began to attribute the new genre to a Japanese authorship. In the 1990s, Japan became the cultural lynchpin of Noise through the term *Japanoise*, which was increasingly distinguished as the most extreme genre of Noise in the world. The overseas reception of Japanoise was solidified through the recorded work of a single artist—Akita Masami, a.k.a. Merzbow—who came to define the genre for a new audience. In music, as is often said of ethnography, one good example is often used to characterize an entire culture. In his global recognition, Merzbow is also the exception that proved the rule of Noise. This archetype could only have taken shape in the distorted feedback of an overflowing media circulation. Merzbow is overwhelmingly cited as the central figure of Noise, by both Japanese and overseas fans. Over the course of three decades of activity, Akita's prolific release of recordings made it possible to argue for the existence of a genre of Noise, even as Merzbow became its singular example. When I begin to describe my research on Noise, most knowledgeable music fans ask which artists I am writing about or simply lead with the obvious answer: "so, like . . . Merzbow?"

I am not arguing that the history of Noise should be traced to any single individual. We would not find its roots in a biographical profile of Akita, in an exhaustive study of his creative works, or even in his multifarious connections to various international music scenes. But the generic narrative of Noise constantly returns to Merzbow like a moon around a planet, thrown into orbit by the sheer number of recordings he has issued from the late 1970s to the present. This enormous body of work—consisting of over three hundred full-length albums, as well as hundreds of contributions to compilations, soundtracks, and remixes—has played a definitive role in the development of transnational Noise networks. Noise's generic history is also strongly influenced by Akita's personal image and by representations of his ideas about Noise. In both Japan and North America, a listener who has never heard of Merzbow has probably never heard of Noise. In many ways, the imaginary of "Japanese Noise Music" depends on Akita's persona. As one fan put it, "I loved Japanese noise music before I even heard it . . . [just for the idea] that there was this bookish guy named Akita who didn't talk much, but who would come out on the stage and make, like, THE MOST EXTREME MUSIC IN THE WORLD" (Huss 2004).

Akita himself does not claim to have invented Noise. Instead, he considers his work as Merzbow as part of an ongoing *detournement* of the international culture industry that connects to political art movements in Europe and the United States, from surrealism to industrial music, performance art, and the cut-ups of William S. Burroughs. His recordings nod to this history by stringing words together in titles like "Cloud Cock OO Grand" or "Noisembryo: Psycho-analytic Study of Coital Noise Posture," and he has published books and articles that link his version of Noise to other aesthetic and political subcultures. Although a handful of Akita's general comments on Noise have been widely reproduced, there have been few English-language translations of his writings. His perspective is most often represented for overseas listeners through selected quotes from English-language interviews, which have usually been heavily edited for publication.[12] But these slight commentaries became the jumping-off point for imagining Japanoise. Akita was described as an isolated genius, and most critics did not draw out his connections to other contemporaneous developments in electroacoustic music, progressive rock, or free jazz. Instead, Japan thematized Merzbow for transnational audiences, and Akita was regularly asked by interviewers to characterize his work in relation to Japanese sociocultural differences.[13]

Akita's eventual refusal of the name "Noise," of course, was partly ordered by the feedback of this reception. While the rich aesthetic frame Akita built around the term had been crucial for its growth as a genre and for his own fame, he told me (in a 1998 interview) that he had abandoned the name. In fact, he argued that he had only "pretended" to use Noise as a term of genre: "When I started, I used the word Noise, but at that time people hated it . . . they thought Noise was just 'no-good music.' I kind of 'pretended' to use the term Noise because it means separation from other music, it was outside of Music. But by the late 1980s, a lot of people began to use the term Noise for different purposes . . . so it's not useful anymore."

Akita used the pretense of Noise to separate from Music, and certainly he could not have predicted its later reception as "Japanoise." But to remain "outside" of Music, the "inside" of Noise demanded to be situated in some distinct and separated self, some original person who could stand for Noise.[14] Akita's identity—and, ultimately, the genre of Noise itself—had to be detached from his own history.

Like Merzbow, the name "Noise" itself operates as a pseudonym that stands in for a hidden reality. Pseudonyms are especially common among oppositional communities, as in the widespread punk rock practice of substituting each musician's last name with the band name (e.g., the Ramones), so that individual identities are surrogated to the familial relations of the punk rock "community."[15] Just as this kind of naming conflates a person with their performative role, recorded media can stand in for musical subjects that could not otherwise be reduced to a consistent identity.[16] As Noise recordings proliferated, the use of pseudonyms created the impression of a larger production. A single individual might release different projects under separate pseudonyms, or a group of musicians might release recordings under multiple band names to differentiate each project's separate aesthetic or sonic goals.[17]

Over time, the name "Merzbow" has taken on a one-to-one correspondence with the figure of Akita, which displaced the search for generic histories onto an inquiry about Akita's persona. Although Akita has clearly been the driving force of Merzbow for more than three decades, the project has also incorporated long-term collaborators who worked with Akita for decades. From 1981 to 1989, Merzbow was a duo with Mizutani Kiyoshi, who remains a well-known solo artist in Tokyo; throughout the 1990s, Akita was joined in live performances and recordings by Azuma Reiko (Reiko A), and Sakaibara Tetsuo (Bara).[18] Although Akita's solo performances are renowned, the sheer quantity of Merzbow releases is what established Akita's reputation in Japan and overseas. I do not mean to suggest that there is nothing distinctive about Merzbow recordings, which are widely recognized as among the most sophisticated, powerful, and uniquely constructed in Noise. But it was the overflowing stream of these releases into transnational circulation that set the stage for Noise's emergence as a distinct musical genre.

Since the late 1970s, Akita has produced recordings constantly and released them in rapid succession. In 1978, Akita created his own label,

Lowest Music and Arts, to produce Merzbow cassettes in small numbers for barter with other musicians; he added another label called ZSF Produkt in the mid-1980s for retail distribution. He soon began sending recordings to be released on international labels, and toured Europe (including the Soviet Union), Korea, and the United States. By the end of the 1980s, the flood of Merzbow cassettes in circulation lent itself to quick parody (the *Bananafish* editor Seymour Glass once quipped that above Chez Merzbow there's a neon sign blinking on and off—"over 12 billion dubbed"). Perhaps most important, Akita's overseas releases were incorporated into a range of different popular music genres. Merzbow recordings could be found on independent labels specializing in different marginal subgenres, from hard-core punk to improvisation to Scandinavian death metal to French computer music (figure 4.3). Because his work circulated at the edges of so many different styles and scenes, Merzbow's range of reception, both within Japan and in Europe and North America, was extremely diverse. Akita has collaborated on recordings with a huge variety of musicians; his work is played at raves and programmed at the Paris Musée d'Art Moderne and the Goethe-Institut; and Merzbow recordings are widely discussed in academic music critiques as the primary sonic texts of Noise.[19] Finally, at the turn of the millennium, Akita gathered up the recordings that had established Merzbow over decades of circulation and collapsed the weight of this overloaded production into a singular commodity.

In 2000, a fifty-CD box set was released on the Australian Extreme label as a collection that compiled thirty Merzbow "classics" from 1979 to 1997, and added twenty more unreleased CDs. The now-infamous *Merzbox* was issued in a limited edition of a thousand boxes, including a "MerzRom" CD-ROM, a hundred-page book with commentary by various artists and music critics, as well as a Merzbow T-shirt and stickers. "There will never be another Merzbox," wrote Roger Richards, head of the Extreme label: "The 50 CDs will never be released again. We made a promise to people that this is it. When all copies of the Merzbox are sold they will not be seen again. . . . The glass masters will be destroyed when the Merzbox is released."[20] The *Merzbox* is clearly a masterstroke of absurdist marketing, but it is also a way of revealing Noise to its truest audience. It is such an over-the-top commodity that its value of "extremeness" carries over from its prolific author to the one thousand consumers who are hard-core enough to buy such a thing (not to mention listen to all of it).[21] The idea of a box

Genre Noise | 135

4.3. Merzbow album covers, mid-1990s.

set of Noise parodies the marketing of similar collections and compilations that wrap up individual creativity in endless reissues and repackaging of musical history. The Merzbox usefully makes a mockery of the commodity circulation of Music. But its form allows fans to get purchase on the uncontainable, overflowing productions of Merzbow, and then to get a handle on the genre of Noise.

The Merzbox, of course, was not the end of Merzbow. Akita continues to release several records a year and says that he has at least another fifty CDs of unreleased material. One release in 2011—a three-CD compilation on British label Dirter Promotions, limited to one thousand copies—was titled simply Another Merzbow Records. The strange, seemingly misprinted title offers two possibilities for reading the word records: first, as a verb, *records* suggests the existence of "another Merzbow," or *records* can be read ungrammatically as a noun, in the strange plurality of broken English. These kinds of slippages remind us that there are always more sounds than the formats of recorded media can contain, and more forms of personal expression than the matrix of genres could ever classify.

The *Merzbox* also represented a codex of Noise that solidified the genre for a broad range of listeners. Far from becoming a lost rarity, copies of the *Merzbox* are furiously traded among fans. More important, its release symbolized the possibility for Noise to be multiple, to become a literature, and ultimately to be consumed as Music. Like Akita himself, the *Merzbox* embodies the history of Noise and shows how circulation generates narratives of musical genre. It compresses the overflowing idea of Noise into a singular production and shows that it really can, and does, exist as Music.

A GHOST STORY

Noise haunts circulation as a kind of "ghost story," as Hiroshige Jojo of Hijokaidan once reminded me: "Noise is not just serious, not just a joke, not just shocking—it includes *many* things . . . but almost no one can know and understand Noise. That's a very good and important thing. Because—there's hardly anything we don't know any more, is there? But there *are* still *mysterious* things, right? Noise is like a ghost, like a ghost story. We know this, too, that there are still some mysterious, but unmistakable, things; Noise must be this kind of mysterious thing." Hiroshige finds Noise in the "mysterious things" (*shimpi-teki na koto*) of musical circulation, but also the "unmistakable things" (*machigai nai koto*) that shadow its presence in the world. The ghost story of Noise relates the creative plurality of a musical genre that endlessly changes its content and disguises its forms. The question becomes not what Noise is, but what we seek in Noise: why we hear it everywhere at once, and why it still cannot be found.

The constitutive paradox of genre, says Jacques Derrida, begins with the law of genre, which demands that they should not be mixed. For a genre to be what it is, it must be separated from other genres. But, he asks, "What if there were, lodged within the heart of the law itself, a law of impurity, or a principle of contamination . . . an axiom of impossibility that would confound its sense, order, and reason? 'I will not mix genres' is a law that requires its own violation" (Derrida 1980:222). As a genre, Noise can be recognized as a part of Music and a meaningful signal in itself. At the same time, it makes musical categorization seem impossible. Noise seems to destroy the possibility of Music altogether. But it constantly conjures up the purity of musical origins and insists that listeners continue to dream of uncategorizable sounds buried within the overproductions of musical media.

> A science which hesitates to forget its founders is lost.
>
> —A. N. Whitehead

CHAPTER 5

FEEDBACK, SUBJECTIVITY, AND PERFORMANCE

Ikeda Keiko (a.k.a. Timisoara) is setting up her gear, preparing for a solo performance as part of an all-night Noise show. A two-feet by four-feet waist-high table has been brought onto the stage—which is really just a section of the floor in one corner of the room—and she is pulling mixers, voltage converters, commercial guitar pedals, tape recorders, and homemade metal boxes of wires and buttons from a small suitcase onto the stage floor. She places the items one by one across the table, throwing the chaos together into a jumble of individual units, each brick-like effect pedal trailing a wire down to a clump of nine-volt power transformers on the floor, stuck like barnacles onto a power strip winding out to the front of the stage, its red "on" light glowing. Bending down to grab a coil of quarter-inch instrument cables, Ikeda quickly connects each piece of electronic gear to the next, plugging the output of a mixer channel into a distortion box, into a digital delay, then into a small graphic equalizer—all of them fed back into her block-like mixer at the center of the table and then back out of the mixer again into another set of pedals—a different distortion, another equalizer, a phaser, a filter, a sampler—as the system builds on itself. The outputs turn back into the inputs, amplifying chains of feedback loops; distortion upon distortion, delay upon delay; carefully—and for the moment, soundlessly—setting the entire system tottering on the edge of overloaded feedback. She completes her connections and is still for a moment, then leans over the table of gear precipitously and the sound suddenly begins, slamming out of the speakers, a precarious whirling roar set on the brink of implosion, revolving back into itself, spinning in shuddering circles through the crackling network of cables and boxes. The air in the room rushes out, replaced with a whirlpool of Noise.

A great challenge of this book is describing Noise without limiting its history to the boundaries of its circulation; to tell something about its creative development while recognizing its open-ended reinventions. A loop seems to be a totally enclosed system. But the changing cycle of feedback is always redirected in motion, transforming itself over and over again. Any circulation might necessarily seem to begin with an original source or input, some action or message that could be identified as an original starting point or event in time. Its path might also be followed to an end, to some place of closure where the source is received and interpreted. But feedback always changes. It generates movement by modulating the relationships between sonic and cultural practices, by constantly erasing and rewriting their beginnings and endings. The subjects of Noise, through their shifting positions in the historical loops of musical circulation, are always moving and changing, too.

In this chapter, I examine Noise's feedback in three different interrelated contexts. First, I describe feedback as part of Noise's electronic sound and the technical structure of its performance systems. This discussion of soundmaking then plugs into feedback as a metaphor for cultural exchange and reciprocity in social science. Finally, I connect Noise's out-of-control performance of sonic feedback to its rewiring of creative identity. In its radical newness and self-invention, Noise has become an antisubject of musical history. Its feedback does not settle in a single place, or author, or moment of discovery. It breaks from continuities and influences, even from the obvious precedents of feedback in experimental rock and electronic music. If it had been hung in the balance of a linear stylistic history, Noise might have become just another "new music" whose time has come and gone. But it continues to build on itself, piling layers upon layers until it can no longer line up with other experiences of musical sound. Where does this feedback loop start? If the emergence of Noise cannot be linked to a particular event or place or work of art, performers must begin with the technical practices of feedback that connect them to their machines.

THE EFFECTS OF FEEDBACK

A classic Noise setup is created from an interconnected assemblage of consumer electronics, often a group of small guitar effect pedals connected through a mixing board (figures 5.1 and 5.2). Although individual setups vary greatly, Noisicians generally work with these inexpensive guitar "stompboxes," also called "effects" (described by Japanese performers with the English transliteration *efekuto*), which are used both in live performance and in recording. True to its name, an effect usually alters the sound of an instrument (in most cases a guitar) by modulating the sound wave electronically. Japanese performers often describe their effects pedals with the word *kizai*, a slightly stiff term used to refer to equipment in a corporate or industrial context, which has been borrowed by tech-oriented hobbyists to lend an aura of purpose to their electronic gear. With its serious connotations of technical equipment, *kizai* implies a pragmatic use for electronics as functional tools of performance. This reference has an ironic undertone in the context of the cheap (and often broken) consumer electronics used to make Noise.

I want to stress that pedal-based feedback systems do not cover the entire range of sound-generating practices of Noise. The creative transformation of sound technology is the primary aesthetic goal for many performers, and few rules apply. Most performers do use consumer music products—often altered in some way—but homemade instruments or modified electronics are also common, and some use very little technical equipment at all.[1] A single live event might include setups ranging from assemblages of broken broadcast equipment to manipulated tapes and amplified metal objects, to laptop computers (whose introduction provoked a crisis among Noise artists), to homemade synthesizers, or simply a distorted electric guitar or microphone smashed against some object or the stage itself. Noisicians are quick to point out that no specific equipment is required to make Noise. As one performer puts it, "It's not about the display of technology—like, 'this is the sound that this object makes.' The 'sound source' is emotion."

Pedals come to the foreground of Noise-making practice for two reasons. First, the common use of pedal-based feedback systems has made

5.1. Defektro's (Uchino Hirofumi) performance setup, March 2003. Photo by Steven Schultz.

5.2. Last Gasp Art Laboratories' "Moouloscillo Fuzz" pedal. Courtesy of Hirofumi Uchino. Photo by the author.

Noise a recognizable style of transnational popular music performance, with its own distinct sound-making practices. Second, the technical conditions of feedback performance powerfully embody Noise's nonlinear representations of musical history. These systems reflect deep investments in cultural self-invention, through which individual Noisicians develop feedback into an individual performance of creative subjectivity. Their self-assembled electronic networks are iconic of Noise's antihistorical discourses of newness. They also reflect Noisicians' challenge to musical ideologies of authorship and stylistic influence and their emphasis on self-reinforcing relationships with technology. A feedback loop can appear as a contained circuit, but its continuity depends on the unpredictable, fluctuating connections between its constitutive parts. Feedback is not created through a linear chain of separate causes and effects (e.g., a guitar tone that goes into a distortion pedal and comes out the other end as a "distorted guitar"). It is a loop that generates sound through the interrelation of all of the individual pedals. A change in one effect changes the entire circulation of energy throughout the system.

Effects pedals are sometimes called "units" to suggest their role as individual elements within a larger system, rather than as distinct sound devices in and of themselves. The term is now used to describe individual Noise performers as well (e.g., "Japanese harsh Noise unit Government Alpha will tour the West Coast in Fall 2005"). This technology-based characterization of individual performers imagines Noise itself as an international electronic feedback loop, in which each discrete "unit" is plugged into a larger network of circulation. This metaphor is in many ways an ironic reference to the global interconnections that might be imagined through electronic music technologies. Noise performers, regardless of location, tend to use ordinary out-of-the-box commercial effects, although some rare and out-of-production items are highly prized, and a cottage industry of "boutique" pedals has sprung up in recent years. Pedals are sometimes handmade by Noise performers and engineered specifically for their ability to produce unusual effects, such as particularly jagged "harsh" distortion sounds, and other pieces are deliberately broken, "bent," or otherwise altered to change their circuitry.

By and large, effects pedals are basic consumer items, made in Japan by companies such as Boss (a subsidiary of Roland), DOD, or Digitech. Because most of the commercial effects used in a Noise setup can be readily purchased, it is not difficult for Noisicians to assemble their own setups, regardless of their training or proximity to other Noisicians. The types of effects used—primarily distortion, delay, and equalization guitar pedals—are common to most setups. However, the effects within the system are less important than the feedback loops that connect them to each other; the distinct sounds of Noise emerge from these nuances of interconnection (figures 5.3–5.5).

Despite the fact that most Noise setups draw from the same pool of commercially available gear, there is a strong expectation that a pedal-based feedback setup should sound original. Audience members and fellow soundmakers often crowd around to scrutinize the gear after the com-

5.3. MSBR setting up at Tokyo livehouse 20000V. Photo by Martin Ekelin.

pletion of a performance, checking out rare equipment and sometimes cribbing ideas. Informed observers can sometimes identify and differentiate between familiar feedback systems. One story tells of a neophyte performer who brought a camera to a show by the well-known Noisician Akita Masami (a.k.a. Merzbow) and took close-up pictures of his pedals, noting the brand of each effect box and also the way they were interconnected on the table. He promptly purchased all of the pedals and set up each and every piece in the same fashion. After a few performances, audiences openly critiqued the performer as an imitator, and he abandoned the system soon afterward. Other fans had already scrutinized Merzbow's setup, so the resemblance was quickly seen in the gear, but also, crucially, heard in the contours created by this particular system. Although the technical elements of the famous Noisician's soundworld were used differently (and possibly ineptly) by the newcomer, a few listeners could still recognize Merzbow's ghost in the machine.[2]

Although digital systems are sometimes used to create feedback, this

5.4. Kenny Sanderson and Filth the Sleep prepare for a duo performance. Photo by the author.

5.5. K2 lays out his effects. Photo by the author.

practice can be controversial. Akita began using a pair of Mac laptops for Merzbow performances around 1999. For many fans, the performative aspect of Merzbow was lost when Akita sat down behind the computer. His gestures became less visible, and the transformative machinery of feedback was hidden behind the flat glow of a translucent white apple. Despite his high-profile status, Akita's turn to the laptop did not inspire a widespread move toward digital systems in Noise.[3] In fact, it has become even more common in recent years for "harsh" Noise artists to perform with exclusively analog setups.[4] This attachment to analog gear is not necessarily a nostalgic fetish for "vintage" musical equipment. I once asked a Noisician why he forced himself to haul a pile of unwieldy, unreliable electronic gear through the backstreets of Osaka for a twenty-minute performance, instead of using a laptop, digital sampler, or stand-alone synthesizer. Rather than stressing the unique qualities of his analog gear, he emphasized his manual labor in struggling with his electronics, describing his meticulous way of putting things together and the physical act of creating the system before tearing the whole thing down again.

The interconnections between these basic units of consumer electronic gear are at the core of Noise's feedback process. Although a pedal-based Noise system employs many separate pieces of equipment, the sound of feedback is not created by the individual machines, as in an array of synthesizers, whose separate sounds are mixed together in performance. Even when they are obviously instrumental to the creation of a feedback loop, effects pedals do not simply become "Noise instruments." They do not *create* Noise in themselves, nor are they used for their intended purpose to alter the sound of an instrument, the way a fuzz box distorts the signal of an electric guitar. Rather, the sound of Noise is the feedback of the entire interconnected system.

Feedback occurs when the output of a system is fed back into the input. Plugging a microphone into an amplifier and holding it up to the speaker exemplifies a simple feedback loop. This audible, self-reinforcing feedback is called positive feedback. Because any amplifier inherently creates some low-level internal noise, its latent hum is played through the speaker, is picked up by the microphone, and then comes out of the speaker again at an increased volume, and so on. The cycle perpetually adds more "gain" to itself until the amplifier reaches the threshold of saturation—the absolute limit of amplification, where the sound loops back into itself, over and over again. Because audio feedback loops respond to changes in their ambient conditions (for example, moving the microphone to a different place in front of the speaker), a feedback loop can generate a number of different sounds.

Bell Labs engineers initially described the feedback sound of self-oscillating loops as "singing" (Mindell 2002). But the sounds associated with positive feedback were not recognized as musical or even as any kind of deliberate signal in themselves. Audio feedback was noise that interfered with the lines of communication: when we hear feedback, it means something has gone wrong. The classic example is that of a PA system accidentally feeding back during a speech, which signifies the speaker's lack of control. But feedback is not merely a kind of sound; it is a process of electronic transformation. This audible feedback, which marks the excessive overload of a technological system gone out of control, is the raw material of Noise's sonic production.

Popular musicians occasionally use amplifier feedback as textural or improvisational material, especially in the techniques of electric guitar in rock performance made famous by Jimi Hendrix, the Who, Link Wray, and the Velvet Underground, among others. Feedback guitar was popularized in recordings such as the Beatles' "I Feel Fine" and the Who's "My Generation" (in 1964 and 1965, respectively), although feedback had been used in performance since the 1950s by early rock guitarists such as Link Wray and Albert Collins. Many independent discoveries of feedback are reported in rock music histories. For example, in recounting the history of the mid-1960s garage group the Monks, Eddie Shaw describes his stunned sensation when guitarist Gary Burger accidentally left his guitar leaning against his amplifier: "Sound exploded. The effect was instant. It was like discovering fire. . . . We began to jump up and down, as small children do when they find something that totally amazes them and yet could be forbidden. No one would call this music" (Shaw and Klemke 1995:157).

Noisicians take advantage of the sonic palette of feedback developed in rock, partly by using the same equipment that modulates and amplifies electric guitars. But the feedback loops they create are made much more complex, first by the number of different pedals—perhaps five or six, or as many as twenty—introduced into the effects chain. The effects are linked together and their outputs are fed into a central mixer; finally, the mixer's outputs are plugged back into the effects units' inputs to create the feedback loop. The sound travels through every one of the effects with each cycle, and the feedback fluctuates according to changes in the total system. A Noisician, then, does not use a pedal to "turn on" a particular sound (as when a guitarist steps on a wah-wah pedal to create a "crying" tone). Instead, a change to one effect changes the productive conditions of the whole system.

The core process in the creation of a Noise feedback loop is the transformative effect of overload. Overload is the cumulative buildup of sound through a cycle of massively distorted amplifications. An input signal—a voice shouting, a microphone scraped on a piece of metal, or simply the internal noise generated by the system—is run through a series of amplifications, distorting the signal over and over again, eventually reaching the threshold of amplitude and overloading the channel. The sound is radically transformed through this additive chain of amplifications, which then is fed back into itself. The cumulative overload of the feedback loop piles distortions on top of distortions, massively compressing and mutating the original sound.

Overload is a kind of distortion that uses the limits of an amplification system to create and change sound. Neither the English nor the Japanese words for "amplify" are really adequate to describe the transformative qualities of overload. Though the English word suggests that a quiet sound is aurally magnified and made louder, the Japanese term zôfuku, based in the root zô (increase), implies a staged additive change that raises the gain from one distinct dynamic level to another.[5] In a feedback loop, amplification does not merely increase a sound's volume to make it louder; it changes it entirely by saturating the entire system. The process is something like magnifying and photocopying an image over and over again, until the details of the original form are totally unrecognizable.

When other effects (such as delay and equalization) are added into this overloaded cycle, the performer can cause complexly interrelated changes in the overall timbre and texture by adjusting the settings of each pedal or triggering microphonic elements in the loop. In Filth the Sleep's off-the-cuff rendition of his overload setup (sketched by the artist in figure 5.6), the sound source is a metal plate attached to a contact mic, which acts as a trigger for the amped-up effects chain of three layers of "fuzz" or distortion, two delays, reverb, and an EQ filter. The mixer feeds the whole thing back so that the chain loops back into itself when plugged into an amplifier on stage. It is important to recognize that the sound of this setup is not simply the result of the metal plate "played" through the system; it is the sound of the whole electronic circuit overloaded back into itself.

5.6. Sketch of pedal feedback setup by Filth the Sleep.

CYBERNETIC NETWORKS, CULTURAL RECIPROCITY, AND POSITIVE FEEDBACK

Radio engineers coined the term *feedback* to identify broadcasting problems in the early twentieth century, but the concept is part of a technological history of engineering that dates back to the Watt steam engine. Beyond its technical reference, the concept of feedback has come to describe a broad field of interactive sociocultural and economic relationships. Variations on this idea have been foundational in social scientific theories of exchange, from the analysis of economic markets to center–periphery models of cultural transmission to mass communication and information theory. The logics of feedback are the basis of Adam Smith's theory of a liberal self-regulating market and connect to contemporary systems dynamics, social policy and management, biological homeostasis, and recent models of artificial intelligence and Internet network flow (Mayr 1971; Richardson 1991).[6] Its loops can represent the enclosed coherence of social networks, as well as the tipping points that drive systems into interaction, collapse, and change.

The term became crucial to postwar social theory through the project of cybernetics, famously developed by the influential work of Norbert Wiener (1948, 1950), as well as by information theorists Claude Shannon and Warren Weaver (1949). Their descriptions of feedback were initially intended to help technologists develop automated solutions to reduce noise and increase efficiency in mechanical systems. But feedback was quickly incorporated into the social scientific analysis of cultural systems and human behavior in postwar visions of a self-regulating modern society. In his first two books, *Cybernetics: Or Control and Communication in the Animal and the Machine* (1948) and *The Human Use of Human Beings* (1950), Wiener described social behavior in relation to the emerging development of automated mechano-electrical control devices, many of which were initially developed as self-correcting systems for military and communications applications.[7] Wiener's theory of cybernetics proposed to use the productive overlaps between human and mechanical capacities to organize and improve modern social function. Cybernetics also imagined society at large as a balanced hermeneutic system, which could be made more efficient by feeding back from its historical outcomes and developmental knowledge. "Feedback," as Wiener put it, "is a method of controlling a system by reinserting into it the results of its past performance" (Wiener 1950:61).

Wiener's ideas about feedback were widely adopted in cognitive psychology, linguistics, and postwar anthropology. Margaret Mead, Gregory Bateson, and Roman Jakobson were among a number of scholars who collaborated with Wiener in the Macy conferences between 1942 and 1953. Cybernetic models of feedback had a powerful influence on Claude Lévi-Strauss's structuralism, Talcott Parsons's theories of social evolution, Jacques Lacan's notions of self-reproducing language, Bateson's later views on cultural reproduction, and Anthony Giddens's theory of structuration. Wiener's visions of communication technology as an extension of the human sensorium were popularized by Marshall McLuhan's theories of network cultures where "the medium is the message." Cybernetic versions of feedback have continued to influence proposals of technologically "wired" subjectivity, from embodied cyborgian myths to expectations and critiques of a pending "posthuman" condition (Axel 2006; Haraway 1991; Hayles 1999; McLuhan 1964).

For anthropology, the central insight of cybernetic feedback was that communication was not necessarily about content but about cultural patterns of transmission. From this perspective, it became clear that cultural feedback was not a historical chain of "contact" through which knowledge was passed from one site or historical moment to another. Feedback represented the technical interplay through which societies regulate themselves into balance: it showed that cultural groups evolved through continuous interaction, rather than progressing through stages determined by heightened moments of creative innovation or conflict. Cybernetics-influenced social science used insights from neurology and linguistics to develop a symbolic analysis of the intentions, goals, and errors inherent to the historical interplay of any given system, and predict the optimal flow of energy within the entire structure. But cybernetics disregarded the effects of cultural performance and participation that might diverge from the "central nervous system" of social interaction. By privileging holistic networks over semantic content, cybernetic theory disregarded the power of creative subjectivity—the variable forces of individualism, improvisation, and especially accident and failure—to short-circuit the continuity of cultural signals and cause sudden, ungovernable changes.

The complicated outcomes of cultural feedback were outlined in earlier anthropological theories of exchange, most implicitly in Marcel Mauss's comparative study of gift circulation. In the *kula* ring of the Trobriand Islands, necklaces of shells were exchanged in a circular loop of gifts, giving rise to a cultural force that compels the recipient to return the gift. This circuit of gift-giving creates an autopoetic social network, in which each participant is related to others through a "system of total services." In this context, the feedback between independent subjects generates an iconic power to create cultural relations. Circulation represents and reproduces society: "The objects," Mauss says, "are never completely separated from the men who exchange them" (Mauss 1990 [1923–24]: 31). Subjects are compelled to participate in the cycles of reciprocity, and in so doing, they create and maintain a cultural system.

Mauss famously describes other, destructive trajectories of the gift, particularly the agonistic form of the potlatch practiced by Pacific Northwestern cultures. In the potlatch, objects of wealth and power are not maintained, but are ritually destroyed in compulsory displays of excessive consumption, which necessarily "go beyond all bounds" of mutuality. In grand conflagrations, clan leaders burned vast storehouses of resources—food, oil, canoes, blankets, and ceremonial objects—to generate social prestige by dissolving their own wealth. With each performance, the potlatch escalated cultural feedback to the point of transformation. Each gift must be returned with interest, building to a level of excess at which simple reciprocation becomes impossible. The existing social balance breaks into new networks of hierarchical power, as gift recipients who fail to respond are (in the case of the potlatch, quite literally) enslaved through the involuntary effects of exchange. Over generations, these lags and failures repeat themselves and create their own patterns. Creative destruction forms a positive feedback loop, which is driven by forces of excess, distortion, and overload.

Cybernetics and information theory were strongly focused on the engineering of "negative" feedback, which diminishes or acts against change to establish systemwide efficiency and stability. Negative feedback loops are crucial to advanced circuit design because they allow electronic systems to regulate themselves, just as a driver uses sensory and physiological feedback to steer a car. Negative feedback circuits use the difference between one variable and another to establish control of the system. A classic example of negative feedback is the thermostat, which uses information from a sensor to control ambient temperature. The vast majority of engineered feedback systems are examples of negative loops, which harness feedback to correct difference and adjust for efficiency. The optimization of the gestalt network is the primary goal.

Negative feedback is fundamentally comparative and reductive; the differences between intention and actual performance are used only to create a steady state for the entire system. Rather than being absorbed in homeostasis and control, individual differences can also be accumulated and amplified. In fact, feedback often spins out of control precisely because senders and receivers are not invested in continuing a holistic social field of transmission or in emulating past performances. Instead, they change direction. When feedback becomes generative of something new—in the case of audio circuits, when it becomes a sound in itself—it is described as "positive."[8] Positive feedback loops are not self-regulating but self-reinforcing. They amplify change with each cycle, emphasizing the gain of new results over continuity and balance.

Although positive and negative feedback systems occur simultaneously and sometimes morph into one another, they represent very different trajectories of circulation. Negative feedback establishes cultural stability as part of a controlled adaptation to environmental conditions. Positive feedback, on the other hand, moves away from social equilibrium to emphasize the cumulative effects of newness and change. Bateson described this process as "schismogenesis," caused by progressive differentiation between individuals, which amplifies intercultural distortions and imbalances within groups.[9] These unbalanced cycles quickly go out of control. In political economies, positive feedback manifests crisis and breakdown. It creates chain reactions of creative destruction exemplified by violent conflict, market bubbles, social cults, and other unstable productions. It is population explosion, nuclear proliferation (and the chain reaction of fission itself), and the excessive booms and busts of a self-reinforcing capitalism that distorts the proposal of a balanced free market. In other words, positive feedback represents the vicious circle that shifts a system away from historical stability and toward a saturation point of change that overloads the original content.

OVERLOADING MUSICAL CREATIVITY

The history of Noise, of course, is a project of positive feedback. For every critic or writer who claims that Noise has newly sprung forth sui generis in a new place with a new set of artists, there are others who claim that the form has long been atrophied, with its creative direction buried in the wake of whichever time period they have assigned as its heyday. The origins of Noise are sometimes attributed to Japanese performers, especially Merzbow but also Hijokaidan and Hanatarashi. Others argue that Noise was sparked in Europe with groups like Throbbing Gristle and Whitehouse in London and Einstürzende Neubauten in Berlin, or in North America, with the release of Lou Reed's *Metal Machine Music* in 1975. Uses of noise sounds in music are dated back to the experimental compositions and writings of John Cage, or even earlier to the authorship of *The Art of Noises* and the construction of *intonarumori* instruments by the Italian futurist Luigi Russolo in 1913.[10] Music writers often reference one or more of these contexts as starting points for later aesthetic developments of Noise, but they do little else to document historical influences or make connections between its divergent forms.

Feedback is not generated by the influence of an individual genius, the global spread of a local cultural form, or a singular history of discovery. Most Noisicians developed their sounds haphazardly, through individual trial and error with consumer music gear. Their stories do not reflect a linear chain of historical influence that could extend into the narratives of experimental music. Instead, their overlapping discoveries of feedback occur through common accidents and mistakes, as separate individuals find new ways of overloading machines on their own. The newness of Noise is based in isolated and self-regenerating personal encounters with technological equipment. This, Ônishi Aya (formerly of Osaka's Sekiri, now of London, Ontario's Nihilist Spasm Band) told me, is why Noise cannot be tied to any particular cultural location but is instead the product of individual difference: "[Noisicians] don't like to read instructions. Say they get some new electronics; they have to set it up their own way, they want to experience it themselves. That's a good thing, to me. When you start listening to music, some people check out the history, look at the label, stuff like that, but that's not what happens with experimental musicians. And you know, that's not a difference in country; it's more of a 'human being difference.'"

Noisicians often describe their initial forays into pedal-based feedback systems through their departures from more traditional popular music ensembles, usually rock or punk bands. Many Noise acts were born in the wake of a rock group's collapse, as former members developed electronic systems from disassembled band equipment. Performers plugged into feedback as they began disconnecting from their instrumental control over musical performance. They put down their guitars and began making sounds by connecting their effects pedals together. Kenny Sanderson, a British Noisician who has lived in Tokyo since 1994, said that his initial experiments with feedback developed entirely without any sense that what he was doing could be connected with other performers at all: "I'd been making Noise since 1991. I didn't know what I was doing at the time—I knew that was what I wanted to make, and I liked the sounds, but I didn't know that people actually *got away* with it. I was playing guitar and I bought effects pedals and things like that, and I always found it more pleasurable playing around with effects knobs and things like that rather than learning chords . . . After I while I learned about Merzbow and Masonna, and I moved to Japan and I was blown away: I was like, 'Fucking hell, people *do* this!'" Sanderson's story is echoed by many other Noisicians who describe their discovery of the genre as an outcome of their solitary experimentation. Although a few had heard of Noise through recordings before beginning to perform, a majority of Noise performers developed their feedback systems in isolation from public examples.

These separate moments of creative discovery challenge linear histories of musical influence and technological invention. Tape delay feedback, for example, is a studio technique that was crucial in the recorded history of popular music, most distinctly in experimental and psychedelic rock. But tape delay or "sound-on-sound" feedback loops were accidentally encountered many times in isolated experiments with audiotape, from the earliest uses of the technology in the 1950s to the contexts of more widespread consumer availability in the 1980s and 1990s. Although histories of music recording often attribute the first use of tape delay on record to American inventor and musician Les Paul (who is also credited, controversially, with the invention of the electric guitar), other attributions of the invention of tape feedback are numerous, including engineers at Abbey Road Studios in London; dub reggae producers like King Tubby in Kingston, Jamaica; and jazz/experimental composer Sun Ra. Practitioners often report their independent discoveries of the technique as an accidental by-product of their isolated use of tape machines. But these incidental, unsynchronized moments of sonic discovery do not add up to a linear history of technical invention or produce a singular model of stylistic development. They cycle back into distinct creative projects and separated moments of innovation. The process of feedback delay was discovered by mistake, over and over again.

These repetitive experiences of feedback are iconic of its technological production. When the output channel of a tape machine is accidentally plugged into the input channel, it feeds the signal from the playback head back into the recording head, so the sound is printed back onto the tape as an echo. Depending on how loudly the output sound is returned to the input, the delay can be repeated once or twice—like the "slapback" echo used on Elvis's voice—or fed back for more repetitions until it fades away. If the return signal is continually louder than the initial input, the repetition builds into a feedback loop. Anyone experimenting with a tape recorder might stumble on and "invent" this process for themselves, re-creating the same technological conditions of discovery to hear the sounds of feedback for the first time.

For example, North American composer Terry Riley's use of long, extended tape feedback loops became central in his early pieces, such as *A Rainbow in Curved Air* and *Music for the Gift*, which are now canonized among the first works of minimalism and live experimental music. But Riley did not learn of tape feedback until it was described by a Radio France recording engineer in 1963. He then asked a friend to reproduce the technique: "I wanted this long, repeated loop and I said 'can you create something like that?' He got it by stringing the tape between two tape recorders and feeding the signal from the second machine back to the first to recycle along with the new incoming signals. By varying the intensity of the feedback you could form the sound either into a single image without any delay or increase the intensity until it became a dense chaotic kind of sound . . . this engineer was the first to create this technique that I know of" (Riley 1995). Riley describes his tape delay as "time-lag accumulation," a process of continuous addition and modulation that mirrors the overloaded historical discourse of feedback as a musical form.[11] Feedback, he says, "generates a lot of distortion very quickly. Each generation brings its noise from the previous generation and adds on to that. After five or six layers of sound on sound, you have a lot of information on the tape" (Riley 1995).

Because of this overlapping technological environment, Noise can be related to more established histories of postwar experimental music, especially of certain American composers whose live electronic performances might be described as formal precedents for Noise's feedback. Noisicians are deeply involved in the search for a sound-producing environment that is neither determined by a distinct composer nor fully controlled by the performer. Noise feedback, then, might have been directly influenced by the well-known concept of indeterminacy developed by composer John Cage, and especially the related performance practices of Cage's longtime collaborator David Tudor, which employed feedback systems based in homemade electronics, guitar pedals, and mixing boards.[12] Even in these live performances of feedback—in which Tudor's feedback systems very closely resemble Noise performance setups, and the sounds might also be considered precedent to those of Noise—there are significant differences. Tudor used the context of feedback networks to reduce the intentional role of the individual performer as much as possible. Noise's feedback instead represents a transformative personal struggle, in which the performer's intentions are subverted by an out-of-control relationship with an electronic system.

Tudor's feedback works were foundational for a new generation of live electronic music. His performances, mostly to support the Cunningham Dance Company, were a radical departure for contemporary electronic music, and stood as the antithesis of the laboratory-style technological progress represented by national studios for electronic music and *musique concrète* (based primarily in Western Europe, but also in the United States and Japan). Tudor created a more open-ended improvisational space for experimental music technology, and he is often described as an unsung hero of live electronic performance. Tudor used mixer feedback and commercial pedals (such as the Electro-Harmonix effect "Bass Balls") similar to those used in Noise setups (figures 5.7 and 5.8). Moreover, his description of nonlinear sound production is strikingly similar to the sourceless, nondirectional ideal of feedback in Noise. In his 1972 essay "From Piano to Electronics," Tudor explains "I no longer think, 'I'm going to do this, so I'll start with this,' and start out somewhere and then go through lots of processes in a straight line. Instead I don't start anywhere, but make a

5.7. David Tudor with his live electronics performance setup, late 1970s. Photo by Lowell Cross, courtesy of the Getty Research Institute, Los Angeles (980039) and the David Tudor Trust.

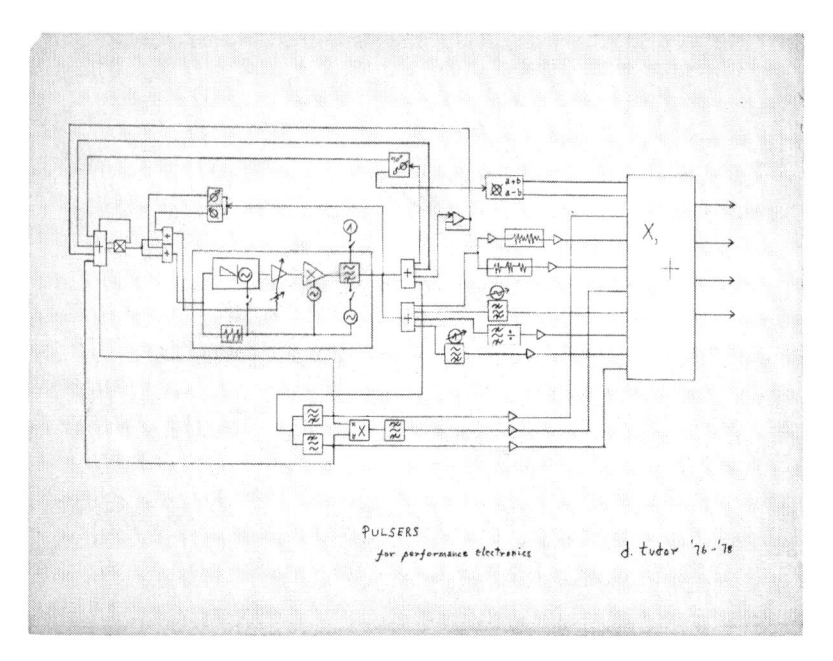

5.8. Schematic drawing for the feedback-based piece Pulsers. Courtesy of the Getty Research Institute, Los Angeles (980039) and the David Tudor Trust.

process such that a signal will be created somewhere within it, you don't know where. . . . I found out that if the components don't match, then one component is able to influence the next, so that signals are created at many points within the circuit" (Tudor 1997 [1972]:29).[13] Certainly Noise's feedback systems bear comparison with Tudor's approaches to electronic music performance. But these different uses of feedback are not correlated within a shared lineage of historical influence. Many Noise performers, as I have described, only learned about postwar experimental music after they had already invented their own feedback systems. Any attempts to construct retroactive connections with historical precedents of experimental music break down even further when considering the different ways that feedback can be performed.[14] The core difference between Noise and Tudor lies not in the sound created or the equipment used but in their different enactments of the technological relationship of feedback.

In postwar experimental music, feedback offered a way of creating unpredictable performance structures that blurred compositional intentions. Michael Nyman has described how Tudor, alongside other experimental composers such as David Behrman, Max Neuhaus, Steve Reich, and Robert

Ashley, used feedback "as the 'controlled' subject of their pieces" to create "an accumulative growth of sound mass" that "arises of its own accord" (Nyman 1999 [1974]:100). In Tudor's systems, the performer sets up a loop "such that a signal will be created somewhere within it," and then works within this "neural" environment of self-regulating feedback.[15] Noisicians, in contrast, use their electronics to embody the self-destructive imbalances of positive feedback. Personal expression is transformed in conflict with the system, through a process that Japanese performers describe as "out-of-control" (*bôsô suru*). This is not a relationship that creates a balanced sound environment. On the contrary, Noisicians appear to be in the midst of battle with their machines. Pushing against their own performance, they reveal the internal conflicts of technological subjectivity.

Performance is itself an embodied context of feedback between sound and the musical self. Musicians learn to play by reinforcing their control over their instrument as part of the process of musical learning. The musician makes a sound and listens to it in the same moment, continually adjusting the instrument to direct the sound. Physiological feedback is inherent to this training, as performers master the nuances of a physical object—their instrument—by embodying the limits of its (and their own) capabilities. In the process of learning to perform, a musician links the creation of sound to bodily self-control and internalized musical knowledge. Noisicians deliberately attempt to keep themselves from naturalizing this instrumental self-expression. To perform their own loss of control as authoritative human subjects, they cannot fully learn the system. In this, Noise's *techne* of feedback diverges from epistemologies of musical intentionality. Its modes and techniques are abstracted beyond self-expression, beyond even the flexible constructs of improvisation and experimental sound. Noise is more than merely indeterminate: it is out of control.

Noisicians are constantly adjusting and interacting with their systems, reaching across the table to pinch a tiny knob and turn it slightly, riding the fader on a micro-mixer while turning a dial across the table, or pushing both hands down into the table to shut one pedal off and another on simultaneously. Others perform their out-of-control electronics like a driver trying to steer a vehicle that has gone off the road or an industrial worker desperately working the controls of a giant machine gone haywire. In this displacement of personal agency, Noise separates itself from identities of musical improvisation. Although Noisicians often perform solo, feedback does not stress the expressive voice of an individual. It can be deeply evocative of personal emotion, but Noise is not "my sound," or even "this sound I make," but "a Noise that surrounds me and becomes my world." Feedback creates "this Noise that I am part of," not "this sound that I speak from myself."

Pedal-based systems reveal the unstable connections between Noise performers and their electronic systems. The small size of pedal effects allows a performer to crowd as many as twenty pedals onto a small table, allowing for direct and rapid access to their controls. Although a Noisician may know how to quickly locate and manipulate a specific piece of gear, the sonic results of feedback are clearly not under their control. It is certainly possible to learn the technical parameters of any electronic system, yet many Noisicians deliberately avoid becoming too familiar with their equipment. Most choose to change the components of their setups regularly to maximize accidents and unpredictable elements, even as they struggle in performance to adjust the sounds emitted by the system. On one hand, a performer passively observing the effects of an unchanging feedback loop would not be interesting. On the other hand, a result that sounded too masterfully manipulated—that sounded "played"—would lack the instability crucial to feedback performance and foreclose the ever-present possibility of breakdown and failure.

At first, it surprised me when prominent performers showed little technical knowledge of their equipment. Many claimed to be uninterested in new musical gear; they don't know how their stuff works and don't want to know. One Noisician told me that although he knows how to control his setup to some degree, "unimagined sounds happen" every time he sets up his gear, and he added that these were the sounds that made Noise interesting. When I asked him to describe the gear he had used in a recent show, he told me that he couldn't recall but pointed out that the exact setup of the gear is not important. He changed his pedals very often, he added, but even with the same gear, the feedback could nonetheless be unique for each performance. Others stressed their ability to mechanically control individual pieces of electronic equipment, without having control over the sounds produced by the system as a whole: "I totally know how to control my gear, so I can try to 'output' my favorite sounds when I play, but I can't predict the sounds—only about half of them come out like I expect them to, the rest are all accidental." Most reject the very idea of controlling their performances, arguing that they do not want to understand their feedback systems or regulate their technical operations. The American experimentalist Mike Patton put it this way: "[Electronic music] had this strange myth about it that you have to know what you are doing to get into it. It was intimidating, and it scared me away for a long time. I didn't want to buy anything because I didn't know what anything did . . . [but] when I started realizing that most of it is highly uncontrollable and illogical, it appealed to me even more, because I don't have that kind of a brain that would process that kind of information anyway. I just want to turn a fucking knob and have it make a hideous racket" (Sajbel n.d.). Yamazaki Maso (a.k.a. Masonna) similarly disclaimed any musical intentions, telling me, "I don't know how to control everything and I'm too lazy to learn—I'm not a musician, I just make Noise."

Performers constantly disrupt the feedback of their own Noise-making processes. It is common to use broken or repurposed electronics, or to destroy or violently disconnect their gear during a performance. For example, when the Tokyo-based Noisician Yoshida Yasutoshi (a.k.a. Government Alpha) set up for one performance I attended in a small bar in Providence, Rhode Island, he began by slowly plugging all of his pedals together on a small table in the middle of the room, spending a good deal of time on this process as the small audience watched. Immediately after turning on the amplifier, he climbed up a pole and dropped onto the table feet first, breaking the feedback loop apart and scattering the pedals everywhere. Yoshida immediately fell to the floor, scrabbling among the pedals to plug them back together as quickly as possible. As soon as everything was reconnected, he climbed back up the pole and scattered the pedals again, repeating this process for several minutes until he became exhausted, switching off his amplifier and abandoning the scattered jumble of gear.

BENDING THE CIRCUITS OF CONSUMER TECHNOLOGY

One of the most interesting and paradoxical aspects of Noise performance is the profound physical intimacy Noisicians have with their setups, which ultimately leaves them vulnerable to the equipment they use. Even as they destroy their electronic gear, they reveal that they are beholden to its technological authority. Despite the fact that many shows end with an out-of-control collapse, they typically begin with a ritual display of technical competence. Performers step onto the stage and immediately begin pulling gear out of zippered duffel bags or beat-up suitcases, connecting them together as quickly as possible, knowing exactly which pedal fits where.

It often takes longer to set up than to actually perform. A musician might be on stage for twenty minutes, busy with the technical tasks of unpacking equipment, connecting it together, and adjusting the whole system before performing a set that lasts a mere ten or fifteen minutes. Some Noisicians set up their gear in advance, on small portable tables at the side of the stage. Even then, just checking the connections and ensuring that the power is working properly can take several minutes. Audience members watch this setup as closely as the performance itself, knowing that this carefully controlled presentation of the system culminates in the moment it all falls apart.

Crucially, feedback can fail. Despite the expectation that their systems will go out of control, Noisicians may nonetheless lose technological control in ways that detract from their performance. During a show by Guilty Connector in the tiny Tokyo livehouse Bin Spark, one fan was so overcome that he began to throw his body onto the floor and roll around in spasms directly in front of the table of gear, with its trailing curtain of wires and cords draped over the front. After a few minutes, he finally rolled over the on/off switch on the power strip delivering current to the entire setup, which immediately snapped off; the Noise abruptly stopped and a strange silence rushed in to fill the space. The performer looked around to fix the problem, but even after the power was restored (and a couple of angry audience members dragged the fan off stage), it was difficult to build up the energy of the feedback again. After a few minutes of attempting to recover, his movements became more active and forceful, suddenly culminating as he stood to quickly overturn the table full of equipment. Though this is a common practice of Noise performance, this particular overload was especially intense because it seemed uncommonly willful. As the pedals, mixers, and cords crashed to the floor, the emotional tension of the system's failure poured into this final, deliberate collapse.

Noisicians often construct feedback systems from discarded junk. Live performances by Dan Greenwood (a.k.a. Diagram A) are cataclysmic struggles with a mountain of broken technology. It takes him a considerable amount of time to set up his electronics, due to the size and delicacy (and sheer quantity) of the gear that he employs in a typical setup (including some pieces, he told me, that do not make or alter sound at all but merely add to the visual element of the assemblage). For one concert at the New York venue Knitting Factory, his system (all of which had been packed and driven down from Massachusetts during a blinding snowstorm) included rewired antique telephone systems, broken computer displays, and large metal contraptions amplified with contact microphones, all wired together into a primitive patch bay that left black cables strewn around the stage and dangling across the floor.

As all of this equipment is pushed into a pile and pieces are stacked on top of one another, it can be hard to determine the exact moment when the setup is complete. The performance seems to emerge from within the technical arrangement of the gear: sounds just begin to emanate from the pile as Greenwood reaches around, plugging things in and turning knobs. He straps on a rubber military gas mask containing microphones, concealing his face entirely, and attaches other electronic pieces onto his body. He dashes back and forth in front of the equipment he has amassed in the center of the floor, turning on switches, pushing buttons, pulling cords out of one area and pushing them into another, pulling things apart. Occasionally he bends forward at the waist, drops to his knees, reels backward, or falls to the floor in front of the heaps of gear, a shout becoming audible from inside the mask. Holding onto some piece of the assemblage, Greenwood jerks his body back and forth violently in front of his machines. It is unclear how the machines function—which pieces are altering the sound, which are not, and which are disconnected or never worked at all. As the performance builds, sections of the pile of gear collapse or are pulled out and thrown to the side of the stage. Somehow, this dismantling process doesn't seem deliberate—though it must be—as he smashes things together, punching parts, grabbing cords, and moving the telephone receiver around in a buzzing feedback loop.

Greenwood had started in a punk rock band, but under his influence, the band "just kept getting noisier and noisier," and eventually everyone quit. Alone with the gear, he broke the instruments down and fed the equipment back into itself. "I was in a band, and used to play with a distortion pedal when I played bass, and I'd just start doing it on my own. I started Proof of the Shooting with John Brown, and we'd just do a lot of stuff messing with the four-track [cassette recorder], and making feedback with the guitar . . . pitch-shift it, stuff like that; plugging microphones into effects. Eventually we figured out how to patch the outputs of effects into their inputs, and we just went from there." Greenwood acquired his equipment haphazardly, buying gear in bulk as cheaply as possible, regardless of make or condition. He began to pick up junked electronics deliberately for the purpose of altering, or "glitching" the original circuit:

With a lot of the junk I use to make Noise, I feel like I'm taking garbage and making something out of it.... I'd get some machine at a flea market or something, and take it apart, and find a resistor in there that I can jump across to reduce or increase the resistance, and that'll sometimes make a pitch-shifting sound, or something like that. Sometimes I'll stumble across something else, like things will go into some kind of a . . . I don't know what you call it. It'll just start glitching, making sounds.... I'll make oscillators out of radios by putting the output into the input, things like that. In the beginning I think I just played with stuff until I found a good sound, and it would usually last as long as a recording, and as soon as I got it, I'd lose it again.

The term *glitch* is used to describe an audible malfunction of electronic sound—the sound of a circuit being shorted out and "confused" into blurting out an error, some broken noise.[16]

The manipulation of consumer electronics by altering factory-printed circuit boards is often described as "circuit-bending." This is usually done by opening up some piece of equipment (often a small synthesizer, clock, or toy) that generates sound with a preprinted circuit board and rerouting the electrical charge. To "bend" a circuit, a resistor is used to "jump" the electricity away from its intended path, forcing the signal into an alternate route or feedback loop that radically changes the parameters of the original sound. Though Noisicians often perform and record "bent" sounds in the temporary, improvised manner described by Greenwood—by randomly jumping the current on an open circuit board—new connections can be made permanent with the introduction of variable resistors. Control knobs are soldered into the existing circuit along with other modifications (mods) that allow a user to create a unique electronic device from a mass-produced piece.[17] Some instruments are modified to expand their sound-making parameters (i.e., adding controls to toy keyboards) and others to produce randomly generated electronic sounds. A classic example is the repurposed Speak 'n' Spell developed by Qubais Reed Ghazala, in which the performer rolls a steel ball over the circuit board, causing the children's toy to randomly spit out strings of the synthesized phonemes that it uses to construct and "speak" words.[18]

Not only is circuit-bending a technically simple way to produce unusual electronic sounds—by using a wire or even one's finger to short-circuit a connection—it is also inexpensive, because new instruments can be made out of junk. But these junk electronics are more than just an adaptation of technology: they demonstrate how original sound-making contexts are created by feeding back the circuits of consumer gear. At the annual Bent Festival in New York City, for example, performances and installations are produced with altered consumer electronics, while hands-on workshops teach neophytes to use these techniques ("basically, just rip apart a toy, pull out the circuit board and start messing with it").[19]

Circuit-bending intervenes in standard consumptions of music technology. In this, it can be related to audiophile modifications of stereo gear and other forms of hobbyist tinkering that alter stock equipment. Musicians often alter their instruments to increase their control over them, and tinkering with electric guitars and other gear has been crucial to the development of technologies in rock music (Waksman 2004). Most often, tinkering takes the form of elaborate personalization of consumer gear, especially home stereo equipment. In Japan, tinkering is an especially common kind of amateur play with consumer technology. It is not unusual for hobbyists to construct elaborate audiophile sound systems or build electronic kits from magazines such as *Otona no Kagaku* (Experiments for Adults). User-driven "improvements" are sometimes viewed as a self-regulating reciprocity of consumer "feedback," in which industrial producers respond to the creative input of users by redesigning products to reflect their needs.[20]

Circuit-bending, on the other hand, makes commodities into idiosyncratic junk. Nozu Kanami, former owner of Bar Noise in Osaka, began to create noise-making machines in the late 1990s, first in the group Power Surprises and then as Destroyed Robot, although he had no formal knowledge of engineering. He describes his junk machines as a manifestation of *hansoku waza* (rule-breaking techniques) as opposed to the improvement of corporate technologies in individual consumption: "People from an engineering department make machines simply because they enjoy making machines. I'm not like that.... Tamiya [an electronics hobbyist company] has this huge contest, but they have this rule that you can't enter unless you use genuine parts manufactured by Tamiya. That's what I mean ... I think many Japanese toys hinder creativity. And I think it's wrong for people to be satisfied with such toys" (Nozu 1998). In Noise electronics, circuit-bending becomes a kind of "reverse engineering" that takes apart the objects of musical consumption and reassembles them into a new form of technological subjectivity.

5.9. Haco with her Pencil Organ. Photo by Uchiike Hideto.

Circuit-bending shows that a network can be creatively manipulated by individual presence, which makes a flow of energy diverge from its established path. Even a person's body, if put into a low-current circuit, can change an electronic sound by the flesh acting as a crude resistor. For example, in Haco's "Pencil Organ," made from a home electronics kit, she holds electrodes in her hands as she traces pencil marks across a piece of paper (figure 5.9). The natural resistance of her body changes the sound of the system; her wired body, too, changes the whole circuit when touched by something else. By connecting the loop of the Pencil Organ to one's own personal energy, Haco says, "a person can become a part—the resistance—of an electronic circuit" (Haco 2004).

Noisicians do not separate their own input from the system. Despite foregrounding the technological context of performance, their feedback stresses the human element of the human–machine relationship. Even when they are screaming within the Noise, performers are careful not to describe feedback as the outcome of personal intention or as simply their own expressive voice, amplified by an instrumental chain of sound-making gear. Noisicians prevent themselves from learning to "play" feedback, to reveal the outcome of human confrontation with an uncontrollable technological environment. Control over feedback would inevitably return it to the self-regulating realm of musical technique, and also, crucially, would distract from the inevitable overload and collapse of the system. "When I start," Greenwood told me, "I don't want to know what's going to happen. Sometimes it just rolls along and things happen and it seems like it's building up and building up—and then it can just fall apart."

FEEDING BACK FROM EVERYWHERE AT ONCE

The out-of-control performance of feedback in Noise reveals what Alfred Gell calls "the technology of enchantment," the cultural process through which societies come to believe in art as an autonomous practice, which is distinct from other forms of human creativity. By isolating artistic production as a technique beyond ordinary ability, people construct art's supernatural qualities. Objects and performances that were previously perceived as instrumental are transformed into transcendent aesthetic symbols. Through technical practices that transcend normal understanding, virtuosic performance is invested with occult power. Art becomes magical, Gell tells us, when people place its transformative powers outside of their own hands. This technology of enchantment then feeds back into "the enchantment of technology," which generates the "power that technical processes have of casting a spell over us so that we see the real world in an enchanted form" (Gell 1994:163). Performance represents a mysterious, special, and isolated technical skill, "oriented towards the production of the social consequences" that ensue from its own instrumental context. Technology, then, becomes a magical system when we conceive of its outcomes as beyond our own personal control. As GX Jupiter-Larsen puts it (in a personal history of his Noise group the Haters), "people take leadership from electricity; even more so than from the person behind the on-off switch" (Jupiter-Larsen 2010).

This is how Noise turns into Music and back again. Feedback reveals technology's creative power, and its potential for unpredictable change. It also performs the effects of mechanical repetition that threaten the autonomous status of musical authorship. Noise is simultaneously the effect and the cause of this feedback. It is a self-reinforcing loop that does not simply maintain its place in a historical lineage of styles. Noisicians grind the gears of the machine, spitting out unresolved difference in their creative reinventions of musical history and out-of-control embodiments of technology. They weave consumer electronics into a positive loop of aesthetic connections between human and machine. But this feedback must go on, repeating and building, until the whole thing collapses on itself.

CHAPTER 6

JAPANOISE AND TECHNOCULTURE

On April 28, 2011, a month and a half after the earthquake and tsunami that triggered the disaster at the Fukushima Daiichi Nuclear Power Plant, Ôtomo Yoshihide delivered a lecture at the Tokyo University of the Arts titled "The Role of Culture: After the Earthquake and Man-Made Disasters in Fukushima."[1] Ôtomo, together with the local poet Wago Ryoichi and Endô Michirô, founder of the pioneering Tokyo punk band the Stalin, had begun to organize an experimental music and art festival in Fukushima to be held in August.[2] But he opened his lecture by questioning the relevance of producing a cultural event in this circumstance, first by expressing his deep ambivalence about Japan "returning to normal." The nuclear disaster was a man-made massacre in slow motion, one that conjoined the effects of radiation leakage with the long-term subjection of Japanese people to the progress of a technocultural state.

Ôtomo further noted that the damage to Fukushima, similar to many other middle-sized cities in Japan, had begun many years prior to the earthquake. Even before the tsunami, the city's population had begun to be abandoned in ways that resonated beyond the evacuation: "They're gradually making this place unsuitable for living, in a way that's not against the law." People had been pushed out of their homes; even more damaging was the perception that Fukushima had become a doomed place. By extension, the growing sense that Japan's national infrastructure was damaged beyond repair could lead to global economic disinvestment. The built-up effects of economic negligence were now conflated with those of the nuclear disaster: "Go to any provincial city and you'll find that there are no people and the shutters are closed. It's not because of radiation. But when it's reported like that on the news, it appears as though some place that used to be vibrant has suddenly become a ghost town. It's TV magic. . . . It's easier [for viewers] to understand because everything is destroyed."

As the Japanese government desperately tried to manage widespread fears about the extent of the meltdown, counterreports filtered in from overseas scientists and independent news sources. Nuclear officials in the United States openly accused Japan of covering up the severity of ongoing radiation emissions in the Fukushima region and in Tokyo, as well as into the oceans and skies around the archipelago. Ôtomo, a Fukushima native who now lives in Tokyo, described his helplessness in the aftershock, struggling to make sense of the technological nightmare unfolding two hundred kilometers to the north. "I became a makeshift scientist, muttering things like 'What's a sievert?' and 'Becquerel?' . . . One's lack of education becomes apparent during times like this." Government updates had underreported radiation levels, cesium was soon detected in the Tokyo water supply, and the public was quickly losing confidence. Many had already abandoned the possibility of learning the truth about the situation, seeking instead to protect themselves by the few and untested means available to them (iodine tablets, homemade Geiger counters, staying indoors) in an atmosphere of disinformation and infrastructural breakdown.

Building nuclear power plants in a country riddled with fault lines had always been a Faustian bargain in Japan's postwar development. Like any mega-industrial city, Tokyo draws a huge amount of electrical power. Without power plants like Fukushima Daiichi, Japan's growth into a competitive global economy would likely have been impossible. Would Japan be what it is today without nuclear power? At the same time, what would it mean for Japan's future to turn back? Refusing the prospect of infrastructural development was unthinkable, even if disaster would inevitably be visited on the Japanese public. The violence of this deterministic rationale for technological progress begins with its invisibility. Modern publics are coerced to accept an inhumane sacrifice as part of the necessary exposure to risk that accompanies industrial global economies. In the most dystopian projections of national technoculture, an unconsenting citizenry is forced to adapt to the demands of technological development, no matter how nightmarish the consequences for human survival.

Ôtomo wearily conceded that antinuclear activism would probably have little impact for Fukushima; it would be like holding an antiknife rally after a stabbing instead of doing something for the wounded. Bringing an audience to a concert in Fukushima six months after the earthquake, even as some reports registered nearly lethal levels of radiation near the city, might make even less sense. But what could an individual artist do to stop this pain? In the context of a technological crisis, what is the role of culture? The situation, Ôtomo said, is "like a feedback machine that's squealing continuously, without a switch to stop it": "So I was thinking of making a machine like that. It'll be called *Genpatsu-kun* ["Lil' Reactor Boy"] No. 1, and it won't have a switch to shut it down. It just keeps leaking Noise and can't be stopped. When you turn it on with a bang, this sound just keeps coming out from it for about twenty thousand years. Bang, buzz! Or it explodes when you cut the power supply. I'm sure Genpatsu-kun No. 1 will dominate the world of Noise music as the most powerful Noise machine ever. I'm just really disappointed that I don't possess the skill to build something like that." The idea of Genpatsu-kun No. 1 is, as Ôtomo admits, an imprudent joke.[3] But it is not entirely unreasonable to suggest that a Noise machine could reveal the inexorable cycles of a technocultural society, in which production is always intimately linked to destruction.

Radiation cannot be detected by human senses. It cannot be seen, smelled, or heard. Once released, it will never disappear; but without a machine to detect its presence, one cannot even know that it exists. The public only feels its effects in strange, slow bodily transformations, and only after it is too late. Noise might offer a way to make sensible this invisible, inexorable feedback, which ties the fate of humanity to the balance of technological progress—somehow, perhaps, to change its loops from within. What else is there to do, Ôtomo argued, but attempt to reveal this harsh reality? What good is culture if it does not keep attention on the human consequences of societal change? Despite his ambivalence about the function of music in responding to the nuclear disaster, Ôtomo nonetheless challenged his audience: "Will you shut up and assist the quiet massacre," he asked, "or will you dream about creating the future?" Dreaming of a new society means awakening to the nightmares of technoculture.

One of the questions that haunted this project is whether Noise can be described as political. On one hand, how could it not be? Its transnational channels of connection came about during the same period as grassroots antiglobalization organizations, and some of its historical developments overlapped with countercultural underground movements. It drew from free jazz and punk, two of the most explicitly politicized genres in popular music. Noisicians, however, were reticent on the subject of political change. Most disclaimed the notion that Noise represented any explicit political statement and stressed the highly individual and emotional aspects of their performance over any social agenda. As I described in chapter 5, their misuse of electronics can be heard as a context of transformation that repurposes consumer technology and wrests the conditions of cultural production back into the hands of resistant social agents. But their creative destruction also reinforces the inexorable effects of mechanization on private consciousness and fatalistically abandons the possibility of broad collective resistance to technological control.

How have Japanese Noisicians revealed what is at stake for individual subjects in national formations of—and resistances to—technology? Ambivalence about the cultural impact of technology has long been a theme of modern social criticism, which tied the technoscientific progression of the nation-state to future developments of human consciousness. For Cold War–era critics like Lewis Mumford, early utopian visions of human-machine relations quickly shifted to paranoia about a global monoculture based in "megatechnics" of rationalized bureaucratic and militaristic control, industrial automation, and networked surveillance (Mumford 1938, 1967, 1970). Others saw the possibility of increasing human autonomy through technological adaptations. Marshall McLuhan famously described the "prosthetic" extension of social communication into a holistic electronic network that would accelerate global societies. "The effects of technology," claimed McLuhan, "do not occur at the level of opinions or concepts, but alter sense-ratios and patterns of perception steadily and without resistance" (McLuhan 1964:18). Adaptations of technology, he argued, would eventually create a consensus of human experience by extending the individual sensory field beyond the existing limits of culture.[4]

The global interconnections of modernity have often been described as projects of "transculturation" that transform the conflicts of intercultural contact in cross-cultural synthesis and mutual influence.[5] Japanoise does not stage its feedback as a form of cosmopolitan hybridity. It is not a transculture, but a technoculture, in which technological crisis becomes essential to the global politics of cultural identity. Technocultures produce ambivalent subjects, who ironically juxtapose the "futurist ethos" of rationalized capitalism against their own individualized machinations (Carey 1989; Penley and Ross 1991). Even as people are coerced to adapt to a deterministic environment of technological power, they attempt to maximize their own control over their daily lives to master the machine. The need for private mastery also demands that consumers pour their energy into an endless cycle of technological power that uses up its users. This feedback does not flow steadily into distinct states of convergence or hybridity, but suddenly crashes into new modes of sensing oneself and being in the world. The subjects of Japanoise do not absorb technology simply to repurpose Japanese national culture into the "soft power" of global capitalism. They perform the effects of technological adaptation on creative subjects by making futile demands for a purely human-generated individual causality in a technological system.

In this chapter, I describe Japanoise as a humanistic critique of technoculture, which was embedded in the geopolitical and economic sensibilities of Japan in the 1980s and 1990s. It is not coincidental that the notion of Japanoise surfaced in transnational circulation during this period, as the electronic futurism of "New Japan" helped the world imagine the fantastic possibilities and existential fears of technology. As Japan's national exceptionalism was increasingly bound to its technological preeminence, its cultural productions gradually became imbued with darker fantasies of social dissolution. Postapocalyptic narratives of Japanese science fiction recalled the psychic trauma of nuclear warfare and fantasized about human transformation in the collapse of industrial cities. Japanese technopop parodied the robotic subjects of a technoscientific state, which ironically raised fears about music's decline into synthesized automation. As electronic goods increasingly came to symbolize Japan's economic power, Japanoise made an art out of destroying electronic gear on stage.

In the decades leading up to the turn of the millennium, these dystopian counternarratives of Japanese popular media were increasingly taken up by a transnational audience. Japanoise connected to a global undercurrent of "technoscientific angst," which generates ethical debates about public trust in technological progress and the protective authority of the nation-state (Sassower 1997). Anxiety about the hazards of technology can undermine its influence on social values by revealing that individual subjects produce and sustain its material power, even when that power goes out of control. In an era of hopeful fusions, Noisicians embodied the inevitable malfunction of the human-machine to show how technological mastery is chained to endless cycles of creative destruction. Noisicians performed the effects of technology within their own identifications with its power. By highlighting its destructive cycles within their own selves, they asked users and creators everywhere to recognize their personal responsibility in the feedback of technoculture.

RESIST THE MACHINES

As I have argued throughout this book, Japanoise should not be seen as an isolated invention of Japanese culture. Similarly, its critique of technological subjectivity is a transnational co-construction, in which "the future of Japan" became crucial in focusing millennial anxieties about technology. As Japan's economic power fell into doubt at the end of the 1980s, Americans began to reinvest Japanese culture with assessments of its "gross national cool" (McGray 2002). In the United States, Japanoise was seen as part of Japan's edgy new wave of postmodern art, film, and music. But its subjects did not seem to align with many other channels of Japanese popular culture.[6] Japanese Noisicians did not embrace technological advancement. Not only did their analog gear fail to reflect new threads of Japanese innovation in the 1990s, a lot of it was simply unidentifiable detritus that bore little resemblance to the shiny electronic gear of technopop. Their stress on solo performance undermined the conventional wisdom of Japan's social collectivity, and their random assemblages of electronic junk defied the rigid "Japan, Inc." stereotype of imitation, improvement, and quality control. In this realm, Japanese artists were not copying or perfecting the tools of electronic music, but misusing them and destroying them.

As Merzbow, C.C.C.C., Masonna, Solmania, and others toured North America in the late 1980s, Japanoise symbolized personal resistance to technology for a new underground audience. The vision of a Japanese performer like Akita Masami calmly stepping on stage and unleashing a howling maelstrom of electronic feedback seemed like the ultimate triumph of individual originality over national-corporate hegemony. Moreover, the coup was accomplished by a forceful deconstruction of Japan-made consumer electronics that turned the weapons of a mass cultural agenda against itself. Instruments were wrecked, gear was broken, and (on at least one occasion that I observed) speakers burst into flames. But if Japanoise represented a new style of Japanese electronic music performance, its creative destruction could not be identified as a regional production. Japanoise tapped into global anxieties about posthuman subjectivity, which were difficult to resolve under existing terms of cultural resistance.

Most Noisicians are critical of scientific progress, even in acknowledging that their sound production is a mix of human and mechanical resources. While Dan Greenwood (a.k.a. Diagram A) is very invested in a project of electronic soundmaking, he is deeply conflicted about the incorporation of technology within his own life. A photographic insert included in one CD shows Greenwood surrounded by destroyed gear, subtitled with the words "Resist the Machines" (figures 6.1 and 6.2). I asked Greenwood about the paradoxes in "resisting machines," even as Diagram A performances clearly depend on electronic gear. Although Greenwood insisted that he's not "antitechnology" ("I'd be living in the woods if I was"): "I do see it as a bad thing that will ultimately destroy us. Even so, it's so much of my life that I don't think I can step away from it. I rely on it so much . . . I guess that's why I put that ["Resist the Machines" text] in there. I guess it's kind of a ridiculous statement to make, but that's why that's in there, because it's hard for me to feel like I could pull away from technology. So it's almost like I have a fantasy of a world without it—or that it's going to damage us somehow." The resistance to technological progress might connect Noise with transnational networks of political activism, especially environmental and antiglobalization protesters who sabotage industrial and technological projects (e.g., Earth First!). Even when sympathetic, most performers and listeners reject the notion that Noise could represent these social agendas of collective political action. They describe it instead as a project of personal transformation, which recognizes human feelings and reactions that cannot be adapted into a technological system. The only way to resist the machines, they argue, is to perform the disruptive effects of this mismatched energy within their own selves.

Casual listeners are often surprised to learn that many Noisicians, although heavily invested in the social and musical effects of technology, are not tech-savvy people. Although their performances depend on an intricate knowledge of consumer electronics, they do not demonstrate mastery over their machines. Instead, they remain out of step with new developments in the electronics sector and ritually destroy their own technological creations. In this, Noise does not align with the musical futurism typical of

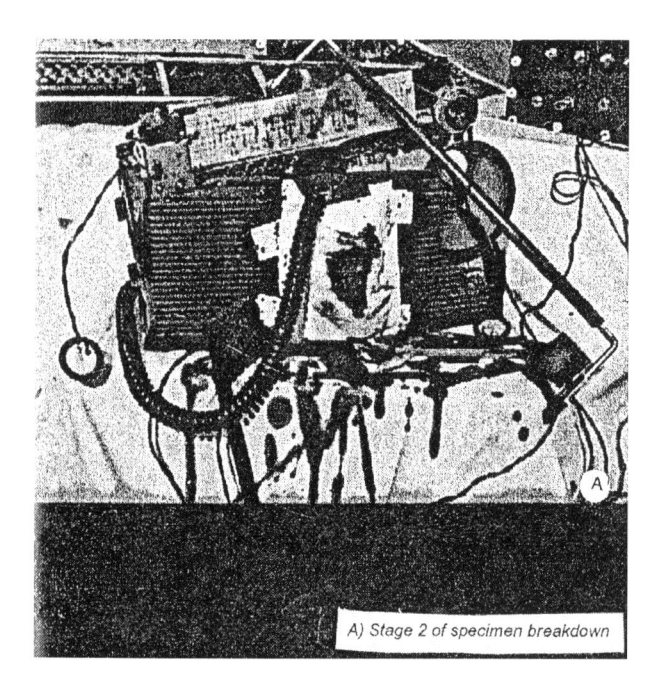

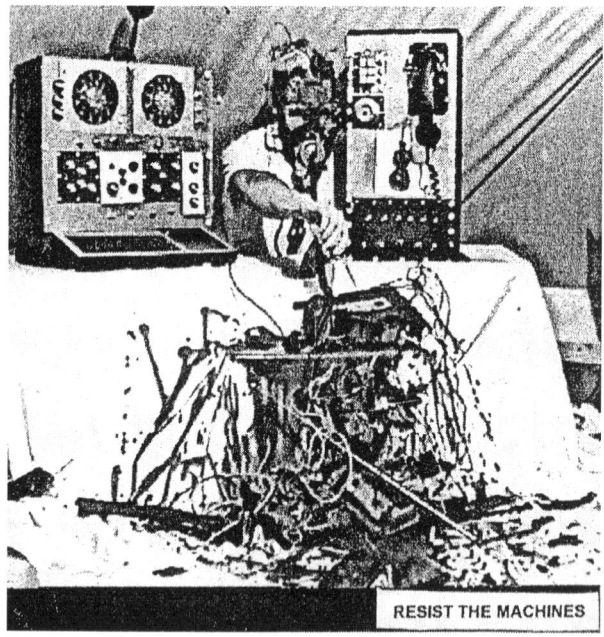

6.1 and 6.2. Diagram A, "Specimen Breakdown"; "Resist the Machines." Courtesy of Daniel Greenwood.

contemporary electronic music and new media art. It is not interactive, not multimediated, not virtual, and usually not even digital. It does not represent the fluid possibilities but the limitations of human creativity in a technological cybersphere. Noise drove electronic music crazy. It embodied the productive use of technology as a destructive force.

Hiroshige Jojo of Hijokaidan, for example, made tape collages of guitars being smashed, isolating these destructive sounds and looping them over and over again: "I loved the moment when Jimi Hendrix smashed the guitar—but the rest of his music is so normal. I wanted to play only the 'high-tension' scenes. I made a tape of all of these moments, the sounds of breaking guitars, all edited together onto one tape." Hijokaidan's live shows extended this high-tension quality of sonic destruction into their performance, endlessly feeding the crashing, chordless, and rhythmless climax of rock's final chord back into a constant, crashing blast of Noise. As I mentioned in chapter 3, Hijokaidan's destruction was not always purely sonic. The group became infamous for their early performances in Kyoto, during which they augmented their Noise by smashing up stage equipment, shattering floorboards, and attacking the audience with fire extinguishers.

Some of Hijokaidan's contemporaries were even more notorious. The duo Hanatarashi (Snotnose), featuring Taketani Ikuo and Yamatsuka Eye, only managed to play a handful of performances in the mid-1980s before they were banned from most clubs. Although the group only played a few times, their shows have become canonical tales of Noise's out-of-control destruction. During one performance, Eye cut his leg open with a chainsaw and terrorized the audience with flying chunks of metal. In the most infamous episode, in 1985, Eye destroyed a Tokyo club, Toritsu Kasei Super Loft, by driving an abandoned backhoe though the room (figure 6.3). As David Hopkins (of Kansai label Public Bath) recalled to me, "He didn't know how to drive it, so he put the shovel up and the whole thing tipped over, it was leaking gasoline onto the floor. . . . The audience held him down because he acted like he was going to light fire to the gasoline." Eye recounts the chaotic event in vivid detail:

> We got on this thing and rode it—bang!—through the doors of the hall. It'll spin a full 360 degrees, so we were spinning and driving through the audience, chasing them around, when suddenly there was this wall we spun into and opened a rather large hole in. The wind came blowing in.

The shovel part got stuck in the hole and, trying to get it out, we pushed a switch that started the tractor tipping up, like it was about to go over backwards. . . . Nobody got hurt there, but it cost us several thousand bucks to pay for all the damage. We'd also broken the backhoe and had to pay for that . . . the place was all concrete walls and no windows. We smashed everything. (Higashiseto 1991)

Ironically, because Hanatarashi's performance generally consisted of simply smashing unamplified objects, the sound was actually not very loud, and the noise of the audience often drowned it out. Remembering the performance, Eye commented, "It's amazing, really, how little sound comes out of something you're smashing with all your might."

As a sonic embodiment of technological power, Japanoise is strongly connected to the Industrial genre popularized in the 1980s by European groups including Throbbing Gristle, Einstürzende Neubauten, Whitehouse, Nocturnal Emissions, and SPK, as well as Americans such as NON and Z'ev (Duguid 1995; Ford 1999; Neal 2001; Vale and Juno 1983). Industrial groups—often in combination with experimental film, performance art, and agitprop political theater—incorporated junk metal, homemade electronic devices, drum machines, amplified motors, and power tools

6.3. Eye destroys machines on stage in the legendary Hanatarashi performance at Toritsu Kasei Super Loft, August 4, 1985. Photo by Satoh Gin.

into musical performance. By bringing these explicitly mechanical sounds into live performance, Industrial music was a powerful aesthetic influence on Japanese and American Noise, even if most Industrial groups organized their noise sounds into rhythmic structures, often accompanied by lyrics, and made more use of recognizable musical instruments (particularly synthesizers and drums). More than by sound, Noise was linked to Industrial music's ambivalent representations of technological authority. Both genres performed a highly abject sensibility of personal control, in which individual artistic expression is embedded in displays of technological power and powerlessness (figures 6.4–6.6).

The human–machine relationship is particularly explicit in the Industrial subgenre "power electronics," a phrase coined by William Bennett to describe his performances and recordings as Whitehouse in the British Industrial scene of the 1980s. Whitehouse is well known for extreme levels of amplification and electronic distortion (as well as for sinister images of violence and subjection in their song titles and lyrics).[7] Bennett developed several sonic techniques that became common in Noise, particularly the concentration of extremely high and low frequencies in pulsing, rhythmless clusters of static. But he also showed that electronics cannot be used simply as a tool to achieve control over sound. Rather, its force always subverts aesthetic goals and expressions into ambivalent relationships of alienation and violence. The user generates this brutal power, which their audience—and they themselves—must then resist, even though resistance is futile. Power electronics, then, does not celebrate the power of electronic music as the mastery of technology. It shows how all forms of technocultural power are generated by the breakdown of human autonomy.

Like Noise, Industrial music stressed the destructive power of machines over people. Covers for recordings and performance flyers often depicted machines of war, or abject imagery displaying the effects of military technology on vulnerable bodies. Titles invoked technologies of medical and sexual violence, imprisonment, and other mechanisms of bodily destruction and social control. In this, Industrial groups tapped into a humanistic impulse to reveal the inhuman effects of mechanization. But their political commentary was obscured by deeply ambivalent representations of technological power. On one hand, Industrial music presented an unmistakable critique of the use of machines to sublimate and control individuals. But performers also reveled in authorizing the technological power of machines to dominate human sensibility. They forced audiences to endure a sound en-

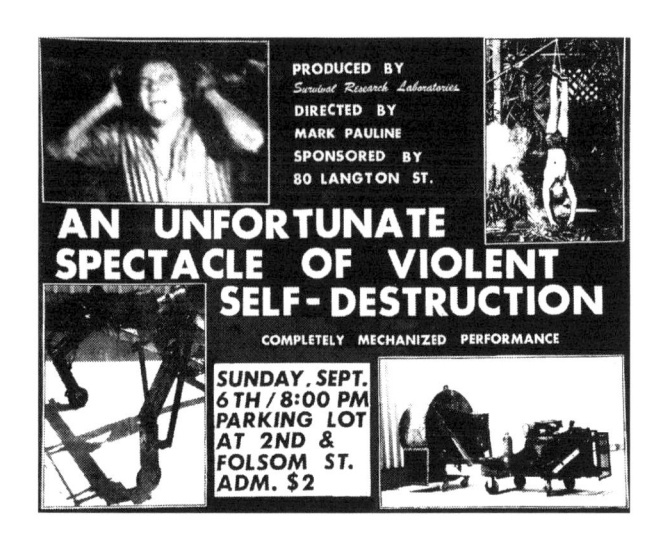

6.4. "An Unfortunate Spectacle of Violent Self-Destruction." Courtesy of Mark Pauline and Survival Research Laboratories.

6.5. The 6-Barrel Shockwave Cannon. Photo by Timothy Childs.

6.6. Flyer for a Noise show, incorporating images of military weapons to symbolize technological power.

vironment filled with repetitive and brutally loud noises, which cut off the possibility of public interaction beyond simply witnessing the spectacle.

Mark Pauline, the founder of San Francisco–based Survival Research Laboratories (SRL), began creating monstrous and deafening assemblages from abandoned industrial junk around 1979. Performances by SRL were and are extremely dangerous affairs, held in warehouses or abandoned buildings where the audience is in close proximity to enormously loud hydraulic pumps, flame-throwing engines, and other frightening constructions.[8] Pauline came to personally embody aspects of a human-machine after creating a robotic claw to replace his own hand, which he had destroyed with explosives while preparing a rocket motor for a show. He describes his love for machines in direct contrast to his ambivalence about the uses of technology: "Ever since I had my first manufacturing job as a teenager, I was struck by how much I loved the process and how little I believed in the products I was making. One of the reasons I started SRL was to have access to the best tools and technology and never have to say I was sorry for not doing something 'useful' with it" (Pauline 2009).

The impact of an overpowering mechanical environment has been associated with industrial modernity throughout the twentieth century and inspired between the wars art movements of Italian futurism and surrealist automatism. Modernist ideas of mechanized personhood became part of the first transnational imaginings of industrial society, which toggled between celebrations of technology's power and fears of its dehumanizing effects. The sudden violence of mechanical noise was symbolized by its spectacular relationship with the explosive growth of cities, factories, and technological warfare. Noise sounds were famously brought into the discourse of modern musical composition by the Italian futurist Luigi Russolo, who sought to expand musical sound to include the noises of the city—"the throbbing of valves, the pounding of pistons, the screeching of gears," and the "new noises of modern warfare"—with a set of new noise-making instruments he called *intonarumori* (Russolo 1986 [1913]). Noise became an important theme of modern music. Charles Ives imitated city noises in *Central Park in the Dark*, Edgard Varèse used sirens in *Amériques*, George Antheil created his *Ballet Mécanique*, and pieces such as Sergei Prokofiev's *Le Pas D'Acier Suite* and Alexander Mosolov's *Factory: Machine Music, Op. 19 (Iron Foundry)* programmatically represented industrial noises in musical forms (Bijsterveld 2008).[9]

However, by the end of the twentieth century, despite the common inclusion of electronic instruments and manipulations of recorded noises, noise had not yet been absorbed (as such) into musical aesthetics. Instead, its sound represented the incursions of a mechanical environment that could not be reconciled with human sensibilities, even as its presence came to dominate public space. Noise abatement policies were enacted in many modern cities, but the triumph of noise in industrial societies seemed inevitable (Thompson 2002). There were only two obvious routes of escape from the advance of noise into public culture: the alienated retreat into private property, or the internal embodiment of noise by changing human perception. If privately controlled space offered to decouple human from machine, this separation lasted only as long as one could hide away from a debased technological environment. On the other hand, internal transformation might return control to the subject by making noise a normal part of the individual sensorium.

Murasaki Hyakurô, a writer and longtime Kansai Noise fan, began attending Noise shows in the early 1980s while working as a machine operator at a local flour mill. In the Japanese underground music magazine Eater, he described his interest in attending Noise concerts as a way of internalizing the ambient noise he was involuntarily forced to experience at work:

> The flour milling machine made an incredibly loud noise, like the noise of an airplane taking off, when it was grinding down the raw material. And the material, imported from Brazil, was cheap and inferior in quality—sometimes something unbelievable was mixed into it, like an iron screw, things like that. When that kind of thing went down into the machine, its teeth would make an incredible noise—it was like four or five bolts of lightning striking at the same time. It was unbelievably loud, and I thought my heart would be crushed. But eventually I got used to it.... The violence of Noise music is not much compared with that of the flour milling machine, which I had to hear even if I didn't want to, in sickness and in health, that almost ground down my brain.... I think I was subconsciously preparing for the noise of the mill breaking down because of an iron screw (laughs). The machine had lots of big teeth inside and they spun around at tremendous speed. And all of them would break in an instant, and to me, that was like the jackpot of the end of the world. (Murasaki 1999)

Murasaki's story is by no means typical, but it captures something of Noise's complex embodiment of technological violence. He began to attend Noise concerts out of a desire to regain control over his own perception by "offsetting one noise with another . . . I wanted to create a noise superior to the noise in my head." To do so, he had to transform the sensory by-products of the industrial environment imposed daily on his unwilling body—in "sickness and in health," like the enforcement of vows in a shotgun wedding of man and machine—into an aestheticized Noise. This is a vision not of synthesis or adaptation but of an impacted human consciousness that internalizes repetitive loops of everyday conflict and violence. The "jackpot" of this overloaded feedback between mechanical and human experience is bound to its inevitable collapse. Listening to Noise became one way to dream the destruction of the entire thing, perhaps even to hear the echo of oneself in the sound of its breakdown.

THE JACKPOT OF THE END OF THE WORLD

Before returning to the creative destruction of Japanoise in the 1990s, it is worth contextualizing its emergence within a Japanese mediascape known for dystopian narratives. Media scholars have argued that the recurrent trope of apocalypse in Japanese science fiction films reflected the desires and fears of postwar Japanese audiences. Susan Napier describes the urban destruction of Toho's *Godzilla* series as "both cathartic and compensatory" for the Japanese public, even in the false promise that the nation's science could save its citizens from the monstrous results of U.S. nuclear weapons (Napier 1993). There was more to this atomic grotesque than the endless reconfiguration of Japanese cultural identity in wartime trauma. The repetitive embodiment and "acting out" of nuclear apocalypse in Japanese popular culture helped its audiences imagine the return of individual subjectivity from out of the ruins of a mass technological society. Zygmunt Bauman argues that all post-Holocaust societies confront the moral ambivalence of global modernity by "imagining the unimaginable" in fantastic displays of violence and power (Bauman 1991). The technocultural imaginary of "Cool Japan," then, strikes this uneasy balance between representing and reproducing the traumatic effects of Japan's modernity. In Japanese science fiction, postapocalyptic fantasies of global destruction became a "complete horizon of experience," which, by projecting the potential outcomes of present-day technology through its ambivalent future, could set "a productive limit to the present time, raising the possibility of seeing out into something new and different" (Looser 2006:94). If these special insights into technocultural subjectivity are now canonically imposed on Japan's national identity, it is partly because these Japanese artworks rehearsed their violent outcomes for a global audience.[10]

The figure of the human-machine became a key symbol of the moral violence of technological adaptation. Science fiction manga and anime raised existential questions about the human integration of mechanical functions in cyborgs, androids, and transformative *mecha* (mechanical "suits").[11] Robotic superheroes such as Tezuka Osamu's *Tetsuwan Atomu* (Atom Boy) were among the first subjects of Japanese popular media to be widely distributed in the United States, followed by the Transformers, the Power Rangers, and a string of others. Their stories were generally celebratory of individual capabilities bestowed by technological power, even as nuclear subtexts were suppressed in American remediations (*Atom Boy*, for example, was distributed in the United States as *Astro Boy*). By the end of the 1980s, bleaker projections of mechanical subjectivity began to narrate technological development as a self-destructive process of psychic violence and deep emotional conflict. Anime and manga such as *Ghost in the Shell*, *Akira*, and *Neon Genesis Evangelion* were hailed in the United States as futuristic masterpieces based in Japan's fluid technological hybridity. But they subverted its national success story into a tale that ends "with the hero dead, Tokyo in smoldering ruins, and fears of apocalypse only briefly alleviated" (Tsutsui 2010).

A handful of cult films have been particularly recognized for their powerful impact on the transnational formation of "cyberpunk" aesthetics.[12] Ôtomo Katsuhiro's breakthrough anime adaptation of his cult manga series *Akira* (1988) is widely associated with the creation of a critical audience for Japanimation in the United States. In *Akira*, a teenage biker named Tetsuo is possessed by telekinetic powers that he cannot control in the postapocalyptic city of Neo-Tokyo, circa 2019, which had been destroyed three decades earlier by a psychic child named Akira. After discovering the remains of the cryogenically frozen boy beneath the city, Tetsuo mutates into a gigantic metallic creature. Finally, out of control with pain and emotion and overwhelmed by his own power, he lays waste to the city of Neo-Tokyo. Following closely on the heels of *Akira* was Tsukamoto Shinya's 1988 live-action film *Tetsuo* (Iron Man), a nightmarish avant-garde tale of violent bodily transformation set to Ishikawa Chu's grating, intensely noisy Industrial soundtrack of synthesizers and metal percussion. The main character (the Salaryman) accidentally kills a monstrous figure (the Metal Fetishist) that triggers his mutation into a being made of junk metal. This is not a progressive cyborgian adaptation but a bloody, violent rupture of the human form by technology. The Salaryman's limbs are not replaced with shiny prostheses; he does not slip into an efficient sheath of robotic armor. Instead, his vulnerable body is broken down internally by a growing mechanical infection. His flesh is punctured; his phallus turns into a power drill that kills his lover. Finally, the Metal Fetishist shows him that all of Tokyo will eventually turn into junk metal, and the two demonic figures join forces to rust the world and scatter its dust into the universe.

Tatsumi Takayuki argues that this "Japanoid" version of the human-machine compressed the transnational techno-imaginary of postwar Japan into a form of national identity (Tatsumi 2006). Japan's technological dependence was embodied in the "creative masochism" of cyborgian and *mecha* (robotic suit) characters, exemplified by anime films like *Patlabor* and *Neon Genesis Evangelion*. These films absorbed the Western insistence on Japan's advanced technological status into a "techno-orientalism," which projected the neo-Tokyo of Ridley Scott's cyberpunk classic *Blade Runner* (1982) back onto a national identity defined by its reception in the political unconscious of the United States (Ueno 1996, 1998). These human-machine narratives, then, did not transgress Japanese social norms into new transcultural hybrids through spectacular adaptations of Western technology. Instead, their "Japanoid" subjects symbolized the internal embodiment of Japan's postwar technological determinism. But this rationalization of technology "inside" the Japanese national subject clearly excluded the coercive historical impact of "outside" forces of transnational capitalism. Postwar adaptations of technology grew out of Japan's compulsory economic relationships with the United States. From the immediate postwar period through the recessionary 1990s, Japan's geopolitical position was marked by its dependency on the foreign market for consumer electronics, which generated new forms of electronic consumption within the constructs of national identity.

One of the paradoxical mandates of postwar Japan was that individuality should be cultivated to prevent the reemergence of a fascist state, even as the ideology of national reconstruction called for the sacrifice of the individual to the state (Cazdyn 2002). The rise of personal electronics helped Japanese citizens imbue their individual consumption with a kind of heroism, conflating it with national production of consumer technologies. Even if the mastery of technology was no longer a question of political or military independence, industrial policy fed culturalist interpretations back into Japan's technological consumption. In the 1950s, the "bright life" (akarui seikatsu) was identified by ownership of a washing machine, refrigerator, and color TV, reified as the "three sacred treasures" of modern Japan (Partner 1999; Yoshimi 1999).[13] In the 1960s and 1970s, research and development led to radical new improvements on American inventions through miniaturization, and the Japanese public championed its engineers as visionary heroes for their development of the transistor, creation of the quartz watch, and implementation of advanced robotics and LED lasers (Johnstone 1999).[14] By the 1980s, the production of personal electronics had begun to represent Japanese cultural aesthetics as part of a new technological consciousness. Products such as the Sony Walkman appeared to incorporate Japan's native perception into the local format of a global technological program, even as it cultivated an electronic individualism that demanded the private isolation of individual senses (duGay and Hall 1997; Hosokawa 1984; Kogawa 1984; Morris-Suzuki 1998). Japanese social critics began to describe their Generation X—children of the 1960s who came of age in the "bubble" economy of the 1980s—as shinjinrui, a "new species" said to be more individualistic than older generations. Shinjinrui could integrate technology fluidly into everyday behavior, but they had lost some of the basic traits of Japanese collectivity through their absorption in electronic products like video games, VCRs, and personal stereos, and in more spectacular forms such as robotic pets. A "new person" might become socially isolated in this private hall of mirrors, but once inside, they could reinvent the world as an adaptive, participatory culture that reorganizes technological media to conform to individual experience.

By the 1990s, obsessive anime fans known as *otaku* had refigured electronic individualism with radical techniques of reception. For most Japanese, the assignation has negative connotations comparable to terms like "geek," "pervert," and "junkie" that identify an unhealthy relationship with anime, video games, and online culture. But otaku reconfigured media narratives in ways that reflected a counterpublic movement within Japanese identity, even if it was difficult to describe as social organization or politically motivated resistance. Otaku incorporated consumption and production into a personalized "media mix," by detaching subelements of anime films from their narrative structures and rearranging them for personal consumption (Azuma 2001; LaMarre 2004; Okada 1996; Steinberg 2004).

Azuma Hiroki has influentially described otaku reception as a "database consumption" that represented an "animalizing" postmodern form of social individuation.[15] But the self-reflexive world of otaku, he explained, also created a "pseudo-Japan, manufactured from U.S.-produced material." Otaku fetishized the anachronistic futurism of 1980s "cutting-edge" Japan, reflecting a narcissistic refusal to acknowledge the links between the trauma of World War II defeat and rapid postwar economic growth.[16] They participated in the technological fragmentation of social narratives, even as their practices embodied a new sociality based in reconfigurable consumer identity.

New subjectivities of fandom and consumption became hallmarks of Japan's cultural power among transnational audiences. Anne Allison describes how Japan's obsession with technological commodities conjured an alternative capitalism, particularly in the intermediated games, toys, and electronic goods that captivated a global market in the 1990s. In the fantasy world of the video game *Pokémon*, for example, players assemble identities from a "bricolage of assorted and interchangeable (machine/organic/human) parts where familiar forms have broken down and reassembled into new hybridities" (Allison 2006:13). These fantasies of flexible consumption, Allison argues, allow individuals to "engage in a continual breakdown and recombination of multiple bodies, powers and parts ... that not only reproduces a lived world of flux, fragmentation, and mobility but also gives kids the opportunity to both mimic and reweave such particle-ization" (30). Players could break the world down into pieces, sometimes violently, to make new connections between the parts. The objects of Japanese "techno-animism" became intelligible on a global scale because they represented more than abstracted curiosities of a marginal popular culture; they embodied the fragmented effects of commodity capitalism on human consciousness, while allowing their users to improvise new technological selves.

The mediated circulations of "Cool Japan" appeared to repair Japan's global connections at a time of increasing economic rupture. Anime, manga, J-pop, and other fan cultures offered a Japanese form of soft power as a panacea for national economic decline (Nye 2004). But as Japan moved deeper into recession throughout the "lost decade" of the 1990s, an alternative capitalism was slow to materialize. Japanese national identity fell into an uncertain self-critique that toggled between cause (a flawed, imitative version of technological capitalism) and effect (the collapse of social collectivity). The bubble economy of the 1980s had spun out of the artificially inflated currency and credit values known as *zaiteku* (financial technologies, from *zaimu*, "finance," and *teku*, "tech"). After these assets crashed in 1991, the cultural suppressions of Japan's postwar growth were exposed by a shocking series of catastrophes and violent events that reopened an anxious discourse about the future. As Japan approached the millennium, the failure of the "Japanese system" suddenly came into view through this "sudden malfunction," which had in fact been building for decades (Yoda 2001).

RETURNING JAPANOISE TO MILLENNIAL JAPAN

By the mid-1990s, Japanoise had begun to filter back into local reception. Although it had been practiced locally for over a decade, Japanoise was reintroduced as a newly minted form. Because its positive overseas reception had been widely publicized, Japanoise could now be described as a Japanese brand of global electronic music, ready to be reimported as a local production. But Japanoise was not readily absorbed into the flexible consumptions of popular music or the alternative youth countercultures associated with other electronic music genres in the 1990s. Instead, it echoed the destructive aspects of advanced technocapitalism, which were becoming increasingly obvious to the Japanese public. National consensus had collapsed in the shock waves of the 1995 Hanshin earthquake and the release of deadly sarin gas into the Tokyo subway system by the Aum Shinrikyo cult. The failure of the postwar *jôhô shakai* (information society) was revealed through bureaucratic and technological inefficiencies that spectacularized a decaying infrastructure through train wrecks, collapsed buildings, and nuclear accidents (McCormack 1996). Japan's political and economic autonomy, as well as its postwar "partnership" with the United States, appeared to be a nostalgic Cold War–era fiction. The projection of a downward spiral was reinforced by analysts in the United States, who predicted that the Japanese public would continue into further stages of introversion, spurred on by its aging population, declining birthrate, and lack of resources.

Iida Yumiko depicts the 1990s as a breaking point for Japanese subjectivity. Individuals fought for personal autonomy in a commercial sphere that had "suffused the realms of subjectivity and the social imaginary with notions of fragmentation, disembodiment and ambiguity" (Iida 2000:8).

Disjunct subcultural forces emerged, from the historical revisionism of a growing neonational movement to the detached identifications of part-time workers known as *furitaa* (derived from "free work"), whose labor propped up a destructive form of flexible capitalism. The socially disintegrated cases of *hikikomori* (shut-ins, who withdraw completely from public life) typified a demoralized and fragmented culture, whose technological solipsism embodied the likelihood that Japanese modernization had reached a dead end. A list of spectacular media events was invoked to represent the decline of youth in 1990s Japan—the Shônen A case (in which a teen boy killed two younger children in Kobe); spectacular murders and suicides among otaku; and the notorious practice of *enjo kôsai* (in which disaffected schoolgirls sell themselves to older men as "compensated dating"). The moral panic around the status of Japanese society was folded back into the socioeconomic violence of rampant neoliberal speculation, collapse, and subsequent bailout in repetitive cycles of recessionary failure (Driscoll 2007; Ivy 2001). Given this millennialist moment, it is not surprising that the brief notoriety of Noise in Japan reached a peak at the end of the 1990s. This was a Japan where Noise finally made sense.

Features on Japanoise began to appear in magazines like *Quick Japan*, *Studio Voice*, and *Music Magazine* (figure 6.7). The American bands Sonic Youth and the Flaming Lips expounded on the virtues of Japanoise in interviews with the Japanese press. A two-hour documentary on the Osaka Noise scene (*Music for Psychological Liberation*, hosted by Public Bath label owner David Hopkins and punk legend Alice Sailor) was broadcast on Kansai television. Boredoms members Yoshimi P-We and Eye briefly appeared on celebrity panels on television variety shows and in high-profile fashion shoots; Boredoms signed to a management contract with giant entertainment conglomerate Yoshimoto Kogyo, known for breaking Osaka comedians into the national mainstream. By the mid-1990s, the hype on Japanoise was fast and furious. Ôno Masahiko (Solmania) was featured in guitar magazines that breathlessly described his effects pedals and deconstructed instruments; a giant cardboard cutout figure of Masonna adorned the first-floor entrance of Shinsaibashi Tower Records in Osaka; a major-label record by Nakahara Masaya (Boryoku Onsen Geisha, a.k.a. Violent Onsen Geisha) on Toshiba EMI even made the national sales charts, and Nakahara popped up on national television several times as a "Noise idol."

Noise entered the public consciousness of Japan as a branch of transnational subcultures, such as rave scenes, modern primitives, and so forth,

6.7. "Addicted to Noise," *Studio Voice* magazine. Photo by Nakafuji Takehiko.

which seemed to constitute an alternative wave of cultural globalization. The idea of Japanoise also reflected a new identification of local youth with domestic culture, even if this alternative Japan was built from the commodity forms of its popular media (a process caustically labeled the "return to J" by the popular social critic Asada Akira, 2000). Taken on the most superficial level, Japanoise could become fodder for this new subcultural essentialism. The spectacle of Noise performance might collect its audiences into some sort of subcultural "tribe" (*zoku*). Critics began to translate Japanoise into local form as *Noizu-kei*, adding a suffix traditionally used to indicate a Japanese "school" or social group. As Noizu-kei, the aesthetics of Noise could be characterized as culturally Japanese, even though it represented a sound that had become globally influential. For a brief moment, images of Noise flowed back into Japan in a reverse importation that, like Japanese star players in U.S. major league baseball, inspired national identifications through the reflections of overseas success. Japanoise, of course, was not destined to become part of the J-culture boom, and its oblique relationship with consumer identity soon dissolved in this fleeting burst of recognition.

Even for those desperate to uncover a new local scene, Japanoise was far too confusing to be marketed as a new musical trend. If the recordings alone weren't a bit too much to swallow, images of Noisicians did not exactly conform to the standards of mass cultural fandom either. Their album covers were oblique blurs or unprintable pornography; some performed behind a screen, in front of projected images, or with their backs to the audience. If they appeared in photographs, most established Noisicians were too middle-aged to become trendy idols of "J-Noise." Still, there was something weirdly charismatic about the idea of a Japanoise subculture that fed back into a global cycle, even if the sound itself seemed destined to remain underground. Were these people serious? Were they a social movement, or just some strange cluster of marginal loners who had somehow learned to express themselves on stage? Unlike most popular musicians in Japan, Noisicians were openly alienated from normal channels of mass culture. But they were not exactly fine artists, either. Their controversial references to industrial, sexual, and social violence were too raw and prurient to be received as intellectual commentary, and their harsh sounds were guaranteed to escape public broadcast.

Meanwhile, Noisicians further pulled the punch of their brief social influence with an oddball sense of humor. They responded to Japan's anxious celebration of popular culture with an absurdist mode of irony, mocking their own image as local rock stars. Hijokaidan began producing T-shirts pronouncing themselves as "King of Noise," and Eye created a lucrative market for rarities with a series of one-off Hanatarashi CD-Rs (featuring, for example, a solo performance recorded in a karaoke booth screaming along to Steppenwolf's "Born to be Wild"). Others pranked the media whenever they could. Reporters faithfully repeated Nakahara's assertion that his group Violent Onsen Geisha had only become a solo act because all of the other original members had died. Most Noisicians reacted skeptically to the proposal that Japanoise represented a new alternative subculture. Part of the irony was that many Noisicians were office workers or small business owners whose everyday lives were tied into the mechanics of Japan's economic motors. A few worked corporate jobs and made no attempt to separate this reality from their Noise. Mikawa Toshiji of Incapacitants referenced his day job as a banker through a series of oblique inside jokes in the group's mid-1990s titles "I Hate Derivatives," "Mental Derivatives," "Asset without Liability," and "Alcoholic Speculation."[17] But even as Noisicians caricatured the failures of Japan's consumer society, they gestured toward a personal aesthetics of creative destruction.

When Akita Masami began performing as Merzbow in the early 1980s, he viewed Noise as a project that could help unravel the social effects of Japanese consumerism. In his seminal collection of essays *Noise War: Noise Music and Its Development* (Noizu Wô: Noizu myûjikku to sono tenkai), Akita connects Merzbow to a history of subversive art (Akita 1992). Detailing his argument with examples from the transnational art movements of mail networks, cut-up techniques, and power electronics, Akita described Noise as a way to "hide something in the media," producing an anonymous context of subliminal private experience. *Noise War* recounts a marginal history of what Andrew Ross calls protopolitical projects of technoculture, in which people "make their own independent sense of the stories that are told within and about an advanced technological society" to "turn technocommodities into resources for waging a communications revolution from below" (Ross 1991:xv–xvi). But unlike contemporaneous projects of culture-jamming, Merzbow was not a postmodern *détournement* that hijacked mainstream media to deliver an alternative message of social resistance. For Akita, the political subversion of Japanese consumer society was embedded in private experiences of Noise.

Akita describes himself as a "Dadaist of the *danchi*," referring to the block-like self-contained "new town" housing projects that symbolize Japan's midcentury urbanization, in which postwar cities were razed, divided, reconstructed, and then torn down and rebuilt over and over again.[18] For Akita, the danchi aestheticized the destructive progress of industrial development. After the war, the Japanese public had become voyeuristically involved in an endless cycle of self-destruction and reconstruction, which eventually became a "kind of a Japanese way [of being] out of control." As the older buildings decayed behind a wave of new developments, the once-futuristic danchi began to evoke nostalgic memories. They became a set of modern ruins that were romanticized and held apart as a memorial for Japan's once-hopeful postwar future.

Merzbow became Akita's way of making audible these excesses of Japan's self-destructive capitalism.[19] Noise, he told me, could sound out the frozen modern landscape of Japanese consumption:

6.8. Merzbow amid the rubble. Photo by Jenny, courtesy of Akita Masami.

> Noise was an idea about capitalism: the overload of capitalism, that kind of consumer overload. For me, it's a consumer sound.... If capitalism goes into catastrophe, it freezes the consumer. In fact, in the late '80s, Japan was frozen with consuming economically—the "bubble," you know? So when I made Noise in that same period—well, I'm not a salaryman, and I'm not consuming with money, but it's the same idea.... It's very difficult to escape from our system. We're already involved in the system. So if I can put something into the system, I want to change its direction to one kind of way, a private way.

Akita considers Merzbow an unfinished lifework of personal transformation, which he symbolized by naming his Noise project after the Bauhaus-era *Merzbau* by German Dada artist Kurt Schwitters. The *Merzbau* began inside Schwitters's family house, which was in a constant state of reconstruction as the artist endlessly added materials, incorporating artworks and garbage stolen from friends into every surface. The danchi were iconic of modern Japan's exterior cycles of public construction and destruction; the *Merzbau* was constructed in layers of private absorption and internal accumulation.

Merzbow was similarly conceived as an endless buildup of junk materials. Through this "gastronomic" process, he told me, musical commodities were transformed into an endless stream of Noise ("We eat many kinds of music, and create Noise"). Merzbow recordings sometimes inspired other transformative performances that destroyed his works or used them to destroy other things. In one infamous one-off "release" titled *Noisembryo Car*, the owner of the Swedish label Releasing Eskimo sealed a copy of the Merzbow CD *Noisembryo* in a car stereo set at full volume. Because it was impossible to either shut off or turn down the stereo, the Mercedes 230 became practically unusable. Although *Noisembryo Car* was put up for sale, it was essentially unbuyable. Others embodied the violence of consumption in their own Noise performances (in more than one instance I have seen Noisicians attempt to chew up and swallow Merzbow CDs and vinyl records).

Merzbow's creative destruction departs from Joseph Schumpeter's version, which envisioned a capitalism that "revolutionizes the economic structure from within, incessantly destroying the old one, incessantly creating a new one" (Schumpeter 2005 [1942]: 83). For Schumpeter, radical innovation was the "essential fact" about capitalism that established its evolutionary cycles of adaptation, as existing technologies are constantly destroyed to enable new contexts of production. But production always demands an equal force of consumption—a term that, as Raymond Williams reminds us, has historically carried the unfavorable meanings "to destroy, to use up, to waste, to exhaust" (Williams 1977:78). Any cultural identity modeled on the progress of technology must endlessly be broken and replaced. Everything that feeds into the commodity cycle, Akita argues, will eventually turn into valueless junk. The only way to change this outcome is to refuse to abandon the junk: to bring the trash back into the house and live with it.

FEEDING BACK TO THE HUMAN

In the apocalyptic world of Aoyama Shinji's extraordinary film Eli, Eli, Lema Sabachthani (2005), it turns out that Noise has the power to cure humanity. In 2015, the world's population is threatened by the rapid spread of a virus called the lemming syndrome. The disease makes people want to kill themselves, and it has begun to spread through cities across the globe. Eight million have died already in the United States, and three million Japanese so far; Japan has a 38 percent unemployment rate, and scientists and government agents are helpless to stop the spread of the disease. A young woman, Hana (Miyazaki Aoi), has been infected and is filled with the feelings of despair and misery that are symptomatic of the disease. Meanwhile, Mizui (the actor-musician Asano Tadanobu) and Asuhara (Nakahara Masaya of Violent Onsen Geisha) are living far from the city. They have abandoned fruitful careers as famous Noise performers to pursue their private inventions, creating new instruments from abandoned junk and experimenting with sounds in a rustic country house. Hana's grandfather locates the hermits with the aid of a detective, learning that somehow their innovative experimentations with Noise may hold out the possibility of an antidote to the suicidal depression brought on by the virus. In a desperate attempt to cure her affliction, Hana's grandfather and the detective bring her to the Noise compound.

They drive Hana to an open, grassy field overlooking the ocean, where Mizui stands with a guitar, a pile of electronic effects, and several mysterious spinning instruments at the edge of a clearing marked by a set of four gigantic speakers. The grandfather strides across the grass, pleading, "Hurry! We're almost out of time!" The afflicted girl paces, dressed

6.9. Hana awaits the curing blast of Noise. Photo still from
Eli, Eli, Lema Sabachthani (2005, Aoyama Shinji).

in black, shielding herself from the sunny day with a black umbrella. The Noisician blindfolds her and leads her to stand in front of the enormous PA system. "You may not be able to see," he tells her, "but you will know the right place when you find it." As he begins to strum the guitar, she stumbles out into the field until she is standing directly between the four monolithic speakers. Mizui leans down to adjust his equipment and then begins to play. For several minutes, the camera pans slowly around blindfolded Hana, and the landscape begins to blur in the blast of sound (figure 6.9). The Noise surrounds her in flashes of memory: inside a club; a pyre (for Asuhara, who has succumbed to suicide) burning on a beach. Finally, she collapses onto the grass. She has survived the lemming syndrome, but, as Mizui later writes, "if you want to keep your will to live, you must return," to be healed again by Noise.

The creative destruction of Noise always cycles back to the critical status of human consciousness within a technological system. But this feedback does not align with the futuristic syntheses that spin out of science fiction, postmodern electronic and experimental music, new formats of configurable media, or the flexible social identities of millennial youth. On the contrary, its transcendent antistructural subject—one that could jam the gears of the system through its unassimilated agency—is conservative, romantic, and almost classically modernist. David Harvey links the aesthetic of creative destruction to the rise of modernism, which isolated personal consciousness as a resistant force. Harvey argues that the process of industrial modernization was "creatively destructive" in demanding the sacrifice of individual differences to construct the technologically rationalized nation-state. Modernist aesthetics valorized the potential of being "destructively creative" within this context by creating new modes of subjectivity that could resist totalizing models of culture from within. Against the endless progression of technologies, "the only path to affirmation of self was to act, to manifest will" by revealing the immutable, submerged forces of humanity, "even if the outcome was bound to be tragic" (Harvey 1990:16).

Japanoise tells a John Henry story. Like that tale of a man bound in fatal contest with a machine, it relates a moral narrative of crisis, in which modern industry endlessly triumphs over the individual subject. Humanity is thrown under the bullet train of technology; the man becomes a man-machine and dies with his hammer in his hand. By acting out this failure over and over again, Noisicians expose the ruse that technology can free humanity. Instead, they show how a mechanical society feeds human energy back into the machine and measure just how deeply creative subjectivity has become embedded in this cycle. Noise's aesthetic mechanisms—its obsolete analog junk, its sounds of malfunction, its performance of automatism and mechanical breakdown—are all attempts to mark the pain and struggle of remaining human in the midst of a dangerous technological world. Noisicians feed the energy of technoculture back into itself to use the shock of the accident to reveal the nature of the underlying system. Within their destructive performances of collapse and overload lies a romantic dream of pure experience and the promise of an original self, somewhere beneath the rubble—even if this dream is a dream-despite-all, in which people can exceed their own control over the technologies that surround them.

CHAPTER 7

THE FUTURE OF CASSETTE CULTURE

At the end of the first decade of the 2000s, the audiocassette has become the object of a strange anachronous revival in the North American Noise scene. I am handed new cassette releases by Noisicians; tapes are sold at Noise shows, in small stores, and by online distributors; and cassettes are reviewed in fanzines and blogs. Many new Noise recordings are issued on tape only, and several cassette labels have sprung up over the past few years. Dominic Fernow (a.k.a. Prurient) of Hospital Productions argues that cassette tapes are essential to the spirit of Noise: "I can't imagine ever fully stopping tapes, they are the symbol of the underground. . . . What they represent in terms of availability also ties back into that original Noise ideology. Tapes are precious and sacred items, not disposable. . . . It's incredibly personal, it's not something I want to just have anyone pick up because it's two dollars and they don't give a fuck" (Fernow 2006). All of this takes place years after the cassette has vanished from music retail and its playback equipment has become technologically obsolescent.[1] Although a very few small independent stores carry newly released cassettes, new Noise tapes are more commonly distributed via mail order or through in-person exchange, most often directly with the artist. Cassettes, too, are everywhere in contemporary visual arts and fashion, both as nostalgic symbols of 1980s pop culture and as iconic forms of new independent design. But at the end of the new millennium's first decade, many years into a global move toward digital formats and Internet-based systems of distribution, why hold on to the analog cassette?

In this final chapter, I relate the current circulation of Noise cassettes to an earlier mail-based exchange, which its participants named "cassette culture." In the 1980s, the person-to-person barter of homemade Noise cassettes grew into a participatory network of anonymous but connected users. The cassette culture set the stage for the rise of independent music in the 1990s and framed the possibility of a shared global underground based in decentralized, user-controlled distribution of recordings. But the present-day cassette represents a different goal: to impose technological, social, and aesthetic limits on the omnipresence of new media, which can return Noise to its marginal position at the edge of circulation.

Cassette tapes relocalize Noise by distinguishing interpersonal exchanges of physical media from the ubiquity of online access. The renewed emphasis on social copresence in independent music has strongly impacted the orientation of cassette exchange networks, which have shifted away from transnational connections to stress the reinvention of local scenes. Even as cassettes move Noise's circulation "back" into the realm of a physical medium, they do not remain fixed in place in the analog realm. Cassettes are reduplicated in parallel circuits of digital distribution, peer-to-peer networks of file sharing and crowd-sourced information, which are in turn dubbed back onto local social life. This push-and-pull cycle—between new and old media, and between virtual and physical contexts of exchange—extends the face-to-face encounter of the local scene into online networks. But even as new publics emerge in the open access projects of Internet circulation, the skeletons of cassette culture keep Noise underground.

CASSETTE CULTURE

The cassette culture of Noise, of course, is only one of the listener-circulated social networks that grew up around the audiocassette. The mass introduction of cassette technology in the late 1970s and 1980s changed musical landscapes on a global level. Audiocassettes initiated new social and economic relationships around sound recordings, allowing individual users to reproduce, remix, and distribute their own material. Cassettes also set the first substantial wave of informal music piracy into motion, radically changing local music industries and further entrenching recorded music in homes, vehicles, and public spaces around the world. As Peter Manuel argues in his influential study of media distribution in North India, the audiocassette offered a "two-way, potentially interactive micro-medium whose low expense [made] it conducive to localized grassroots control and corresponding diversity of content" (Manuel 1993:2). Cassettes enabled new political functions for "small media" in mass communication networks, such as the channels of audiocassette exchange that affected the outcome of the Iranian revolution (Sreberny-Mohammadi and Mohammadi 1994). New circulations of cassettes changed local music performance contexts of traditional gamelan music in Java, generated new contexts of religious listening in Egypt, and influenced the textual aesthetics of poetry and song in Yemen (Hirschkind 2006; Miller 2007; Sutton 1985). Audio- and videocassette technologies also helped new media publics form, as inexpensive analog reproductions created informal markets for music and film (Greene and Porcello 2005; Larkin 2008).

The global advent of the audiocassette demonstrated how musical cultures could be radically transformed and even reconstructed in circulation. The cassette also generated new discourses of participatory democratic media, in grassroots networks of distribution that offered economic and social independence from state and industrial controls. Nowadays, digital productions possess this radical emancipatory status, whereas analog formats appear limited and archaic. But the newness of new media often hides their continuities with ongoing social values of old media.[2] From the mid-1980s until the mid-1990s, the analog cassette tape represented many of the technological attributes now associated with digital files.[3] Cassettes offered transportability, mutability of content, and smaller size, but most significant, they created opportunities to produce and share music that enabled an alternative to industrial modes of distribution. Like the MP3, the sound quality of cassette tape was not regarded as an improvement from previous formats, but its ease of use encouraged new possibilities of homemade production, flexible user-controlled distribution, remixing, and the proliferation of marginalized styles. Contemporary narratives about the participatory networks of online digital media, too, follow from older storylines of "independent music," which developed in the context of analog physical media.

Audiocassettes catalyzed a powerful backlash against media users by music industries, from international litigation to public and private campaigns against illegal duplication (memorialized in the cassette-and-crossbones logo developed by a British industrial antipiracy group, which famously announced that "Home Taping Is Killing Music"). Amateur home taping became a crucial background for the legal doctrine of fair use in U.S. copyright law, and qualities of analog degeneration and erasure became markers of the "aesthetics of access" that accrued to decentralized exchanges of bootleg audio and videotapes (Hilderbrand 2009). Cassettes helped popularize amateur "lo-fi" recording practices with the introduction of inexpensive cassette recorders in the 1970s, followed by the four-track cassette recorder in the 1980s. Audiocassettes also fostered newly personalized modes of configurable media in the form of the compilation mix tape. Mix tapes are indexes of person-to-person social networks, often as concentrated musical representations of friendships and romantic relationships.[4] The gift of a mix tape allowed listeners new opportunities to narrate and share their experiences of media by sequencing materials to reflect personal histories and express individual aesthetics. Cassette mixing techniques also provoked new sounds and performance styles, especially in hip-hop, in which the mix tape remains a powerful metaphor of populism.[5]

What extends to the social imaginary of new media from the old media contexts of cassette culture? I have argued that Noise's inaccessibility was crucial to motivating its circulation between Japan and the United States in the 1980s and 1990s. These hard-to-get values might seem incommensurable with a contemporary digital mediascape based in open access. Peer-to-peer file sharing, torrent networks, MP3 blogs, streaming audio, and a growing host of commercial outlets like iTunes, Rhapsody, Last.fm, Spotify, and YouTube have made even the most rare and obscure sound recordings widely available. Websites, blogs, and discussion boards allow participants to pass on information about Noise, post photographs and video clips of live performances, generate collective content about artists and styles, and share, identify, and discuss new recordings almost instantly. Things that were once an enduring mystery, even for the most hardcore collectors, can easily be discovered just by opening a search engine to locate a fan site, blog, stream, or torrent that allows direct access to once-rare material. Previously hidden sounds can be located much more simply, and perhaps more important, historical background about Noise is suddenly available as online networks drag even the most marginalized, sub-subcultural forms of underground media to the surface (and up into the cloud). If Noise has now become knowable, downloadable, and easily contextualized as a subject through online networks, how can it retain its unclassifiable character and regenerate its valued aesthetics of obscurity? Everything, it seems, has changed.

The revival of the cassette might merely memorialize a lost golden age, rather than a move toward recognizing the radical changes of digital culture. I argue that the contemporary exchange of Noise cassettes is a production of "residual media," in which old, technologically obsolescent formats continue to influence new media contexts (Acland 2007).[6] In the 1980s, the cassette facilitated the expansion of Noise into anonymous circuits of mail exchange, which became skeletal frameworks for later retail distributions of independent music recordings in the 1990s. But in the early 2010s, its physical and technical limitations represent Noise's offline divergence from digital networks. The contemporary production of Noise cassettes, then, is more than nostalgic inertia or Luddite resistance to online culture. It marks a radical attempt to redefine the social independence of independent music, by using the residue of past exchanges to define Noise in emergent contexts of new media. The cassette tape has become a magical object of media circulation. In its physical housing, we hear the echo of older, apparently obsolete social values and aesthetic goals, which "print-through" from the analog cassette culture onto digital distributions of Noise.[7] The cassette persists, even in its technological obsolescence, as a stubborn reminder of a deep and continuous effort to stay underground.

POSTING NEW MEDIA

> Here at the edge of the East Village, I'm sitting on the sidewalk, on a tossed out
>   sofa letting the cassette tape recorder roll on
> the midsummer sun searing
> lively chatter of people meld into the salsa rhythms that waft by from somewhere
>   footsteps cross my vision, somehow familiar
> like pressing my ear to her breast, hearing the pulse of her heart
> this cumulation of memory, piling up over this city New York
> where is it they vanish to, these sounds once emitted?
>
> —Onda Aki, "Cassette Memories"

During the 1980s, the decade in which Noise began to coalesce into a transnational imaginary of popular music, you had to really want it to find it—

and if you found it, you found it on cassette. Mason Jones (author of the influential Noise zine *Ongaku Otaku*, and owner of the label Charnel House) became involved in international cassette exchange while living in Michigan, where mail order seemed like the best opportunity to reach out into the underground. "I discovered the cassette underground through *Sound Choice*, and some other zines dedicated to home recording. Nothing was going on in Ann Arbor in 1985, so I turned to mail order. . . . Eventually I got into the habit of writing to the artists I liked, and they usually responded to me." For home recordists like Jones, mail-order cassettes created an alternative to retail media distribution, which led to a new social network. Cassettes held out the possibility for a democratic independent media exchange that could leave industrial distribution behind, in a new world of grassroots access and reciprocity. By the mid-1980s, cassettes were included with magazines and sold at performances, and cassette-only programs had become a staple of college and local independent radio around the United States.

The emerging distribution networks of cassette culture provoked a sense of populist liberation from the recording industry. In his edited collection of essays, *Cassette Mythos*, Robin James captured the moment of radical democratization offered by cassette technology:

> The audiocassette is the perfect vehicle: inexpensive, portable . . . and accessible to anyone and everyone. They can be purchased in a department store or drug store for a dollar or two apiece. So if you have a couple of cassette recorders, you're ready to record, duplicate, and distribute cassettes of your music (or whatever) to as many or as few people as your desire and pocketbook allow. The cassette is the counterculture's most dangerous and subversive weapon. It is a threat, an incendiary device, the perfect tool for the cultural anarchist. It's a letter to your best friend in Wichita, or a record of your secret dream diary. You can use a cassette to make recordings of those new songs you just wrote—just you, your old guitar, a few pots and pans, a microphone, and a 4-track cassette recorder. . . . The mass media and big entertainment companies feel their monopoly on information and its dissemination slipping away—cassettes truly are the most democratic art form! (James 1992:vii–viii)

For James, the cassette was the ideal people's medium for sound. It was cheap, it was reusable, and its production could be individually controlled.

The cassette allowed its users to escape the role of passive consumption; perhaps most important for Noise, it could contain things beyond the scope of music.

Cassettes embodied the nascent ideologies of independent music, linking the open-ended accessibility of do-it-yourself production to a diversity of musical styles. Although audiotape technology had existed for decades, the spread of the cassette in the 1980s allowed small-scale amateur productions to be distributed as equivalents to commercial musical products. It was easy to make a recording outside of a studio, and recorders and media were inexpensive. Audiotape was a medium that could be under a single producer's control from start to finish, and the durability and size of the cassette made the final product mobile. The cassette culture offered a new world of music that could become practically and aesthetically independent from industrial production. Its social networks were as individualized and personal as its sonic objects were anonymous and obscure. As Robin James writes: "Every time you go to your mailbox you could be picking up little packages that contain impossible sounds: the stage whispers in empty rooms, the sound of echoing oceans, pop-tones—heck, it could be a message from someone you don't know, will never meet, and probably wouldn't know what to do if you met them anyway. Or someone with the key to what you need" (James 1992:ix).

Early cassette culture was socially grounded in a loose network of interpersonal contacts. Almost all cassette traders were musicians—whether primarily as performers or home recordists—and had discovered other experimentalists through print or broadcast media or in their travels. They began to send out cassettes in mail art exchanges, similar to those made famous by Fluxus and New York School of Correspondence artists who used the postal system to distribute their pieces to one another (Friedman 1995). Through these activities, many artists had amassed lists of addresses by direct person-to-person trading of unique homemade cassette recordings, and a few began to use these as a kind of micro-distribution network for new releases. These lists began to be shared in fanzines such as *Sound Choice*, *File 13*, and *Option*, which printed contact indexes for anyone interested in exchanging tapes.[8] Though composed primarily of North Americans, trading lists in magazines included contacts from Central and South America to Australia to Eastern Europe and, of course, Japan. Despite the rapid growth of the cassette culture in the 1980s through person-to-person contacts, its larger contours remained shadowy and fragmented. Listeners

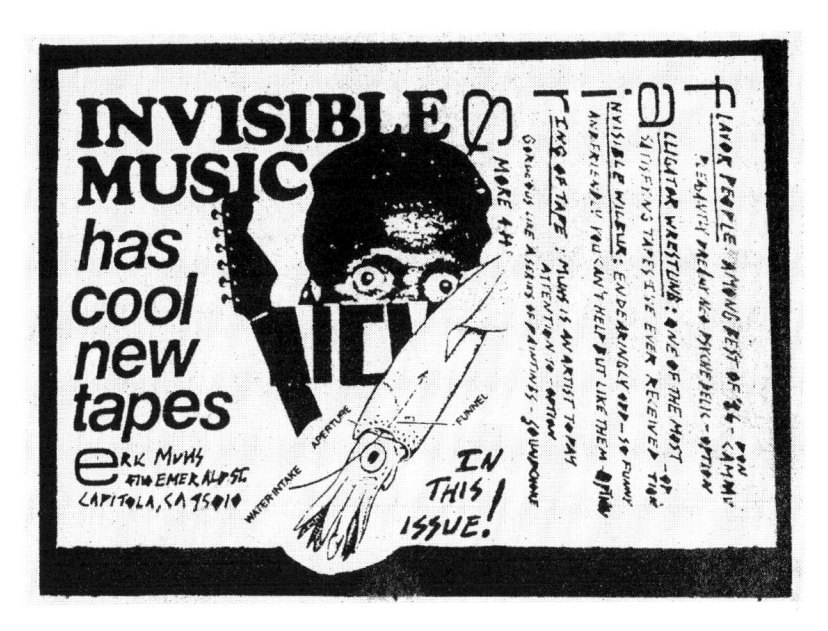

FREE CASSETTE CATALOG!-- Unknown musicians still roam the Earth. New Hat Music Co, 6751, N. Blackstone Ave. #108, Fresno, CA 93710.
MAILING LIST of Independent Radio Stations. More than 360 stations in the U.S., Canada and elsewhere. Stations playing cassettes are noted. Xerox or printed mailing labels--$12. Both for $20. Send check or money order to Lee Scott, P.O. Box 185, Newhall, CA 91321.
CASSETTE ONLY RADIO SHOW seeks cassettes for Canadian/U.S. airplay on CJAM-FM, to be hosted by independent cassette producer. We play all styles, the stranger, the better. Contact: Frank Pahl, P.O. Box 531, Wyandotte,

7.1. *Invisible Music* cassette label advertisement, mid-1980s.

7.2. *Sound Choice* "Unclassifieds," mid-1980s.

received tapes from friends, and also from total strangers, and they usually made sense of these mysterious new sounds in the absence of any background information at all beyond the creator's name and address.

The brief existence of Generator, a retail store and performance space opened by "Gen" Ken Montgomery in Manhattan's Lower East Side in 1984, illustrates the newly decentralized context of cassette culture. Generator eventually became a small, mail-order-only distribution company, but it briefly existed as a retail space for the cassette culture, offering the fruits of connections made through Montgomery's long-running personal trading. Generator's clientele reflected the density of experimental music listeners in downtown Manhattan, but its wares were not limited to the local scene. The tapes represented a diffused collection of isolated artists from anywhere and everywhere:

> It was all from people who lived somewhere by themselves and didn't have anyone to talk to, that really got into their thing, and sent out a cassette. And I remember at one point, someone came into Generator saying, "this could only happen in New York, New York is so rich [with] all this stuff here." But most of the stuff—the most interesting things at least—wasn't from any one place. The experimentation was coming from all over the world. It could be from Kansas or Spain or Long Island—it wasn't that there were more things from New York, it was just that I was located there.

For musicians who typically received little or no local response for their recordings, linking up with artists from distant countries could be especially motivating. Daniel Menche, based in the Pacific Northwest, told me that the first letter he received after sending out copies of his first recording was from a Japanese tape trader, who turned out to be Tano Koji (MSBR), a well-known Noisician from Tokyo: "I couldn't believe it. I had barely played any shows, and someone from JAPAN just wrote me! After that, it was just writing back and forth to people all the time—my postal bill got pretty significant each month."

The flexibility of cassette recorders also encouraged new experimental recording practices, such as collecting "found sounds" encountered in everyday life and creating spontaneous montages by editing directly in handheld machines. Like instant cameras, cassette recorders could capture daily experience in an almost accidental way. As New York City–based cassette sound artist Onda Aki relates, these casual recording practices could fuse the passing moments of everyday life into a layered sonic juxtaposition:

> Going about my life, walking about town, on my travels, I would press the record button whenever I came across a sound that I liked, and magnetically imprinted its memory onto tape. It was like a diary of sound. . . . After a while, the tapes began to pile up. They just piled up and soon storage space became a problem, so I then took these recorded tapes and randomly began layering new sounds onto them. It was fun to simply collect these sounds recklessly, innocently. After repeating this for a while, I realized that I had now wound up with some incredible sonic collages that just invented themselves. (Onda 2002)

With cassettes, one could capture sounds without being a recording artist and create music without inscribing it in a permanent record.

Through the collective anonymity of the mail networks, cassette traders also developed new techniques of mixing that blurred the lines of musical authorship. Using the newly minted technology of four-track cassette machines (first with the Teac 144, followed by the Tascam Porta series a few years later), tapers began to create multisited recordings based in layering individual contributions on top of one another. Recordists circulated tapes through the mail, each creating a track to add to the previous ones in a sort of auditory Exquisite Corpse, erasing sounds and recording again until all tracks were full or someone decided the collaboration was finished. Mail-based concerts, such as Conrad Schnitzler's famous Cassette Concerts series in Berlin, presented a selection of taped music to a remote audience, which was live-mixed by a local tape operator. Other cassette concerts were live-mediated collaborations, in which a performer improvised along with a preprepared recording by a distant contributor.[9] Cassette-only radio shows represented global "scene reports" as free-form sound mixes. "In 1988," Peter Courtemanche remembers, "I was doing radio, a weekly program of live noise art," which featured

> feedback, intense collage, crashing and banging, tape loops, field recordings (found sound), ethereal phone-in manifestations, everything from rough recordings (to be used as components of a larger mix) to finished works and cassette releases. Ron Lessard of RRRecords used to have an open call for cassette tapes. People from around the world would send him material, and he would use it live on-air and send

out copies of the resulting collages. In response to mail outs, artists sent back a variety of materials: audiotapes, CDs (which were very new back then), poems, books, zines, et cetera. (Courtemanche 2008)

Sometimes different cassettes were remixed into indistinguishable masses of sound. For example, when Sean Wolf Hill solicited cassettes for his *Tape Worm* compilation, he mixed the results freely by layering Noise tapes together with materials he qualified as "Pieces." Hill describes his spontaneous editing process: "What I got was a mixture of things: some simply-read prose and poetry, some semi-produced prose and poetry (with sounds in the background), some very long noise pieces, some cut-up noise, some multi-track noise, one sampler-derived alteration of an interview, some live readings, some media collages from records, radio, and TV, and one spontaneous alone-in-the-car drunk-driving rave-up. . . . Somewhat at random, I began to record the various submitted chunks of sound (Pieces and Noise) on different tracks . . . [in] kind of a wave effect, with one wave dying and another beginning" (Hill 1992).

Over time, the aesthetics of the cassette culture became iconic with sonic effects of its informal distribution. Copying an analog tape reduces or "rolls off" the treble frequencies. When an analog tape is copied over and over, each successive reproduction becomes increasingly murky and noisy. As cassettes were distributed in a person-to-person chain, the sound gradually degraded in particular ways. Cassettes emphasized midrange frequencies, tape hiss, wow-and-flutter, and effects of cumulative distortion generally described as "lo-fi" sounds. These textures eventually became aesthetic markers of the "classic" Noise recordings of the 1980s, which heavily influenced the sound of contemporary "harsh" Noise.[10] With each copy, the blurry contours of the original sound were further eroded, and the sound of Noise became more embedded within the cassette culture.

A STEREO RAINBOW OF JAPANOISE

In the 1990s, person-to-person mail exchanges ran parallel to a growing range of mail-order catalogs and fanzines, which eventually helped carve out a retail space for Noise in the indie music boom of the 1990s. In the United States, new distribution networks brought long-dormant underground styles to the surface of musical consumption in ways that threatened their integrity; 1991, to borrow the filmmaker Dave Markey's ironic phrase, was "the year Punk broke" (Markey 1992). In this context, participants in the cassette culture continued to amplify the value of marginality through linguistic and cultural differences of media circulation. If a cassette *could* contain anything—as James describes, "almost anything from anybody to anyone else"—the particular aesthetic priorities of the cassette culture grew out of the limitations of its self-reproducing network. As transnational media distribution strengthened in the 1990s, the anonymous networks of the cassette culture came under greater stress.

Thurston Moore (a member of the influential band Sonic Youth and an active cassette trader) reports the conflicted fallout from his 1996 remix of Ono Yoko's track "Rising," which incorporated material from Japanese Noise cassettes. Moore has long been an obsessive collector of Noise, and he regularly tours and collaborates with Japanese musicians.[11] After several tours of Japan and years of active postal correspondence, he had amassed, to his increasing anxiety, a huge collection of over nine hundred rare Japanese Noise cassettes (much of which, he admitted, he had never had a chance to listen to). When asked to provide a remix of Ono's song, Moore decided to put the Noise cassette collection to use:

> I went to this amazing studio in Manhattan. The Yoko tapes were there, as were two studio engineers prepared for a good two-days-minimum pro-remix. I brought my box of Noise. I pulled out cassettes, some wrapped in homemade gunk, and had the engineer fill up every open track on the song. There were many open tracks. I cranked Yoko's voice, closed my eyes and listened to the playback. When I yelled, "Go!" the engineer would toggle-switch the stereo rainbow of MSBR, The Geriogerigegege, Hanatarashi, Masonna, Solmania, Incapacitants, Violent Onsen Geisha, C.C.C.C., Hijokaidan, Aube, Monde Bruits and Keiji Haino into the mix, completely obliterating everything in its path. And when I yelled, "Stop!" he'd toggle it off. (Moore 1995:13)

But Moore's remix of Japanese Noise into Ono's song had to be sorted out retroactively with the individual participants: "Only problem: I didn't ask any of the artists for their permission. I told the record company to get clearance from each artist, and to compensate them fairly. The label received two responses from Japan. One was, 'Please use my music freely anywhere, anytime, anyplace!' and the other was, 'How dare Thurston Moore use our music and tell us afterward?!' I responded to all who had animosity and everything was ironed out, but I did get called a weird Japanese name by Hijokaidan" (Moore 1995:13). Moore had tapped into a seemingly endless flow of Japanese Noise as a dedicated participant in the cassette culture and found a creative way to project its anonymous force into a work by Japan's most famous experimentalist. But in the process of remixing Ono's song, the cassette culture was compressed into industrial contexts of authorship and intellectual property.

Ron Lessard's release of a demo cassette by Yamatsuka Eye's group Hanatarash on his RRR label in 1989 represents another controversial remediation of Japanese Noise cassettes. The story has become legendary gossip among Noise fans, and it reveals the fractures in the transition from the informal cassette culture of the 1980s to the burgeoning independent music circulation of the 1990s. As part of Lessard's desire to see Noise "graduate" from the cassette culture to vinyl, RRR took existing cassette releases and made them available in retail distribution on LP and CD. As Lessard recalls:

> Eye had mailed me a demo on a cassette with a simple hand written note that said "Will you release this as LP." So I listened to the cassette and said, "Okay, this is great, no problem." I wrote him back and said, "Okay, I will release this as an LP, please make me a cover." And he made me a cover, and I put the record out. But I made the record from his cassette, and apparently it was a demo, and he had made a reel-to-reel master and didn't tell me about it yet. If he had said "Don't release the cassette, I'm making a master," I wouldn't have, but I misunderstood what he was trying to tell me.

Lessard's story calls attention to the impact of linguistic and cultural differences in the transnational circulation of Noise. It also reflects the confusion between two overlapping contexts of musical distribution, represented by two different media formats. Eye viewed his cassette as an initial phase in the process of releasing an "official" record on an overseas label. He expected the recording would progress toward completion in several stages and presumed that nothing would be done until he sent a proper master on a professional media format (at that time, reel-to-reel tape), designed a cover, and so forth. Lessard, on the other hand, was used to receiving cassettes that were already being informally circulated as completed releases. RRR simply transferred their contents to the retail-ready formats of LP and CD, which enabled the cassettes to enter into a wider distribution to record stores. *Hanatarash 3* was caught between two overlapping media contexts—the participatory democracy of the cassette culture, and the entrepreneurial retail distribution of independent music.

The amorphous anonymity of mail exchange had made it easy to imagine the cassette culture as an open global network that connected individuals through shared experiences of sound. Noise tapes were not integrated into the retail marketplace, and they also avoided or actively deconstructed social identifications based in regional history, individual biography, genre, performance style, and so on. But by the mid-1990s, mail-based tape networks began to be challenged by the introduction of the CD and the growth of transnational retail distribution around the new digital format.[12] Many tapers continued to circulate their work exclusively in person-to-person barter networks of cassettes. But the equanimity of the 1980s cassette culture was threatened by the growing retail distribution of independent music in the 1990s. Small labels began to distribute their products through major labels, and the border between underground and mainstream circulation became increasingly stratified.

Marcel Mauss's notion of the gift economy, as David Graeber has pointed out, showed that barter networks are not merely unsophisticated premodern versions of commodity markets. Rather, they are ethical systems whose subjects emphasize social relations over economic efficiency and refuse to calculate exchange purely in terms of profit (Graeber 2004:21). In the 1980s, the cassette was an ideal object to cultivate independent circulations of Noise though the peculiar "in-between-ness" of barter. But cassettes had to remain separate from other modes of distribution, in a self-enclosed loop within which participants could "exchange things without the constraints of sociality on the one hand, and the complications of money on the other" (Appadurai 1986:9). In a contemporary barter system, objects of exchange must be made equivalent to one another by creating an alternative system of value outside of existing market and social forces. Noise cassettes continued to be traded, one-to-one, in a decentralized participatory network: to get Noise, you had to make Noise. As Noise recordings began to circulate into the rapidly consolidating consumer market for independent music in the 1990s, tape traders closed ranks around their interpersonal contacts.

One of the most active Japanese participants was Kyoto-based Nakajima Akifumi, whose G.R.O.S.S. label distributed his own recordings (as Aube), as well as Noise cassettes from Japanese, North American, and European artists. Nakajima gathered his initial list of contacts from the cover information on cassettes he bought through mail order: "During the late 1980s, I wrote a lot of letters to cassette labels, because I wanted to buy Noise cassettes from all around the world.... We communicated by letter often, and as we got to know each other, I began to write the artists whose cassettes I bought. I decided to make my own cassettes and sent everyone I knew letters about it, and eventually, through G.R.O.S.S., I turned from a big buyer into a big seller."

But the terms *buying* and *selling* do not exactly capture how Nakajima distributed G.R.O.S.S. tapes into the cassette culture. He sent most tapes to overseas musicians with whom he had begun to cultivate relationships, and because almost all of these "customers" were producers themselves, direct sales were usually supplanted by a tape-for-tape barter exchange. About 80 percent of his cassettes were distributed outside of Japan—40 percent to North America and 40 percent to Europe, almost all mailed directly to individual Noise artists of Nakajima's acquaintance. The remaining tapes were given away or traded with local Kansai musicians, and only a few cassettes were made available for purchase beyond the initial circle. Degrees of access were further marked by the quality of cassette tape. G.R.O.S.S. releases were often issued in a limited run of 50 type IV metal tapes, followed by a larger release of about 150 on cheaper type II chrome tapes. The notion of a "limited release" cassette tape seems completely arbitrary, because one obvious advantage of home-duplicated cassettes was the ability to generate new copies on demand. But because there were only two hundred tapes out there, a G.R.O.S.S. cassette was, from the first moment of its release, practically inaccessible to anyone who wasn't already in the loop.

Mail exchange of cassettes remained a robust context for Noise distribution through the end of the 1990s and into the early 2000s, even as home-burned CD-Rs, digital audiotapes (DAT), and MiniDiscs began to circulate alongside cassettes. Although physical formats of digital media had become increasingly affordable to produce, cassettes retained an inertial force among those already linked into cassette culture. Compared with CD-Rs, too, tapes simply worked better for international mail. The plastic housing of a cassette tape was more robust and more difficult to damage in transit than a CD, and they were predictably compatible with existing consumer playback equipment. Perhaps most important, the cassette culture had come to "house" Noise in ways that discouraged the adaptation of newer formats of physical media. Tape networks, developed over two decades, had helped a transnational group of participants create a self-constructed underground that sheltered Noise from the changing forces of the musical marketplace. In the space of only a few years, the cassette culture crashed directly into the social networks of the Internet, and then reformed in the shadow of online discourse.

REELING IN THE INTERNET

By the early 2000s, file sharing and other forms of digital distribution had radically rescaled the boundaries of global media circulation. Separated from physical formats, recordings could potentially be instantly available (to press a well-worn phrase into service) "to anyone with an Internet connection." Digital networks opened up a range of new possibilities to define and represent independent music in intermediated contexts of websites, blogs, and discussion boards. Most of these networks were developed in North America by young fans who began to make Noise recordings—and even more crucially, information and critical discourse about Noise—newly accessible online. In this context, the resurgence of the cassette culture can be seen as a reaction against the concentration of knowledge production in online networks, which privileged face-to-face contact and live performance to regenerate a social network of Noise outside of the Internet. This meant that cassette trading could become provincialized in local music scenes, even as Noise's online culture detached from existing contexts of transnational exchange.

By any account, Noise has a robust online presence, which continued to expand through the end of the first decade of the 2000s. Most first-time listeners now discover Noise online. Noisicians in any location can post their releases directly to web boards, MP3 blogs, and file sharing services like uTorrent and Soulseek. One can view video clips of shows on YouTube, read about the personal histories of performers, learn about upcoming performances, buy homemade electronic equipment, and discuss and trade recordings with other listeners on message boards, chat groups, and social networking sites. Curious browsers can find some form of historical information and access a variety of recordings almost immediately, even as the sudden abundance of online resources obviously clashes with underground values that prize obscurity and rarity (as in, for example, the ironic self-description of the MP3 blog *Terror Noise Audio* as "your one stop place for the best/hard-to-find extreme electronic music on the net").[13]

Japanese participants were relatively isolated from emergent online networks. As Costa Caspary and Wolfram Manzenreiter showed in an early study of Noise's online circulation, the development of Noise websites in the mid- to late 1990s did not immediately contribute to greater communication between Japanese and North Americans (Caspary and Manzenreiter 2003). Furthermore, the rapid growth of online channels had a fragmentary effect on existing contexts of transnational exchange, as North American Internet users increasingly predominated in the circulations and web representations of Noise. North American Noise networks now dwarf the presence of Japanese Noise, which, even in the 1980s and 1990s, was defined more by rumor than anything else. Even when Japanese Noisicians have created websites, they often remain beyond the scope of U.S.-based search engines, and there are few Japanese posters on the most established message boards or online exchanges of recordings.

These intercultural gaps reframe the putatively global scale of an online public sphere. Language difference is a powerful obstacle, both in the early predominance of English-language sites and in the difficulty of representing Japanese characters in HTML.[14] Despite common presumptions of its "ahead-of-the-curve" technological advancement, Japan was also slow to develop online infrastructures, and its Internet services took a different trajectory than that of U.S. networks. It might be expected that the tech-friendly and trend-obsessed Japanese would be early adopters of web-based technologies. But early Japanese Internet providers were stymied by Nippon Telegraph and Telephone's dominance of national telecommunications channels (Coates and Holroyd 2003; Ducke 2007). Even after a major government initiative in 2001 revamped platforms for Internet access over the next several years, Japanese have continued to use online services less than other industrialized publics (Esaki, Sunahara, and Murai 2008). Japanese computer users did not immediately take to online services like email and web browsing, in part because existing mobile phone (*keitai*) technologies were strongly established as resources for messaging and photo sharing (not to mention inspiring a new literary genre, the *ketai shôsetsu* or "phone novel"; Ito, Okabe, and Matsuda 2005). Home computers and laptops remained relatively uncommon into the early 2000s, as Internet access was structured by phone-based platforms for streaming, downloading, and sending media, instead of the computer-based browsing and file sharing tools that developed during the same period in United States. The rapid development of 3G phone technologies also allowed the

Japanese music industry to create resources for phone-based music downloads, which further reduced user migration to online channels of file sharing and web distribution (Condry 2004; Manabe 2009). In addition to linguistic and cultural barriers, these differences of digital media infrastructure further slowed Japanese participation in Internet music circulations, including early peer-to-peer and torrent networks.[15]

The online presence of Noise in the early 2000s, then, was defined among North Americans who developed an intermediated network of fan-created web pages, MP3 and video blogs, discussion boards, and social networking sites (i.e., MySpace, Facebook, Bandcamp, Last.fm) and collectively authored representations (e.g., Wikipedia entries). The majority of websites about Noise—harshnoise.com, iheartnoise.com, noisefanatics.com, noiseguide.com, and a few others—have been organized and frequented by North American participants (as are Facebook groups such as Harsh Noise Enthusiasts). Although there are a handful of bilingual Japan-based sites, most are posted in English only.[16] Even by the early 2010s, many well-known Japanese Noisicians do not yet have websites, and only a handful of Japanese labels have developed web-based sales portals to allow their recordings to be downloaded or ordered online. In addition, not many Japanese authors post recordings online or contribute directly to discussion boards about Noise. Individual posters can choose to remain anonymous, of course, and might change their names regularly (or lurk voyeuristically in ways that make their identity and even their presence difficult to register). But regular participants can quickly become known by their pseudonyms, and those who faithfully add or update material and engage in discussion with others rise quickly to the surface of group consciousness. The contributions of frequent posters are often referenced in links by other regular contributors, and frequently asked questions can quickly be resolved by pointing to an archive of earlier discussions about Noise.

Like the cassette culture, the online Noise network was built around the contributions of its most active participants. Whereas the cassette culture grew through barter exchange of recordings between fellow producers, Noise's online communities converged through open access to crowd-sourced knowledge. Individuals could participate in knowledge construction in ways that reflected little or no stake in Noise's complexities. In an especially ironic example, the wiki for the Japanese Noisician Guilty Connector was deleted from Wikipedia in April 2008 (although a dead link still lingers in the "List of Japanoise artists" page). The user Jon513, who nominated the article for deletion, argued that Guilty Connector was not "notable" under the criteria for "musicians" in the guidelines for the WikiProject on Music. At this time, the criteria for notability as a musician on Wikipedia included being the subject of "reliable" and "non-trivial" (e.g., non-self-published) articles and books; the production of music that has won awards, been certified gold, placed on national music charts, or received significant rotation on broadcast media; or the release of recordings on a major label or "one of the more important indie labels" that has "a history of more than a few years and with a roster of performers, many of which are notable." Jon513's challenge was cited under the tag "Musician fails WP:Music."[17]

Predictably, the backlash against Internet Noise communities was forceful among those invested in earlier contexts of exchange. Even for Japanese participants, the problem was not necessarily the overabundance of North American representatives or their lack of connection to existing social networks of Noise. Few objected to the open exchange of Noise recordings on anonymous file sharing platforms either, and many took advantage of the opportunity to freely distribute their recordings digitally in peer-to-peer and torrent networks.[18] Rather, it was the shift toward the production of discourse *about* Noise that violated the social and aesthetic values of the cassette culture. Noise recordings circulated online with other information—historical background, discographies, criticism, and other commentary—which predominated over the unmarked exchange of sound content. One Noisician complained bitterly (in the context of requesting anonymity in this book) about the advent of the Internet: "I hate *information*! Fuck the Internet world! When we were children, there were so many mysteries . . . that was fun for me. I want people to focus on *sounds*, not *information*."

Despite these protests, Noise was an ideal subject for the "recursive publics" of online culture, which constantly generate, modify, document, and maintain their own infrastructures (Kelty 2008). Active participants construct the network by contributing new materials, correcting and expanding existing knowledge, reiterating common references, and developing open archival structures that can be searched and linked to other bodies of shared information. Community formation also produces conflicts and internal struggles. Working against the consensus of crowdsourced knowledge are "trolls" and "griefers" who take advantage of the transparent open process of Internet dialogues by posting antagonistic, irrelevant, and disruptive messages on Noise discussion forums and edit online content by replacing commentary with nonsensical and often prurient responses, "just for the lulz" (just for laughs).[19] For most who came in search of Noise online, this simply meant that a Google search would produce more results. Even if many of these links did not necessarily match up with one another, they formed a breadcrumb trail back into the loops of online discourse.

In this context, the audiocassette returned Noise to the underground with a vengeance. Through its persistent materiality, the cassette helped listeners imagine a participatory network that was not just socially and aesthetically divergent but seemingly incommensurable with online circulation. Even as the contents of Noise cassettes were mediated into open digital networks, the tapes themselves became increasingly inaccessible.

PLAYING HARD TO GET

The cassette is a symbol of everything that independent music once was (but is not), and everything that the Internet could be (but is not): something free from commercial production, and also something not immediately available—a *thing* that takes effort to find, but that you can hold on to, and that stays in place. In this, the cassette mirrors the cultural authenticity of the vinyl LP, which remains the strongest contemporary icon of analog music and its most tangible fetish object. But unlike cassettes, LPs evoke the face-to-face sociality of the record shop, a public sphere of music consumption that remains a crucial aspect of their continued appeal.[20] In contrast to the nostalgic audiophilia of vinyl—often claimed to possess superior "natural" sound and acoustic "warmth" lacking from digital reproductions—the cassette represents sonic degradation and material flimsiness, marking its lesser status as a medium of musical preservation. Because it must be physically traded, transported, and stored, the cassette tape embodies the creative limits and the efforts of exchange that separate Noise from digital circulations. In a context of open digital access, the cassette serves as a reminder of Noise's aesthetics of inaccessibility.

Noise cassettes are manipulated and reconstructed to represent the "hard-to-get" qualities of their circulation. In their overworked physical forms, they sometimes seem more like conceptual artworks than containers of musical content (figure 7.3). Since the early days of the cassette culture, Noise tape makers have transformed the physical appearance of cassettes by altering or building onto their cases or onto the plastic housing of the cassettes themselves. Cassettes are wrapped in gauze, burned and bent, glued to books or leaves, and hung in spools of wire. Tapes are covered in paint or hardened epoxy, requiring the listener to chip the excess material away and possibly damage the housing beyond repair before it can even be played. By complicating the listener's access to the sound within, the physical design of Noise cassettes symbolizes their separation from the world of musical commodities. Sometimes the sound is literally inaccessible—for example, by encasing a cassette in concrete or melting the housing so it cannot be played at all. In other cases, recorded content is completely absent. *This Is Shaking Box Music / You Are Noisemaker*, a release by Yamanouchi Juntaro's Geriogerigegege, consisted of a metal box full of one hundred blank "C-0" tapes; as the title suggests, recipients must make the Noise for themselves.[21]

Other cassettes simply make the listener work harder to access the recorded sound. For one tape on his Soundprobe label, Seth Misterka attached each copy (of twenty in the limited edition of the release) to a small board, screwing the cassette down through the sprocket holes with two large wood screws. ("I felt like it should take a little more effort to hear this," he told me, "since it took so much more effort get it out there.") A few altered cassettes are literally unique, having been issued in an edition of a single copy. Although Noise cassettes can be released as one-off editions and collected as singular pieces, they rarely cross over to be cataloged or sold as artwork. On the other hand, there is not enough critical mass in Noise circulations to standardize the values of cassettes in an independent collectors' market (like that of jazz records, for example). Instead, Noise cassettes remain unintegrated, floating between separated individual encounters. Their appearance in the marketplace is strange and divergent, like a unique personal mix tape that somehow accidentally turned up for sale.

Some Noise labels record new releases over discarded copies of commercial cassettes. The *RRRecycled* series, for example, was created by dubbing new recordings by Noise artists over random cassettes by pop megastars (e.g., REO Speedwagon). As part of a series of "cheap Noise," *RRRecycled* tapes are reproduced on misaligned recording decks, and ghostly echoes of the original tracks seep up through the imprinted layers of Noise. Faint traces of Mötley Crüe can be heard beneath the blasts of sound on a Masonna recording, or the tail end of a track by Cher will suddenly pop up at the end of a tape by Burning Star Core. Of course, any Noise recording,

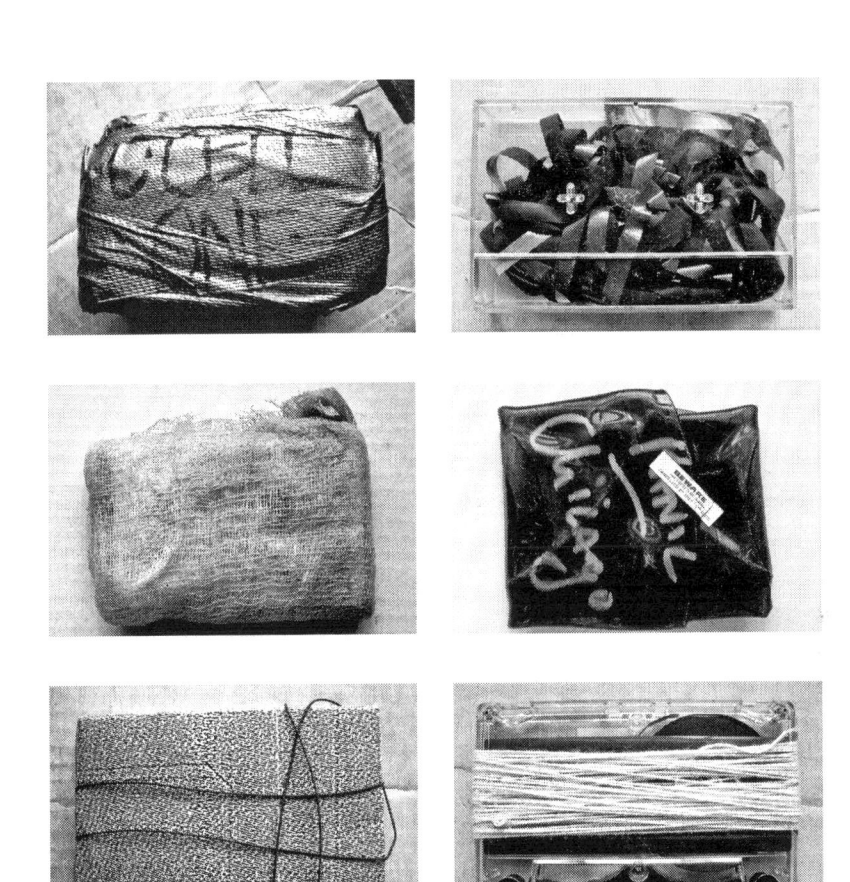

7.3. Cassette tapes from the collection of Generator Sound Art.
Photos by the author.

too, could easily be dubbed over and erased by something else. The cassette calls out to the listener's judgment, to decide whether this particular thing contains something singular and beautiful, or something cheap and disposable. It inspires attention to the ephemeral qualities of musical creativity in a commodity cycle, asking its recipients to recognize the fleeting life of a sound that begins to fade away almost as soon as it has been heard. But the cassette also stresses the personal effort involved in creating something and giving it to someone else. The handicraft of analog reproduction reminds listeners of the need for social reciprocity in participatory networks. If you're going to bother to hold on to Noise, the cassette seems to tell its recipients, make it a handle to something else.

The Future of Cassette Culture | 219

HOME TAPING IS KILLING MUSIC (BUT SAVING NOISE)

Since the end of the first decade of the 2000s, there has been a resurgence of new Noise labels in cities across the United States, including Heavy Tapes, American Tapes, Fuck It Tapes, Baked Tapes, Hanson Records, Hidden Fortress, Gods of Tundra, and many others. Most of these are heavily oriented toward cassettes; many release cassettes exclusively, often focusing on productions of a specific local scene. Prices tend to be particularly low in comparison with other formats—between $3 and $7 per cassette—and labels typically trade as many tapes as they sell. Like the 1980s cassette culture, labels often release cassettes in limited editions of fifty to seventy-five tapes, and sometimes as few as ten. One might wonder what kind of public could be formed by such a limited context of exchange, or whether this circulation should be considered public at all. But Noise cassettes are remediated into a parallel world of digital representation on the Internet. Tapes are photographed and described in online reviews, and their sonic contents are digitized and posted for download on Noise web boards, file sharing services, or cassette-oriented MP3 blogs such as *Cassette Gods* (figure 7.4), *Chewed Tapes*, and *Noise Not Music*. Cassette labels post images and sound samples on their websites, and some make the contents of cassettes available for online downloading. Noise cassettes, then, did not remain offline, but fed back into digital circulation.

Mirror Universe Tapes, for example, sells cassette tapes online via mail order but includes free download codes that allow the purchaser to download a digital version ("we ripped the tape so you don't have to").[22] The majority of Mirror Universe's tapes are limited to one hundred copies or fewer, and most cassettes are listed as sold out. Many can be hunted down on blogs that repost the cassettes as streaming audio or provide download links hosted at file lockers (RapidShare, MediaFire, MultiUpload, and so on). This does not necessarily constitute a digital archive of Noise recordings, which might be permanently accessed online. Download links go out of date quickly and blog posts—as well as the blogs themselves—disappear. But more important, the physical instability of the cassette reveals its origins in a hidden world of Noise that cannot properly be accessed on the Internet. For example, a post on Patient Sounds' site announced the availability of a new four-tape package: the cassettes could be ordered via mail for $25, but they were also freely accessible for immediate download. The poetic blurb for the release contrasts the openness of digital distribu-

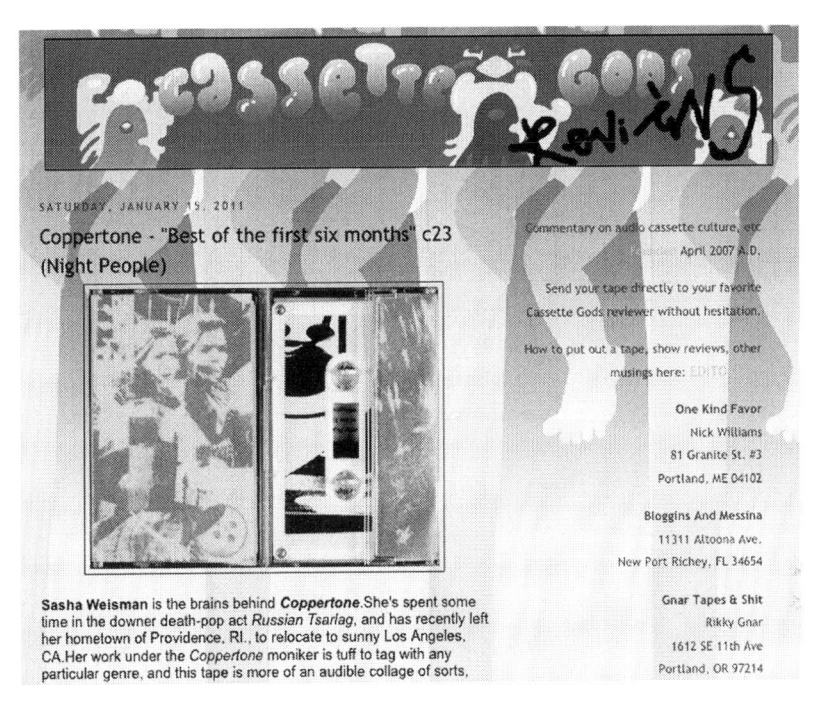

7.4. Front page of *Cassette Gods* blogspot site, January 15, 2011. Courtesy of George Myers.

tion with the limitations of physical exchange that represent the promise of social connections in the real "scene":

> remember to download for free....
> forever...
> and give to your friends
> but remember that we are only making 100 of each of these tapes EVER
> so
> order up friends
> and see you soon[23]

Online remediations of cassette culture join two seemingly contradictory movements, which tack differently toward the goal of musical independence. Noise tapes revitalize the person-to-person barter exchange of physical media ("we are only making 100 of each of these tapes EVER") to renew a self-contained North American independent music scene based in face-to-face social contact ("see you soon"). At the same time, their self-contained limits encourage a profusion of Internet circulations, in which cassettes are digitized, cataloged, reviewed, discussed, photographed, and redistributed in an unrestricted context ("download for free . . . and give to your friends"). The social copresence of contemporary local Noise scenes is imbued with these ghostly traces of digital circulation. In the new cassette culture, independent media exchange is balanced against "virtual" online formations of knowledge.

The idea of a digital cassette complicates the social mediation of the Internet that Henry Jenkins describes as "convergence culture." Media convergence broadly describes the concentration of media networks in centralized infrastructures—Internet resources such as blogs, web pages, search engines, and so forth—which generate new audiences and combine different formats in "intermediated" modes of consumption and representation (Higgins 1989 [1966]; Jenkins 2006; van Dijk 1999). As a medium that is, at least in its material form, divergent from digital circulations, the Noise cassette puts pressure on the convergence of online culture in two ways. First, it represents an idealized object of musical creativity that cannot be fully absorbed into new media, even as its contents are remediated for digital exchange. Second, its obstinate material form requires Noise audiences to maintain systems of distribution based in face-to-face encounters. Cassette networks appear to occupy a separate world from the Internet, even as their conditions of circulation cannot fully diverge from those of online access. In this, the contemporary Noise cassette flips the circulatory project of the 1980s cassette culture on its head. Where the cassette was once the anonymous vehicle of global grassroots media, it is now a talisman of the discrete local scene.

Cassettes tapes highlight the coincidental, ephemeral qualities that accrue to social participation in a musical underground. Person-to-person exchanges distinguish individual constructions of Noise from the collective archives of digitally accessible materials. Like many other North American Noisicians, Jessica Rylan (a.k.a. Can't) rarely buys or downloads recordings but chooses instead to trade cassettes directly with fellow performers in the course of her touring schedule. She described tape trading as a way of restricting her musical consumption to a network of friends: "I guess I'm prejudiced about recordings. It's so easy to make recordings now that in a way, it's hard to listen to a recording unless I know something about it and have some personal connection—like I know who made it, or kind of what it's about, or that a good friend liked it or something." In an overflowing production of musical objects, cassettes carry the uncommon virtue of allowing their listeners to reconstruct Noise in a sphere of personal encounter. By limiting her consumption of recordings to tapes made by friends (or friends of friends), Rylan stresses the heightened meanings of a "handmade" social context.

Noise cassettes are distributed through unpredictable person-to-person encounters that undermine standard timetables of media production. Rather than producing tapes as "releases" in a media cycle, Noisicians make tapes available on an ad hoc basis through exchange at shows or on the street. These do not always represent the latest "album" by an individual artist. They can be mix tapes, older solo projects, collaborations or "splits" with other artists, or unique one-offs that are made for a single listener. One Noisician described cassettes as "calling cards" that are given to make people aware of his work in general. As he explained, the gift of a cassette is also imbued with a social force that surpasses its content: "It's something that I can just give you, that I can hand to you and you can take home and maybe listen to; but even if you don't, it's like—here's something between me and you, that I gave to you." Playback depends on a technical requirement that further distinguishes participants in the cassette culture by requiring that they own and maintain obsolete hardware. After attending a number of live shows and slowly amassing a collection of tapes given by potential friends and collaborators, an uninitiated new listener must find a way to listen. Tape decks equip the listener to access the hard-to-get sounds of the cassette culture. But they also allow their owners the possibility of further participation by recording their own tapes to trade with others.

Beyond one's own contacts, it is difficult to keep track of what is going on in the cassette culture. To really know where a tape is coming from, you have to receive it from someone personally or put it into circulation yourself. As the local scene is brought into relief, the horizon of Noise's larger circuitry becomes increasingly blurry, and distant contacts can easily fade into the background. Of course, this distinction was always the point: to close the loops of participatory media back down to personal experience. Standing on this self-determined ground, a larger world of Noise is built from coincidental encounters and mysterious discoveries. As one Brooklyn-based taper put it, "We know most of the people in our circle, and it's a big city . . . [but] maybe, on the opposite side of the street, there's a parallel circle" (Jarnow 2009).

ENJOY IT (WILL YOU HAVE IT)

Social networks, and their objects, change quickly. In less than a decade, the audiocassette was transformed from a standard, taken-for-granted commodity of popular media to a resistant emblem of underground culture. Its visual trace has become increasingly important in contemporary art and design, sometimes as a kitschy, retro item of nostalgic irony. For some, the image of the cassette reflects the superficial innocence of 1980s pop culture and channels a purer, simpler, and more authentic relationship to popular music consumption. But the cassette is also a symbol of populist resistance to copyright law and corporate enforcements of intellectual property ownership, symbolized by a recent flood of ironic appropriations of the famous cassette-and-crossbones logo, originally developed by British record industry groups as part of an antibootlegging campaign in the mid-1980s. In one example, the online advocacy group Downhill Battle used the image in a T-shirt campaign to raise money for the defendants of copyright violation lawsuits, but they changed the famous caption "Home Taping Is Killing Music (and It's Illegal)" to "Home Taping Is Killing the Music Industry (and It's Fun)" (figure 7.5).

In the early decades of the twenty-first century, the commodity form of music seems increasingly up for grabs. Corporate-driven political anxiety about digital media impacts the growth of online music communities, even as media piracy and access to illegal content become entrenched in everyday life. In January 2012, this was marked by the takedown of file-hosting service MegaUpload, a few days after the public pushback against proposed antipiracy legislation forced the U.S. Congress to reconsider laws that would restrict access to sites and networks accused of copyright infringement.[24] National regulations of Internet media have influenced geopolitical developments, as well as impacting the subjectivities of citizens around the world. As musical circulations continue to become concentrated in informal online economies, they also endanger their own continuity, as entire channels of exchange and consumption are made illegal (even if, as in the case of MegaUpload, most content is not illegal). In this context, any circulation that appears to be independent from the extreme freedoms and controls of the Internet can generate a powerful, almost magical context of social remediation.

The cassette returns attention to social values of underground media that have been radically redefined in the context of digital networks. It

7.5. "Home Taping Is Killing the Music Industry" T-shirt. Courtesy of Nicholas Reville of Downhill Battle.

demonstrates how the marginal, seemingly inconsequential productions of Noise contribute to the cultural imaginaries of participatory media. Cassette culture shows that participation in a social network is a hard-fought aspect of creative work and not just a given aspect of communication. Its limitations also show that accessibility and creativity do not always progress in equal measure and reveal how the Internet can overshadow and restrict coterminous forms of offline social exchange. Finally, the cassette has allowed Noise to duck back and forth between contexts of online circulation and the darkness of a different kind of anonymous sociality. Its bearers carry the flame of Noise forward, into the productive mysteries of future undergrounds.

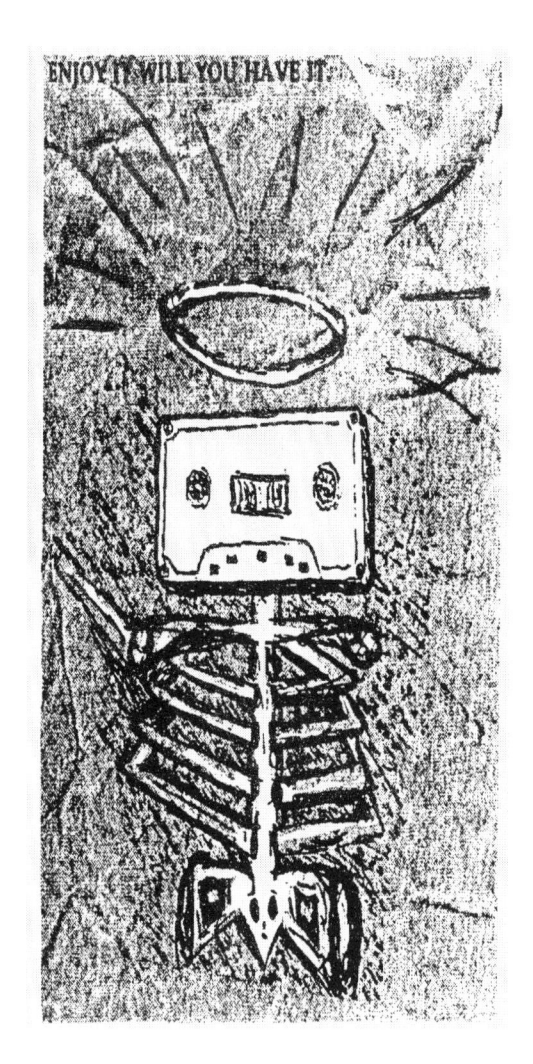

7.6. "Enjoy It Will You Have It," drawing by mR. dAS from Big City Orchestra's *The Four Cassettes of the Apocalypse* (1991; The Subelectrick Institute 1). Courtesy of mR. dAS.

EPILOGUE

"can't" understand music—

a dream
an antagonism
a way to live like you wished
a way to face the horror—
a way of testing limits
a way to transgress—
(or to transcend?)

—Jessica Rylan (Can't)

A STRANGE HISTORY

As I complete this book in 2012, the world of Noise I encountered in my fieldwork can only be considered historical. Noise has proliferated well beyond the contexts I describe in my ethnographic research, and its cultural locations shifted many times during the course of my writing. In the later part of the first decade of the 2000s, Noise experienced a major surge in the United States, with performers such as Wolf Eyes, Jessica Rylan, Nautical Almanac, John Weise, Prurient, Burning Star Core, Yellow Swans, and others cresting on its newest wave. Influential local Noise scenes continue to develop, and Noise performance festivals are now common across North America, from Rhode Island to Michigan to Oregon.[1] Some long-term participants have even described the current moment to me as a "golden age of Noise," in which "Americanoise" is more popular and diverse than ever before. Japan is no longer at the center of this narrative. After a decade defined by the combination of continued economic downturn and the global restructuring of media distribution in online networks, Japanese performers have only recently begun to reestablish a presence in North American Noise. This, too, has often been limited to select legendary figures of Japanoise, such as Incapacitants and Merzbow, who now belong to a "classic" early period in Noise's stylistic development. Even as this unstable cycle spins forward into its fourth decade, its feedback is still experienced as a new and unheard-of sound—now emanating from a North American scene at the global center of Noise.

In all of these ways, Noise might seem to trace a developmental arc instead of a loop. But Noise is not a stable object of history. It is always at the threshold of newness, at the edge of some moment just about to happen. Noise is not always emergent, it is endlessly submergent. Sounds are called "noise" before they are recognized for any specific creative or communicative function. In the annals of musical history, from Stravinsky, to jazz, to rock, to rap, new musical forms have always first been heard as noise. To extend the rule into contemporary musical consumptions, it seems as if anything now called Noise must inevitably one day become generally accepted as music; as if all forms of newness and difference will eventually become normal and ordinary in the future. But this staging of musical circulation does not adequately describe the productive obscurity of Noise, which cycles in and out of recognition with unpredictable and incomplete movements. As long as it continues to be submerged in circulation, Noise has a special power. Its definitive form is always held off, even as its creative force can be experienced here and now by anyone willing to listen.

I have described Noise in this process of musical and cultural feedback, marked by its capital N, as a specific genre created through its special aesthetics of recording and performance; through techniques of listening and social interpretations of sound; in practices of international exchange and the formation of individual subjectivities. I have also shown the relationship of Noise to more general frames of "noise" (with a lowercase n) that circulate in public discourse. Increasingly, the concept of noise has become an essential reference for the incalculable effects of globalization and technological fragmentation on the human condition. The rise of noise has become the new grand narrative of transnational circulation, but at the same time it is recognized as an essential object of cultural relativism. It is in our senses of sound, of communication, place, experience, and subjectivity. It is everywhere and nowhere to be found.

Over the past few years, noise has become a subject of scholarly attention that cuts across history, anthropology, musicology and ethnomusicology, comparative literature, media studies, cognitive science, and studies of science and technology. Historians and critical theorists have shown that noise was used to characterize racial, ethnic, and class differences in contexts ranging from the earliest projects of colonialism to contemporary urban societies (Cockayne 2007; Cruz 1999; Picker 2003; Radano 2003; Rath 2003; Smith 2001; Schwartz 2011; Thompson 2002). Social identifications of noise are embedded in the soundscapes of modernizing nations, inscribed by new technologies of communication, transportation, mechanization, and military force (Bijsterveld 2008; Evens 2005; Goodman 2009; Sterne 2003). Environmental contexts of noise echo the destructive impact of the built world on the human senses; noise represents the suppression of social discourse in the clamor of industrial societies, and the loss of natural silence (Keizer 2010; Nakajima 1996; Prochnik 2010; Sim 2007). But noise might also represent an emergent cosmopolitan sensibility, which can fold the radical incommensurabilities of global culture into new social identities (Ferguson 1999; Povinelli 2001).

Noise is an attractively fluid metaphor to revitalize scholarly inquiries about music and culture. Its unclassifiable nature undermines constructions of knowledge and conjures universal human experience even from the incalculable differences of global modernities. But cultural productions of noise often fade into the background. Too often, noise occupies a negative space. Its borders can never be filled in, but are otherwise isomorphic with what is called "culture." Like the term *culture* itself, it is easy to make a *thing* of noise without ever saying what kind of thing it is or what it does. The discourse of noise has been expanded with sweeping theoretical gestures and expansive claims of its synchronic recurrence across history. Some narratives take for granted its unity as a sonic object; others render its psychic effects as sonic excess, pain, and even torture, without touching on the diverse embodiments and interpretations of sound that they press into service for an ideal aural subjectivity.

As a universal opposite, Noise frames many dialectical forms of knowledge:

Noise is the opposite of music, as the antithesis of beautiful things admissible as art; this noise pertains to aesthetics and affective modes of cultural expression.
Noise is the opposite of classification, in its violations of categorical objectivity; this noise stands at the margins of musical history and typologies of style and form.
Noise is the opposite of communication, against meaningful transmis-

sions of information; this noise embeds discourse in a binary signal-to-noise relationship.

Noise is the opposite of the natural world, and its silence; this noise emerges from the urban industrialized environment and in technological conditions of social production, regulation, and control.

Noise is the opposite of public consensus and corporate and state-ordered collectivity; this noise relates to the mediation of subjectivity by overlapping projects of globalization, cultural nationalism, local infrastructure, and subcultural identity.

Finally, the oppositional subject of noise requires its own opposite: a stable and continuous culture against which it can take shape as an interruptive force of creativity and change. Noise—like music used to—offers a new universal language of difference. It is a black box that allows a vast array of systems, structures, and processes to be transposed against its own unknowable form. In discovering the rich possibilities of noise as an independent subject, we cannot lose sight of its constitutive role in specific formations of musical culture. Noise is constantly feeding back into music. Noises circulate as music, are perceived as music, are spoken about and compared to music, and are made meaningful in the reflexive loops of musical consciousness.

Jacques Attali's book *Noise: The Political Economy of Music* (1977) has been among the most influential critical theories of noise. In Attali's utopian Marxist critique of musical production, noise is a subversive, antihegemonic force of social resistance. For him, noise was the foundation of human expression before it was absorbed into late capitalist cultural production. In this context, where music represents "a society of repetition in which nothing will happen anymore," he argues that noise can prophesy social futures and become an oracle of cultural change (Attali 1985 [1977]:5). But on its entry into the market economy, noise is transformed into music through a ritual "sacrifice" that channels its creative newness into rationalized production. In becoming a commodity, music becomes a tool of regulatory power. Music makes people forget about violence and disorder, represses their subjectivity and silences their embodied experiences of sound, and then makes them believe in the spectacle of its harmonious social order. Noise represents the elemental forces of creativity that interrupt these commercial and technological repetitions. It is a herald of change that "creates a problem in order to solve it": "by listening to noise, we can better understand . . . what hopes it is still possible to have" (Attali 1985 [1977]:2, 29).

Attali's great insight was to recognize that noise always precedes, and then eventually becomes, music. But his dream of a purely oppositional noise is difficult to reconcile with cultural practice. In his formulation, noise constantly feeds into musical culture, yet noise itself can never be integrated into cultural subjectivity. How can noise remain outside of music, when it is constantly absorbed in musical circulations? Music began as noise, Attali argues, until it was unlinked from its creative origins and silenced through repetition. To distinguish creative noise from the commodity form of music, he redefines "composition" as new processes of soundmaking, "in which the musician plays primarily for himself, outside any operationality, spectacle, or accumulation of value": the creation of noise, then, is "an activity that is an end in itself" (Attali 1985 [1977]:135). Attali's notion of composition is particularly focused on then-emergent styles of free jazz and electronic music, which he celebrates as embodied but socially unintegrated forms of noise. But no noise begins or ends in itself. As Attali recognizes, these countercultural projects were already feeding back into musical circulation at the moment of their emergence: "what is noise to the old order," he says, "is harmony to the new" (Attali 1985 [1977]:35).

This eternal "suicide of form" ensures that despite its oppositional force, Attali's noise cannot be unbound from a Romantic, transcendent context of music. Because it represents an unintegrated creativity, its practices and traits can never enter into the spinning wheel of musical systems. For Attali, noise can only exist outside of technological mediation. Its open-ended forms must remain separate from their own political agency and from their role in developing spectacular differences of representation and repetition. Because Attali's noise is prophetic, it cannot be functional in the present, and it cannot be mixed with or influenced by existing musical practices. It cannot be collected, evaluated, or exchanged beyond unique moments of performance. Most crucially, this noise cannot address the differences among its creative subjects, even in their starring role as icons of pure difference. In proposing a process of composition that could exist outside of the eternal struggle between music and noise, Attali does not move far enough away from the site of resistance to imagine a productive culture of noise. Instead, he splits the cycle of noise and music down the middle, freezing both sides in place. But a separate realm of noise can only emerge in relation to a noise-free musical culture, and no such thing could ever exist.

Noise exceeds its formulation as a totalizing category of difference, whether in sound or social discourse. The Noise I describe here did not emerge through its pure distinctions from Music but in the overlapping and repetitive feedback between "noise" and "music," "local" and "global," "old" and "new" that generates new modes of musical and social experience. Even when these fluctuations of identity, production, mediation, and creative practice are drawn into specific and observable loops of sound and performance, Noise does not settle. Its identity is continually absorbed, restructured, and regenerated by musical circulation. As people learn to hear, feel, and create Noise, its movements flow into a circle that might appear to be continuous and unbroken. But without the constant ruptures of feedback, it fades into the background.

Noise, it almost goes without saying, has changed. When I came into this loop, it had already changed beyond comprehension. "Noise is over," some said, and moved on to new ground; others stayed and renamed the territory. People changed, their playing changed, their listening changed. These changes faded into an ongoing field of creativity. Over time, things unfold, and build up in people's lives. Noise becomes part of a personal cycle. Some artists who were reluctant to historicize Noise have begun to write narratives about their past, including the members of Hijokaidan, who recently collaborated on the memoir *Hijokaidan: A Story of the King of Noise* (Hiroshige et al. 2010). Going the way of many other niche record stores over the past few years, the Alchemy Music Store in Shinsaibashi has closed down, but still distributes label material through an online storefront.[2] Yamazaki Takushi (Masonna) and Fusao Toda (Angel'in Heavy Syrup, Christine 23 Onna) continue to run their brick-and-mortar vintage clothing store Freak Scene in the same building. Akita Masami continues making Merzbow recordings, now as part of a new political mission to raise consciousness about animal rights. Many of his recent recordings—including *Bloody Sea* (which makes reference to controversial Japanese whaling practices), *F.I.D.* ("Fur Is Dead"), and *13 Japanese Birds* (a set of thirteen CDs each based on an individual species)—support the activist group PETA (People for the Ethical Treatment of Animals), and he writes about veganism on his blog and in his recent book *My Vegetarian Life* (Akita 2005).[3]

Filth the Sleep, who spearheaded the regeneration of harsh Noise in the early 2000s, has begun to work more closely in Kansai's grindcore circles, even as he moved to a remote mountaintop between Osaka and Kobe. Fujiwara Hide returned to Kyoto after fifteen years in New York City to live with his aging parents, re-form a Japanese version of his long-running group Ultra Bidé, and create a weekly performance series called "Happy Noise Monday." Hiroshige Jojo closed his baseball card shop and moved back to Osaka to begin a new career as a fortune-teller (his shop, named after the Can album of the same name, is called Future Days). The rebirth of Noise in the United States, exemplified by projects like the No Fun Fest, is now long past its infancy. In 2010, the No Fun Fest became a victim of its own success, as organizer Carlos Giffoni put the project on hold to "refocus energies and plan new directions," but there are new Noise festivals starting every year.[4] Some passed on during the course of this research, including much regretted lost friends Tano Koji (MSBR), Iwasaki Shohei (Monde Bruits), and Hugh McIntyre (Nihilist Spasm Band), whose gifts of words and sounds I hope are returned in this book.

I close with a final story that returns to the beginning. I am sitting on a bench with Hiroshige Jojo during a brief North American tour in 2005. We are outside of the recording studio at a local radio station in London, Ontario, where the members of Hijokaidan await the interview that I described in the introductory pages of this book. I have been filming and taking photographs of the group all morning at Art Pratten's house, as the group prepared their equipment for that evening's performance at the Forest City Gallery downtown. We sit in silence in the lobby. After a few minutes, Jojo turns to me with a curious look and says, "So . . . why are you still interested in this? Why do you care about Noise?" I answer with a confused list of all the reasons and motivations that come to the front of my mind—recounting my initial surprise that this extreme style seemed to emerge from Japan, the fascination with the sounds that I had encountered so far, the interesting people who were involved and their perspectives on music and life, the possibilities to describe cultural politics and global relationships through sound—but the only real answer, I tell him, is that I still don't know what Noise is, and I didn't think I was going to end up knowing anyway. Jojo looks relieved—he leans back against the wall again, nods, laughs, and says, "Good."

NOTES

INTRODUCTION

1 I conducted fieldwork in Japan beginning with short research trips in 1998 and 2001, and returned for a year for primary fieldwork in 2002–2003. I spent another year of fieldwork in the United States (New York, Providence, and San Francisco) and Canada (London, Ontario) during 2003–2004, and returned to Japan again in 2007 and 2012. I acknowledge the support of Fulbright, the Social Science Research Council, the Andrew W. Mellon Foundation, and the Society of Fellows in the Humanities at Columbia University for funding my research.

2 Noise performers sometimes describe themselves with the word *Noisician* to differentiate their practices from the instrumental performance of musicians. Others consider this word unbearably corny, but I use it here to maintain the crucial difference it implies between Noise performance and musicianship.

3 As I describe in chapter 6, Japanese anime has populated North American television since 1961 when Tezuka Osamu's *Atom Boy* was distributed in the U.S. market as *Astro Boy*. A continuous succession of exports followed (including *Speed Racer*, *Star Blazers*, *G-Force*, *Pokémon*, *Yu-Gi-Oh!*, etc.), all of which were adapted from Japanese programs (Allison 2000). While a recent fandom has arisen around anime that strongly recognizes (even fetishizes) its Japaneseness, early adaptations in the U.S. market were most often left without any trace of Japanese

sources. Asian adaptations of Japanese pop culture, on the other hand, reveal different relationships with Japanese sociocultural content. See Iwabuchi (2002) for an extensive look at Japanese hegemony in Asia's increasingly globalizing popular culture consumption patterns, and Ching (2000) for a discussion of Asian mass culture formations and the Japanese involvement in developing "Asianist" regionalism.

4 The release was distributed by Dutch East India Trading Company, an important early independent music consolidator that jump-started the U.S. retail network of smaller labels in the mid-1980s.

5 A definitive event in the naming of Noise Music was the nine-day Noise Fest organized by Thurston Moore at the Manhattan art gallery White Columns in 1981 (Masters 2007; Moore and Coley 2008).

6 Kawabata Makoto's rejection of the connections between "Noise Music" and his band Acid Mothers Temple in a 2006 interview is typical: "Even though my music may be noisy, it is never 'Noise Music'" (Baron 2006).

7 In addition to collaborating with many Japanese artists both in New York and Tokyo during the 1990s, Zorn created important channels of distribution for Japanese artists in the 1990s with the "New Japan" series of his well-regarded Tzadik label.

8 A short list of Boredoms-related side projects includes Audio Sports, AOA, Dendoba, Destroy 2, DJ Pika Pika Pika, Concrete Octopus, Hanadensha, Hanatarashi, Noise Ramones, Omoide Hatoba, OOIOO, Puzzle Punks, Rashinban, and UFO or Die. A complete discography would take up several pages, as Dave Watson has demonstrated on his exhaustive Boredoms website Sore Diamonds (http://eyevocal.ottawa-anime.org/boredoms/boreside.htm).

9 Satoh Gin's photograph, reproduced as the frontispiece, depicts the infamous Hanatarashi concert during which Eye drove a backhoe into a Kyoto club. This event is discussed in more detail in chapter 6.

10 Perhaps the most obvious example of gyaku-yunyu in Japanese media is the doting attention to Japanese baseball stars that play in the U.S. major leagues (e.g., Hideki Matsui). This kind of transnational feedback is essential to a cultural politics of popular music, in which local cultural producers first become "prophets abroad" to generate a domestic presence (many African American jazz performers, for example, had to become validated by European audiences before they were recognized as artists in the United States).

11 Recent literature that discusses Noise as a subject of electronic and experimental music includes Bailey (2009), Corbett (2000), Demers (2010), Dyson (2009), Hegarty (2007), Henritzi (2001), Jones (1999), Kelly (2009), Kahn (1999), LaBelle (2006), Licht (2007), Rodgers (2010), Ross (2007), and Voegelin (2010).

12 I have written more extensively elsewhere on musical untranslation in the electroacoustic improvisational genre called onkyô (Novak 2010a). My thinking about

intercultural translation is strongly influenced by the work of Sakai Naoki, particularly his crucial *Translation and Subjectivity* (Sakai 1997).

13 The increasing recognition of media circulation as a context of cultural expression is strongly reflected in the anthropological turn to media in the 1990s and early 2000s. See Castells (1996), Ginsburg, Abu-Lughod, and Larkin (2002), Iwabuchi (2002), Marcus and Myers (1995), Morley and Robins (1995), and Spitulnik (1993).

14 As Casey further notes, art itself is a kind of cultural "edge-work," as it defines and regenerates possibilities for future creativity on the "cutting edge," beyond existing expectations and knowledge, where all new forms take shape (Casey 2004).

15 As I describe in chapter 5, the geopolitical context of mass mediation was crucial for developing the idea of feedback in information theory, especially in the postwar United States with the work of mathematicians Claude Shannon and Warren Weaver, who developed the idea of noise in transmission, and Norbert Wiener, who popularized the notion of feedback in his theory of cybernetics.

16 The preeminent postwar musical folklorist and collector Alan Lomax, for example, proposed a "cultural feedback system" that would return cultural materials to their source by repatriating media gathered for scholarly research to the documented populations (Lomax 1968).

17 See Bohlman (2004) for a useful critique of musical nationalism, and Hutnyk (2000) on musical hybridity and fusion.

18 On the tensions between cosmopolitanism and industrial hegemony in "world music," see Erlmann (1996), Feld (1996, 2000), Lipsitz (1994), Negus (1999), Novak (2011), Stokes (2004), and Taylor (1997).

19 For some examples, see Keil (1994), Schloss (2004), Veal (2007), and Waxer (2002).

20 In this, I hope also that *Japanoise* adds to the recent critique of experimental music's genre construction, following literature (Born 1995; Demers 2010; Lewis 2008; Piekut 2011; Plourde 2009; Whitesell 2001) that challenges its historical and cultural restriction to a narrow lineage of influential postwar American composers (Holmes 2008; Nyman 1999 [1974]; Saunders 2009).

21 Cox (2007) and contributors contextualize theories of Japanese imitation, both in culturally embedded practices (such as the imitative learning patterns called *kata*) and as a transcultural history of creative exchanges. The Japanese identification with copying has been broadly critiqued by popular musicians as well. Technopop artists from the 1980s like NYC-based Japanese band Plastics, for example, flatly parodied the idea of Japanese cultural imitation in the lyrics of their song "Copy": "Copy People / Copy this and copy that / Tokyo Copy Town / Atchimo Kotchimo Copy Darake [over there, over here, copy everywhere]."

22 Miyoshi and Harootunian (2002) and their contributors critique the institutional

history of East Asian area studies in *Learning Places: The Afterlives of Area Studies*; for a recent discussion about globalizing American studies, see Edwards and Gaonkar (2010).

23 It is also worth noting the extensive but often underrecognized participation of Japanese classical musicians and composers within North American musical institutions. See Thornbury (2013), Wade (n.d. and 2004), and Yoshihara (2007).

24 Here I am indebted to George Marcus's framing of "complicity" as a deconstruction of ethnographic models of insider rapport and cross-cultural collaborations of producing local discourse. I invoke complicity in this generative sense, as the "awareness of existential doubleness on the part of *both* anthropologist and subject" that makes "elsewhere" present, both in ethnographic narratives and reflexive local discourses (Marcus 1997).

1. SCENES OF LIVENESS AND DEADNESS

1 This is usually called the *noruma* ("norm") system, in which the promoter or the musicians must cover the minimum fee for the use of the livehouse. The rise of noruma in Japanese live music scenes has led to a decline of organized tours for foreign Noise musicians since the mid-1990s. Most concerts are promoted individually by local artists and promoters, and bringing a performer from overseas is especially expensive and risky. During my fieldwork, almost all of the tours for overseas Noise artists lost money; individual promoters were rarely paid and usually contributed significantly toward the final costs of the booking.

2 For example, Manhattan club CBGB became emblematic of authentic punk music, despite the fact that most histories of the genre insist on its emergence from the English working class and point to London groups such as the Sex Pistols as stylistic originators. On the other hand, the short-lived Roxy—which, for its three-month life in London in 1977, housed punk in its nascent stages in England—is usually cited only in insider accounts and detailed histories of the English scene. Although CBGB was an equally important locale for New York's 1970s punk and New Wave scene, its conflation with punk's origin depends on the representational power enabled by its longevity (1973–2006) and its location in a media center of the United States (and, of course, its T-shirt sales).

3 Aside from Bears, a few other Osaka livehouses, including Fandango, Club Water, and Club Quattro, feature Noise performances on a regular basis.

4 The duo's name, Mikawa says, refers to nonlethal military weapons that render their victims incapable of resistance.

5 "The feeling of the sublime," Immanuel Kant argued, "is a pleasure which arises only indirectly, produced by the feeling of a blocking of vital forces for a brief instant, followed by an even stronger release of them" (Kant 1978:245). As a form of negative beauty, the Kantian sublime aestheticizes the collapse of self-control in the presence of more powerful forces.

6 See Feld and Basso (1996). Feld has described elsewhere how reverberation metaphorizes the social and musical emplacement of Kaluli people in highland Papua New Guinea. For Kaluli, the "reflection" of human and bird voices in the shared environment of the Bosavi rain forest sonically represents the "intuitive nature of a felt worldview" (Feld 1994:128, 132). Ihde (1976) discusses the sonic value of reverberation as a facet of the phenomenological experience of echolocation, through which humans navigate spatial environments and construct individual understandings of the heard world.

7 Joe Meek–branded electronic reverberation units, for example, offer to emulate Meek's classic sounds, whereas the presets for some computer reverberation programs are named after famous studio rooms (i.e., Abbey Road's Studio One). Even mechanical reverbs can become associated with specific people and creative places. It is not uncommon today for dub producers worldwide to pore over—literally with magnifying glasses—the single existing photograph of Lee "Scratch" Perry's former Kingston studio Black Ark, in hopes of identifying and possibly purchasing the echo machines he used to produce early dub's famed qualities of liveness (Veal 2007).

8 Throughout the history of the music industry, private listening was marketed as a sublime individual experience. The image of silhouetted figures of listeners tethered to their iPods is now iconic of this isolated immersion in listening. In the 1980s, a famous ad for Maxell cassettes portrayed a listener slouched in a chair directly in front of a speaker, pushed back into the cushions and holding on tight, his long hair blown back by the power of the sound, wearing sunglasses to further suggest his sensory isolation.

9 The frequency range around one kilohertz is considered critical in the evolution of human aurality. Human hearing is more finely attuned to this range because it is the region in which most vocal formants are located, and thus is crucial to linguistic communication.

10 Studies on the frequency sensitivity of human hearing are based on equal-loudness contours, commonly known as Fletcher-Munson curves from the research done by Harvey Fletcher and Walter Munson on the perception of loudness in the 1930s, which was followed and revised by psychoacousticians in the 1960s and 1970s (Fletcher and Munson 1933; Robinson and Dadson 1957).

11 Like "extreme sports," the enjoyment of Noise reflects an uncommon distinction of personal endurance and experiential challenge. The term "extreme" valorized personal challenges to physiological limits, embodied in sports such as snowboarding or bungee jumping. But the "extreme" youth culture of the 1990s overlapped with many other areas of consumption, including an explosion in consumer audiovisual technologies—here represented in the domain of sound by the higher frequency definition of CDs.

12 Aube often manipulates only a single sound source for the duration of a performance. For instance, his earliest piece, *Torpedo* (1991, Vanilla Records), used only

recordings of water, whereas others are derived solely from rusty metal plates, human heartbeats, or light bulbs.

13 Most of the posts on Google Image, Flickr, and YouTube under the search term "Incapacitants" consist of clips and photos from the 2007 No Fun Fest performance, even as I write this note five years later.

2. SONIC MAPS OF THE JAPANESE UNDERGROUND

1 The record store owner is inevitably male, as are his customers, in Japan as elsewhere in the world (Straw 1997).

2 Even within Tokyo, there are other epicenters of record collecting, including Shibuya and Shimokitazawa.

3 A recent literature dealing with cartographic relativity includes Black (1997), Harley and Woodward (1987), King (1996), Monmonier (1991), and Wood (1992), with John Pickles's *A History of Spaces* (2003) providing an overview of this critical history. This work also relates to geographies of consumption (Jackson and Thrift 1995), geographies of media and communication (Adams 2009), and theories of place and space (Casey 2002).

4 Donald Richie, for example, chronicles Tokyo as an "impermanent capital," which fails to produce an underlying logical plan, instead existing in a continual and organic state of transience (Richie 1987). But Tokyo's hypermodern imagescape has also been critiqued as an artifact of Western imagination. Iwabuchi Koichi describes how Tokyo is mediated as a hermeneutic, claustrophobic space of cultural reclusion in Sofia Coppola's 2003 film *Lost in Translation*, which he contrasts to recent political crises of globalization and multiculturalism triggered by the city's growing immigrant labor population in the 1990s (Iwabuchi 2008).

5 The search for direction in the layers of cosmopolitan experience can also mark the differences and almost-sames between oneself and other people. The trajectories of Barthes's Tokyo quest are given further depth by D. A. Miller, who reveals in *Bringing Out Roland Barthes* that *Empire*'s hastily drawn map of Shinjuku in fact directs readers to one of the city's best-known gay bars of the time (Miller 1992).

6 Marilyn Ivy touches on this effect in her well-known discussion of the 1980s-era Japan National Railway tourism campaign "Discover Japan," which used the term *tabi* to characterize domestic travel as self-discovery. The invocation of tabi, an old-fashioned word for spiritual pilgrimage, encourages a searching return to a unique cultural landscape. But this is a nostalgic home that can be encountered only by a cosmopolitan outsider. Japan's citizens became strangers to rediscover the local world from outside: "one 'discovers myself' [*jisukabaa maiserufu*], a self that is authentic, but lost" (Ivy 1995:41). The "Discover Japan" advertising campaign, too, was doubled by transnational influence, having been based directly on an American tourism campaign called "Discover America."

7 Popular music can become definitive of local identity in smaller cities like Austin or Liverpool, where live music scenes contribute heavily to the management of urban social space through mediated forms of musical tourism (Cohen 1991; Porcello 2005).
8 As Thomas Bey William Bailey writes in a recent report on Japanese independent record stores, "Japanese select shops reward the patience that it takes to actually find them," so that any customer who does actually find the place is "in," "even if they were local salarymen or other people who appeared to be the polar opposite of people involved with 'the scene'" (Bailey 2008).
9 The editors of *Rekôdo Mappu* now also run an English-language blog profiling Tokyo record stores (http://blog.cdandlp.com).
10 In an attempt to create complete collections even when no recording is available, some fans buy records for the album jacket cover alone, a practice known among Japanese collectors as *jake-gai* ("jacket buy").
11 Caroliner (a.k.a. Caroliner Rainbow) was well known for their eccentric packaging of LPs, which were enclosed within hand-colored drawings in boxes with assorted scrap material—confusingly, the same album would often be released with different covers, or the same cover might contain different records. The mystery of the recordings helped set the stage for their extremely successful Japanese tours. One fan, recalling seeing a Caroliner record in the store, stuffed into a plastic bag with a handful of leaves and a small paper flyer, told me, "I could only think: 'What the hell? Why is this in the store?' Of course I bought it. And it sounded just like it looked!"
12 Throughout the period of my research, the primary Noise-specialized shops—Ned's in Tokyo and AMS (Alchemy Music Store) in Osaka—were managed by internationally active Noise artists MSBR (Tano Koji) and Masonna (Yamazaki Maso), respectively.
13 For example, the prominent producer and musician Jim O'Rourke, who now lives in Tokyo, began his initial contact with Japan in mail correspondence with Higashiseto, who helped O'Rourke to set up his early tours in Osaka and connected him to Kansai underground music circles. O'Rourke's collecting has led to other musical collaborations as well. During my fieldwork in Japan in 2002, O'Rourke toured with Mirror, a group that formed after he and German musician Christoph Heemann met through record collecting circles, years before either of them began making music.
14 Released by, respectively, PSF in 1991, Charnel Music in 1993, and Susan Lawly in 1994. Other important foreign compilations of Japanese Noise scenes in the 1980s and '90s include *Dead Tech* volumes I–III (released in 1986 and 1988 on Dossier, and in 1994 on Charnel Music).
15 Here Merzbow again represents a controversial and deeply complicated exception. Akita's interest in kinbaku, bondage, and other alternative sexual practices is well documented and has been strongly productive of associations between

Noise and taboo sexuality and violence, but many crucial details are lost to overseas audiences. He has written many articles and books on photographic representations of sexuality and censorship, including one about between-the-wars Japanese sex magazines and scientific research on "abnormal" sexuality titled *Bizarre Sex Moderne* (1994, Seikyûsha), served as a cameraman for several videos made by the bondage cinema collective Kinbiken in the 1980s, and directed a video that represents the *seppuku* suicide ritual of a young woman. In contrast to this artistic regime of bondage photography, which he describes as an antiauthoritarian project of performance based in sexual parody and psychological transformation, Akita considers pornography as a subversive by-product of capitalist commodity fetishism. The connection between pornography and Noise is often explained by his well-known and often repeated quip: "If music is sex, Merzbow would be pornography." He materialized the metaphor with his *Pornoise* series, which wrapped Merzbow cassettes in cut-up pornographic images.

Akita now disavows the relationship between Merzbow and bondage sexuality. To fully explain the complexities and changes of his perspective would require a more extensive reading than is possible here, and demands more privileged ethnographic knowledge than I possess. But for the purposes of detailing the representational field of Noise, it is important to note that the use of bondage images transfixed overseas audiences in the early days of Noise, heavily contributed to the attribution of Japanese cultural specificity, and eventually led Akita to move away from this practice. In a widely republished interview, Akita argued that his purposes in using bondage photographs were undermined by the proliferation of other sexual images in Noise's transnational circulation: "This is very different from people using Xeroxed bondage images from Japanese magazines. I know that there are many bondage images associated with Merzbow releases. But many of these releases use stupid images without my permission. I should control all of them but it is very difficult to control all products abroad. . . . It's meaningless to create ideology by using pornography without the correct knowledge of the image itself" (Akita 1999).

3. LISTENING TO NOISE IN KANSAI

1 A *jokyû*, as Silverberg describes, was a kind of erotic hostess (but not a prostitute) whose role in creating a sexualized public space metaphorized the contestation of sexuality within the radical cultural transformations of early modern Japan (Silverberg 1998). However, despite the increasing public role of women in cafés, whether as servers or customers, listening to recordings remained a male-coded pleasure in jazu-kissa. As jazu-kissa became more conservative in the 1970s and 1980s, the increased participation of women as listeners in experimental and "free" kissa helped differentiate the later countercultural goals of social justice

and "alternative" internationalization from the earlier embrace of democratic modernity in jazz.
2 Most Japanese writing on jazu-kissa fixes its historical center in the 1960s. Much of the existing literature consists of anecdotal memories by generational representatives (Adoribu 1989 and Soejima 2002, among others).
3 The institutional strictness of silent listening in jazu-kissa is legendary. Atkins cites a sign listing the "house rules" of one Shibuya kissa: "Welcome. This is a powerful listening space. Please 'dig' your jazz. We ask that you observe silence while the music is playing" (Atkins 2001:4).
4 A similar cost differential between imported and domestic media influenced film's reception in Japan. Japanese theaters often increased entrance fees for imported films to cover the higher rental costs, a move that gave American film a higher prestige but limited its audience (Freiberg 1987).
5 Compounding the exclusivity of the relationship between a kissa and its clientele is the "bottle keep" system, where a large sum is paid for a personal bottle of liquor, which is then marked with the customer's name and kept behind the bar. This makes the relationship between customer and master more homey and comfortable, eliminating the need for the awkward direct exchange of money and allowing the customer to treat his friends without overtly paying for their drinks.
6 Japanese instrumental learning is traditionally organized within hierarchical "guilds" called *iemoto*, which maintain a historical lineage of forms and styles through oral transmission in a familial organizational structure. Linda Fujie notes that the social conditions of the iemoto system "not only transmit knowledge; they also control quality," regulating the number of individuals licensed to perform, teach, or otherwise represent their music in society at large (Fujie 1996:386).
7 However, during their 1960s heyday, jazu-kissa were centers of bohemian progressivism on all fronts, and so were briefly aligned with nascent feminist politics in spite of their ultimately male-dominated social frame. There have been several famous jazu-kissas run by couples, one or two female musicians, and women have occasionally (though rarely in the authoritative and authorial role of masters) become famous and influential participants in Japanese jazz circles. Compared to postwar jazu-kissa, female participation expanded exponentially in later free kissa, and women are distinctly present as listeners and performers in most experimental music events in Japan.
8 The male identification with sound technology is typical elsewhere in the world, especially in the United States, where "hi-fi" culture became a common masculine household project (Keightly 1996; Taylor 2001). But there are specific precedents for gendering sound aesthetics in the Japanese language as well. Inoue Miyako describes how women's vocal character and language use have been monitored,

contained, and marginalized by male practices of listening, which have reduced the sounds of progressive female speech styles—and modern female sociality more generally—to nonreferential "unpleasant" sounds (Inoue 2003).

9 This passage is cited in a slightly different translation in Derschmidt (1998:308). Ôshima's reminiscence is drawn from a collected volume featuring several authors nostalgically memorializing their student days spent in endless listening sessions in jazu-kissa (Adoribu 1989). The obi (belt-cover) of the book describes the contents with the following sentimentally self-deprecating blurb, which can only be understood as a generational invocation of sempai-kôhai context (literally "senior-junior"; a reciprocal social institution of elder–younger power relations and mentorship), meant to mark the ownership of subcultural jazz cool: "To the young jazz fans: We, the retread middle aged members of the baby-boom generation [dankai no sedai, 'mass' or 'cluster' generation], want you to know that in the past there were days in our youth when we were excited by going to jazu-kissa." The reaction to the generational curation of jazz motivated younger artists to move toward experimental genres. Experimentalist Kudo Tori—who visits jazu-kissa frequently enough to think about having his grave marked "He loved coffee shops"—complains that "all the current critics have become totally middle-aged, and it feels like they're just enjoying some communication while waiting for their lives to end."

10 The special sense of atmosphere created by this listening behavior is regularly noted by touring musicians, who describe Japanese audiences as especially serious. Critic Sasaki Atsushi has described this hyperattentive listening style as "clarified listening" (mimi wo sumasu), which he identifies in the careful audition associated with the recent Tokyo-based onkyô genre (Sasaki 2001). See also Plourde (2008) on "disciplined listening" in Japanese experimental music audiences.

11 As I describe in chapter 2, the weight given to recordings influenced the terms for concert performance used among popular music fans; a concertgoer attends a raibu, from the English word "live," and small concert spaces have come to be called raibuhausu (livehouses).

12 The Japanese conflation of recordings and live music is perhaps most transparently illustrated by the now-global practice of karaoke (literally, "empty orchestra"). Charles Keil has described karaoke as a "mediated-but-live" experience, in which unchanging recordings highlight the singular efforts and distinct expressions of an individual performer, as the singer sings along with a prerecorded tape (Keil 1994). Noting how Japanese have fluidly assimilated electronic media into their everyday lives, Keil suggests that karaoke represents a special cultural adaptation to mediated music, through which mechanical processes of reproduction are "humanized," or "personalized" in a new mode of performing-listening. Rey Chow further notes that the crux of karaoke affect is the continued presence of a distinct individual human voice in the context of mass mediation.

The karaoke machine "liberates" the singer from the objective requirements of musical skill but turns their listenership into a creative performance: "One is literally performing as a listener, with all the 'defects' that a performer is not supposed to have" (Chow 1993).

13 The Japanese JVC corporation, for instance, was formed out of the Yokohama subsidiary of the Victor Company, breaking ties with RCA-Victor at the outbreak of World War II.

14 Modern listening was being transformed around the world through what Jonathan Sterne calls "audile techniques" that linked the rise of urban bourgeois society to sound reproduction technologies (Sterne 2003). Sterne argues that modern listeners' critical aesthetic judgments about sound were transformed before recordings, with turn-of-the-century developments in medical science and communication technologies, specifically the inventions of the stethoscope and the telegraph. Jonathan Crary shows that a similar process of increased observation and attention to seeing created a "productive and manageable subjectivity" of modern visuality, which regulated its subjects through "purified aesthetic perception" (Crary 1990).

15 Immediately following the end of the war, U.S. forces issued orders for four million radio sets, and by 1948 Japanese factories were already producing a volume of 800,000 radios per year for the domestic market (Nakayama, Boulton, and Pect 1999:29). The rapid reintroduction of radio in postwar Japan was abetted by occupation demands that the Japanese populace receive "educational" broadcasts that carried information about the nation's reconstruction efforts and also American popular music. The eventual miniaturization of transistor technology in the decade following the occupation allowed Japan to begin major exports of radios in the 1960s, triggering the "economic miracle" (managed through imbalanced trade agreements with the United States) that brought the nation to an economic par with Western industrial nations.

16 The *angura* moment of Japan in the late 1960s and 1970s produced influential aesthetic movements and lasting stylistic innovations in several different areas of popular culture, centered in Tokyo's Shinjuku district and exemplified by the underground theater of Terayama Shuji and the Tokyo Kid Brothers troupe; the new performance/dance style of Ankoku Butoh; the experimental films of Iimura Takahiko, Matsumoto Toshio, and the Image Forum collective; the art movements of Gutai and High Red Center; and the "free" music of Takayanagi Masayuki, Abe Kaoru, Kosugi Takehisa, Haino Keiji, and others, all of which were often presented together in multimedia events that conjoined sociopolitical and aesthetic goals. See Goodman (1999) for an interesting introduction to the poster artwork of *angura* theatre, Ridgely (2011) on Terayama's role in the counterculture, Munroe (1994) on postwar avant-garde art, and Klein (1988) on Butoh performance.

17 See Murai (2002) and Derschmidt (1998) for further commentary on the jazu-

kissa's decline into traditionalism in the 1980s and 1990s, and Molasky (2005) for a rebuttal of the nostalgic mythos that accrues to histories of 1960s jazu-kissa. However, some Japanese critics continue to argue for the potential of jazz as a flexible source of innovation, despite the recent encroachment of totalizing genre histories. Soejima Teruto argues that "free jazz" should not be seen as the last subgenre in a historical line and that "genuine jazz has no goal. It's music that keeps changing, permanently" (Soejima 2002:77).

18 Ironically, the term *free* here is derived from the 1960s African American countercultural music "free jazz," but was quickly negotiated away from this social history to become "free music." Although there has been an active free jazz scene in Japan—Soejima (2002) attempts a detailed history—"free" here implies a broader freedom from all existing idiomatic musical and social structures and was concurrently employed in generic constructions such as "free rock" and "free improvisation." These naming discourses were crucial to the cultural decontextualization of improvisation in the ideological projects of experimental music (Lewis 2004; Novak 2010a).

19 Drugstore was especially crucial in the lives of Hiroshige Jojo and Junko, as the backdrop for the friendship that led to their marriage and the founding of their important Noise group Hijokaidan.

20 The word *maniakku* is borrowed from English and is commonly used to refer to an obsessive fan. Maniakku is slightly more forgiving than the related Japanese term *otaku*, which translates as "geek" or "junkie," and often bears a darker connotation of antisocial fetishism. The coexistence of the English and Japanese terms to describe two different states of fandom in a single media consumption reflects a split in popular cultural identity in Japan, in which media is classified into native and foreign contexts of origin (e.g., *yôgaku* as a term for all foreign music; *hôgaku* for Japanese).

21 Minor, which evolved in the bohemian West Tokyo neighborhood of Kichijoji from a jazu-kissa to a free performance space, was pivotal in providing cross-genre "sound workshops" and starting the careers of underground legends Mukai Chie, Shiraishi Tamio, Kudo Tori, and others during its brief life from 1978 to 1980 (documented on the 1980 compilation *Aikyoku Jinmin Juji Gekijo*) (Cummings 2009).

22 Zenkyôtô was formed as a national federation of student self-government, similar to Students for a Democratic Society on U.S. campuses, which became crucial in the 1968 student uprising (Marotti 2009; Steinhoff 1984). In the 1970s, zenkyôtô had a less formalized agenda and a more fluid membership, organizing public musical and theatrical events as well as mobilizing political action.

23 Rallizes (a.k.a. Les Rallizes Denudes) had a vast influence in the Kansai underground, particularly in their excessively loud stage volume. The group was nationally controversial for reasons beyond their music. Though the band had become famous by playing at the 1969 Barricades A Go-Go concert (accompanied by a

massive student demonstration and occupation of Kyoto University), the group was blacklisted for several years after member Wakabayashi became involved in the actions of the radical communist group Sekigun, or Red Army, and participated in the 1970 Yodo-gô hijacking, when the fringe group infamously seized a jet airliner and took its passengers to North Korea. See Cope (2007) for a brief English-language summary of the event and its relevance for Rallizes.

24 Although his music and performance range beyond what is commonly identified as Noise, Haino Keiji's influence, within local histories of Japanese experimental music and in formations of Noise, cannot be understated. Haino's first band, Lost Aaraaf, and his later famed improvised rock band Fushitsusha were heavily influential; he often performs solo shows and collaborates with others as well. Much of Haino's recorded material is available on the Tokyo-based label P.S.F.

25 While Inu was among the most well-known punk groups in Kansai, Machida eventually became more famous for his novels, winning the Akutagawa Prize in 2000 for *Kiregire* and the Tanizaki Prize in 2005 for *Kokuhaku*.

26 Kosakai Fumio, later Mikawa's partner in Incapacitants, recalled the inspired chaos of seeing Hijokaidan at Keio University in 1981: "Within the first five minutes a fight broke out between the convulsing, rampaging members of the group and the venue's soundmen who were trying to stop them. An organ flew through the air and landed in the audience, smashing into pieces. Jojo Hiroshige suddenly appeared with a fire extinguisher and as he struggled with the venue staff, the extinguisher fell to the ground and began spurting out foam" (Kosakai 2009).

27 Mikawa (2009). Mikawa began Incapacitants as a solo recording project immediately following this period and did not perform live for several years.

28 In discussing the idea of alchemy, Hiroshige uses the Japanese term *renkinjutsu* for the magical process of transforming objects from one state to another, while the label name is rendered in English.

29 *Sore wa chotto chigau ne?* This phrase could also be interpreted as "that's sort of getting it wrong, isn't it?"

4. GENRE NOISE

1 Kahn (1999) points out that the Italian futurist Luigi Russolo, inventor of the *intonarumori* Noise instruments, contested Helmholtz's identification of noise sounds with nonperiodic waveforms. Russolo believed it was the continuity of noise that distinguished it from music, as well as the rich timbres of mechanical noises produced in modern life.

2 Noise components contribute many of the defining aural cues for the recognition of musical sounds. Without the "attack transients" at the beginning of a tone, listeners cannot identify the difference between one instrument and another (Russo and Warner 2004:49).

3 Though the group names itself "Nihilist," its members deny any meaningful as-

sociations with nihilist philosophy. Cofounder Murray Favro sums it up: "I don't give a shit about Nihilism. . . . I am myself, not a collection of ideas" (Paes 2003).

4 Art Pratten worked at a local newspaper; Bill Exley as a schoolteacher; Greg Curnoe, John Boyle, and Murray Favro were visual artists; Hugh McIntyre was a librarian; and John Clement was a doctor. One of the original members, Archie Leitch, disappeared at some point in the 1960s and has not been heard from since.

5 The availability of the early NSB records via Alchemy's CD reissues greatly inflated the price of the rare original vinyl LPs: in the mid-1990s, mint condition copies of *No Record* sold for as much as US$900 in Japan.

6 There are important exceptions, particularly in the modern pop ballad form *enka* and the related metageneric term *kayôkyoku*, both of which carry a general connotation of Japanese origin (Yano 2002). See also Hosokawa (1994) and Stevens (2007) for surveys of popular music styles and naming contexts in postwar Japan.

7 For example, pop recordings by the Rolling Stones and the Beatles were imported into Japan under the local category "Group Sounds" (a genre name subsequently shortened, as is typical in colloquial Japanese, to the initials GS). In the GS boom of the 1960s, thousands of "copy groups" were spawned to emulate the *ereki* (electric) tones of instrumental surf ensembles, such as the Ventures (whose popularity has been much more enduring in Japan than in the United States). See Bourdaghs (2012).

8 A further irony is that J-pop, along with a variety of other Japanese popular media productions, is heavily consumed in export markets throughout Asia and has become a marker of Japan's "soft" economic power in the region (Ching 2000; Iwabuchi 2002).

9 The concepts of "noise" and "music" are not oppositional in Japanese taxonomies of sound, either (for instance, *sô-on* [noise] and *ongaku* [music] both use the same root for sound [*on*]). The use of *Noizu*, then, enabled a distinction from Music that is not present in Japanese linguistic taxonomies of sound, as well as stressing associations with a translocal sphere of popular music.

10 The Japanese Society for the Rights of Authors, Composers and Publishers, like foreign copyright societies such as BMI and ASCAP, registers most industrially produced records in Japan and administers the collection of royalties.

11 Other circulations of Western popular music were not reworked into a generalized local genre because they connoted highly marked categories of racial or national origin. As Ian Condry describes, Japanese hip-hop has complex and contradictory relationships with genre that have been strongly defined by Japanese difference from its African American origins. The media productions of Japanese hip-hop, however, are eminently indigenous in consumption, not least as a result of being delivered in the Japanese language (Condry 2006).

12 For example, although the otherwise excellent 1999 catalog *Merzbook: The Pleasuredome of Noise* (released by Extreme Records to accompany the fifty-CD Merzbox)

describes itself as a detailed history of Merzbow, it contains little substantive writing or historical contribution by Akita himself beyond short segments from English-language interviews and some fragmentary comments.

13 For a widely circulated example, see Akita (1999) (excerpted in Cox and Warner 2004).

14 Akita often uses the English word *outside* to describe the placement of his music. The term *outside*, or *out*, is an especially common descriptor in jazz's genre discourse, where it carries an ambivalent connotation of difference that was formative in the avant-garde status of postwar bebop and free jazz. Performers are described as "out" to connote the extreme styles that are difficult to recover into standard repertoires.

15 As in other cases of pseudonymic naming, the name "Ramones" covers up the diverse ethnicities of individual members of the group, allowing them to appear as members of the same punk rock "family."

16 Pseudonymic practices are also prominent among non-music-making participants and fans in independent music scenes (e.g., the author of the long-term punk-scene chronicle *Cometbus* is known as Aaron Cometbus).

17 For example, Yamazaki Maso became well known for his solo performances as Masonna (playing on the pronunciation of "Madonna") and then began to perform solo under the moniker Space Machine to distance his newer work from his older identity; he also played with others in the group Christine 23 Onna (detaching *onna*, the word for "woman," from Masonna).

18 Reiko A currently performs under her own performance name, solo and in collaboration with Hasegawa Hiroshi of Astro.

19 See, for example, Hegarty (2007) and Woodward (1999). Hegarty notes that "even within the prolific production of Japanese noise musicians . . . Akita could constitute a genre in his own right" (Hegarty 2007:155).

20 See the *Merzbox* web page at http://www.xtr.com/merzbox/swf/index.htm (accessed June 23, 2009). Richards goes on to suggest that shards of the glass master might be sold on an Internet auction site. To my knowledge, the sale has never materialized.

21 There are, of course, many fans that distinguish themselves by having listened to the entire *Merzbox*. Some reviewers have attempted to describe the cumulative experience of listening to each of the fifty CDs one after the other (Burns 2002; Haynes 2003).

5. FEEDBACK, SUBJECTIVITY, AND PERFORMANCE

1 In one exceptional experiment, a Japanese label solicited contributions for a "Noise unplugged" record that required each of its contributors to make a two-minute Noise piece without the use of any amplification whatsoever (the recordings have never been released).

2 Despite this initial controversy, the performer eventually became a well-respected Noisician.
3 Probably the most basic reason for this is that most Noisicians simply cannot afford to destroy a laptop computer (although I have witnessed this once).
4 The situation is markedly different in Europe, however, where many performers use laptops.
5 *Zôfuku* is the most common verb for electronic sound amplification, but the English loanword *anpurifai* is also used.
6 Richardson (1991) describes the economic industrial analysis developed as systems dynamics by Richard M. Goodwin, Herbert Simon, and Jay Forrester as a servomechanisms theory of feedback, which attempts to conceptualize the dynamic behavior of socioeconomic systems.
7 On the technological and military history of cybernetics, see Bennett (1993), Edwards (2007), Gallison (1994), and Mindell (2002).
8 There are, however, some applications in which positive feedback is not necessarily generative as a self-reinforcing loop but can be used as a stabilizing force in a larger electronic system.
9 Bateson describes schismogenesis in "complementary" and "symmetrical" relations, both of which lead to inevitable breakdown in binary exchanges. In complementary schismogenesis, A is more and more assertive and B is more and more submissive; in symmetrical schismogenesis, both A and B become increasingly assertive (Bateson 1935). Bateson later used the negative feedback theory developed in cybernetics to analyze processes of learning and epistemologies of alcoholism and recovery (Bateson 1964, 1971), and he also went on to critique the "systematic distortions" of humankind and the global ecology that result from the implementations of modern technology (M. C. Bateson 1972).
10 Cage (1961) and Russolo (1986 [1913]). See also Marinetti (1973 [1909]) on noise sounds in warfare.
11 For example, a similar long delay time-lag technique was discovered a few years later by Brian Eno in collaboration with Robert Fripp, who renamed the feedback system "Frippertronics."
12 Indeterminacy became a hallmark of institutional narratives of postwar American composition. Cage viewed indeterminacy as an intervention in the European avant-garde that defined "experimental music" in a specifically American postwar environment of radical newness. In his essay "History of Experimental Music in the United States," published in 1961 in the hugely influential volume *Silence*, Cage argues that the United States "has an intellectual climate suitable for radical experimentation," and reports a remark he made to a Dutch musician that "it must be very difficult for you in Europe to write music, for you are so close to the centers of tradition" (Cage 1961:73). Cage rehearses a particularly U.S.-based version of hegemonic globalization at the end of the essay: "It will not be easy . . .

for Europe to give up being Europe. It will, nevertheless, and must: for the world is one world now" (Cage 1961:75).

13 In the first draft of this 1972 essay, Tudor had written this last sentence as "one component *overloads* the next so that *you can create signals*" but ultimately changed "overload" to "influence" and "you can create" to the passively voiced "signals are created" (Tudor 1997 [1972]:29).

14 For example, when I first had a chance to closely observe Merzbow's pedal-based system in 1997, I had recently been introduced to some of Tudor's equipment and recognized some similarities in his electronics. When I mentioned this, Akita explained that although he had been conscious of Tudor through the work of John Cage, he had not known Tudor's electronic pieces when he began making Noise.

15 Tudor shied away from losing control of his feedback systems completely. In a 1984 interview, he commented that he doesn't like it when feedback "takes off" on its own, and that in those cases, he will shut off the system and start over. In some of Cage's "indeterminate" pieces, too, the electronic systems are clearly controlled (such as *Variations IV*, which appears to be an open-form electroacoustic improvisation). Cage's contradictory positions on indeterminacy as a separate realm from improvisation are equally complex and resonate with a desire to distinguish his "experimental music" from emergent contemporary genres such as "free improvisation."

16 Glitch, a term often used to describe the sounds of CDs skipping, also describes a nascent genre of experimental electronic music at the end of the 1990s (which is probably why Greenwood hesitated, during this 2004 interview, to invoke the overused and abandoned term). Glitch was created largely on laptops by emphasizing the digital errors created when sound software is forced to malfunction, resulting in clicking and interruption (Bates 2004; Cascone 2000; Kelley 2009; Sangild 2004).

17 Mods can also be created for software and are often produced in an environment of oppositional experimentation similar to physical circuit-bending (Lysloff 2003). Naturally, there are degrees of creativity inherent both in modding software and in circuit-bending. A mod for an existing electronic instrument (for example, the commonly modded sampler/synthesizer Casio SK-1) might be as simple as adding potentiometer knobs to extend the range of its existing parameters while maintaining its basic form, which some consider pointlessly unoriginal. One experimentalist exhorted circuit-benders to "stop doing mods and start actually probing circuits, maybe even leave the SK-1s alone, leave the Speak-and-Spells alone, and find something of your own" (Sajbel n.d.).

18 Ghazala, an American electronic musician who began circuit-bending in the late 1960s, is often called "the father of circuit-bending," and he has published a book of how-to articles (Ghazala 2005). His close association with the term has, of course, led many experimental electronic musicians, especially outside the

United States, to reject circuit-bending as a description for what they insist is an inventorless practice.
19 A note posted at the 2006 Bent Festival was indicative of the casual, hands-on approach to experimental learning in circuit-bending communities: "If you plan on attending Wednesday afternoon's Walkman bending workshop, in this workshop you will learn how to make a tape loop from an audio cassette and pitch-shift it with a variable resistor . . . please bring the following with you: cassette tapes—scissors—Walkmans (that you can destroy)—thin adhesive tape." A guide to a few basic mods for toys is available at Peter Edwards's website (http://casperelectronics.com/finished-pieces/casio-sa2), as well as the "circuit-bending: a bender's guide" page online at http://www.anti-theory.com/soundart/circuitbend/cb02.html.
20 Theorists in social construction of technology (SCOT) and history of science have proposed that user feedback creates a counternarrative to technological determinism through actor–network relations, showing how consumers' dialogic evaluations and remediations of technology have influenced the history of scientific development (Gitelman 2006, 1999; Pinch and Bijker 1984).

6. JAPANOISE AND TECHNOCULTURE

1 A transcription of the lecture, translated into English by Isozaki Mia, is available at http://www.japanimprov.com/yotomo/fukushima/lecture.html. All quotes here are from this translation.
2 See Project Fukushima's mission statement on their website, at http://www.pj-fukushima.jp/en/manifesto_en.html. Also see Ôtomo Yoshihide, "Let's Make 'Fukushima' a Positive Word!" at http://japanecho.net/society/0099/ (2011).
3 The joke about Genpatsu-kun had other iterations, including those of the media artist Yatani Kazuhiko, whose popular tweets in the weeks following the Fukushima meltdown represented the faulty reactor as a small boy with a stomachache. Yatani's tweets inspired a short animated film, depicting a charmingly humiliated "Lil' Reactor Boy," who struggles to keep his radiation-emitting poops and farts from leaking out and contaminating the population (like his infamous classmate Chernobyl-chan). Genpatsu-kun helped remediate an unfathomable context of public violence by literally "characterizing" the reactor into an endearing figure that might bring people closer to understanding what could happen in the aftermath of the meltdown. This disarming cuteness—through which even the catastrophic events at Fukushima can be anthropomorphized into an anime character—resonates with a familiar mode of Japanese cultural production, described by Christine Yano as "pink globalization," that ironically subverts the monstrosities of Japanese capitalism into cute and childish objects of affective identification and empathy (Yano 2006, 2009). Ôtomo's Noise machine Genpatsu-kun reveals the flip side of this cultural production, which focuses attention on the darkness of technoculture in postwar Japan.

4 Sound recordings played an especially important role in diversifying technological environments to create new modes of social interaction with media. According to Walter Ong, "tactile" aural media existed as an electronic "secondary orality" that shifted media from the tool of a compartmentalized "print culture" to that of a culturally transcendent global "tribe" with the potential for universal participation (Ong 1982).

5 The concept of transculturation has a complex intellectual history, particularly as a term of Latin American postcolonial theory. Fernando Ortiz initially coined the term to distinguish the dynamism of cultural transformation from the acculturation of center-periphery power relations in colonial histories (Ortiz 1995 [1940]). The idea has since been taken up to describe multidirectional transformations of globalization and cosmopolitan identity in counterhegemonic literature (Rama 1989), performances of cultural identity (Taylor 1991), and "contact zones" of mutual intercultural influence (Pratt 1992), as well as sonic epistemologies of modernity (Ochoa Gautier 2006).

6 For example, they were certainly not "cute" (*kawaii*), an attribute increasingly regarded as central to the globalization of Japanese popular culture (Yano 2006, 2009).

7 Whitehouse is notable for having popularized the phrase "extreme music," which Bennett used to describe the group's alienating combination of aggressive sounds with shocking lyrics and often chillingly misogynistic portrayals of sexual violence.

8 At one mid-1990s SRL performance I attended at an abandoned warehouse in San Francisco, volunteers blasted air horns to keep the crowd at a reasonable distance from the machines, adding to the incredible density of sound and the chaotic, apocalyptic atmosphere.

9 Bijsterveld (2008) further notes that despite their futuristic rhetoric, many twentieth-century modernist composers echoed the humanistic orientation of antinoise abaters. Both movements aestheticized technological noise as a violent disruption of human life and natural phenomenologies—whether attempting to harness its powerful affective complexities or to eliminate its harmful presence—and shared romantic and elitist ideologies of social activism.

10 An extensive scholarly commentary is captured in the *Mechademia* series edited by Frenchy Lunning, particularly volume 3 (Lunning 2008).

11 On science fiction narratives of posthuman identity, see Allison (2006), Balsamo (1996), Haraway (1991), Hayles (1999), LaMarre (2008, 2009), Napier (1993), Schodt (2007), and Ueno (1998).

12 On Japanese influences and realizations of cyberpunk, see Bolton (2007), Brown (2010), Napier (2000), and Tatsumi (2006).

13 The term *Sanshu no Jingi* here references the three imperial treasures—sword, jewel, and mirror—that authenticate the Japanese nation. As Simon Partner notes, the "three sacred treasures" of the 1950s were swiftly followed by the

"three Cs" (car, cooler, color TV) in the 1960s, and by the "three Js" (jewels, jet travel, and *jûtaku* [home ownership]) in the 1980s. Despite the skepticism and lack of buying power that marked the initial introduction of these goods to the Japanese public, industry ideologies strongly encouraged consumers to quickly invest themselves in rationalized lifestyle improvements, which compressed the technological process of modernization into quotidian consumer behavior (Partner 1999).

14 The occupation of engineer is viewed as a highly prestigious and respected position in Japan, and the encouragement of individual innovation was instituted as corporate policy. In the 1970s, 40 percent of graduate degrees in Japan were in engineering compared to 5 percent in the United States, and the budget for research and development in Japanese electronics companies was much larger in Japan than elsewhere, with 60 percent of Japanese engineers involved in R&D compared to 20 percent in the United States (Gregory 1985:120).

15 Thomas LaMarre usefully summarizes these ideas in his introduction to Azuma's article "The Animalization of Otaku Culture" (LaMarre 2007).

16 Murakami Takashi (2001) more cuttingly described the otaku perspective on national identity as "impotence culture."

17 Incapacitants also released a seven-inch vinyl EP identifying the sarin gas attacks in Tokyo, titled "Sarin Will Kill Every Bad AUM" (1996; Dirter Promotions).

18 In the early days of development in the 1960s, new laws allowed developers sweeping rights of eminent domain to build in outlying rural areas at the edges of Japanese cities (famously resisted during the construction of Narita Airport in years of protests that galvanized the left-wing student movement). Danchi were given names such as Senri New Town and Tsukuba Science City, reflecting futuristic visions of a self-contained urban development (Mizushima 2006). By the end of the 1980s, danchi had become symbols of a failed urban policy and a deeply corrupt construction state (*doken kokka*) that hastened the collapse of the Japanese economy. I am indebted to Anne McKnight for highlighting Akita's reference to danchi.

19 Akita's turn to veganism and animal rights in the 2000s became another personal method of altering a technocultural system through alternate subjectivities of embodiment. His 2005 book *My Vegetarian Life* [*Watashi no Saishoku Seikatsu*] brings attention to global technologies of food production that depend on the mechanical subversion of animals (Akita 2005).

7. THE FUTURE OF CASSETTE CULTURE

1 In 2011, the term *cassette tape* was removed from the *Concise Oxford English Dictionary* (added terms included *retweet* and *cyberbullying*). But there are many contexts in which the audiocassette remains in use globally in the early 2010s and a few

in the United States as well (particularly in car stereos). Interestingly, cassettes continue to be the primary format in some U.S. prisons, where Internet use is forbidden and CDs are banned as possible weapons ("Music Retailer Thrives Serving Captive Audience," Reuters, July 19, 2008, http://www.reuters.com/article/2008/07/20/us-jailhouse-idUSN1945795120080720).

2 Online networks, of course, have their own residual histories as countercultural projects of "virtual community," many of which were developed during the same period as the cassette culture (Turner 2005). On relationships of old and new media, see also Acland (2007), Bolter and Grusin (2000), Gitelman (2006), Jenkins (2006), Kittler (1990), Manovich (2002), and Novak (2011).

3 Some of the cassette's sonic and circulatory qualities fall into what Jonathan Sterne (2012) describes as "compression practices" that create new kinds of aesthetic experiences through the technological materialities of media formats.

4 For example, the website (and now book) *Cassette from My Ex* and the novel *Love Is a Mixtape: Life and Loss, One Song at a Time*, as well as Thurston Moore's collection of annotated photographs of mix tapes made by his friends and colleagues (Bitner 2009; Moore 2005; Sheffield 2007).

5 On hip-hop mix tapes, see Driscoll (2009), Forman (2002), Keyes (2004), and Rose (1994). The portability of the cassette "boombox," like that of the Walkman and car cassette deck, is emblematic of public recorded music consumption in the 1980s, and of the emergence of DJ culture in street performance.

6 Williams (1977) defines as residual those "experiences, meanings and values, which cannot be verified or cannot be expressed in terms of the dominant culture [but] are nevertheless lived and practiced on the basis of the residue—cultural as well as social—of some previous social formation."

7 I am indebted here to Tom Porcello's development of "print-through" in magnetic audiotape as a metaphor for the social mediation developed through cumulative experiences of listening (Porcello 1998).

8 On U.S. fanzine culture of this era, see Duncombe (1997).

9 Although multisited simultaneous live events have recently become popular via Internet streaming services, live/recorded collaborations also persist in the "soundmail" performance mode. In 2003, for example, I heard performances of such collaborations at the Festival Beyond Innocence, a five-day concert at Bridge in Osaka, in which local musicians Haco, Samm Bennett, and Yoshida Ami improvised with prerecorded tapes sent by Christian Marclay, Wayne Horvitz, and Hatanaka Masao.

10 One of the most fascinating uses of audiocassette sounds can be heard on *Blank Tapes*, a 2000 release (on CD) by the Argentine Noise group Reynols. The group processed the audible hiss from a collection of blank tapes spanning the commercial production of the format from 1978 to 1999, amplifying the medium's inherent self-noise into a powerful textural aesthetic of Noise.

11 Moore recently edited a book titled *Mixtape: The Art of Cassette Culture*, compiling photos of favorite mix tapes together with short tales about their contents and personal meaning (Moore 2005).

12 This period oversaw the introduction of factory-pressed CDs as an industrial retail format, which allowed mainstream and independent music markets alike to expand dramatically in the 1990s with a digital medium that was predictable and affordable to manufacture and transport. For most musicians, home-burnable CD-Rs were still a few years away in the 1990s and did not yet represent an alternative possibility of individualized production. Although CD-Rs did enter into Noise circulations over the next few years, they did not overcome the cassette as a primary medium of barter exchange until the early 2000s, and, as I explain later, were quickly supplanted by online file sharing by the end of the decade.

13 *Terror Noise Audio* redistributes old and new Noise recordings via file sharing sites, though its activity has diminished since the shutdown of MegaUpload in January 2012 (http://terrornoiseaudio.blogspot.com).

14 Partly because of language, not least the problems of displaying characters on HTML webpages, Japanese Internet users have developed alternate web resources that prioritize national over transnational exchanges. For example, networks of record collecting have been strongly impacted by the fact that most Japanese use the Japanese-language Yahoo auction service rather than eBay, which is predominant in the United States and most of Europe.

15 As Condry (2004, 2013) shows, the slow development of Internet file sharing also contributed to a less stringent enforcement of copyright by Japanese media industries. This has allowed a more robust fan remixing culture (typified by self-published fan products known as *dôjinshi*) to develop around music, manga, and anime, which, in turn, feed back into continued economic and social support for industrial publishing.

16 One of the most useful Japanese-language sites is http://www.japanoise.net, and Akita Masami often posts new recordings on his blog at http://www.blog.merzbow.net. Japanese artists have occasionally set up bilingual web pages, including a site run by MSBR from the late 1990s until his death in 2005.

17 See the Wikipedia entry on Guilty Connector, http://en.wikipedia.org/wiki/Guilty_Connector. Accessed June 23, 2010.

18 There are a couple of notable exceptions, such as Whitehouse, who reportedly aggressively go after anyone who posts their recordings.

19 For example, Merzbow fan pages have regularly been subject to troll attacks (including streams of non sequiturs that filled the Shoutbox commentary page for Merzbow on Last.fm). In the case of Noise's online representation, it is tough to distinguish trolls from true fans. The transgressive tactics of trolls and griefers, as Gabriella Coleman (2012) has argued, reflect a "drive toward cultural obfuscation" that extends from the complicated ethical politics of hacker culture, which overlaps considerably with the historical social networks of the cassette culture.

20 See, for example, the recent inception of Record Store Day, an annual event held on the third Saturday of April since 2007.
21 Another Geriogerigegege release, *Art Is Over*, consisted of a single octopus tentacle taped to the inside of the cassette box (limited to fifty copies).
22 See "MU01 Ophibre/Brian Grainger split #3 C44," from Mirror Universe Tapes, http://mirroruniversetapes.blogspot.com/2009/03/mu01-ophibrebrian-grainger-split-3.html.
23 From the Patient Sounds blog, http://patientsounds.blogspot.com/2010/04/patient-sounds-bundle-package.html. Accessed April 26, 2010.
24 Protests by online communities led to a flood of critique against the proposed SOPA (Stop Online Piracy Act) and PIPA (Protect Intellectual Property Act) legislation, leading to a blackout by many services, including Wikipedia in the United States, on January 18, 2012.

EPILOGUE

Epigraph: Jessica Rylan, n.d., http://www.irfp.net/Cant.html. Accessed July 1, 2010, cited by permission.

1 For a concise recent overview of Noise scenes in the United States, see Masters (2009).
2 See Alchemy Records' Alchemy Music Store online at http://www.kt.rim.or.jp/~jojo_h/ar/p_ams/index.html.
3 See also Merzblog at http://blog.merzbow.net.
4 See "No Fun Fest New York 2010," at http://www.nofunfest.com/2010.html.

REFERENCES

Acland, Charles R., ed. 2007. *Residual Media*. Minneapolis: University of Minnesota Press.
Adams, Paul C., ed. 2009. *Geographies of Media and Communication: A Critical Introduction*. London: Wiley-Blackwell.
Adoribu, ed. 1989. *Tokyo Jazu-kissa Monogatari* [The story of Tokyo jazu-kissa]. Tokyo: Adoriubu.
Akita, Masami. 1992. *Noizu Wô: Noizu myûjikku to sono tenkai* [Noise war: Noise music and its development]. Tokyo: Seikyusha.
———. 1999. "The Beauty of Noise." Interview by Chad Hensley. *EsoTerra* no. 8.
———. 2005. *Watashi no Saishoku Seikatsu* [My vegetarian life]. Tokyo: Ohta.
Allison, Anne. 2000. "A Challenge to Hollywood? Japanese Character Goods Hit the US." *Japanese Studies* 20(1):67–88.
———. 2006. *Millennial Monsters: Japanese Toys and the Global Imagination*. Berkeley: University of California Press.
Althusser, Louis. 1971. "Ideology and Ideological State Apparatuses." *Lenin and Philosophy, and Other Essays*, trans. Ben Brewster. London: New Left Books.
Aoyama, Shinji. 2005. *Eli, Eli, Lema Sabachthani* (film). VAP.
Appadurai, Arjun. 1986. "Introduction: Commodities and the Politics of Value." *The Social Life of Things: Commodities in Cultural Perspective*, ed. Arjun Appadurai, 3–64. Cambridge: Cambridge University Press.

———. 1996. *Modernity at Large: Cultural Dimensions of Globalization*. Minneapolis: University of Minnesota Press.

Asada, Akira. 2000. "J-kaiki no yukue" [Future of the return to "J"]. *Voices* 267:58–59.

Asher, Zev. 2003. *What about Me? The Rise of the Nihilist Spasm Band* (DVD). Tokyo: Uplink Factory.

Atkins, Taylor E. 2001. *Blue Nippon: Authenticating Jazz in Japan*. Durham: Duke University Press.

Attali, Jacques. 1985 (1977). *Noise: The Political Economy of Music*. Trans. B. Massumi. Minneapolis: University of Minnesota Press.

Auslander, Philip. 1999. *Liveness: Performance in a Mediatized Culture*. London: Routledge.

Avan Myûjikku Gaido [Avant music guide]. 1999. Ed. S. Shiba. Tokyo: Sakuhinsha.

Axel, Brian. 2006. "Anthropology and the New Technologies of Communication." *Cultural Anthropology* 21(3):354–84.

Azerrad, Michael. 2001. *Our Band Could Be Your Life: Scenes from the American Indie Underground, 1981–1991*. New York: Back Bay.

Azuma, Hiroki. 2001. *Dôbutsuka suru posutomodan: Otaku kara mita Nihon shakai* [Animalizing postmodernity: Otaku and postmodern Japanese society]. Tokyo: Kodansha.

Bailey, Thomas Bey William. 2008. "Singing Doctors and Friendly Time Bombs: A Salute to Japan's Independent Record Shops." Perfect Sound Forever website. http://www.furious.com/perfect/japaneserecordstores.html.

———. 2009. *Micro-bionic: Radical Electronic Music and Sound Art in the 21st Century*. London: Creation Books.

Bakhtin, Mikhail. 1986. *Speech Genres and Other Late Essays*. Austin: University of Texas Press.

Balsamo, Anne. 1996. *Technologies of the Gendered Body: Reading Cyborg Women*. Durham: Duke University Press.

Baron, Zach. 2006. "Don't Call it Noise Music." *Village Voice*, February 28.

Barthes, Roland. 1982 (1970). *Empire of Signs*. Trans. Richard Howard. New York: Hill and Wang.

Basso, Keith. 1992. "Speaking with Names: Language and Landscape among the Western Apache." *Rereading Cultural Anthropology*, ed. George Marcus, 220–51. Durham: Duke University Press.

———. 1996. *Wisdom Sits in Places: Language and Landscape among the Western Apache*. Albuquerque: University of New Mexico Press.

Bates, Elliot. 2004. "Glitches, Bugs, and Hisses: The Degeneration of Musical Recordings and the Contemporary Musical Work." *Bad Music: The Music We Love to Hate*, ed. C. Washburne and M. Derno, 275–94. New York: Routledge.

Bateson, Gregory. 1935. "Culture Contact and Schismogenesis." *Man* 35:178–83.

———. 1971. "The Cybernetics of 'Self': A Theory of Alcoholism." *Psychiatry: Journal for the Study of Interpersonal Processes* 34(1):1–18.

———. 1972 (1964). "The Logical Categories of Learning and Communication." *Steps to an Ecology of Mind*. New York: Ballantine.

Bateson, Mary Catherine. 1972. *Our Own Metaphor: A Personal Account of a Conference on the Effects of Conscious Purpose on Human Adaptation*. New York: Knopf.

Bauman, Richard, and Charles Briggs. 1999. "Genre." *Journal of Linguistic Anthropology* 9:1–2.

———. 2003. *Voices of Modernity: Language Ideologies and the Politics of Inequality*. Cambridge: Cambridge University Press.

Bauman, Zygmunt. 1991. *Modernity and Ambivalence*. Oxford: Polity.

Benjamin, Walter. 1969. *Illuminations*. Ed. H. Arendt, trans. H. Zohn. New York: Schocken.

Bennett, Andy, and Richard Peterson, eds. 2004. *Music Scenes: Local, Translocal, and Virtual*. Nashville: Vanderbilt University Press.

Bennett, Stuart. 1993. *A History of Control Engineering, 1930–1955*. Stevenage, U.K.: Peter Peregrinus for the IEE.

Berger, Harris. 1999. *Metal, Rock, and Jazz: Perception and the Phenomenology of Musical Experience*. Hanover, N.H.: Wesleyan University Press.

Bey, Hakim. 1991. *T.A.Z.: The Temporary Autonomous Zone, Ontological Anarchy, Poetic Terrorism*. New York: Autonomedia.

Bijsterveld, Karin. 2008. *Mechanical Sound: Technology, Culture, and Public Problems of Noise in the Twentieth Century*. Cambridge: MIT Press.

Bitner, Jason. 2009. *Cassette from My Ex: Stories and Soundtracks of Lost Loves*. New York: St. Martin's.

Black, Jeremy. 1997. *Maps and Politics*. Chicago: University of Chicago Press.

Boellstorff, Tom. 2008. *Coming of Age in Second Life: An Anthropologist Explores the Virtually Human*. Princeton: Princeton University Press.

Bohlman, Philip. 2004. *The Music of European Nationalism: Cultural Identity and Modern History*. Santa Barbara: ABC-CLIO.

Bolter, Jay David, and Richard Grusin. 2000. *Remediation: Understanding New Media*. Cambridge: MIT Press.

Bolton, Christopher. 2007. "The Mecha's Blind Spot: Patlabor and the Phenomenology of Anime." *Robot Ghosts and Wired Dreams: Japanese Science Fiction from Origins to Anime*, ed. C. Bolton, I. Csicsery-Ronay Jr., and T. Tatsumi, 123–47. Minneapolis: University of Minnesota Press.

Born, Georgina. 1995. *Rationalizing Culture: IRCAM, Boulez, and the Institutionalization of the Musical Avant-Garde*. Berkeley: University of California Press.

Bourdaghs, Michael. 2012. *Sayonara Amerika, Sayonara Nippon: A Geopolitical Prehistory of J-Pop*. New York: Columbia University Press.

Bourdieu, Pierre. 1977 (1972). *Outline of a Theory of Practice*. Trans. R. Nice. Cambridge: Cambridge University Press.

———. 1980. *The Logic of Practice*. Trans. R. Nice. Cambridge: Polity/Blackwell.

Brackett, David. 2003. "What a Difference a Name Makes: Two Instances of

African-American Popular Music." *The Cultural Study of Music: A Critical Introduction*, ed. M. Clayton, T. Herbert, and R. Middleton, 238–51. London: Routledge.

Briggs, Charles L., and Richard Bauman. 1992. "Genre, Intertextuality, and Social Power." *Journal of Linguistic Anthropology* 2(2):131–72.

Brown, Steven T. 2010. *Tokyo Cyberpunk: Posthumanism in Japanese Visual Culture*. New York: Palgrave Macmillan.

Bürger, Peter. 1984. *Theory of the Avant-Garde*. Minneapolis: University of Minnesota Press.

Burns, Todd. 2002. "Deconstructing the Merzbox." *Stylus Magazine*, http://www.stylusmagazine.com/articles/weekly_article/deconstructing-the-merzbox.htm.

Butler, Judith. 1997. *The Psychic Life of Power: Theories in Subjection*. Stanford: Stanford University Press.

Cage, John. 1961. *Silence*. Middletown, Conn.: Wesleyan University Press.

Carey, James W. 1989. *Communication as Culture: Essays on Media and Society*. Boston: Unwin Hyman.

Cascone, Kim. 2000. "The Aesthetics of Failure: 'Post-digital' Tendencies in Contemporary Computer Music." *Computer Music Journal* 24(4):12–18.

Casey, Edward S. 2002. *Representing Place: Landscape Painting and Maps*. Minneapolis: University of Minnesota Press.

———. 2004. "Keeping Art to Its Edge." *Angelaki: Journal of the Theoretical Humanities* 9(2):145–53.

———. 2008. "Edges and the In-Between." *Phaenex: Journal of Existential and Phenomenological Theory and Culture* 3(2):1–13.

Caspary, Costa, and Wolfram Manzenreiter. 2003. "From Subculture to Cyberculture? The Japanese Noise Alliance and the Internet." *Japanese Cybercultures*, ed. Nanette Gottleib and Mark McLelland, 60–74. London: Routledge.

Castells, Manuel. 1996. *The Rise of the Network Society*. Vol. 1 of *The Information Age: Economy, Society and Culture*. Cambridge, Mass.: Blackwell.

———1997. *The Power of Identity*. Oxford: Blackwell.

Cazdyn, Eric M. 2002. *The Flash of Capital: Film and Geopolitics in Japan*. Durham: Duke University Press.

Chasny, Ben. 2005. "Fighting Shadows, Finding Light: A Close Encounter with Enigmatic Psychedelic Folk Adventurer Ben Chasny of Six Organs of Admittance." Interview by Jay Babcock. *Arthur* 1(15):12–15, 60.

Ching, Leo. 2000. "Globalizing the Regional, Regionalizing the Global: Mass Culture and Asianism in the Age of Late Capital." *Public Culture* 12(1):233–57.

Chow, Rey. 1993. "Listening Otherwise: Music Miniatured: A Different Type of Question about Revolution." *The Cultural Studies Reader*, ed. S. During, 462–78. London: Routledge.

Coates, Ken, and Carin Holroyd. 2003. *Japan and the Internet Revolution*. New York: Palgrave Macmillan.

Cockayne, Emily. 2007. *Hubbub: Filth, Noise and Stench in England, 1600–1770.* New Haven: Yale University Press.

Cohen, Sara. 1991. *Rock Culture in Liverpool: Popular Music in the Making.* New York: Oxford University Press.

Coleman, Gabriella. 2012. "Phreaks, Hackers, and Trolls and the Politics of Transgression and Spectacle." *The Social Media Reader*, ed. Michael Mandiberg. New York: New York University Press.

Condry, Ian. 2004. "Cultures of Music Piracy: An Ethnographic Comparison of the U.S. and Japan." *International Journal of Cultural Studies* 7(3):343–63.

———. 2006. *Hip-Hop Japan: Rap and the Paths of Cultural Globalization.* Durham: Duke University Press.

———. 2013. *The Soul of Anime: Collaborative Creativity and Japan's Media Success Story.* Durham: Duke University Press.

Cope, Julian. 2007. *Japrocksampler: How the Postwar Japanese Blew Their Minds on Rock 'n' Roll.* London: Bloomsbury.

Corbett, John. 2000. "Experimental Oriental: New Music and Other Others." *Western Music and Its Others: Difference, Representation, and Appropriation in Music*, ed. Georgina Born and David Hesmondhalgh, 163–86. Berkeley: University of California Press.

Couldry, Nick. 2004. "Liveness, 'Reality,' and the Mediated Habitus from Television to the Mobile Phone." *Communication Review* 7:353–61.

Courtemanche, Peter. 2008. "The Imaginary Network." *Re-inventing Radio: Aspects of Radio as Art*, ed. Heidi Grundmann et al., 329–46. Frankfurt: Revolver.

Cox, Christopher, and Daniel Warner, eds. 2004. *Audio Culture: Readings in Modern Music.* New York: Continuum.

Cox, Rupert, ed. 2007. *The Culture of Copying in Japan: Critical and Historical Perspectives.* New York: Routledge.

Crary, Jonathan. 1990. *Techniques of the Observer: On Vision and Modernity in the 19th Century.* Cambridge: MIT Press.

Cruz, Jon. 1999. *Culture on the Margins: The Black Spiritual and the Rise of American Cultural Interpretation.* Princeton: Princeton University Press.

Cummings, Alan. 2009. "Alan Cummings on the Origins of the Tokyo Underground Sound." *The Wire* no. 300.

Dee, Jimmy. 2001. "Tokyo Soundings." *Ongaku Otaku* 1(4):62–71.

Demers, Joanna. 2010. *Listening through the Noise: The Aesthetics of Experimental Electronic Music.* New York: Oxford University Press.

Derrida, Jacques. 1980. "The Law of Genre." *Glyph* 7:202–13.

Derschmidt, Eckhart. 1998. "The Disappearance of the 'Jazu-Kissa': Some Considerations about Japanese 'Jazz-Cafes' and Jazz-Listeners." *The Culture of Japan as Seen through Its Leisure*, ed. Sepp Linhart and Sabine Frühstück, 303–15. Albany: State University of New York Press.

Dewey, John. 1980 (1934). *Art as Experience*. New York: Perigee.
Doyle, Peter. 2005. *Echo and Reverb: Fabricating Space in Popular Music Recording 1900–1960*. Middletown, Conn.: Wesleyan University Press.
Driscoll, Kevin. 2009. "Stepping Your Game Up: Technical Innovation among Young People of Color in Hip-Hop." Master's thesis, MIT. http://hdl.handle.net/1721.1/54503.
Driscoll, Mark. 2007. "Debt and Denunciation in Post-bubble Japan: On the Two Freeters." *Cultural Critique* 65:164–87.
Ducke, Isa. 2007. *Civil Society and the Internet in Japan*. London: Routledge.
duGay, Paul, Stuart Hall, et al. 1997. *Doing Cultural Studies: The Story of the Sony Walkman*. London: Sage.
Duguid, Brian. 1995. "Prehistory of Industrial Music." EST, http://www.media.hyperreal.org/zines/est/articles/preindex.html.
Duncombe, Stephen. 1997. *Notes from the Underground: Zines and the Politics of Alternative Culture*. London: Verso.
Dyson, Frances. 2009. *Sounding New Media: Immersion and Embodiment in the Arts and Culture*. Berkeley: University of California Press.
Edwards, Brian T., and Dilip Parameshwar Gaonkar, eds. 2010. *Globalizing American Studies*. Chicago: University of Chicago Press.
Edwards, Paul N. 2007. *The Closed World: Computers and the Politics of Discourse in Cold War America*. Cambridge: MIT Press.
Erlmann, Veit. 1996. "Aesthetics of the Global Imagination: Reflections on World Music in the 1990s." *Public Culture* 8(3):467–88.
Esaki, Hiroshi, Hideki Sunahara, and Jun Murai, eds. 2008. *Broadband Internet Deployment in Japan*. Tokyo: Ohmsha/IOS Press.
Evens, Aden. 2005. *Sound Ideas: Music, Machines and Experience*. Minneapolis: University of Minnesota Press.
Feld, Steven. 1994. "Aesthetics as Iconicity, or 'Lift-Up-Over Sounding.'" *Music Grooves*, ed. Charles Keil and Steven Feld, 109–50. Chicago: University of Chicago Press.
———. 1996. "Pygmy POP: A Genealogy of Schizophonic Mimesis." *Yearbook for Traditional Music* 28:1–35.
———. 2000. "A Sweet Lullaby for World Music." *Public Culture* 12(1):145–71.
Feld, Steven, and Keith Basso, eds. 1996. *Senses of Place*. Santa Fe, N.M.: School of American Research Press.
Feld, Steven, and Aaron Fox. 1994. "Music and Language." *Annual Review of Anthropology* 23:25–53.
Ferguson, James. 1999. *Expectations of Modernity: Myths and Meanings of Urban Life on the Zambian Copperbelt*. Berkeley: University of California Press.
Fernow, Dominic. 2006. Interview. *Night Science III*.
Feuer, Jane. 1983. "The Concept of Live Television: Ontology as Ideology." *Regarding Television*, ed. E. A. Kaplan. Los Angeles: American Film Institute.

Fletcher, H., and W. A. Munson. 1933. "Loudness, Its Definition, Measurement and Calculation." *Journal of the Acoustical Society of America* 5:82–108.

Ford, Simon. 1999. *Wreckers of Civilization: The Story of Coum Transmissions and Throbbing Gristle*. London: Black Dog.

Forman, Murray. 2002. *The Hood Comes First: Race, Space and Place in Rap and Hip-Hop*. Middletown, Conn.: Wesleyan University Press.

Freiberg, Freda. 1987. "The Transition to Sound in Japan." *History on/and/in Film*, ed. T. O'Regan and B. Shoesmith, 76–80. Perth: History and Film Association of Australia.

Friedman, Ken. 1995. "The Early Days of Mail Art: An Historical Overview." *Eternal Network: A Mail Art Anthology*, ed. Chuck Welch, 3–16. Calgary, Alberta: University of Calgary Press.

Frith, Fred. 1985. Liner notes to *Welcome to Dreamland: Another Japan*. LP. Celluloid.

Fujie, Linda. 1996. "East Asia/Japan." *Worlds of Music*, 3rd ed., ed. J. Titon, 369–427. New York: Schirmer.

Gallison, Peter. 1994. "The Ontology of the Enemy: Norbert Wiener and the Cybernetic Vision." *Critical Inquiry* 21:228–66.

Gaonkar, Dilip. 2001. "On Alternative Modernities." *Alternative Modernities*, ed. Dilip Gaonkar, 1–23. Durham: Duke University Press.

Gell, Alfred. 1994. "The Technology of Enchantment and the Enchantment of Technology." *Anthropology, Art and Aesthetics*, ed. J. Coote and A. Sheldon. Oxford: Oxford University Press.

Ghazala, Reed Qubais. 2005. *Circuit-Bending: How to Build Your Own Alien Instruments*. Hoboken, N.J.: Wiley.

Ginsburg, Faye, Lila Abu-Lughod, and Brian Larkin, eds. 2002. *Media Worlds: Anthropology on New Terrain*. Berkeley: University of California Press.

Gitelman, Lisa. 1999. *Scripts, Grooves, and Writing Machines: Representing Technology in the Edison Era*. Stanford: Stanford University Press.

———. 2006. *Always Already New: Media, History, and the Data of Culture*. Cambridge: MIT Press.

Gluck, Carol. 1993. "The Past in the Present." *Postwar Japan as History*, ed. Andrew Gordon, 64–99. Berkeley: University of California Press.

Goodman, David G. 1999. *Angura: Posters of the Japanese Avant-Garde*. New York: Princeton Architectural Press.

Goodman, Steve. 2009. *Sonic Warfare: Sound, Affect, and the Ecology of Fear*. Cambridge: MIT Press.

Gracyk, Theodore. 1996. *Rhythm and Noise: An Aesthetics of Rock*. Durham: Duke University Press.

Graeber, David. 2004. *Fragments of an Anarchist Anthropology*. Chicago: Prickly Paradigm.

Greene, Paul, and Thomas Porcello, eds. 2005. *Wired for Sound: Engineering and Technologies in Sonic Culture*. Middletown, Conn.: Wesleyan University Press.

Gregory, Gene. 1985. *Japanese Electronics Technology: Enterprise and Innovation.* Tokyo: Japan Times.

Gupta, Akhil, and James Ferguson. 1997. "Beyond 'Culture': Space, Identity and the Politics of Difference." *Culture, Power and Place*, ed. Akhil Gupta and James Ferguson, 33–51. Durham: Duke University Press.

Haco. 2004. "Sound-Art." Improvised Music from Japan website. http://www.japanimprov.com/haco/sound-art.

Haraway, Donna J. 1991. *Simians, Cyborgs, and Women: The Reinvention of Nature.* New York: Routledge.

Harley, J. B. 2002. "Deconstructing the Map." *The Spaces of Postmodernity*, ed. Michael Dear and Steven Flusty, 277–90. Malden, Mass.: Blackwell.

Harley, J. B., and David Woodward, eds. 1987. *The History of Cartography*, vol. 1. Chicago: University of Chicago Press.

Harootunian, Harry D. 2000. *History's Disquiet: Modernity, Cultural Practice, and the Question of Everyday Life.* New York: Columbia University Press.

Harvey, David. 1990. *The Condition of Postmodernity: An Enquiry into the Origins of Cultural Change.* Cambridge, Mass.: Blackwell.

Hayles, Katherine N. 1999. *How We Became Posthuman: Virtual Bodies in Cybernetics, Literature, and Informatics.* Chicago: University of Chicago Press.

Haynes, Jim. 2003. "The Merzbox." *Chunklet* 4, http://www.chunklet.com/index.cfm?section=article&IssueID=4&ID=115.

Hebdige, Dick. 1979. *Subculture: The Meaning of Style.* London: Methuen.

Hegarty, Paul. 2007. *Noise/Music: A History.* New York: Continuum.

Helmholtz, Hermann. 1954 (1877). *On the Sensations of Tone as a Physiological Basis for the Theory of Music.* New York: Dover.

Henritzi, Michel. 2001. "Extreme Contemporary: Japanese Music as Radical Exoticism." *Japanese Independent Music* (various authors). Bordeaux, France: Sonore.

Higashiseto, Satoru. 1991. "An Oral History of the Hanatarashi." *Bananafish* 6.

Higgins, Dick. 1989 (1966). "Intermedia." *Esthetics Contemporary*, ed. Richard Kostelanetz, 173–76. New York: Prometheus Books.

Hilderbrand, Lucas. 2009. *Inherent Vice: Bootleg Histories of Videotape and Copyright.* Durham: Duke University Press.

Hill, Sean Wolf. 1992. "Tape Worm." *Cassette Mythos*, ed. Robin James, 78–80. Brooklyn, N.Y.: Autonomedia Press.

Hiroshige, Jojo, et al. 2010. 非常階段: *A Story of the King of Noise.* Tokyo: K&B.

Hirschkind, Charles. 2004. "Hearing Modernity: Egypt, Islam, and the Pious Ear." *Hearing Cultures: Essays on Sound, Listening, and Modernity*, ed. Veit Erlmann, 131–53. Oxford: Berg.

———. 2006. *The Ethical Soundscape: Cassette Sermons and Islamic Counterpublics.* New York: Columbia University Press.

Holmes, Thom. 2008. *Electronic and Experimental Music: Technology, Music, and Culture.* New York: Routledge.

Hosokawa, Shuhei. 1984. "The Walkman Effect." *Popular Music* 4:165–80.

———. 1994. *Japanese Popular Music of the Past Twenty Years: Its Mainstream and Underground*. Tokyo: Japan Foundation.

———. 2007. "Jazu-kissa no bunkashi senzen hen: Fukusei gijutsu jidai no ongaku kanshô kûkan" [A cultural history of jazz coffee houses in prewar Japan: Music appreciation in the age of reproductive technology]. *Nihon Kenkyû* 34:209–48.

Hosokawa, Shuhei, and Hideaki Matsuoka. 2004. "Vinyl Record Collecting as Material Practice: The Japanese Case." *Fanning the Flames: Fans and Consumer Culture in Contemporary Culture*, ed. William W. Kelly, 151–69. Stonybrook: State University of New York Press.

Huss, Mattias. 2004. "Eastern Storm: Random Bursts of Japanoise." *Release*, October 8, http://www.releasemagazine.net/Spotlight/spotlightjapanoise.htm.

Hutnyk, John. 2000. *Critique of Exotica: Music, Politics and Culture Industry*. London: Pluto Press.

Huyssen, Andreas. 1986. *After the Great Divide: Modernism, Mass Culture, Postmodernism*. Bloomington: Indiana University Press.

Ihde, Don. 1976. *Listening and Voice: A Phenomenology of Sound*. Athens: Ohio University Press.

Iida, Yumiko. 2000. "Between the Technique of Living an Endless Routing and the Madness of Absolute Degree Zero: Japanese Identity and the Crisis of Modernity in the 1990s." *positions: East Asia Cultures Critique* 8(2):423–64.

———. 2001. *Rethinking Identity in Modern Japan: Nationalism as Aesthetics*. London: Routledge.

Ilic, David. 1994. "Extreme Noise Terrors." *Wire* no. 129.

Industrial Culture Handbook. 1983. San Francisco: RE/Search Publications.

Inoue, Miyako. 2003. "The Listening Subject of Japanese Modernity and His Auditory Double: Citing, Sighting, and Siting the Modern Japanese Woman." *Cultural Anthropology* 18(2):156–93.

Ito, Mizuko, Daisuke Okabe, and Misa Matsuda, eds. 2005. *Personal, Portable, Pedestrian: Mobile Phones in Japanese Life*. Cambridge: MIT Press.

Ivy, Marilyn. 1995. *Discourses of the Vanishing: Modernity, Phantasm, Japan*. Chicago: University of Chicago Press.

———. 2001. "Revenge and Recapitation in Recessionary Japan." *South Atlantic Quarterly* 99(4):819–40.

Iwabuchi, Koichi. 2002. *Recentering Globalization: Popular Culture and Japanese Transnationalism*. Durham: Duke University Press.

———. 2004. "How 'Japanese' Is Pokémon?" *Pikachu's Global Adventure: The Rise and Fall of Pokémon*, ed. Joseph Tobin. Durham: Duke University Press.

———. 2008. "Lost in TransNation: Tokyo and the Urban Imaginary in the Era of Globalization." *Inter-Asia Cultural Studies* 9(4):543–56.

Jackson, Michael. 1995. *At Home in the World*. Durham: Duke University Press.

Jackson, Peter, and Nigel Thrift. 1995. "Geographies of Consumption." *Acknowl-

edging Consumption: A Review of New Studies, ed. Daniel Miller, 204–37. London: Routledge.

James, Robin, ed. 1992. *Cassette Mythos*. Brooklyn, N.Y.: Autonomedia.

Jameson, Frederic. 2001 (1991). *Postmodernism, or, the Cultural Logic of Late Capitalism*. Durham: Duke University Press.

Jarnow, Jesse. 2009. "On the Abandon Ship Label and Its Noise-Tape-Trading Brethren." *Village Voice*, August 11.

Jenkins, Henry. 2006. *Convergence Culture: Where Old and New Media Colide*. New York: New York University Press.

Jinnai, Hidenobu. 1995. *Tôkyo no kûkan jinruigaku* [Tokyo, a spatial anthropology]. Trans. Kimiko Nishimura. Berkeley: University of California Press.

Johnson, Henry. 1999. "The Sounds of Myûjikku: An Exploration of Concepts and Classifications in Japanese Sound Aesthetics." *Journal of Musicological Research* 18(4):291–306.

Johnstone, Bob. 1999. *We Were Burning: Japanese Entrepreneurs and the Forging of the Electronic Age*. New York: Perseus.

Jones, Mason. 1999. "Noise." *Japan Edge: The Insider's Guide to Japanese Pop Subculture*, ed. A. Roman, 75–100. San Francisco: Cadence.

Jupiter-Larsen, GX. 2010. "30 Years of the Haters." *As Loud as Possible* 1:28.

Kahn, Douglas. 1999. *Noise Water Meat: A History of Sound in the Arts*. Cambridge: MIT Press.

Kahn-Harris, Keith. 2007. *Extreme Metal: Music and Culture on the Edge*. Oxford: Berg.

Kant, Immanuel. 1978. *The Critique of Judgment*. Oxford: Oxford University Press.

Keightly, Keir. 1996. "'Turn It Down!' She Shrieked: Gender, Domestic Space and High Fidelity, 1948–59." *Popular Music* 15(2):149–77.

Keil, Charles. 1994. "Music Live and Mediated in Japan." *Music Grooves*, ed. Charles Keil and Steven Feld, 247–56. Chicago: University of Chicago Press.

Keizer, Garret. 2010. *The Unwanted Sound of Everything We Want: A Book about Noise*. New York: Perseus.

Kelly, Caleb. 2009. *Cracked Media: The Sound of Malfunction*. Cambridge: MIT Press.

Kelty, Christopher. 2008. *Two Bits: The Cultural Significance of Free Software*. Durham: Duke University Press.

Keyes, Cheryl. 2004. *Rap Music and Street Consciousness*. Urbana-Champaign: University of Illinois Press.

King, Geoff. 1996. *Mapping Reality: An Exploration of Cultural Cartographies*. New York: St. Martin's.

Kittler, Friedrich A. 1990. *Discourse Networks 1800/1900*. Trans. Michael Mettler with Chris Cullens. Stanford: Stanford University Press.

———. 1999 (1986). *Gramophone, Film, Typewriter*. Trans. Geoffrey Winthrop-Young and Michael Wutz. Stanford: Stanford University Press.

Klein, Susan Blakely. 1988. *Ankoku Buto: The Premodern and Postmodern Influences on the*

Dance of Utter Darkness. Cornell University East Asia Papers no. 49. Ithaca, N.Y.: Cornell University Press.

Kogawa, Testuo. 1984. "Beyond Electronic Individualism." *Canadian Journal of Political and Social Theory* 8(3):15–19.

Kondo, Dorinne K. 1997. *About Face: Performing Race in Fashion and Theater*. New York: Routledge.

Kosakai, Fumio. 2009. Liner notes to *Box Is Stupid*. Picadisk. Trans. Alan Cummings.

Krauss, Rosalind. 1986. *The Originality of the Avant-Garde and Other Modernist Myths*. Cambridge: MIT Press.

Kruse, Holly. 1993. "Subcultural Identity in Alternative Music Culture." *Popular Music* 12(1):31–43.

Labelle, Brandon. 2006. *Background Noise: Perspectives on Sound Art*. New York: Continuum.

LaMarre, Thomas. 2004. "An Introduction to Otaku Movement." *EnterText* 4(1):151–87.

———. 2007. Introduction to Azuma Hiroki, "The Animalization of Otaku Culture." *Mechademia 2: Networks of Desire*, ed. F. Lunning, 175–87. Minneapolis: University of Minnesota Press.

———. 2008. "Born of Trauma: Akira and Capitalist Modes of Destruction." *positions: East Asia Cultures Critique* 16(1):131–56.

———. 2009. *The Anime Machine: A Media Theory of Animation*. Minneapolis: University of Minnesota Press.

Larkin, Brian. 2008. *Signal and Noise: Media, Infrastructure, and Urban Culture in Nigeria*. Durham: Duke University Press.

Lee, Benjamin, and Edward LiPuma. 2002. "Cultures of Circulation: The Imaginations of Modernity." *Public Culture* 14(1):191–213.

Lefebvre, Henri. 2001 (1974). *The Production of Space*. Trans. D. Nicholson-Smith. Oxford: Blackwell.

Lewis, George. 2004. "Improvised Music after 1950: Afrological and Eurological Perspectives." *The Other Side of Nowhere: Jazz, Improvisation, and Communities in Dialogue*, ed. D. Fischlin and A. Heble, 131–63. Hanover, N.H.: Wesleyan University Press.

———. 2008. *A Power Stronger Than Itself: The AACM and Experimental Music*. Chicago: University of Chicago Press.

Licht, Alan. 2007. *Sound Art: Beyond Music, Between Categories*. New York: Rizzoli.

Lipsitz, George. 1994. *Dangerous Crossroads: Popular Music, Postmodernism and the Poetics of Place*. London: Verso.

Lomax, Alan. 1968. *Folk Song Style and Culture*. Washington: American Association for the Advancement of Science.

Looser, Thomas. 2006. "Superflat and the Layers of Image and History in 1990s Japan." *Mechademia 1: Emerging Worlds of Anime and Manga*, ed. F. Lunning. Minneapolis: University of Minnesota Press.

Lunning, Frenchy, ed. 2008. *Mechademia 3: Limits of the Human*. Minneapolis: University of Minnesota Press.

Lyotard, Jean-Francois. 1984. *The Postmodern Condition: A Report on Knowledge*. Trans. G. Bennington and B. Massumi. Minneapolis: University of Minnesota Press.

Lysloff, Rene. 2003. "Musical Life in Softcity: An Internet Ethnography." *Music and Technoculture*, ed. Rene Lysloff and Leslie Gay. Hanover, N.H.: Wesleyan University Press.

Manabe, Noriko. 2009. "Going Mobile: The Mobile Internet, Ringtones, and the Music Market in Japan." *Internationalizing Internet Studies*, ed. Gerard Goggin and Mark McLelland, 316–32. New York: Routledge.

Manovich, Lev. 2002. *The Language of New Media*. Cambridge: MIT Press.

Manuel, Peter. 1993. *Cassette Culture: Popular Music and Technology in North India*. Chicago: University of Chicago Press.

Marcus, George E. 1997. "The Uses of Complicity in the Changing Mise-en-Scène of Anthropological Fieldwork." *Representations* 59:85–108.

Marcus, George E., and Fred R. Myers, eds. 1995. *The Traffic in Culture: Refiguring Art and Anthropology*. Berkeley: University of California Press.

Marinetti, F. T. 1973 (1909). "The Futurist Manifesto." *Futurist Manifestos: The Documents of 20th-Century Art*, ed. Umbro Apollonio, trans. Robert Brain, R. W. Flint, J. C. Higgitt, and Caroline Tisdall, 19–24. New York: Viking.

Markey, Dave. 1992. *1991: The Year Punk Rock Broke* (film). We Got Power Films.

Marotti, William. 2009. "Japan 1968: The Performance of Violence and the Theater of Protest." *American Historical Review* 114(1):97–135.

———. 2013. *Money, Trains, and Guillotines: Art and Revolution in 1960s Japan*. Durham: Duke University Press.

Masters, Marc. 2007. *No Wave*. London: Black Dog.

———. 2009. "The Decade in Noise." Pitchfork.com, September 19, http://pitchfork.com/features/articles/7702-the-decade-in-noise/1.

Matsue, Jennifer Milioto. 2009. *Making Music in Japan's Underground: The Tokyo Hardcore Scene*. New York: Routledge.

Mauss, Marcel. 1990 (1923–24). *The Gift: The Form and Reason for Exchange in Archaic Societies*. New York: Routledge.

Mayr, Otto. 1971. "Adam Smith and the Concept of the Feedback System: Economic Thought and Technology in 18th-Century Britain." *Technology and Culture* 12(1): 1–22.

McCormack, Gavin. 1996. *The Emptiness of Japanese Affluence*. Armonk, N.Y.: M. E. Sharpe.

McGray, Douglas. 2002. "Japan's Gross National Cool." *Foreign Policy* 130 (May/June):44–54.

McKinlay, Sam. 2006. Interview. *Night Science III*.

McLuhan, Marshall. 1964. *Understanding Media: The Extensions of Man*. New York: McGraw-Hill.

Meintjes, Louise. 2003. *Sound of Africa! Making Music Zulu in a South African Recording Studio.* Durham: Duke University Press.

Merleau-Ponty, Maurice. 1962. *The Phenomenology of Perception.* London: Routledge.

Mikawa, Toshiji. 1992. "Hijokaidan no Monogatari" [The Hijokaidan story]. *G-Modern* 3. Trans. Alan Cummings.

———. 2002 (1994). "'Nihon no Noizu' futatatabi (tte? . . .)" ["Japanese Noise" again, you say?]. *G-Modern* 23:40–43. Trans. Sakuramoto Yuzo and David Novak. Reprinted at http://japanoise.net/j/incapa15.htm.

———. 1999. Interview. *Eater.* Trans. Yamamoto Yuka and David Novak.

———. 2009. Liner notes to *Box Is Stupid.* Picadisk. Trans. Alan Cummings.

Miller, D. A. 1992. *Bringing Out Roland Barthes.* Berkeley: University of California Press.

Miller, Flagg. 2007. *The Moral Resonance of Arab Media: Audiocassette Poetry and Culture in Yemen.* Cambridge: Harvard University Press.

Mindell, David E. 2002. *Between Human and Machine: Feedback, Control and Computing before Cybernetics.* Baltimore: Johns Hopkins University Press.

Minor, William. 2004. *Jazz Journeys to Japan: The Heart Within.* Ann Arbor: University of Michigan Press.

Miyoshi, Masao. 1991. *Off Center: Power and Culture Relations between Japan and the United States.* Cambridge: Harvard University Press.

Miyoshi, Masao, and H. D. Harootunian, eds. 1993. *Japan in the World.* Durham: Duke University Press.

———, eds. 2002. *Learning Places: The Afterlives of Area Studies.* Durham: Duke University Press.

Mizushima, Takaji. 2006. "Transformation of Cities." *A Social History of Science and Technology in Contemporary Japan,* vol. 3, ed. Nakayama Shigeru and Gotô Kunio, 430–41. Melbourne: Transpacific.

Molasky, Michael. 2005. *Sengo Nihon no Jazu Bunka: Eiga, Bungaku, Sabukaruchaa* [The jazz culture of postwar Japan: Film, literature, subculture]. Tokyo: Seidosha.

Monmonier, Mark. 1991. *How to Lie with Maps.* Chicago: University of Chicago Press.

Monson, Ingrid. 1997. *Saying Something: Jazz Improvisation and Interaction.* Chicago: University of Chicago Press.

Moore, Thurston. 1995. "Trash and Dirt." *Resonance* 4(2):12–13.

———. 2005. *Mixtape: The Art of Cassette Culture.* New York: Universe Publications.

Moore, Thurston, and Byron Coley. 2008. *No Wave: Post-punk. Underground. New York. 1976–1980.* New York: Abrams Image.

Morley, David, and Kevin Robins. 1995. *Spaces of Identity: Global Media, Electronic Landscapes and Cultural Boundaries.* London: Routledge.

Morris-Suzuki, Tessa. 1998. *Re-inventing Japan: Time, Space, Nation.* New York: M. E. Sharpe.

Mumford, Lewis. 1938. *The Culture of Cities.* London: M. Secker and Warburg.

———. 1967. *Technics and Human Development.* Vol. 1 of *The Myth of the Machine.* San Diego: Harcourt Brace Jovanovich.

———. 1970. *Pentagon of Power*. Vol. 2 of *The Myth of the Machine*. San Diego: Harcourt Brace Jovanovich.
Munroe, Alexandra. 1994. *Japanese Art after 1945: Scream against the Sky*. New York: H. N. Abrams.
Murai, Kôji. 2002. *Jazu kissa ni Hanataba* [A bouquet for the jazz café]. Japan: Kawade DTP.
Murakami, Takashi. 2000. *Superflat*. Tokyo: Madora Shuppan.
———. 2001. "Impotence Culture-Anime." *My Reality: Contemporary Art and the Culture of Japanese Animation*, 55–66. Des Moines, Iowa: Des Moines Art Center.
Murasaki, Hyakurô. 1999. "*Dempi-teki*" [Radio-wave-esque]. *Eater*.
Nakajima, Yoshimichi.1996. *Urusai nihon no watashi* [Myself, of noisy Japan]. Tokyo: Shinchôbunko.
Nakayama, Wataru, W. Boulton, and M. G. Pecht. 1999. *The Japanese Electronics Industry*. Boca Raton, Fla.: CRC Press.
Napier, Susan Joliffe. 1993. "Panic Sites: The Japanese Imagination of Disaster from Godzilla to Akira." *Journal of Japanese Studies* 19(2):327–51.
———. 2000. *Anime from Akira to Princess Mononoke: Experiencing Contemporary Japanese Animation*. New York: Palgrave.
Neal, Charles. 2001(1987). *Tape Delay: Confessions from the Eighties Underground*. London: SAF Publishing.
Negus, Keith. 1999. *Music Genres and Corporate Cultures*. London: Routledge.
Novak, David. 2010a. "Playing Off Site: The Untranslation of Onkyô." *Asian Music* 41(1):36–59.
———. 2010b. "Cosmopolitanism, Remediation and the Ghost World of Bollywood." *Cultural Anthropology* 25(1):40–72.
———. 2011. "The Sublime Frequencies of New Old Media." *Public Culture* 23(3):603–34.
Nozu, Kanami. 1998. Interview by Shinsuke Inoue. *ReSist* 1(spring).
Nye, Joseph. 2004. *Soft Power: The Means to Success in World Politics*. New York: Public Affairs.
Nyman, Michael. 1999 (1974). *Experimental Music: Cage and Beyond*, 2nd ed. Cambridge: Cambridge University Press.
Ochoa Gautier, Ana María. 2006. "Sonic Transculturation, Epistemologies of Purification, and the Aural Public Sphere in Latin America." *Social Identities* 12(6):802–25.
Okada, Toshio. 1996. *Otaku-gaku Nyûmon* [Introduction to Otakuology]. Tokyo: Ota Verlag.
Onda, Aki. 2002. "Cassette Memories." Liner notes to CD *Bon Voyage! Cassette Memories Vol. 2*. Improvised Music from Japan IMJ-510.
Ong, Walter J. 1982. *Orality and Literacy: The Technologizing of the Word*. New York: Methuen.

Ortiz, Fernando. 1995 (1940). *Cuban Counterpoint: Tobacco and Sugar*. Trans. Harriet de Onís. Durham: Duke University Press.

Ôsuki, Takayuki. 2002. "Shikago to Nyûyôku shiin no genjô" [The present situation in the Chicago and New York scenes]. *Afutaa Awaazu* [After hours] 16:17–19.

Ôtomo, Yoshihide. 1995. "Leaving the Jazz Café." *Resonance* 4(2):4–8.

———. 2011. "The Role of Culture: After the Earthquake and Man-Made Disasters in Fukushima." Lecture at Tokyo University of the Arts, April 28. Trans. Isozaki Mia. http://www.japanimprov.com/yotomo/fukushima/lecture.html.

Paes, Rui Eduardo. 2003. "Nihilist Spasm Band: The Godfathers of Noise." Interview with Nihilist Spasm Band. http://rep.no.sapo.pt/entrevistas3.htm.

Partner, Simon. 1999. *Assembled in Japan: Electrical Goods and the Making of the Japanese Consumer*. Berkeley: University of California Press.

Pauline, Mark. 2009. Interview. *Neural* 32:9.

Penley, Constance, and Andrew Ross, eds. 1991. *Technoculture*. Minneapolis: University of Minnesota Press.

Peters, John Durham. 1999. *Speaking into the Air: A History of the Idea of Communication*. Chicago: University of Chicago Press.

Picker, John. 2003. *Victorian Soundscapes*. New York: Oxford University Press.

Pickles, John. 2003. *A History of Spaces: Cartographic Reason, Mapping and the Geo-coded World*. London: Routledge.

Piekut, Benjamin. 2011. *Experimentalism Otherwise: The New York Avant-Garde and Its Limits*. Berkeley: University of California Press.

Pinch, Trevor J., and Wiebe E. Bijker. 1984. "The Social Construction of Facts and Artefacts: Or How the Sociology of Science and the Sociology of Technology Might Benefit Each Other." *Social Studies of Science* 14(3):399–441.

Plourde, Lorraine. 2008. "Disciplined Listening in Tokyo: Onkyô and Nonintentional Sounds." *Ethnomusicology* 52(2):270–95.

———. 2009. "Difficult Music: An Ethnography of Listening for the Avant-Garde in Tokyo." Ph.D. dissertation, Columbia University.

Poggioli, Renato. 1968. *The Theory of the Avant-Garde*. Cambridge: Harvard University Press.

Porcello, Thomas. 1998. "'Tails Out': Social Phenomenology and the Ethnographic Representation of Technology in Music-Making." *Ethnomusicology* 42(3):485–510.

———. 2005. "Music Mediated as Live in Austin: Sound, Technology and Recording Practice." *Wired for Sound: Engineering and Technologies in Sonic Culture*, ed. Paul Greene and Thomas Porcello, 103–18. Middletown, Conn.: Wesleyan University Press.

Povinelli, Elizabeth. 2001. "Radical Worlds: The Anthropology of Incommensurabilty and Inconceivability." *Annual Review of Anthropology* 30:319–34.

Pratt, Mary Louise. 1992. *Imperial Eyes: Travel Writing and Transculturation*. London: Routledge.

Prochnik, George. 2010. *In Pursuit of Silence: Listening for Meaning in a World of Noise.* New York: Doubleday.

Radano, Ronald. 2003. *Lying Up a Nation: Race and Black Music.* Chicago: University of Chicago Press.

Rama, Angel. 1989. *Transculturación narrativa en América Latina.* Montevideo: Fundación Angel Rama.

Rath, Richard. 2003. *How Early America Sounded.* Ithaca, N.Y.: Cornell University Press.

Rekôdo Mappu 2000 [Record map]. 2000. Tokyo: Gakuyo Shobo.

Richardson, George P. 1991. *Feedback Thought in Social Science and Systems Theory.* Philadelphia: University of Pennsylvania Press.

Richie, Donald. 1987. *A Lateral View: Essays on Culture and Style in Contemporary Japan.* Berkeley, Calif.: Stone Bridge.

Riley, Terry. 1995. Interview. Liner notes to *Music for the Gift.* CD. Organ of Corti 1.

Robinson, D. W., and R. S. Dadson. 1957. "Threshold of Hearing and Equal-Loudness Relations for Pure Tones and the Loudness Function." *Journal of the Acoustical Society of America* 29(1):1284–88.

Rodgers, Tara. 2010. *Pink Noises: Women on Electronic Music and Sound.* Durham: Duke University Press.

Rose, Tricia. 1994. *Black Noise.* Hanover, N.H.: Wesleyan University Press and University Press of New England.

Ross, Alex. 2007. *The Rest Is Noise.* New York: Farrar, Straus and Giroux.

Ross, Andrew. 1991. "Hacking Away at the Counterculture." *Technoculture,* ed. Constance Penley and Andrew Ross, 107–35. Minneapolis: University of Minnesota Press.

Russo, Mary, and Daniel Warner. 2004. "Rough Music, Futurism, and Postpunk Industrial Noise Bands." *Audio Culture: Readings in Modern Music,* ed. Christopher Cox and Daniel Warner, 47–55. New York: Continuum.

Russolo, Luigi. 1986 (1913). *The Art of Noises.* London: Pendragon.

Sajbel, Derek. n.d. *Circuit Bending Documentary* (unreleased film). http://absurdity.biz.

Sakai, Naoki. 1997. *Translation and Subjectivity: On Japan and Cultural Nationalism.* Minneapolis: University of Minneapolis Press.

Sangild, Torben. 2002. *The Aesthetics of Noise.* Copenhagen: Datanom.

———. 2004. "Glitch: The Beauty of Malfunction." *Bad Music: The Music We Love to Hate,* ed. Chris Washburne and Maiken Derno. New York: Routledge.

Sasaki, Atsushi. 2001. "Kêji, Minimarizumu, Onkyô-ha" [Cage, Minimalism, Onkyô-ha]. *Tekunoizu Materiarizumu* [Technoise Materialism]. Tokyo: Seidosha.

Sassower, Raphael, 1997. *Technoscientific Angst: Ethics and Responsibility.* Minneapolis: University of Minnesota Press.

Saunders, James, ed. 2009. *The Ashgate Research Companion to Experimental Music.* Aldershot, U.K.: Ashgate.

Schloss, Joseph. 2004. *Making Beats: The Art of Sample-Based Hip-Hop.* Middletown, Conn.: Wesleyan University Press.

Schodt, Frederick. 2007. *The Astro Boy Essays: Osamu Tezuka, Mighty Atom, and the Manga/Anime Revolution.* Berkeley, Calif.: Stone Bridge.

Schumpeter, Joseph A. 2005 (1942). *Capitalism, Socialism, and Democracy.* New York: Taylor and Francis.

Schwartz, Hillel. 2011. *Making Noise: From Babel to the Big Bang and Beyond.* New York: Zone.

Shank, Barry. 1994. *Dissonant Identities: The Rock'n'Roll Scene in Austin, Texas.* Hanover, N.H.: Wesleyan University Press.

Shannon, Claude Elwood, and Warren Weaver. 1949. *The Mathematical Theory of Communication.* Chicago: University of Illinois Press.

Shaw, Thomas Edward, and Anita Klemke. 1995. *Black Monk Time.* Carson Street.

Sheffield, Rob. 2007. *Love Is a Mix Tape: Live and Loss, One Song at a Time.* New York: Three Rivers.

Silverberg, Miriam. 1993. "Constructing a New Cultural History of Prewar Japan." *Japan in the World,* ed. Masao Miyoshi and H. D. Harootunian, 115–14. Durham: Duke University Press.

———. 1998. "The Café Waitress Serving Modern Japan." *Mirror of Modernity: Invented Traditions of Modern Japan,* ed. Stephen Vlastos, 208–25. Berkeley: University of California Press.

Sim, Stuart. 2007. *Manifesto for Silence: Confronting the Politics and Culture of Noise.* Edinburgh: Edinburgh University Press.

Simmel, Georg. 1950 (1908). "The Stranger." *The Sociology of Georg Simmel,* trans. K. Wolff. New York: Free Press.

Smith, Michael Mark. 2001. *Listening to Nineteenth-Century America.* Chapel Hill: University of North Carolina Press.

Soejima, Teruto. 2002. *Nihon Furii Jazu-shi* [The history of Japanese free jazz]. Tokyo: Seidosha.

Soja, Edward. 1989. *Postmodern Geographies: The Reassertion of Space in Critical Social Theory.* New York: Verso.

Spitulnik, Barbara. 1993. "Anthropology and Mass Media." *Annual Review of Anthropology* 22:293–315.

Sreberny-Mohammadi, Annabelle, and Ali Mohammadi. 1994. *Small Media, Big Revolution: Communication, Culture and the Iranian Revolution.* Minneapolis: University of Minnesota Press.

Steinberg, Marc. 2004. "Otaku Consumption, Superflat Art and the Return to Edo." *Japan Forum* 16(3):449–71.

Steinhoff, Patricia G. 1984. "Student Conflict." *Conflict in Japan,* ed. Ellis S. Krauss, Thomas P. Rohlen, and Patricia G. Steinhoff, 174–213. Honolulu: University of Hawai'i Press.

Sterling, Marvin Dale. 2010. *Babylon East: Performing Dancehall, Roots Reggae, and Rastafari in Japan*. Durham: Duke University Press.

Sterne, Jonathan. 2003. *The Audible Past: Cultural Origins of Sound Reproduction*. Durham: Duke University Press.

———. 2012. *MP3: The Meaning of a Format*. Durham: Duke University Press.

Stevens, Carolyn. 2007. *Japanese Popular Music: Culture, Authenticity and Power*. London: Routledge.

Stewart, Susan. 1993. *On Longing: Narratives of the Miniature, the Gigantic, the Souvenir, the Collection*. Durham: Duke University Press.

Stillman, Nick. 2002. "Welcome to Dreamland." *Sound Collector Audio Review* 3:27.

Stokes, Martin. 2004. "Music and the Global Order." *Annual Review of Anthropology* 33:47–72.

Straw, Will. 1991. "Systems of Articulation, Logics of Change: Communities and Scenes in Popular Music." *Cultural Studies* 5:368–88.

———. 1997. "Sizing Up Record Collections: Gender and Connoisseurship in Rock Music Culture." *Sexing the Groove: Popular Music and Gender*, ed. Sheila Whiteley. London: Routledge.

Sutton, R. Anderson. 1985. "Commercial Cassette Recordings of Traditional Music in Java: Implications for Performers and Scholars." *World of Music* 27(3):23–43.

Takahashi, Yasuo. 1994. "Why You Can't Have Green Tea in a Japanese Coffee Shop." *The Electric Geisha: Exploring Japan's Popular Culture*, ed. Atsushi Ueda, trans. Miriam Eguchi. Tokyo: Kodansha International.

Tatsumi, Takayuki. 2006. *Full Metal Apache: Transactions between Cyberpunk Japan and Avant-Pop America*. Durham: Duke University Press.

Taylor, Diana. 1991. "Transculturating Transculturation." *Performing Arts Journal* 13(2):90–104.

Taylor, Timothy D. 1997. *Global Pop: World Music, World Markets*. New York: Routledge.

———. 2001. *Strange Sounds: Music, Technology and Culture*. New York: Routledge.

Thompson, Emily. 2002. *The Soundscape of Modernity: Architectural Acoustics and the Culture of Listening in America, 1900–1933*. Cambridge: MIT Press.

Thornbury, Barbara. 2013. *America's Japan and Japan's Performing Arts: Cultural Mobility and Exchange in New York, 1952–2011*. Ann Arbor: University of Michigan Press.

Tsing, Anna. 2005. *Friction: An Ethnography of Global Connection*. Princeton: Princeton University Press.

Tsutsui, William M. 2010. *Japanese Popular Culture and Globalization*. Ann Arbor, Mich.: Association for Asian Studies.

Tudor, David. 1997 (1972). "From Piano to Electronics" (facsimile reproduction of original manuscript). *Music* 1(1):27–29.

Tufte, Edward R. 1983. *The Visual Display of Quantitative Information*. Cheshire: Graphics Press.

Turino, Thomas. 2008. *Music as Social Life: The Politics of Participation*. Chicago: University of Chicago Press.

Turner, Fred. 2005. "Where the Counterculture Met the New Economy: The WELL and the Origins of Virtual Community." *Technology and Culture* 46(3):485–512.

Ueno, Toshiya. 1996. "Japanimation and Techno-Orientalism." *Documentary Box* 9:1–5.

———. 1998. *Kurenai no metaru sûtsu: Anime to iu senjô* [Metalsuits, the red: Wars in animation]. Tokyo: Kinokuniya Shoten.

Urban, Greg. 2001. *Metaculture: How Culture Moves through the World*. Minneapolis: University of Minnesota Press.

U.S. *Indii Poppu Mappu* [Indie pop map]. 2000. Tokyo: Cookie Scene Books.

Vale, V., and Andrea Juno, eds. 1983. RE/Search 6/7: *Industrial Culture Handbook*. San Francisco: RE/Search.

van Dijk, Jan. 1999. *The Network Society: Social Aspects of New Media*. London: Sage.

Veal, Michael. 2007. *Dub: Soundscapes and Shattered Songs in Jamaican Reggae*. Middletown, Conn.: Wesleyan University Press.

Vlastos, Stephen, ed. 1998. *Mirror of Modernity: Invented Traditions of Modern Japan*. Berkeley: University of California Press.

Voegelin, Salome. 2010. *Listening to Noise and Silence: Towards a Philosophy of Sound Art*. New York: Continuum.

Wade, Bonnie. 2004. *Music in Japan*. Oxford: Oxford University Press.

———. n.d. "Composing Japanese Musical Modernity." Unpublished manuscript.

Waksman, Steve. 2004. "California Noise: Tinkering with Hardcore and Heavy Metal in Southern California." *Social Studies of Science* 34(5):675–702.

Wallach, Jeremy. 2003. "The Poetics of Electrosonic Presence: Recorded Music and the Materiality of Sound." *Journal of Popular Music Studies* 15(1):34–64.

Walser, Robert. 1993. *Running with the Devil: Power, Gender, and Madness in Heavy Metal Music*. Hanover, N.H.: Wesleyan University Press.

Warner, Michael. 2002. *Publics and Counterpublics*. New York: Zone Books.

Waxer, Lise E. 2002. *The City of Musical Memory: Salsa, Record Grooves, and Popular Culture in Cali, Columbia*. Hanover, N.H.: Wesleyan University Press.

Weidman, Amanda. 2006. *Singing the Classical, Voicing the Modern: The Postcolonial Politics of Music in South India*. Durham: Duke University Press.

Whitesell, Lloyd. 2001. "White Noise: Race and Erasure in the Cultural Avant-Garde." *American Music* 19(2):168–89.

Wiener, Norbert. 1948. *Cybernetics: Or Control and Communication in the Animal and the Machine*. Cambridge: MIT Press.

———. 1950. *The Human Use of Human Beings: Cybernetics and Society*. Boston: Houghton Mifflin.

Williams, Raymond. 1977. *Marxism and Literature*. Oxford: Oxford University Press.

Wood, Denis. 1992. *The Power of Maps*. New York: Guilford Press.

Woodward, Brett, ed. 1999. *Merzbook: The Pleasuredome of Noise*. Melbourne: Extreme.

Yamamoto, Seiichi. 1998. Liner notes to *Bears Are Not Real*. Japan Overseas JO98-41.

Yano, Christine. 2002. *Tears of Longing: Nostalgia and the Nation in Japanese Popular Song*. Harvard East Asian Monographs no. 206. Cambridge: Harvard University Press.

———. 2006, "Monstering the Japanese Cute: Pink Globalization and Its Critics Abroad." *Godzilla's Footsteps*, ed. William Tsutsui, 153–66. New York: Palgrave.

———. 2009. "Wink on Pink: Interpreting Japanese Cute as It Grabs the Global Headlines." *Journal of Asian Studies* 68(3):1–8.

Yoda, Tomiko. 2001. "A Roadmap to Millennial Japan." *South Atlantic Quarterly* 99(4):628–29.

Yoshihara, Mari. 2007. *Musicians from a Different Shore: Asians and Asian Americans in Classical Music*. Philadelphia: Temple University Press.

Yoshimi, Shunya. 1999. "'Made in Japan': The Cultural Politics of 'Home Electrification' in Postwar Japan." *Media, Culture and Society* 21(2):149–71.

———. 2003. "'America' as Desire and Violence: Americanization in Postwar Japan and Asia during the Cold War." *Inter-Asia Cultural Studies* 4(3):432–50.

Zak, Albin. 2001. *The Poetics of Rock: Cutting Tracks, Making Records*. Berkeley: University of California Press.

INDEX

Note: Page numbers in italics indicate figures.

Abbey Road Studios, 154–55
Abe Kaoru, 3, 103
acid folk (genre), 131
Acid Mothers Temple, 11, 236n6
acoustics, 123–24
"Aestheticizing Noise" (panel), 3
aesthetics: audiocassette media and, 198–202, 217–26; avant-gardism and, 20, 23, 118, 194, 250n12; Noise and, 3, 5, 30–31, 36–43, 52, 89–91, 133–34, 141–49, 172, 198–202, 216–26, 238n5, 253n9; Orientalism and, 12, 24, 89–91, 185; recording technology and, 2, 48–53, 141–49, 154; technoculture and, 186–88
affective experience, 31–34, 36–48, 58, 68, 141–49, 238n5

Afutaa Awaazu (magazine), 70–71, 71, 72
Akira (anime), 184
Akita Masami, 119, 132–33, 144, 146, 174, 192, 194, 232, 241n15. See also Merzbow
Albini, Steve, 49
Alchemy Records, 12, 56, 82–83, 94, 106, 108, 111–15, 118, 127, 129, 232, 248n5
Allied Records, 126
Allison, Anne, 25–26, 187
American Tapes, 220
Amériques (Varèse), 181
Angel'in Heavy Syrup, 232
anime, 9–10, 23, 184–88, 235n3, 256n15
Another Merzbow Records, 136
Antheil, George, 181

"Are! Nande Konna Tokoro ni Iru no yo?" (Ôsuki), 72
Art of Noises, The (Russolo), 153, 242n1
Asada Akira, 190
Asano Tadanobu, 195
Asher, Zev, 129
Ashley, Robert, 158–59
Astro (band), 12, 249n18
Atom Boy (manga), 184, 235n3
Attali, Jacques, 230–31
Aube, 12, 56, 82, 129, 209, 211–12, 239n12. See also Nakajima Akifumi
Aum Shinrikyo, 188
Aunt Sally, 109
Auslander, Philip, 32
avant-garde, 20, 23, 118, 194, 250n12
Avant Music Guide, 74, 77
Aya Ônishi, 129
Ayler, Albert, 15–16, 96
Azuma Reiko (Reiko A), 134

Bakhtin, Mikhail, 120
Bananafish, 82, 122, 135
Bar Noise, 165
Bar Noise Full Volume Live Vol. 1 (compilation), 114
Bar None, 73
barter, 211–12. See also gift exchange
Barthes, Roland, 68–69, 240n5
Basso, Keith, 67
Bateson, Gregory, 150, 152, 250n9
Bauman, Richard, 121
Bauman, Zygmunt, 183
Bears (livehouse), 35, 118
Behrman, David, 158
Bell Labs, 147
Benjamin, Walter, 117
Bennett, William, 179. See also Whitehouse
Bent Festival, 165
Bey, Hakim, 36
Blade Runner (Scott), 185

Bloody Sea (Merzbow), 232
Boredoms, 11, 13–14, 44, 79, 81–82, 85–86, 189, 236n8
Bourdieu, Pierre, 32, 68
Boyle, John, 126, 129, 248n4
Brain Ticket Death (Merzbow), 4
Braxton, Anthony, 99–100
Briggs, Charles, 121
Bringing Out Roland Barthes (Miller), 240n5
Brown, John, 121, 163
Brown, Trevor, 89
Burger, Gary, 147
Burning Star Core, 218, 227
Burroughs, William S., 133
Bustmonsters, 82

Cage, John, 153, 156, 250n12, 251n15
Canada: London, Ontario, and, 2, 36, 119; Nihilist Spasm Band and, 124–29, 153, 233, 247n3; Noise's mediation and, 16, 119–25. See also North America
Can't, 222, 227
capitalism: cartography and, 70–73; creative destruction and, 188–95; feedback and, 149, 152; postwar Japan and, 9, 25–26; technoculture and, 184–95; transnational circulation and, 7–10, 20–21, 24–26
Caroliner Rainbow, 79
cartography, 64–70, 74, 75–91, 240n5
Casey, Edward, 19, 237n14
Caspary, Costa, 214
Cassette Concerts, 207
cassette culture, 198–208, 213–26, 239n8, 254n1, 256n11
Cassette Gods (blog), 220, 221
"Cassette Memories" (Onda), 202
Cassette Mythos (James), 203
CBGB, 238n2
C.C.C.C., 12, 174, 209

Charnel House, 89, 203
Chasny, Ben, 131
Chewed Tapes, 220
Chigaihōken, 104
Christine 23 Onna, 232, 249n17
CHRW (radio station), 2
Churko, Kelly, 51–52, 53, 54, 56
circuit-bending, 23, 161–67
circulation: definitions of, 17–18; genre questions and, 117–20; listening practices and, 93–101; liveness and, 30–33, 38–43; maps and, 64–67; Noise's emergence and, 5, 7, 12, 111–14, 124–29, 132–38, 228, 248n11; temporality and, 19–21, 122–23; theoretical importance of, 16–20; transnational networks and, 6, 11, 58–63, 89–91, 93–94, 172–73, 183–88, 208–13
Clement, John, 248n4
CMJ Music Marathon, 3
coffeehouses. *See* jazu-kissa
Coltrane, John, 16, 96
Come Again II, 89
communication theory, 19–20
compilations, 84–91, 109–10, 114, 122, 128, 131, 136, 198–202, 208, 256n11. *See also* cartography; cassette culture; Noise; social networks
Condry, Ian, 34, 248n11
consumption (media), 75–89, 93–103, 191. *See also* cassette culture; listening; Noise; record labels
Cookie Scene, 70, 72, 73
cosmopolitanism, 21, 68–69. *See also* cultural feedback; transnational networks
Courtemanche, Peter, 207
creative destruction, 23, 169–74, 177–88, 195–97
"Crowd Inched Closer and Closer, The" (Incapacitants), 62

cultural feedback: cassette culture and, 199–202, 208–10, 217–26; definitions of, 17–18; ethnography and, 26–27, 139–40, 149–53, 238n24; Japan's postwar history and, 10–14, 24–26, 56, 172–73, 248n11, 252n3; Noise's Japanese–North American loop and, 14–20, 93–94, 103–11, 124–29, 195–97, 230–32, 236n10; Orientalism and, 89–91; temporality and, 20–21
Cunningham Dance Company, 156
Curnoe, Greg, 125, 126, 248n4
cybernetics, 149–53, 237n15
Cybernetics (Wiener), 149

Daigoretsu, 106, 108
danchi (housing), 192, 254n18
Datetenryu, 109
deadness, 30, 33, 48–58
Dee, Jimmy, 77, 78
Deerhoof, 79
Defektro, 142
delay (effect), 2, 143, 154–56
Derrida, Jacques, 137–38
Destroyed Robot, 165
Dewey, John, 57–58
Diagram A, 162. *See also* Greenwood, Dan
discourse theory, 119–21, 131, 216, 238n24
Dokkiri Rekōdo (compilation), 109
Doshisha University, 105, 109
Downhill Battle, 224, 225
Drugstore, 93–94, 101, 103–11, 105, 113–15, 246n19

Earth First!, 175
Eater (magazine), 182
effects, 2, 48–53, 139–49, 154, 156, 160. *See also specific effects*
Eggplant, 109
Einstürzende Neubauten, 153, 178

Index | 281

"Electric Peekaboo" (Merzbow), 4
Eli, Eli, Lema Sabachthani (Aoyama), 195, 196
embodiment, 23, 29–30, 35–46, 67–68, 229. *See also* affective experience; listening; Noise
Empire of Signs (Barthes), 68–69, 240n5
emplacement (concept), 30–36, 48–50. *See also* liveness
Endô Michirô, 169
"Enjoy It Will You Have It" (mR. dAS), 226
equalization, 52–53, 143, 148
ethnography, 5–7, 21, 26–27, 31, 66–68, 238n24. *See also specific concepts and theorists*
ethnopoetics, 55–57
Every Monday Night (Nihilist Spasm Band), 129
Exile Osaka (fanzine), 113
Exley, Bill, 126, 248n4
Extreme Music from Japan (compilation), 85, 89
Extreme Recordings, 55, 135

Facebook, 215
"Factory" (Mosolov), 181
Fake (band), 87
Fandango, 113, 283n3
Favro, Murray, 126, 248n4
feedback: circulation theory and, 17–20; consumer electronics and, 161–67; definitions of, 17, 19, 146–48; genre discourse and, 117–20; human-machine interface and, 188–97; Japanese capitalism and, 188–95; liveness and, 39, 229–30; negative-, 151–52; overload and, 142, 153–61, 172–73; performance and, 22; positive-, 142, 152–61, 177; technological mediation and, 20–21, 50–51, 139–49, 153–59, 250n9; temporality and, 19–21; trans-
national circulation and, 6, 10, 12, 14–20, 93–94, 127, 230–32
Feelies, the (band), 73
Fernow, Dominic, 198
Feuer, Jane, 32
file sharing, 201–2, 213–17, 220, 256n15
File 13, 204
Filth the Sleep, 53, 55, 145, 149, 232. *See also* Guilty Connector
Flaming Lips, 189
F.M.N. Sound Factory, 106
Forced Exposure, 82, 113, 131
Forest City Gallery, 3, 127, 233–34
Forever Records, 80, 81, 113
Four Cassettes of the Apocalypse, The (Big City Orchestra), 226
free jazz, 15, 96, 133, 172, 228, 246n18
free kissa, 103–16, 242n1
Friction (Tsing), 18
Frith, Fred, 86–88
"From Piano to Electronics" (Tudor), 156–57
Fujiwara Hide, 106–7, 109, 233
Fukushima (city), 96
Fukushima Daiichi Nuclear Power Plant, 169–71
Fukushima Tetsuo, 99–100
Fusao Toda, 232
Fushitsusha, 82
futurism, 23, 153, 173, 181, 187, 254n18

Gell, Alfred, 167–68
Generator Sound Art, 206, 219
Genpatsu-kun, 171, 252n3
genre, 117–38, 156–58, 249n14
Geriogerigegege, 12, 82, 209, 217–18
Ghazala, Qubais Reed, 164, 251n18
Ghost (band), 11
Ghost in the Shell (manga), 184
Giddens, Anthony, 150
Giffoni, Carlos, 58–59, 62, 233
Gift, The (Mauss), 151, 211

gift exchange, 151–53, 211–12, 223
Glass, Seymour, 82, 122, 135
Glenn Branca, 13
glitch(ing), 117, 163–64, 251n16
globalization. *See* circulation; cultural feedback; transnational networks
G-Modern (magazine), 89
Gojira (Godzilla) (film), 59–60, 183
Gomi Kohei, 51, 59. *See also* Pain Jerk
Go Shoei, 112–13
Goudreau, Chris, 60–61. *See also* Sickness
Government Alpha, 12, 161. *See also* Yoshida Yasutoshi
Gracyk, Theodore, 46
Graeber, David, 211
Greenwood, Dan, 121, 162–64, 167, 175, 176, 251n16
G.R.O.S.S., 82, 211–12
Ground Zero, 11
Grux, 79. *See also* Caroliner Rainbow
G-Scope (magazine), 113
Guilty Connector, 52, 53, 55, 148, 162, 215–16. *See also* Filth the Sleep
Guru Guru, 104–5
GX Jupiter-Larsen, 167
gyaku-yunyû (reverse importation), 14–15, 189–91, 236n10. *See also* feedback; Japan

Haco, 166
Hadaka no Rallizes, 109, 246n23
Haino Keiji, 11, 58, 87–88, 109, 209, 247n24
Hanatarash 3, 210–11
Hanatarashi, 14, 82, 85, 153, 177–78, 178, 209–10
hardcore (genre), 28, 37, 46
harshness: embodied sensations and, 23, 29–31, 146, 208; ethnopoetics of, 55–56; liveness and, 46–48, 51–52
"Harvest of This Trip, The" (*Afutaa Awaazu*), 72

Harvey, David, 196–97
Hasegawa Hiroshi, 249n18
Hashimoto Tsuneo, 99
Hayakawa Yoshio, 111
Hayashi Naoto, 43, 107, 109–10
"Hello America (excerpt)" (Pain Jerk), 62
Helmholtz, Hermann, 123–24, 247n1
Hendrix, Jimi, 147, 177
Henshin Kirin, 109
Higashiseto Satoru, 80–81, 81, 114, 118, 241n13
Hijokaidan: canonical status of, 12, 14, 82, 86, 153, 191, 209, 247n26; Drugstore and, 106–8, 110, 246n19; influences on, 2–3, 110, 233; Nihilist Spasm Band and, 127; *Noise from Trading Cards*, 83, 84; performances of, 2, 36, 43, 110, 110–11, 129, 177; transnational distribution and, 112. *See also* individual members
Hijokaidan: A Story of the King of Noise (Hijokaidan), 232
Hill, Sean Wolf, 208
hip-hop, 22, 25, 34, 73, 201, 228, 248n11, 255n5
Hiroshige Jojo, 83, 86, 106–7, 110, 115, 118, 127–28, 177, 233. *See also* Hijokaidan
Hiroshige Junko, 36, 107
Hirschkind, Charles, 22
"Home Taping Is Killing Music" (slogan), 201, 224, 225
Hopkins, David, 85–86, 177, 189. *See also* Public Bath Records
Hosokawa Shuhei, 76, 102
Hospital Productions, 198
humanism, 173–74, 188–97
Human Use of Human Beings, The (Wiener), 149–50

"I Feel Fine" (Beatles), 147
Ifukube Akira, 59

Index | 283

Iida Yumiko, 24, 188
Ikeda Keiko, 139–41
Ilic, David, 80
Incapacitants, 12, 14, 29–30, 38–42, 40–41, 42, 51, 56–63, 82, 129, 191–92, 209, 228
independent music, 20, 198–202, 208–13, 217–26. *See also* Noise; underground; *specific artists, genres, labels, and record stores*
Industrial music, 13, 15, 23, 131–33, 178–79
information theory, 149–53, 237n15
Inoue Miyako, 243n8
Internet, 201–2, 213–17, 255n9, 256n15
interpellation, 122
intonarumori, 153, 247n1
Inu, 109, 247n25
Invisible Music, 205
Ishibashi Shôjirô, 106–7, 109
Ishii Akemi, 118
Ishikawa Chu, 184
Ives, Charles, 181
Ivy, Marilyn, 26, 240n6
Iwabuchi Kôichi, 9, 236n3, 240n4
Iwasaki Shohei, 233. *See also* Monde Bruits

Jacks (band), 111
Jackson, Michael (anthropologist), 68–70
Jakobson, Roman, 150
James, Robin, 203–4, 209
Japan: anime and, 9–10, 23, 184–88, 235n3, 256n15; "bubble" economy of, 152, 184–88, 194; cartography and, 64–65, 240n5; collective social structures of, 97, 104–7, 186–88; "Cool Japan" trope and, 9–14, 183–88, 191; cultural feedback and, 56, 129–32, 183–95, 252n3; electronic commodities and, 9, 23, 102–3, 161–67, 184–88, 245n15; Internet usage in, 213–17; jazu-kissa and, 92–104, 109, 113–16, 242n1, 243n3, 244n10; livehouses and, 22–23, 33–36, 113, 118, 162, 238n1; manga and, 96, 184, 235n3, 256n15; media structures in, 11–12, 94–101, 111–14; Noise's emergence and, 3, 7, 15–16, 24, 35, 132–37, 227; postwar history of, 10, 24–26, 102–3, 174–88, 245n15; record stores of, 64–66, 75–83, 101–3, 111–14; sexualized imagery and, 89–91, 241n15; subject formation in, 184–95; technoculture in, 169–88; transnational capitalism and, 7–10, 24–26, 129–32, 174–75, 183–95, 248n11; underground music culture in, 33–36, 64–65; Western representations of, 12, 24–25, 67–70, 89–91, 185, 240n4. *See also* cultural feedback; J-pop; Noise; transnational networks; underground; *specific cities and regions*
Japan Bashing vol. 1 (Public Bath), 85, 85, 86
Japanese-American Noise Treaty, The (Jones), 86, 87
Japanimation. *See* anime
Japanoise. *See* Noise
Japan Overseas (label), 12, 82, 112
JASRAC (Japanese Society for the Rights of Authors, Composers, and Publishers), 131
jazu-kissa, 92–101, 98, 101–4, 109, 113–16, 242n1, 243n3, 244n10
jazz, 15, 25, 93–101, 103–7, 115, 133, 172, 228–31
Jenkins, Henry, 222
Jinnai Hidenobu, 69
Jones, Mason, 12, 86, 203
J-pop, 11, 24, 129–32, 187, 248n8
Junk (genre), 112, 117, 131

Kansai (region), 10–20, 52, 85, 87, 92–94, 103–14, 118, 182
Kant, Immanuel, 238n5
karaoke, 22, 244n12
Kaufman, Matt, 113
Kawabata Makoto, 236n6. *See also* Acid Mothers Temple
Keil, Charles, 244n12
King Tubby, 156
kissaten. *See* free kissa; jazu-kissa
Kittler, Friedrich, 123
K.K. Null, 12. *See also* Zeni Geva
Knitting Factory, 162
Knurl, 129
Kosakai Fumio, 29–30, 38–40, 40–41, 42, 42, 59–63, 247n26. *See also* Incapacitants
Kosugi Takehisa, 3
Kramer, Mark, 73
K Records, 12
K2, 12, 145
Kyoto, 7–9, 24, 93, 103–11

Lacan, Jacques, 150
Land of the Rising Noise (compilation), 85, 89
Last.fm, 201, 215
Last Gasp Art Laboratories, 142
Lee, Benjamin, 17
Lefebvre, Henri, 67
Leitch, Archie, 248n4
Les Rallizes Denudes, 109, 246n23
Lessard, Ron, 82, 210–11
Lévi-Strauss, Claude, 150
Link Wray, 147
LiPuma, Edward, 17
listening: affect and, 33–48; cultural feedback and, 103–11; jazu-kissa conventions and, 92–104, 109, 242n1; liveness and, 30–43, 49–58; North American audiences and, 115–16; techniques of, 21–22, 29–30, 37, 108–9, 114–16, 124, 239n8, 243n8, 244n10
Live at No Fun Fest (Pain Jerk/Incapacitants), 62
livehouses, 33–43, 63, 113, 118, 162, 238n1
Live in Japan (Nihilist Spasm Band), 129
liveness: authenticity and, 31–33, 49; definitions of, 30; emplacement and, 30–36, 48–50; media circulation and, 30–31, 38–43; Noise's aesthetics and, 30–31, 33–36, 39; performance and, 36–45; recording techniques and, 48–51; subject formation and, 46–48
Liveness (Auslander), 32
Lollapalooza (festival), 14
Lomax, Alan, 21, 237n16
Los Angeles Free Music Society, 15
Los Apson, 65, 79
Lost Aaraaf, 247n24
Lost in Translation (Coppola), 240n4
"Lower East Side" (*Avant Music Guide*), 74
Lowest Music and Arts, 135

Machida Machizô (Machida Kô), 109, 247n25
Magical Power Mako, 82
mail order, 82, 97, 112–13, 204–12. *See also* cassette culture; circulation; transnational networks; underground
manga, 96, 184, 235n3, 256n15
Manuel, Peter, 200
Manzenreiter, Wolfram, 214
maps, 64–73, 74, 75–83. *See also* cartography; Noise; transnational networks
Marcus, George, 238n24
Markey, Dave, 208–9
Maru ka Batsu, 113
Mary Jane (jazu-kissa), 99

Index | 285

Masonna, 12, 44, 44–46, 56, 114, 118, 154, 174, 189, 209, 218, 232, 249n17
"master" (jazu-kissa), 98–100
mastering, 23, 48–55, 62
Matsuoka Hideaki, 76, 102
Matsuzaki Satomi, 79. See also Deerhoof
Mauss, Marcel, 151, 211
Maximum Rock'n'Roll (magazine), 75
McIntyre, Hugh, 126, 128–29, 233, 248n4
McKinlay, Sam, 57
McLuhan, Marshall, 150, 172
Mead, Margaret, 150
MediaFire, 220
mediation: cassette culture and, 200–202; convergence culture and, 222; deadness and, 62–63; definitions of, 32; digital circulations and, 201–2, 213–17; jazu-kissa and, 94–101; liveness and, 30–32, 48–51. See also technology; transnational networks
MegaUpload, 224
Meintjes, Louise, 49
Melt Banana, 11, 44
Menche, Daniel, 121–22, 206
Merleau-Ponty, Maurice, 40
Merzbau (Schwitters), 194
Merzbow: *Another Merzbow Records*, 136; "Electric Peekaboo," 4; electronic setup of, 144, 146; generic status of, 12, 14, 82, 119, 131, 133–37, 153–54, 228, 256n19; and history of political art, 192–94, 232; *Merzbox* and, 134–37, 249nn21–22; performances of, 58, 135, 192; politics and, 174, 192, 193, 232; sexual associations of, 89, 241n15; *Venereology*, 54–55
Metal Machine Music (Reed), 153
Mikawa Toshiji, 2, 29–30, 38–42, 40–42, 51, 59–63, 89–90, 105–11, 191–92. See also Incapacitants

Minor (free space), 109
Minor, Bill, 99
Mirror Universe Tapes, 220
Misterka, Seth, 120–21, 218
Mixtape (Moore), 256n11
mix tapes, 201, 218, 223, 255n5, 256n11
Miyake Issei, 25
Miyazaki Aoi, 195, 196
Mizutani Kiyoshi, 134
modernity: alternative modernities and, 22; creative destruction and, 183–97; Japan and, 94–103, 183–95; subjectivities of, 22–23, 33, 46–48, 95–101, 115–16. See also circulation; cultural feedback; technology; transnational networks
Modern Music (record store), 77, 131
Monde Bruits, 12, 209, 233
Monks, the (band), 147
Monson, Ingrid, 122
Montgomery, "Gen" Ken, 206
Moore, Thurston, 82, 129, 209–10, 236n5, 256n11. See also Sonic Youth
Mosolov, Alexander, 181
MSBR, 12, 28–29, 82, 144, 206, 209, 233, 241n12
Mumford, Lewis, 172
Murakami Takashi, 25, 254n16
Murasaki Hyakurô, 182–83
Music: affective experiences of, 29–34, 238n5; circulation and, 5, 70, 75–91, 202–8; discourse theory and, 119–21, 131, 216; independent music and, 20, 198–202, 208–13, 217–26; listening techniques and, 21–23, 30–31, 92–101, 103–4, 109, 239n7, 244n10; mediation and, 20–26; Noise's relation to, 117–25, 133–38, 151–59, 167–68, 228, 230–32, 235n2, 249n14; performance of, 22, 33–48, 159; piracy and, 200–201, 210, 224–26; record-

286 | Index

ing technology and, 48–51, 101–3; subject formation and, 21–23, 33, 43–48, 58, 95–102, 140, 142–49. See also cultural feedback; genre; Noise; technology; *specific labels*
Music for Bondage Performance (Merzbow), 89
Music for Psychological Liberation (documentary), 189
Music for the Gift (Riley), 155
"My Generation" (the Who), 147
My Vegetarian Life (Akita), 232

Nakahara Masaya, 189, 191, 195. See also Violent Onsen Geisha
Nakajima Akifumi, 106, 211–12. See also Aube
Naked City, 14
Napier, Susan, 183
Nautical Almanac, 227
Neon Genesis Evangelion, 184–85
Neuhaus, Max, 158
New York City, 3, 12, 22, 29, 51, 58, 66, 70–73, 74, 233
Nihilist Spasm Band, 2, 119, 124–29, 126, 128, 153, 233, 247n3
Nippon Telegraph and Telephone, 214
Nirvana (band), 14, 81
Nishi-Shinjuku, 64–65
No Fun Fest, 3, 51, 58–63, 233
Noise: aesthetics and aestheticization of, 3, 5, 30–31, 36–43, 50–52, 89–91, 133–34, 141–49, 172, 198–202, 216–26, 238n5, 253n9; capitalism and, 188–97; cartography and, 64–66, 70–73, 75–83, 83, 84–91; cassette culture and, 198–202, 213–26, 256n11; circulation of, 5–6, 24–26, 30–31, 62, 84–89, 132–38, 208–13, 228; collectors and, 75–89, 191, 203–9, 217–26, 219; compilation tapes and, 77–91, 103–16, 122, 128, 131, 136, 208; creative destruction and, 174–83; deadness of, 29–30, 50–58; discourse theory and, 119–21, 131, 216; distribution of, 11, 127, 202–26; Drugstore's association with, 93, 103–11; electronics of, 141–49, 157; embodiment and, 23, 29–30, 35–48, 58, 229, 238n5; emergence of, 5, 10–14, 120–25, 132–37; ethnopoetics of, 54–57; fanzines and, 12, 70, 73, 74, 75, 77, 78, 82, 89–91, 203; feedback and, 6, 16–17, 56, 62, 141–49, 153–61, 229–32; genre and, 117–37, 156, 158; harshness and, 23, 29, 55–56, 146, 208; historical influences on, 2–3, 15–16, 104, 106–11, 147, 178, 247n24; human-machine relationship in, 23, 149–53, 172; Internet and, 213–26, 255n9, 256n15; listening techniques and, 21–23, 57, 92–101, 108, 114–16, 239n7; livehouses and, 33–36, 63, 113, 118; liveness of, 22–23, 29–30, 36–43, 57–63; music scenes and, 6, 28, 36–43; noisy music and, 11–14; North American scenes and, 2, 10–17, 24, 55–56, 89, 201; parodies of, 135–37; performance features of, 3–4, 6, 22, 28–30, 36–43, 40–41, 42, 58–63, 135, 139–41, 159–67, 236n5; political consciousness and, 133, 169–83, 189–95, 232; recording technology and, 48–58, 245n14; relationship with Music of, 117–25, 228, 230–32, 235n2; scholarship on, 15–16, 123–24, 153, 228–31, 236n11, 249n19; sexualization of, 89–91, 241n15, 242n1; sonic classifications of, 123–24; subject formation and, 21–23, 33, 43–48, 58, 140, 142, 161–68, 196–97,

Index | 287

Noise (continued)
228–29; technological mediation
and, 20–26, 30–32, 139–49, 153–59,
161–74, 239n7; transnational circulation and, 12, 14–21, 58–65, 76–89,
111–16, 119–20, 124–29, 131–37,
195–97; volume of, 28–30, 37, 43–48,
50–51, 54, 131–37

Noise (Attali), 230–31

Noise Fest, 236n5

Noise from Trading Cards (Hijokaidan), 83, 84

Noise May-Day 2003, 83

"Noisembryo" (Merzbow), 133, 194

Noisembryo Car, 194

Noise War (Akita), 192

Noisicians, 23, 30–31, 52–60, 89, 141–48, 153–68, 235n2. See also specific Noisicians

No Movie (film), 125

Nomura Araebisu, 102

No Music Festival, 2, 36, 129

NON, 178

No New York (compilation), 73

No Picnic (event), 127, 129

Nord, 29

No Record (Nihilist Spasm Band), 126–27

North America: compilation tapes and, 84–91, 198–202; cultural representations of Japan and, 12, 24, 68–69, 89–91, 165, 240n4; Internet usage in, 215–17; Japanimation and, 9–10, 235n3; listening practices in, 115–16; Noise performances in, 37, 54, 174, 227; Noise's distribution in, 112–14, 131–37; Noise's naming in, 7, 10–14, 16, 24, 130; receptions of Noise in, 10–14, 54–56, 76–83; underground music scenes and, 22, 70–73, 77, 83–89, 198–208, 217–26

No Wave music, 13, 15, 73

Nozu Kanami, 165

nuclear power, 169–71

Nyman, Michael, 158

Omoide Hatoba, 11, 82, 85–86

Omoide Yokocho (Memory Town), 64

Onda Aki, 202, 206–7

Ongaku Otaku, 12, 77, 78, 203

Ônishi Aya, 112, 153

Ôno Masahiko, 189

Ono Yoko, 209

Option (fanzine), 204

O'Rourke, Jim, 241n13

Osaka, 8, 11, 14–20, 22, 24, 35, 44, 46, 79–81, 94, 103–14, 118

Ôshima Yu, 100, 244n9

Ôsuki Takayuki, 72

Otaguro Motoo, 102

otaku, 186–89

Ôtomo Katsuhiro, 184

Ôtomo Yoshihide, 96, 169–71

Otona no Kagaku (magazine), 165

overload, 38–39, 51–53, 148

Pain Jerk, 12, 47, 51, 58–59, 62, 82

Parsons, Talcott, 150

Patient Sounds, 220–22

Patlabor (anime), 185

Patton, Mike, 161

Paul, Les, 154

Pauline, Mark, 180, 181

pedals (effects), 141–42, 153–60

"Pencil Organ" (Haco), 166

Peters, John Durham, 19–20

Phew, 109

piracy, 200, 224–25, 257n24

Pokémon, 25, 187

politics, 133, 169–83, 189–95, 232

Pop Tatari (Boredoms), 14

Power Rangers, 184

Power Surprises, 165

Pratten, Art, 2, 125–26, 126, 127, 233, 248n4

presence (sonic effect), 53–54. *See also* liveness; technology
Pretty Little Baka Guy / Live in Japan (Shonen Knife), 12
progressive rock (genre), 104–6
Prokofiev, Sergei, 181
Providence (Rhode Island), 6, 161
Prurient, 198, 227
P.S.F., 82
Public Bath Records, 12, 82, 85, 85, 86, 177, 189
Pulsers (Tudor), 158
punk rock, 2, 28, 37, 46–47, 134, 163, 172, 209, 238n2
Pussy Galore, 81

Rainbow in Curved Air, A (Riley), 155
Ramones, 12, 134, 249n15
record labels. *See* Noise; *specific labels*
Reed, Lou, 153
reiberu-bon (label book), 75–76, 77
Reich, Steve, 158
Rekôdo Mappu, 75, 76
Relapse (label), 55, 86
"Resist the Machines" (Diagram A), 176
reverberation (effect), 48–51, 148, 239n6
Richards, Roger, 135
Richie, Donald, 240n4
Riley, Terry, 155–56
"Rising" (Ono), 209–10
Rita, The, 57, 63
"Role of Culture, The" (Ôtomo), 169
Rollins, Sonny, 100
Romanticism, 47, 119–20, 238n5
Ross, Andrew, 192
Rough Trade, 80
RRRecords, 82, 210
RRRecycled (series), 218
Ruins, 11, 44, 82
Russolo, Luigi, 153, 181, 247n1
Rylan, Jessica, 222, 227

Sailor, Alice, 189
Sakaibara Tetsuo (Bara), 134
Sanderson, Kenny, 145, 154
Sangild, Torbin, 124
scenes: affective experiences and, 43–46, 58–63, 68; authenticity and, 31–33, 49; emplacement and, 30–36, 48–50; jazu-kissa and, 92–101; livehouses and, 28, 35–46, 238n1; mapping of, 70–73, 79–81; No Fun Fest and, 58–63; Osaka and, 80–81, 103–11; postwar Japanese underground and, 93, 103–11, 245n16; record stores and, 64–66; technological mediation and, 32–33. *See also* Noise; underground
schismogenesis (concept), 152, 250n9. *See also* Bateson, Gregory
Schnitzler, Conrad, 207
Schumpeter, Joseph, 194. *See also* creative destruction
Schwitters, Kurt, 194
Scott, Ridley, 185
Seibu Kôdô (performance space), 109
Sekiri, 129, 153
sexualization, 89–91, 241n15, 242n1
Shannon, Claude, 149, 237n15
Shaw, Eddie, 147
shibaki (method), 55
Shibuya, 77, 78
"Shikago to Nyûyôku Shiin no Genjo" (Ôsuki), 72
Shimmy Disc, 12–13, 73
Shimomoto Taku, 120
Shiramuren (jazu-kissa), 96
Shônen A case, 189
Shonen Knife, 11–12
Shonen Knife (Shonen Knife), 12
Showboat, 63
Shûmatsu Shorijô (compilation), 110
Sickness, 47, 60–61
Silverberg, Miriam, 95

Index | 289

Simmel, Georg, 68
Smith, Adam, 149
social networks, 198–208, 213–26. See also cassette culture; gift exchange; Internet; transnational networks
Solmania, 12, 174, 189, 209
Sonic Youth, 13–14, 81–82, 189, 209
Sony Walkman, 9, 186
Soul Discharge (Boredoms), 13
Soulseek, 213
Sound Choice, 203–4, 205
Soundprobe, 120–21
Space Streakings, 11
Spasmom, 128–29
"Specimen Breakdown" (Diagram A), 176
SPK, 15, 178
Stalin, the (group), 112, 169
Star Blazers (TV series), 8–9
Step across the Border (film), 87
Sterne, Jonathan, 21–22, 124, 245n14
Stravinsky, Igor, 228
Studio Voice (magazine), 189–90
subjectivity: antisubjectivity and, 140, 157–60, 195–97, 230; capitalism and, 185–88; human-machine interaction and, 150–53, 165–68, 184–88; interpellation and, 122; listening techniques and, 102, 115–16; Noise and, 20–26, 33, 43–48, 228–29; technology and, 169–83, 228; transnational feedback loops and, 184–95. *See also* modernity
Suicide (band), 13
Sun Ra, 156
Survival Research Laboratories (SRL), 181, 253n8

Tabata Mitsuru, 92–93. *See also* Zeni Geva
Taj Mahal Travellers, 3
Takayama Kenichi, 107

Takayanagi Masayuki, 103, 245n16
Taketani Ikuo, 177
Taku Taku, 43, 109
Tano Koji, 206, 233. *See also* MSBR
Tape Worm (compilation), 208
Tatsumi Takayuki, 185
technology: audiocassettes and, 202–8; creative destruction and, 169–74, 184–88; dystopian narratives and, 183–88; humanism and, 173–74, 188–97; human-machine relationship and, 23, 149–53, 172, 184–88; Japanese nationalism and, 9, 23, 102–3, 161–67, 184–88, 245n15; listening practices and, 92–94; mediation and, 20–26, 29–32, 62–63, 157–61; Orientalism and, 185; recording technology and, 32, 48–58, 122–23, 245n14; subject formation and, 21–23, 33, 46–48, 58, 102, 142, 157–60, 165–83, 228; technoculture and, 169–95. *See also* deadness; effects; liveness; mediation; Noise
Temporary Autonomous Zone, 36
Terror Noise Audio (blog), 213
Test Dept., 131
Tetsuo (Tsukamoto), 184
13 Japanese Birds (Merzbow), 232
This Is Shaking Box Music / You Are Noisemaker (Geriogerigegege), 218
Throbbing Gristle, 15, 153, 178
Timisoara, 139–41
Tokyo, 11–12, 22, 43, 66, 68, 70–71, 77, 78, 87, 96, 111–14, 162, 241n12
Tokyo Flashback (compilation), 85, 131
Toritsu Kasei Super Loft, 177–78, 178
Torpedo (Aube), 239n12
Transformers (TV show), 184
transnational networks: capitalism and, 7–11, 20–21, 24–26, 184–97; cassette culture and, 198–202, 213–26, 256n11; circulation and, 6, 17–18,

32–33, 172–73; compilation tapes and, 84–89, 109–14, 122, 128–31, 136, 198–202; digital media and, 201–2, 213–17, 255n9, 256n15; feedback loops and, 14–20, 103–11, 127, 188–95, 230–32, 236n10; Japan–North America circulation and, 7, 129–32, 183–88, 201, 208–17; liveness and, 30–33, 38–43; maps of, 64–65, 68; receptions of Noise and, 12, 16, 58–63, 111–16, 119–20, 124–29, 131–37; record stores and, 64–66, 111–14; technology and, 142–49, 169–74. *See also* cultural feedback; Japan; Noise; North America; social networks; technology
Tsing, Anna, 18
Tudor, David, 156, 157, 158, 251nn13–15
Tufte, Edward, 69
Turino, Thomas, 31
20,000V (livehouse), 28
Tzadik (label), 12

Uchino Hirofumi, 142
Uchû Senkan Yamato (TV series), 8–9
UFO (Guru Guru), 105
UFO or Die, 82, 85
Ultra Bidé, 106, 109, 233
Unbalance Records, 110
underground: cartography of, 70–73, 77, 83–89; cassette culture and, 198–208, 217–26; circulatory networks of, 22, 70–73, 77, 78, 83–91; Kansai region and, 11–12, 14–15, 35, 52, 85, 103–14, 118, 182; as political sphere, 174–83, 191; postwar Japan and, 92–101; record stores and, 64–66, 75–83, 111–14; United States and, 22, 29, 66, 72–73, 208–13. *See also* Noise; scenes
"Unfortunate Spectacle of Violent Self-Destruction, An," 180
United States: copyright law and, 201, 210, 224–26; Japan's postwar relationship to, 24–26, 102–3, 129–32, 184–95, 245n15; jazz and, 95; underground scenes in, 22, 29, 66, 72–73, 208–13
"Unpacking My Library" (Benjamin), 117
URC (Underground Records Club), 111
U.S. Indii Poppu Mappu (Cookie Scene), 70, 73
uTorrent, 213

Vanilla, 82
Varèse, Edgard, 181
Velvet Underground, 15, 73, 106, 147
Venereology (Merzbow), 54–55
Victor Talking Machine Company, 102
Viodre, 29
Violent Onsen Geisha, 12, 82, 189, 191, 195, 209
Vol. 2 (Nihilist Spasm Band), 126–27

Wago Ryoichi, 169
Wallach, Jeremy, 53
Warner, Michael, 19
Weaver, Warren, 149, 237n15
Weidman, Amanda, 22
Weise, John, 227
Welcome to Dreamland (compilation), 86–88, 88
Western Apache placenames, 67–68
What About Me? (Asher), 128–29
Whitehead, Alfred North, 139
Whitehouse (band), 15, 153, 178–79, 253n7
Who, the, 147
Wiener, Norbert, 149–50, 237n15
Wikipedia, 215–16, 257n24
Williams, Raymond, 195
Wolf Eyes, 3, 129, 227
World Music (compilation), 128
World War II, 102–3

Yamakazi "Maso" Takushi, 45–46, 114, 232, 249n17. *See also* Masonna

Yamamoto Seiichi, 35, 85–86. *See also* Boredoms

Yamanouchi Juntaro, 218. *See also* Geriogerigegege

Yamatsuka (now Yamataka) Eye, 13–14, 86, 177–78, 178, 189, 191, 210. *See also* Boredoms

Yano, Christine, 252n3

Yatani Kazuhiko, 252n3

Yellow Swans, 227

York Hotel (London, Ontario), 127

Yoshida Yasutoshi, 53, 161. *See also* Government Alpha

Yoshimi P-We, 58, 189. *See also* Boredoms

Yoshimoto Kogyo, 189

YouTube, 62, 201, 213, 240n13

Zeni Geva, 11, 82

Z'ev, 178

Zorn, John, 14

ZSF Produkt, 135

Zunô Keisatsu, 109

Zushi Naoki, 107

Library of Congress Cataloging-in-Publication Data
Novak, David, 1969–
Japanoise : music at the edge of circulation /
David Novak.
p. cm — (Sign, storage, transmission)
Includes bibliographical references and index.
ISBN 978-0-8223-5379-9 (cloth : alk. paper)
ISBN 978-0-8223-5392-8 (pbk. : alk. paper)
1. Noise music—Japan—History and criticism.
2. Japan—Relations—United States. 3. United States—
Relations—Japan. I. Title. II. Series: Sign, storage,
transmission.
ML3534.6.J3N68 2013
781.630952—dc23   2013005282